Robert E. Owens Jr., PhD

Queer Kids
The Challenge and Promise for Lesbian, Gay, and Bisexual Youth

*Pre-publication
REVIEWS,
COMMENTARIES,
EVALUATIONS . . .*

"**T**his is *not* a book that will sit on your shelf gathering dust! Owens's book is useful, comprehensive, thoroughly researched, exceptionally well-written, and focused on information and solutions. A must read for all mental health counselors, counselor educators, counselor trainees, psychotherapists, medical doctors, psychologists, educators and school board members, school counselors, and pastoral counselors. In addition to theory, Owens includes a highly valuable and up-to-date resources section."

Phil Travers, EdS
*Counselor,
Family Violence Prevention
Services, Inc.,
San Antonio, Texas*

"**A**s an advisor to a group for LGBT young people, I really appreciate *Queer Kids,* which provides a learned and accessible introduction to the issues facing queer youth today. Without understating the sometimes life-threatening situations that queer youth often encounter, Owens also offers, as importantly, stories of survival, success, and joy. With a great guide to resources around the U.S. and a wide range of valuable strategies for advocates and activists, *Queer Kids* gives readers both the tools and the imperative to get involved."

Erica Rand
*Advisor,
Outright/Lewiston-Auburn
Maine*

"**D**r. Robert Owens's book is an ideal blend of research and the honest voices of young lesbians, gays, and bisexuals. I'm also impressed with the list of useful books for children and adolescents, as well as the impressive list of national and local organizations. I'd like to see a copy of this book in every high school counselor's office and in every public library."

Margaret Matlin, PhD
Distinguished Teaching
Professor of Psychology,
State University of New York
at Geneseo

"**W**ith a clear writing style, Owens educates about and advocates for the needs of gay teens. His argument is well documented, insightful, and compassionate.

For the uninitiated, *Queer Kids* reviews basic vocabulary and concepts and provides an overview of the developmental processes involved in identifying oneself as a gay adolescent. Owens carefully ex-amines the multiple challenges faced by gay teens across a variety of domains (e.g., emotional, psychological) and social contexts (e.g., within the family, at school, and within the adolescent peer group). Further, he strongly advocates for the needs of gay teens and makes a 'call to action' to all those interested in fostering the development of young people. His advice to parents, teachers, counselors, youth workers, gay adults, and gay teens contains numerous practical suggestions for both addressing societal prejudices and stereotypes and re-sponding to the needs and concerns of gay youth. Owens's sensitivity to the challenges faced by gay teens and his concern for their well-being are evident throughout the book.

I enthusiastically recommend this book to anyone who is concerned about the development of gay youth in America and interested in helping gay adolescents develop and thrive."

Daniel J. Repinski, PhD
Assistant Professor,
Department of Psychology,
State University of New York
at Geneseo

Harrington Park Press
An Imprint of The Haworth Press, Inc.

Queer Kids

The Challenges and Promise for Lesbian, Gay, and Bisexual Youth

HAWORTH Gay & Lesbian Studies
John P. De Cecco, PhD
Editor in Chief

Queer Kids

The Challenges and Promise
for Lesbian, Gay, and Bisexual Youth

Robert E. Owens Jr., PhD

Harrington Park Press
An Imprint of The Haworth Press, Inc.
New York • London

Published by

Harrington Park Press, an imprint of The Haworth Press, Inc., 10 Alice Street, Binghamton, NY 13904-1580

The Haworth Press, Inc., 10 Alice Street, Binghamton, NY 13904-1580

Quotations from *Joining the Tribe* by Linnea Due, copyright © 1995 by Linnea Due. Used by permission of Doubleday, a division of Bantam Doubleday Dell Publishing Group, Inc.

Quotations from *Two Teenagers in Twenty* edited by Ann Heron, copyright © 1994. Reprinted by permission of Alyson Publications.

Poem by Langston Hughes from *Collected Poems* by Langston Hughes, copyright © 1994 by the Estate of Langston Hughes. Reprinted by permission of Alfred A. Knopf, Inc.

Excerpts from *Passages of Pride* by Kurt Chandler, copyright © 1995 by Kurt Chandler. Reprinted by permission of Times Books, a division of Random House, Inc.

Excerpt from *Straight Parents/Gay Children* by Robert A. Bernstein, copyright © 1994. Appears by permission of the publisher, Thunder's Mouth Press.

Quotations from *Free Your Mind* by Ellen Bass and Karen Kaufman, copyright © 1996 by Ellen Bass and Karen Kaufman. Reprinted by permission of HarperCollins Publishers, Inc.

Excerpts from *The Lives of Lesbians, Gays, and Bisexuals: Clinical, Developmental, and Cultural Issues* by Ritch C. Savin-Williams and Kenneth M. Cohen, copyright © 1995 by Harcourt Brace & Company. Reprinted by permission of the publisher.

Cover design by Monica L. Seifert.

The Library of Congress has cataloged the hardcover edition of this book as:

Owens, Robert E.
    Queer kids : the challenges and promise for lesbian, gay, and bisexual youth / Robert E. Owens, Jr.
        p. cm.
    Includes bibliographical references and index.
    ISBN 0-7890-0439-9 (alk. paper)
    1. Gay youth—United States. 2. Lesbian youth—United States. 3. Bisexual youth—United States. 4. Coming out (Sexual orientation)—United States. I. Title.
HQ76.3.U50996 1998
305.235′086′64—dc21
                                             97-39230
                                             CIP

ISBN 1-56023-929-8 (pbk.)

To Tom, who is the love and light of my life

ABOUT THE AUTHOR

Robert E. Owens Jr., PhD, is Professor of Communicative Disorders at the State University of New York at Geneseo. An expert in language development and disorders, Dr. Owens has authored two books, *Language Development: An Introduction* and *Language Disorders: A Functional Approach to Assessment and Intervention,* as well as numerous professional papers, book chapters, and articles. To date, he has presented nearly 150 professional workshops and conferences.

CONTENTS

Preface

In the past thirty years, life for sexual minorities has improved. Human rights protections are in place in some communities, but the country as a whole is a long way from being accepting or even tolerant.

In the United States, lesbians, gays, and bisexuals have failed to gain the same level of acceptance and protection as other minorities. "Faggot," "dyke," and "queer" are among the vilest epithets used in American English, especially by the young. Although discrimination, harassment, or violence based on a person's race, ethnicity, gender, or religion are considered criminal by most, all forms of such behavior toward sexual minorities (lesbians, gays, and bisexuals), no matter the severity, are tolerated and even encouraged in some segments of the population. Unaccepted and unprotected, lesbians, gays, and bisexuals provide a ready target for any demagogue with an audience or any thug with steel-toed boots. Indeed, sexual minorities provide an easily vilified population for ambitious politicians, preachers, and comedians. Although many lesbian, gay, and bisexual adults carry wounds from present and past confrontations, they have managed nevertheless to find fulfilling lives and relationships.

Conditions have also improved for lesbian, gay, and bisexual youths, yet a great need still exists for this population. Lesbian and gay *adults* who may have endured high school in isolation assume that this situation has changed radically for the better. Lesbian and gay *youths* disagree. Author Linnea Due addressed this issue with a group of teens and was surprised when one youth proclaimed that it is worse now than it was before Stonewall. He explained, "Now they know we're here."[1] In a way, this new emerging teen population has become isolated from the adult lesbian, gay, and bisexual community, from social services, and from each other.

The American high school remains one of the most homophobic and change-resistant institutions in the United States. Within the American high school, sexual-minority adolescents are almost nonexistent persons.

In 1989, the Department of Health and Human Services (HHS) squelched a report on teen suicide that concluded, in part, that 30 percent of teen suicides were among lesbian and gay youth and that these were the result of the antigay attitudes within the society. In other words, these deaths were preventable. Although only one of over fifty papers included in the report, the section on lesbian and gay youth created a right-wing backlash when it was leaked to concerned members of Congress.

Representative William Dannemeyer (R-CA) sent a letter to then-Assistant Secretary for HHS, James O. Mason, demanding that the government denounce the report. "The last thing these individuals [lesbians and gays] need is a perception of accommodation from the Bush administration." This letter was followed on August 9 by an even stronger one to then-President Bush suggesting, "If you affirm traditional family values, . . . dismiss from public service all persons still employed who concocted this homosexual pledge of allegiance and . . . seal the lid on these judgments [the report's conclusions] for good."

These letters were followed by meetings between HHS Secretary Louis Sullivan and Representative Dannemeyer. Sullivan finally concluded in a letter to Dannemeyer that the section on lesbian and gay youth did indeed "undermine the institution of the family." As a result, the entire report on teen suicide was suppressed to the detriment of all adolescents. A more watered-down version of the lesbian and gay report was finally released. It did not address adolescent suicide but instead focused on lesbian and gay adults in their twenties and thirties. Secretary Sullivan distanced himself by neither endorsing nor approving the report.

It is in response to these actions and similar ones against young people, especially *queer kids*, that I have undertaken to write this book. Mark Twain once declared the truth to be a very fragile thing. If so, it is my hope that this book, when dropped, will shatter into a million pieces. In the process may it also shatter misunderstanding, discrimination, and hatred.

A word concerning my methods is in order. I am familiar with scholarly writing and hope that readers will excuse the occasional academic nature of my writing. I never met a fact I didn't need to pass along to others. I have tried to be both readable and factual.

As for the subject matter, although I desire to be as inclusive as possible, I primarily will address the issues for lesbian and gay youths, and bisexual youths when possible. The available information necessitates this course. Very little research exists on bisexual teens and none to my knowledge on transgender adolescents. I will use the phrases *lesbian, gay, and bisexual; sexual minority;* and *queer* interchangeably. *Adolescent, teen, youth,* and *kid* also will be used in this fashion to refer to individuals between and including the ages of thirteen to nineteen years. I have chosen the title *Queer Kids* for this book although some may find it a bit pejorative. The title is in recognition of the relatively new phenomenon of adolescents proudly proclaiming themselves to be lesbian, gay, or bisexual, refusing to remain in the closet even as teens.

It is often difficult to definitively say what is lesbian, gay, or bisexual. The cultures of sexual minorities change rapidly and what we write today may be passé tomorrow. Individual sexual persona is a complex concept including sexual orientation, behavior, and identity. Those who disclose publicly may be different from those who do not. It is difficult to study and discuss those who are less open because so little is known. It is ironic that in order to study something that most people keep very personal we must ask individuals to disclose that something.

Once we have defined sexual persona, identifying lesbian, gay, and bisexual youths is equally difficult. Sexual experimentation is prevalent in the adolescent population and, in some ways, less stigmatized than identifying as lesbian, gay, or bisexual. In recognition, I have attempted to let youths speak for themselves and to use adult remembrances of their youth only when particularly illustrative.

Originally, I had intended to interview lesbian, gay, and bisexual teens and to quote them extensively in this book. I have talked with many across the country. A problem arises, not from talking but from quoting in print. It is difficult to get permission to quote from or for underaged teens, especially when they are in the closet. On advice from an editor friend, I decided to paraphrase teens with whom I talked and to supplement this with appropriate quotes from other authors. I believe the combination provides more varied and lively reading.

Finally, it would not be fair to expose readers to my biases without being informed. I am gay. After years of involvement in the civil rights struggles of racial and ethnic minorities, those with differing abilities, and lesbians, gays, and bisexuals, I find it almost impossible to remain objective about human rights. I realize, though, that some measure of objectivity is expected when exploring a subject. I have attempted to let the facts speak for themselves.

My commentary and conclusions are tainted, no doubt, by my biases. I am unable to fully comprehend the thinking of those who are hostile toward diversity. To claim that I am free of prejudice would be, at best, wishful thinking and, at worst, a lie. It is quite another matter, however, to attempt to have these prejudices transformed into laws that violate the human rights of others. Religious conservatives are free to sermonize until next Sunday on the supposed evils of sexual minorities, but they have no right—however sincere their beliefs—to criminalize behaviors and limit the liberties and freedoms of individuals. The rights of one group are not to be erased to satisfy the "beliefs" of another.

When all the facts are examined, I must reach the same conclusion as the suppressed 1989 HHS Report on Teen Suicide. It is society that is responsible for the problems faced by queer kids. In her insightful book *Two Teenagers in Twenty*, Ann Heron states the situation clearly, "[W]e, as a society, are failing to provide critical information and support for young people who feel they may be different."[2] If the result is a victim mentality among some queer kids, my hope is that this book will provide a correction. For the rest of us, I hope it is a call to action.

Acknowledgments

I cannot take sole credit for this manuscript. Many individuals have aided and encouraged me in this project. My earliest attempts to write were aided by four very able consultants and friends. Kurt and Addie Haas, both professors at State University of New York at New Paltz and authors and acknowledged experts in their own fields, kept me academically sound and audience-oriented. In addition, Addie and her thirst for life have added gusto to my own desires for the new, the different, and the changing. She and Kurt are dear friends and I love the all-too-short time that we share together.

John Mitchell, a PhD and counselor at the Rochester Institute of Technology, has been my reality check. I always welcome his perspective and his unique way of tweaking my consciousness. I'm thankful that after losing contact with each other in college, we met by chance in the supermarket hundreds of miles away and fifteen years later.

Harriet Smith, my bestest bud and a genuine human being in the best sense, offered the professional perspective of a college counselor and the personal perspective of the mother of a gay son. Her editing expertise and her personal insight were invaluable. Her move to Maine has been a loss for me but a gain for the continuing human rights struggle in that state.

The list of individuals who have encouraged me is long, and I will, no doubt, forget someone, but I will try to name as many as possible. The following people have never doubted my ability to finish this book: Rob Howell, Kathy Jones, Peggy Meeker and Brita Lilius, Linda Robinson, and Ramona Santorelli.

I must also give a special thanks to the many young people to whom I have spoken over the last few years. Their insight and their personal stories have enriched this book and added to my own knowledge.

Finally, I could not have completed this book without the constant support and love of my partner of fourteen years, Tom Menzel. Somehow he has endured my hyperactivity and my compulsive need to experience life in all the ways possible. I love him more than I can say, in ways that I cannot explain, and with a depth that I do not fully understand. He makes me whole.

DIVERSITY

- Maureen is senior class president. Jacilyn is cheerleading captain. Wayne is on the junior varsity cross country team. Nate is an Eagle Scout and senior patrol leader. Sasha is a basketball co-captain. Sammy is student council president. Nancy is editor of the school paper. Mary Ann is the yearbook photographer. Rosemarie is not in any extracurricular activities. Randy had the lead in the local summer theater production.
- Mike works as a dishwasher after school. Nicole helps in her parent's garden center on weekends and during the summer. Benji tutors kids from low-income families in the evening. Ellen was a counselor-in-training at a local day camp last summer. Bill was just fired. Rachel has worked as a teacher's aide in a preschool for two summers.
- Danielle hopes to be an engineer. O'Dell wants to be a dancer. Walt would like to play professional soccer. Nicki is undecided on her future. Jamie is going to beauty culture school. Kate is planning on becoming a lawyer. Curt is going to be rich some day. Janelle will make a fine teacher. Janey would like to stay home and raise a family. Jose doesn't know. Joe is majoring in chemistry at a private college. Maria will be an audiologist. Nan does not want to grow up.
- Beth sings at weddings. Sondra plays cello. Tony dances with a local group. Christopher composes songs. Bill listens to music. Rich plays bass guitar. Chantelle writes poetry. Harold tries to be a comedian.
- Arlene likes country music. Shanel listens to rap. Rob loves female groups from the sixties. Cheralann prefers classical music. Lynn likes everything.
- Troy's favorite food is pizza. Dale likes Mexican. Sandy will eat any kind of pasta. Kay prefers Chinese. Antoinette orders lobster whenever she eats out with her parents. Kim will take a steak anytime. Charleen prefers home-cooked meals.
- Roger is homeless. Emily lives in the suburbs. Denny's parents are divorced. Mona's father died when she was in preschool. Chuck lives with his mother and stepfather. Benny lives in the projects. Jeri-Ellen is pregnant.
- Jason collects coins. Kristi bums money. Tonya likes to read mysteries. Rochelle prefers romances. Linda writes short stories about women. Fran bakes bread and pastry. Van hangs out. Dane spends too much time on homework.
- Cathy is Catholic. Harriet is Jewish. Ali is Muslim. Jeff is Buddhist. Nicholas doesn't believe in anything. Ed is Methodist. Sean is a Unitarian.
- Reza has cancer. Vic has AIDS.

They have one thing in common.
They are all queer kids.

Chapter 1

Who Are Queer Kids?

Degenerates
some folks say
But God, Nature
or somebody
Made them that way

Langston Hughes

No one ever promised that being a teen would be easy. In addition to the trials and tribulations of acne and fitting in, adolescence can be a time of insecurity and uncertainty. Some youths face the additional daunting task of coming to terms with their sexual orientation in a hostile, often abusive environment. They must make decisions about accepting their sexual orientation that can result in assault or even death. These are queer kids and they face a unique set of stressful and potentially harmful experiences unlike any faced by heterosexuals. It is important to recognize, however, that the life experiences of these teens are as diverse as those of other adolescents. In addition, like all adolescents, they share the usual developmental and maturational issues.

Homosexuality is not just an adult phenomenon, and this fact can be made clear in some very poignant and personal ways. I realize that there are many interpretations to the two stories that follow but because they're *my* stories, I'll add *my* interpretation. Once after a high school presentation on lesbian and gay issues I found myself standing in the doorway to the principal's inner office with another speaker. My hands were behind my back. A student reporter for the school newspaper stood behind me. As the principal discussed the presentation with us, I became aware of a hand being inserted into mine. It remained only briefly, long enough for a squeeze, then it slipped out quickly. The student and I said nothing about our brief encounter, but when we shook hands as we took our departure, I realized how very vital it is for many lesbian, gay, and bisexual teens to have adult role models.

On a second occasion, I presented these same issues in a format in which high school students could choose between several competing presentations on various topics. Six skinheads came to our workshop. Their purpose was a disruptive one, and unfortunately, they achieved their aim. When I returned in a similar format two years later, two of the younger skinheads, now seniors, also returned. Their attitude this time was very different. They listened attentively, asked questions, and added to the discussion. My interpretation is that on my first visit they had been wrestling with issues surrounding sexual orientation and had been trying to deny their feelings; by the second, they had resolved their conflict and were ready to identify themselves as gay.

Lesbian, gay, and bisexual teens are "a forgotten, largely invisible minority."[1] In fact, often the existence of queer kids is denied. When schools attempt to promote and respect individual diversity, the term usually applies to racial/ethnic or religious differences. Notably absent are differences in sexual orientation.

At the same time, there is a brash and growing in-your-face assertiveness among some of these sexual-minority teens. A sense of pride and of self exists that was often absent in past generations. Their presence is increasingly difficult to deny. With this new attitude has come a new set of challenges being faced by younger and younger teens.

These challenges are far more serious than deciding a shade of nail polish or the right move to make a foul shot. Some of these challenges have life threatening consequences and cause extreme stress. For example, Peter wrestled with his decision to tell his parents he was gay, recognizing that it might threaten their support of his college education. One young woman's parents refused to pay for her chemotherapy when she told them she was a lesbian. In 1993, the American Academy of Pediatrics Committee on Adolescence stated that the problems of lesbian, gay, and bisexual youths do not originate with this group but are a consequence of societal defects.

Despite all these challenges, despite everything they must face, most queer kids become well-adjusted lesbian, gay, and bisexual adults. They survive adolescence, as do most teens, and move on with an incredible resilience. Their individual stories are powerful testimony to the trials they have endured. Most become ordinary individuals, remarkable only for their sexual orientation.

A WORKING VOCABULARY

Labels are just labels and their application may signify little. A friend related the following story about Jenny, a preschool child with mental retardation, which illustrates this point.

> Jenny was in the habit of addressing everyone by her or his first name. Her parents became concerned when she began to call the new

neighbors, a rather reserved and stuffy couple, by their first names: David and Lisa. Taking her aside, Jenny's mother explained that they were not David and Lisa but Mr. and Mrs. Smith.

Jenny nodded that she understood but the next day when she spied Mrs. Smith in her yard, she called, "Hi, Lisa!" Jenny's mother snatched her inside and admonished, "It's not Lisa; it's Mrs. Smith, remember?" Jenny nodded again.

Upon reemerging, Jenny looked across to her neighbor's yard, spotting her neighbor. In a very loud voice, she boomed, "Hi, Mrs. Smith, but you sure look a lot like Lisa."

Labels or names often mask rather than illuminate. By lumping people together, we lose their individuality and heterogeneity. Lesbian, gay, and bisexual teens are not a monolithic, homogeneous group. The enormous diversity and complexity of the lesbian, gay, and bisexual community is concealed by the terms that are meant to explain it.

Labels are for things, not for people. Sexuality is an important part of all humans, but it is not the only part. I am a college professor who is gay, not a gay college professor. In the first example, my individuality is emphasized, while in the latter, group identity receives more notice.

There are three aspects to an individual's sexuality: sexual orientation, sexual behavior, and sexual identity.[2] Each is independent but related to the others. For example, an individual may know that she or he is heterosexual (orientation) but still be a virgin and thus have no history of sexual behavior. Similarly, a young man may engage in same-sex erotic behavior but identify himself as heterosexual (identity). The seeming imbalance in the second example can be difficult to maintain. As a married gay man for sixteen years, my orientation to me was clearly homosexual, my sexual behavior was almost exclusively heterosexual, and to very close friends I would self-identify as "slightly" bisexual.

The normal, healthy personality is well integrated. Sexual identity integration occurs when all three aspects of sexuality—orientation, behavior, and identity—are aligned. In general, the healthy, productive lesbian, gay, or bisexual individual feels positive about her or his sexual identity and is not significantly hindered in everyday life by internal conflict.[3] Self-identified lesbian and gay adults have no mental health problems relative to their sexual orientation.[4] Even studies with very diverse populations report the healthy self-esteem of open lesbians and gay men.[5] For myself, a long period of self-searching has resulted in my becoming comfortable with and proud of my homosexual orientation, behavior, and identity.

In 1973, the American Psychiatric Association, which had for decades diagnosed homosexuality as a mental/emotional disorder, discarded this classification. Homosexuality was no longer a psychiatric condition. This decision was followed by similar ones by the American Medical Association and the World Health Organization. The American Academy of Pediatrics recognizes homosexuality as "inherent" in the individual, whether adult or child.

Sexual Orientation

Sexual orientation can be defined as a consistent pattern of arousal that includes sexual feelings, affectional attractions, thoughts, fantasies, and emotional and romantic feelings. It is a predominant erotic attraction for the same or other sex, or for both sexes in varying degrees. Few obvious identifiable mannerisms exist that distinguish between individuals of various sexual orientations. Sexual orientation is not a choice, lifestyle, or behavior. It is a sense of inner identity.[6] Sexual orientation is only one small aspect of a person's being but sometimes to oneself or to others, it can obscure everything else about that individual.[7]

It is important to remember that sexual orientation is a continuum, not a dichotomy: heterosexuality versus homosexuality. Relatively few individuals are exclusively one or the other. The exact number of lesbians, gays, and bisexuals is difficult to determine in a hostile society and varies with the type of study reported. Data are complicated by the inclusion of sexual behavior. Estimates on the percentage of the population who are lesbian and gay vary from highs of 16 to 21 percent to lows of 1 percent. Higher figures generally representing orientation-only studies while the lower ones represent behavior-only within a specified period, often one year.[8] Frequently, studies with low reported percentages were not designed to collect data on sexual orientation and did not ensure adequate confidentiality nor obtain the considerable trust needed to obtain such personal and potentially harmful information from homosexuals. The most recent estimates place the percentage of lesbians and gays at 6 to 10 percent and bisexuals at less than 30 percent.

The source of human sexualities is unknown, although there is evidence of a strong biological and/or early socialization origin. One recent study suggests that the biological origin of sexual orientation may differ somewhat for men and women.[9] Males present a bipolar distribution of heterosexuality and homosexuality with very few bisexuals in between. This suggests a single gene determiner. Women present a more gradual heterosexual-bisexual-homosexual distribution, suggesting more than one determiner and/or the possible influence of sociological factors.

Sexual orientation is evident at a very early age. Sex role modeling by adults is irrelevant and the percentages for each of the sexual orientation categories do not vary greatly regardless of the sexual orientation of the parents.[10] Lesbian and gay parents, whether natural or adoptive, do not have a higher incidence of lesbian or gay children. Older notions that a dominant mother and a weak, aloof father resulted in a gay adult son are ludicrous and have been proven repeatedly to be false. This notion reveals more about the patriarchal bias of researchers than it does about the origin of sexuality.

Sexual Behavior or Activity

Sexual behavior is not a determiner of either orientation or identity. The expression and interpretation of same-sex affection is dependent upon the cultural and situational context and upon personal needs. Individuals engage in sexual behavior for a variety of reasons, such as love and affection, loneliness, experimentation, societal expectations, and coercion.

For adolescents, little synchrony may exist between sexual orientation and sexual behavior, and this asynchrony may cause great individual distress.[11] Some lesbian, gay and bisexual youths are virgins. Our best "guess-timates" are that among thirteen to twenty-three-year-old lesbian and gay youths, 5 to 20 percent of males and 12 to 25 percent of females have had no sexual activity of any type with either gender.[12] These figures are similar for heterosexual youths. As high as 31 percent of gay adults did not engage in same-sex sexual behavior until out of high school.[13]

Same-sex genital behavior is commonplace in adolescence regardless of the sexual orientation of a youth.[14] This fact makes it difficult to accurately measure the prevalence of sexual behavior among groups of teens. Heterosexual teens engage in same-sex behavior and may account for 90 percent of same-sex contacts.[15] Same-sex contacts by heterosexual youths usually are without an affectional component. The motivation for this behavior may be that one's own sex is less threatening than the other sex, that there is reassurance in comparison, and that curiosity is very strong.[16]

The distinction between behavioral and psychosocial aspects of sexuality or between "doing" and "being" are very important.[17] It is one that often is overlooked either deliberately or by accident when sexual orientation is discussed. For example, researchers often use sexual behavior as an indicator of sexual orientation, thus equating the two. Gay individuals who are sexually inactive or in heterosexual marriages would be classified as heterosexual.

Sexual Identity

Sexual identity is a consistent, enduring sense of one's own sexuality and of repeated sexual feelings, thoughts, and/or behaviors.[18] Some youths self-identify as lesbian, gay, or bisexual with no same-sex erotic experiences.[19] Others may self-identify as lesbian or gay but have extensive heterosexual experience. The process of self-identification may not be completed even by adulthood.

Homosexual versus Lesbian and Gay

Lesbians and gay men prefer the terms *lesbian* and *gay* to *homosexual* for a number of reasons. First, *homosexual* has many negative connotations and is a medical and psychological term. *Lesbian* and *gay* have affectional, emotional, spiritual, intellectual, and communal connotations. They are an affirmation of self-acceptance and self-identity. The terms subsume a cultural identity.

Second, lesbians and gays have made a conscious choice to name themselves rather than be named by a hostile society. Just as African Americans reserve the right to name and to define themselves, lesbians, gays, and bisexuals prefer to decide who they will be. It is often difficult to define oneself on one's own terms without reference to the majority. Some lesbians and gay men have adopted *queer* to describe themselves in a frontal assault on the hurtful use of this epithet by nongay individuals.

All of this terminology is relatively new. *Homosexual* is a late-nineteenth-century medical term. *Lesbian* and *gay* are more modern terms; their popularity has increased since the Stonewall riots of 1969. In that year, patrons at the Stonewall, a New York City gay bar, rioted for three days in reaction to police harassment. This event is considered by many to be the watershed for the modern lesbian and gay human rights movement.

Lesbians and gays hail from every race, ethnicity, socioeconomic status, and religion. Our society's obsession with behavior often negates these and other very individual differences. In general, lesbians and gay men have more in common with heterosexual women and men respectively than with each other. What lesbians and gay men do share is a process of "becoming" and an experience of societal oppression. Stereotypes, myths, ignorance, and politicization have delayed societal acceptance of these sexual minorities.

Long considered the mark of an unhealthy mind, homosexuality was declassified as a mental illness in the 1970s by the American Psychiatric Association. Increasingly, the sexuality of lesbians, gays, and bisexuals is viewed as a normal sexual variation and as one dimension of personality.[20]

Unfortunately, many heterosexuals focus exclusively on the sexual orientation of lesbians, gays, and bisexuals, obscuring everything else about the individual.[21] Individuals are reduced to *that gay neighbor, my lesbian professor,* or *your bisexual friend.* Sexual orientation can become the sole characteristic, discrediting all other aspects of identity.

Lesbians, gays, and bisexuals cannot escape the duality of their existence as individuals and also as members of a sexual minority. If they are members of an ethnic minority, other divisions may exist. These various allegiances and, more importantly, other consciousnesses affect the ways in which lesbians, gays, and bisexuals view life.

Bisexuality

Little is known about bisexuality. Research is scant, especially for bisexual women. Few individuals are equally attracted to both genders or truly bisexual. Rather, some attraction to both genders exists; the degree of attraction varying with the individuals to whom the bisexual person is attracted.

Contrary to the conventional wisdom, bisexuality is not a phase in the process of becoming homosexual. It is neither a "cop-out" for homosexuals unable to accept their sexual orientation nor a confusion. Susie, a young bisexual, explains, "I am not questioning; I am not wondering."[22] The issue is confused by the use of the term *bisexual* by some lesbian and gay adolescents to describe themselves until they become comfortable with and accept the terms *lesbian* and *gay.*

In many ways, the pressures on bisexuals to "choose a side" are unfair. Anni, a seventeen-year-old, explains,

> [T]he heterosexual community closes me out for having that gay part and the homosexual community closes me out for having that heterosexual part. I think it's almost harder to be bisexual than to be just gay or straight.[23]

"I'm not at all confused," states Susan. "I think what . . . people are really saying is that my being bisexual confuses them."[24]

Homophobia

Homophobia is an irrational and distorted view of homosexuality and of homosexual individuals. As with other "phobias," it may be symptomatic of deeper psychological disorders. In everyday parlance, the term has come to mean anxiety, disgust, anger, and hatred toward homosexuals.

Homophobia is a societal pathology that has become codified in our laws and social policies, canonized in our religious practices, and internalized in many lesbian and gay youths and adults. So few individuals in our culture lack homophobia that we are left to characterize individuals based on its varying strength, not its presence or absence.

"[T]o be homosexual in American society today," concludes one researcher, "constitutes a profound stigma. Of modern western societies, the United States remains one of the most hostile toward homosexuals."[25] In general, more negative attitudes are present in the South and Midwest portions of the United States than on the coasts, in small towns, and rural areas than in metropolitan areas, among males than females, and among those who are less educated, more conservative religiously, and more traditional in their sexual attitudes.[26] In addition to being more homophobic than females, males are more upset by male homosexuality than by lesbianism. Those with more negative attitudes toward homosexuals have fewer personal contacts, fewer same-sex erotic experiences, more conservative religious beliefs, and more traditional attitudes about sex roles than those with less negative views.

Although sexual orientation and psychological health are not related, homophobia and psychological health definitely are. Highly homophobic individuals tend to be more prejudiced toward all types of difference.

Homophobia and the hostile attitudes it breeds can adversely affect not only lesbian and gay individuals but also those people who perpetuate the prejudice and discrimination. Fear of appearing homosexual can lead to misdirected attempts to prove one's heterosexuality. Males may strut their machismo and refrain from expressing any type of intimacy. Females may take what they perceive to be feminine roles of helplessness and nondominance. Individuals may fail to explore both the male and female aspects of their personalities, thus limiting their range of psychological growth and development. Much of the psychological distress experienced by lesbian and gay adults and teens results from external stress and lack of support from the predominantly heterosexual society.

Heterosexism

Heterosexism is an institutionalized enforcement of heterosexual "normality" that is assumed by our culture.[27] As with sexism and racism, heterosexism is a learned prejudice. Conformity to sex roles is a bulwark of heterosexism which assumes that everyone is or should desire to be heterosexual. Those who are not exclusively heterosexual deserve to be punished, physically or by discrimination, in order to make them conform. Lesbians, gays, and bisexuals, by their ambiguity, challenge the heterosexist prerogative and the inequity inherent in its view of men and women.

Some heterosexuals view homosexuality and bisexuality as incomplete fulfillment of an individual's heterosexual potential. Until 1970, this bias enabled psychologists and psychiatrists to label lesbians and gay men as mentally ill. Early studies of homosexuals were conducted among prison inmates, bar patrons, psychiatric patients, and hustlers as if these populations were representative of the larger lesbian and gay community. Some irresponsible clinicians still insist that some maladjustment exists although no scientific study has found a difference in psychological functioning relative to sexual orientation by any measure so far employed.[28]

Heterosexism has given birth to a widely accepted and destructive myth that all youths are heterosexual and that only adults are homosexual or bisexual. In turn, this assumption has been used to deny services to this very vulnerable adolescent population.

In addition, heterosexism has a profound influence on lesbian, gay, and bisexual youths. In the process of becoming healthy, happy adults, these teens must change their internalized concept of sexual minorities and reverse the heterosexual "programming" to which they have been exposed.[29]

Adolescence

Adolescence, as we know it, is a product of late-twentieth-century America. Throughout most of human history and in much of the world today, puberty marks the transition from childhood to adulthood with little recognition of an extended period which we have labeled adolescence. Modern culture and educational needs push the entry to adulthood to eighteen or twenty-one years of age, expanding the period of immaturity. At the same time, as a result of improved health care and nutrition, sexual maturity—the biological hallmark of adulthood—is occurring earlier and earlier.

Sexual behavior and expression are considered rights of adulthood, not prerogatives of youth. In fact, adolescent sexual behavior is considered a problem by society. Because teens are not sexual, it is reasoned, they cannot have a sexual orientation. Teens are not sexual and are innocent of such things. Those who are lesbian, gay, or bisexual are, therefore, unnatural and definitely not innocent. This attitude reflects the duality of our society's obsession with sex and its fear of sexuality.

Queer Kids

Lesbian, gay, and bisexual youth are an invisible, largely silent minority who are overlooked, ignored, denied, and abused. Until recently, few schools would even acknowledge the presence of sexual-minority students.

"I don't think people really appreciate how lonely it is," concludes John, a sixteen-year-old gay high school student.[30]

One result of this invisibility is a denial of social and emotional self-validation.[31] A second result is that social agencies, educational institutions, and society as a whole are not prepared to help and support lesbian, gay, and bisexual youth.

The recognition of this need for help and support and the call for services have unleashed a backlash from those who want to continue the denial. "Why not just treat them like everybody else?" some ask. "Why do they need special treatment or special rights?" others charge. To these, Damion Martin, co-founder of the Hetrick-Martin Institute, responds, "[G]ay and lesbian youth are not like other adolescents. Their difference stems from their status as members of one of the most hated and despised minority groups in the country."[32] Among these kids, "The experience of being gay or bisexual in our society overwhelms any potential differences in social categories involving age, ethnicity, race, social class, or geographical region of the country."[33]

Even though the condition of queer kids is changing rapidly, especially in some urban and collegiate areas, the overall environment is often hostile to the notion of youth who are lesbian, gay, and bisexual. "Few individuals or organizations have been willing to challenge the myth that homosexuality is a phenomenon of adulthood."[34]

By a conservative estimate, there are three million lesbian and gay youths, although the number who self-identify as such is smaller.[35] A statewide survey found that 26 percent of Minnesota twelve-year-olds are not sure of their sexual orientation. Among older Minnesota high schoolers, 6.4 percent self-identified as homosexual, an amazing figure given that adolescent self-identification is a relatively new phenomenon.[36] Of course, any figures are complicated by large numbers of heterosexual youth who experiment with same-sex behaviors.

One fact is indisputable: More adolescents are *coming out* or disclosing their sexual orientation at an earlier age. Unlike many older lesbians and gay men, teens seem less constrained by stereotypic roles, more independent, and more celebratory. With a wider range and variety of role models, lesbian and gay youths are free to develop in a more individual manner. It is the responsibility of our society to optimize their developmental opportunities.

It is easy to see queer kids as victims of a society that hates them. Fortunately, many of these teens refuse to accept victim status and the helplessness it implies. Doe, a twenty-three-year-old white lesbian, explains,

[L]esbian and gay youth . . . are not just suffering. We're challenging the boundaries[,] . . . the way relationships are viewed[, and] . . . the way sexuality is being defined. We're not apologizing. We're not hiding. We know what we deserve. We're proud of who we are.[37]

By concentrating on the uniqueness of lesbian, gay, and bisexual adolescents, we may miss their similarities with other teens. Although they encounter some serious developmental challenges as a result of their sexual orientation, queer kids have many of the same concerns as their peers for puberty, friendships, family conflict, peer pressure, and their future.[38] Their developmental concerns and processes are similar, and yet, great complexity and heterogeneity exist within the lesbian, gay, and bisexual youth population.

CONCLUSION

The definition of and societal acceptance of homosexuality differs with the culture. Most South American indigenous peoples consider it to be normal, healthy, and accepted. In much of the Mediterranean, homosexuality or bisexuality is an acknowledged, but never discussed, part of life for many men, a reaction to repressive Christian and Islamic strictures.

Being lesbian, gay, or bisexual is a personal matter. In today's world it is also political and possibly very dangerous for the individual. In the United States, the Civil Rights Movement of the 1950s and 1960s spawned the present day Gay Rights Movement. It became a political act to "come out of the closet" and reveal one's same-sex orientation to others as a way of combating invisibility and heterosexism. The openly lesbian, gay, or bisexual individual stands in sharp contrast to notions that sexual minorities are evil, that sexual orientation is a preference, and that lesbians, gays, and bisexuals lead unfulfilling, empty lives.

Lesbians and gays are the targets of stand-up comics, neo-Nazi groups, rappers and rock and roll musicians, and televangelists and their followers. Several well-publicized court cases, the fight over the status of lesbians and gays in the military, the attacks by the religious right on curriculum and textbook coverage of sexual minorities, and the virulent remarks of Senator Jesse Helms (R-NC) and ex-Congressman Robert Dornan (R-CA) are only the most dramatic examples.

With the end of the cold war, the ever-present desire for wealth and power and the unseemly human need to dominate others have come together in the form of the Christian Right and its fund-raising target, the threat to civilization posed by lesbians and gays. Their campaign of hatred sees demons in every tiny advance in lesbian and gay human rights, claiming that "children are becoming subject to an increasing number of influences which encourage them to adopt a homosexual lifestyle. . . ."[39] Despite the fact that no individual has ever become lesbian or gay by seeing a gay positive character in a TV sitcom, this group perpetuates the old homosexual stereotypes and fills its coffers with money collected to attack lesbian and gay individuals who desire only to be able to work and live free of discrimination. The power of the antigay forces was demonstrated recently when a commercial using the recorded antigay messages of some televangelists with a backdrop of hate crime statistics was blocked from airing by the threat of law suits from these same televangelists.

One message from the Christian Right is love the sinner, hate the sin; love the homosexual, hate the homosexuality. In practice, the two are never differentiated by these supposed lovers of homosexuals. "Couching venomous rhetoric within the pretense of love," states the mother of a gay son, "does not diminish the hatred of the message."[40]

The AIDS epidemic has been used to justify condemnation of lesbians and gays with little thought to the human tragedy of illness. In his landmark study, *Growing Up Gay in the South* (1991a), researcher James Sears concludes, "In the era of AIDS, 'faggots' have become the new 'niggers' of the American South."[41] Michigan State Senator Doug Carl allegedly told two nongay Sterling Heights students researching a term paper that AIDS stands for "anal inserted death sentence."[42] Ironically, the positive image of lesbian and gay adults caring for their loved ones has earned some degree of acceptance for sexual minorities.

At the same time, some individuals, in the name of Christianity, have made the world a more dangerous place for lesbian and gay youth, a minefield which must be successfully traversed on the way to a fulfilling and happy adulthood. Today's lesbian, gay, and bisexual youths face increasing amounts of fear, intolerance, and violence. Addressing the religious right, one mother claimed, "Your 'values' are killing many of our children."[43] In 1991, the American School Health Association called for an end to discrimination against lesbian and gay youth.

Why have openly lesbian, gay, and bisexual teens become a target? For the simple reason that their very being challenges the Religious Right's axiom that sexual minority teens do not exist. This belief is a correlary of their thesis that lesbian and gay adults choose their "lifestyle" over their inherent heterosexual nature.

In some ways the very success of the lesbian, gay, and bisexual rights movement has made it more difficult for sexual minority teens by stripping them of their invisibility.[44] Visibility is fine unless you're a high school kid in a hostile environment, who is not ready to disclose her or his same-sex orientation.

The oppression of sexual minorities is not accidental.[45] It is well designed, coordinated, and financed. It is surprising that so many lesbian, gay, and bisexual youth make it to adulthood relatively unscathed.

> The cumulative effects of being either an invisible or outcast segment of society are often that sexual minority youth feel bad about themselves, have a poor self-image and low self-esteem, and more than other teenagers, feel totally alone.[46]

Still, positive changes are occurring. Queer kids are becoming proactive and refusing to accept victim status. "It's an exciting time to be queer," declares Vic, a young lesbian college student.[47]

Chapter 2

"Becoming" Lesbian, Gay, and Bisexual

> Dear God, I am fourteen years old. . . .
> [L]et me know what is happening to me.
>
> Alice Walker, *The Color Purple*

Although many educators and professionals deny the existence of queer kids, the process of becoming lesbian, gay, or bisexual is very much an adolescent rite of passage. Sexual identification is not embraced immediately upon self-recognition and there is a gradual process of "coming out" to oneself. Most individuals pass from awareness to positive self-identity between ages thirteen and twenty, and a positive lesbian, gay, or bisexual identity is being established earlier today than in the past.[1] Relatively few middle school youths self-identify as lesbian, gay, or bisexual in contrast to as high as 6 to 7 percent of older high school males who describe themselves as primarily homosexual.[2]

This chapter describes a "generic" pattern of becoming. Many individual variations exist. The process seems to differ for men and women. In general, on issues of relational expectations, sexual awareness, and equality, young lesbians have more in common with young heterosexual women and young gays have more in common with young heterosexual men than young lesbians and gay men have with each other.[3] It is possible that being male or female is more important overall than being gay or lesbian. As has been observed, "Female homosexuality is to be understood as a unique female phenomenon, rather than a state which is either the same as or the reverse of male homosexuality."[4]

Even with these differences, the questions asked along the journey are surprisingly similar.

> *Am I really lesbian (or gay)?*
> *Why me?*
> *What will my parents think?*
> *Am I the only one?*
> *Should I tell my best friend?*

In general, over a period of years and against a backdrop of stigmatization, lesbian, gay, and bisexual youths gradually accept the label homosexual or bisexual for themselves as they interact with the sexual-minority community and increasingly disclose their sexual orientation.[5]

This chapter will describe a four-step process of "becoming." From their initial feelings of being different, gay, lesbian, and bisexual individuals gradually become aware of their same-sex attractions, engage in same-sex erotic behavior and dating, and finally self-identify as lesbian, gay, or bisexual.

FEELING DIFFERENT

Seventy percent or more of lesbian, gay, and bisexual adolescents and adults report feeling different at an early age, often as early as age four or five.[6] A fourteen-year-old gay male writes in his school paper,

> [T]here was always something I knew was a little bit different about me. I didn't know exactly what that might have been. It was just something that was there and I learned to accept it. . . .

Seventeen-year-old Kenneth recalls, "I've known I was different since I was five or six."[7] For some lesbian, gay, and bisexual adults the feeling of difference centered on a vague attraction to, or curiosity about, their own gender.

For most youths, these feelings are not sexual as we will see later in this section.[8] Early childhood experiences may later be interpreted in light of sexual orientation identification.

Many sexual-minority youths state that before they even knew what the difference was they were convinced of its importance. Linda recalls, "Quietly I knew."[9] From second grade on Tony knew instinctively that he was unlike other boys. They knew it too and targeted Tony for ridicule. Philip, a high schooler with deafness, recalls, "I didn't know what it was . . . , but I just knew I was different."[10] In contrast to reports from lesbians and gays, only about 10 percent of heterosexual adults report feeling different or odd as a child.[11]

Many lesbian and gay adults report that as children they felt like an "outsider" within their peer group and their family. They describe isolation, low popularity, scant dating, and lack of interest in the other sex, little participation in same-sex games, and gender nonconformity.[12] Derek, an African-American teen, had physical relations with other boys from age five on. He reports engaging in prepubescent games such as *doctor* and *I'll show you mine if you'll . . .* with boys, but never with girls. Furtive mutual fondling also occurred with other boys.[13]

As children, some but certainly not a majority of gay and bisexual male youths found men to be "enigmatic and unapproachable"[14] and felt more comfortable with women and girls. In general, these youth did not enjoy rough or athletic activities, especially team sports, and the coercion to participate, preferring instead books, art, and fantasy play. Doug, a very bright child, enjoyed problem-solving tasks such as puzzles and word games. Some gay male youths attribute their sexuality to a failure to develop "masculine" characteristics and to being "feminized" through ostracism by boys and association with girls with whom they shared more interests.[15] Jim, a young white gay male, was an isolate in his class except for the occasional female friend. He was labeled a *sissy* by the other children.

Many gay males report that they were more sensitive than other boys and had their feelings hurt more easily; cried more easily; had more aesthetic interests; were drawn to other "sensitive" boys, girls, and adults; and felt and acted less aggressively than their peers.[16] A young student recalls,

> I never felt like I fit in. I don't know why for sure. I feel different. I thought it was because I was more sensitive.[17]

"I had a keener interest in the arts," recalls a young gay man. "I never learned to fight; I just didn't feel I was like other boys. I was very fond of pretty things like ribbons and flowers and music; I was indifferent to boys' games, . . . I was more interested in watching insects and reflecting on certain things. . . ."[18] Male youths may experience the dichotomy of being attracted to the very bullies who are tormenting him.

Approximately 70 percent of lesbian and gay adults report gender nonconforming behaviors in contrast to 16 percent and 3 percent for heterosexual females and males respectively.[19] These figures must be treated carefully because they are based on subject reports. In contrast, very few lesbian and gay adults exhibit gender or sex role inappropriate behaviors.[20]

The actual incidence of gender nonconformity is unknown and does not seem to be related to the amount of masculine or feminine behavior seen in an adult. "I was more masculine," recalls a young lesbian, "more independent, more aggressive, more outdoorish. . . ."[21] For the child who doesn't conform, whispers and innuendo about her or his sexual orientation may begin early. Parental admonitions to avoid another child who seems different can plant the seeds of homophobia early. Linda, a young lesbian, recalls her distaste for Barbie and learning in first grade to sneak on a pair of shorts under the dresses her mother made her wear to church.

Gender nonconformity seems to be related to socioeconomic status with the most exaggerated behavior found in lower income groups.[22] In general, those who are most different in gender behavior are the most pressured to change.[23] Malcolm, an African-American youth, was a devoutly religious child. Commenting on the boy's effeminate mannerisms, one congregant told Malcolm, "You're degrading God's name." To which the minister added, "You're a disgrace."[24] Often lesbian and gay children are teased for their gender nonconformity. The impact of teasing seems to be more severe for boys than for girls.[25] Miles, a very agile child, became awkward and less willing to try physical activity when at age five, someone stated that he ran "like a girl." "When the others called me names and stuff," recalls Malcolm, "I assumed they were right. I had very low self-esteem."[26] Boys may be viewed as weird and be rejected as undesirable playmates. For their part, some gay and bisexual boys reject play with other boys as unsafe and unenjoyable.[27]

At some level, both the child and the family recognize that a difference exists.[28] This recognition can lead to conflict within both the family and the individual. For me, it meant enrollment by my parents in Cub Scouts and Boy Scouts and an endless stream of failed attempts to play Little League. As for Malcolm, mentioned above, "I was embarrassing to them [his family], especially to my father." He continues,

> When we were in the projects and I would play with other kids, there were times when my mom would tell me to come in. She would say, "Those kids don't want you to play with them." She always made me feel like there was something wrong with me.[29]

For many individuals, feeling lesbian or gay is a natural part of themselves. Most lesbians, gays, and bisexuals state emphatically that they did not choose their sexual orientation and that they were not in control of their feelings. Kevin, now an adult, remembers that he had known he was gay, even before he heard the word or knew its meaning.[30] His older brothers' friends elicited very different feelings in him than in his brothers.

AWARENESS OF SAME-SEX ATTRACTIONS

Sexual awareness usually begins in early adolescence. Awareness is not a sudden event but a gradual sensitivity and consciousness, a growing realization that "I might be homosexual." Most individuals develop feelings and awareness before they ever have a label for them. For some youths, awareness is better described as confusion. Labeling of these feelings may become very frightening.[31] Edmund White in *A Boy's Own Story* (1982) recalled, "I see now that what I wanted was to be loved by men and to love them back but not to be a homosexual. . . ."[32] It is important to remember that while initial awareness may be met with some shock among self-identified youths, only 30 percent of lesbians and 20 percent of gay males report that they experienced negative feelings about themselves.[33] Dan realized he was gay when he was eleven. "It just gave me a sense of wholeness."[34]

The mean age for same-sex awareness and attractions is 10.9 to 13.2 years with a reported range of 10 to 18 years.[35] In a recent survey called *Sex on Campus,* 87 percent of lesbian college students and 63 percent of gay male college students report that they were aware of their sexual orientation by high school, although some knew their orientation in elementary school.

Recalling her confusion, Linda remembers that nobody felt as passionate about members of their own gender as she felt about two of her friends.[36] As a group, boys report being aware before girls. Approximately one-third of gay male youths report same-sex attractions prior to the onset of puberty.[37] In one study, a third of lesbian and gay teens claim that they knew they were homosexual prior to age ten.[38] Mickey, age eighteen, reports an awareness of such feelings at age four or five, concluding, "I've always wanted to touch and be touched by guys."[39] He began to realize that he was not heterosexual in seventh grade. Similarly, Andrew, a young white gay man, remembers noticing at age eight the beauty of his swimming instructor, an older boy of sixteen. Henry, a young college student, recalls, "What I wanted ever since I was five or six watching Marlo Thomas' boyfriend on television, was to have a man in my bed!"[40]

Often these early attractions are vague and impressionistic. One young gay teen recalled,

> My first memory of being attracted to men was a dream I had when I was six or seven. I was in a bathtub with a man in the middle of the forest. I remember this was a happy dream for me, and I dreamt it over and over again for years.[41]

More common is the fifth grade experience of Nathaniel, a middle-class African-American teen. "I was noticing guys," he recalls. "Not knowing that I was gay—just curious about guys."[42] Derek, also African American, recalls,

> In every grade, there was at least one boy that I had a certain fond-
> ness for. . . . And later on, . . . I recognized this as crushes. I wanted
> to spend as much time as I could with them.[43]

The vague same-sex attractions of childhood become eroticized in
adolescence. The mean age for same-sex erotic fantasies among males is
reported to be 13.9 years, for females somewhat later. "I had homosexual
fantasies consistently," recalls Audrey, a young gay man. "If I had a heterosexual fantasy it was because I forced it upon myself."[44] At age fifteen,
Mike began to collect photos of his best friend and to write his friend's
name all over his notebooks. "It was like I was a junior high girl," he
recalls. "I didn't know I had fallen in love with my best friend."[45] Norma
Jean became aware of her sexual feelings while working as a store clerk.

> Some women runners kept coming by the store. . . . After they
> finished practicing, all of those gorgeous bodies would just pile into
> the store to get something to drink. I became very sexually excited
> about that. I made sure that I worked the nights they practiced.[46]

In his book *What the Dead Remember*, Harlan Green recalls from boy-
hood:

> I picked up the *Saturday Evening Post* . . . I turned the page and
> stopped. . . . I breathed out, transfixed at what I saw. . . . a picture of
> men and boys in black-and-white advertising Hanes or BVD's.[47]

Similarly, Darrell remembers scanning underwear ads closely in second
grade, looking for an outline of what lay beneath. Erotic feelings can come
from pictures, words, and voices that others might not consider erotic in
the least.

Same-sex attractions are reported by many queer kids to have always
been present, deep within the "natural self."[48] Richard, age nineteen,
summarizes, "I have always been gay, although I did not know what that
meant at the time."[49] In seventh grade, Amy, a young lesbian, recalls that
she suddenly changed to a more gender-neutral manner of dress with the
defense that "I just want to be myself."[50]

Gay male youths report that they first experienced an obsession to be
near masculinity. Mickey, age eighteen, recalls,

> At eight I fell in love with Neal, this guy who rode my bus. . . . I guess
> he was fourteen. . . . I always wanted to sit with him or be next to him.
> . . . I spent my childhood fantasizing about men, not sexually . . . , but
> just being close to them and having them hold me or hug me.[51]

Former NFL running back David Kopay recalls a high school football captain two years older than himself. At the time, David did everything possible to be close to this teammate.[52] At age eleven, Tony developed nonsexual "crushes" on other boys in his scout troop. A seventeen-year-old Chinese-American youth recalls, "In high school . . . I had a crush on a guy I didn't even know."[53] Cory became obsessed with Jessie when both were in seventh grade. He recalls,

> I started going crazy. He looked better every day. I did not do anything during that time; I just looked a lot. . . . I just couldn't go up to him and say, "Hey, Jessie, I'm horny for you.[54]

Although occasionally a peer, the object of the obsession is more often an older male, such as a teacher, scout leader, coach, or older cousin. As a child, Denny's interest in big league sports masked his secretive crushes on the players he admired. A former neighbor, now an adult gay man, confided in me that he had wanted to have sex with me since we met when he was age thirteen and I was thirty-four. "These are often cases of unrequited love," explains Paul Gibson, author of the 1989 DHHS report on adolescent suicide, "with the youth never revealing their true feelings."[55]

Some lesbians report that they were attracted to women in authority positions. Maria had a crush on her third grade teacher. Tara, enamored with her softball coach recalls, "I would fantasize about being a man, so I could kiss her."[56] Other lesbian girls are attracted to peers. Lynn, a lesbian student, developed a crush on her best friend with whom she often danced to recorded music in the dark, took long walks, and slept over.

The reverse of the "typical" heterosexual pattern may occur in which a lesbian or gay teen is drawn to members of the other sex as friends but sexually attracted to members of the same sex. Gay male teens may have many female friends but not be sexually attracted to females. "I was real attracted to pretty women," explains Elisa, "but I identified more with men. But there was no attraction between us."[57]

An erotically aroused teen may or may not have engaged in same-sex sexual behavior. In fact, same-sex feelings and attractions almost always precede same-sex behavior.[58] Usually, erotic feelings appear in the early teens, although some adults report that they had same-sex fantasies and arousal as early as late preschool. Scott, an adolescent, recalls sexual interests at age six or seven. Approximately 70 percent of lesbians and 95 percent of gay men report same-sex arousal by age nineteen. In contrast, only 6 percent of heterosexual women and 20 percent of heterosexual men report same-sex arousal by this age.[59]

Most gay and bisexual male adolescents report that they initially believed that all boys felt as they did about other males.[60] Eventually they learned otherwise and the inner conflict of self versus society began, along with its accompanying confusion. Having defined himself along societal expectations, a youth may be concerned about the discrepancy that is now developing. An increasing doubt grows as both males and females become aware of their inability to fulfill heterosexual expectations. At age thirteen, Martin, an African-American student, was struck by the realization that his sexual feeling and being gay were one in the same. Chris, an eighteen-year-old male, adds, "I was under the impression that since I was gay, I wouldn't be able to do anything substantial with my life."[61]

Initial realization may be accompanied by intense anxiety and an identity crisis. Mike, a gay middle school student, spent hours in the counselor's office with vague school-related problems. He refused to face the sexual issue and recalls, "I was convinced they'd kick me out of school and send me to jail."[62] "[S]uddenly all the feelings . . . came together." recalls eighteen-year-old Joanne, "and pointed to the label, lesbian. As a result, I walked around like a shell shock victim for days."[63] "I was frightened," explains Linda. "Although I'd become somewhat comfortable with my label as 'the weird one,' lesbianism was *too* weird."[64] At age thirteen, Michelle kept a dream journal and she dreamt that she and a female friend kissed. "I immediately stopped keeping my journal," she recalls.[65] A sixteen-year-old Chinese-American Texan confides, "It was a total shock. . . . I simply could not accept myself. All the confidence I had in me disappeared."[66]

Positive self-regard and the plans for a bright future may appear to be lost as a teen recognizes that she or he is a member of a despised minority. Conflict can occur between a teen's positive self-esteem and her or his own internalized homophobia with its negative connotations.

Although this conflict easily resolves for some, others incorporate familial and societal values of the homosexual as sick, wrong, and undesirable, a member of a despised minority. Paul became aware of his attraction to other boys and to male TV stars at age eleven. "When the feelings did not go away I became distraught; the problem seemed beyond my control," he recalls. "I spent whole days crying alone in my room, and my family and friends didn't know what to make of me."[67] A fourteen-year-old bisexual girl reports, "I'd been thinking about it but I didn't want to believe what I was thinking."[68] She had first begun to be attracted to both boys and girls at age eleven. Having "bought into" society's negative values and social conditioning, queer kids may begin to hate themselves intensely.

Many gay and bisexual male youths report that sexual thoughts and feelings intrude on everything else.[69] They report being frightened by their awareness, threatened by the possibilities, and energized by the intensity of their feelings and the sense of the forbidden. "I knew I was clearly checking out the guys in the shower after soccer practice," a young gay man recalls. "This scared the shit out of me."[70] With little except negative feedback from home or school, these adolescents have no context within which to make sense of their feelings.

Myths and stereotypes of lesbians, gays, and bisexuals are a source of much of their confusion. A nineteen-year-old lesbian recalls, "I heard so many times, 'You look straight.' I thought that was stupid. . . . What's looking straight, what's looking gay?"[71] A young gay male or lesbian may try to fulfill the stereotype or be repelled by it. Lack of appropriate role models only exacerbates the situation.

The extreme loneliness of this period, as described by lesbian, gay, and bisexual adults, may be even more acute for younger adolescents who do not have the maturity to explore these complex feelings. This isolation may be made more harsh by a youth's active avoidance of other students suspected of being lesbian, gay, or bisexual. A queer kid can become the loneliest person in the high school.[72] Vulnerable and afraid of being revealed, a sexual-minority teen may be incapable of withstanding peer pressure to conform to a heterosexual standard that does not fit. Anti-homosexual jokes or ridicule are especially painful.

Youths may learn to hide their desires as wrong, believing that they will change or decrease. "Over the years, these tiny denials have a cumulative effect."[73] The youth may hate herself or himself for feeling a certain way but the sexual feelings continue to come. The result may be acting out, rebellion, dangerous sexual behavior, depression, and/or suicide.

In similar fashion, those youth who are very open about their sexual orientation may also experience isolation. Former "friends" may ridicule or stop associating. When Jill began to dress in a more "butch" manner, her phone fell silent as more and more girls she had considered friends avoided her. At school, she became an isolate.

The sense of isolation increases with the fear of discovery and rejection, especially for teens who belong to racial minorities. Many honestly believe that they are the only lesbian or gay student in their high school.[74]

Early recognition of sexual orientation by today's teens contrasts sharply with the lengthy process of self-acceptance and identification reported by many older lesbian, gay, and bisexual adults. Few resources or guides exist to facilitate this process for the young adolescent.

Coping Strategies

The three most common coping strategies for defending one's self against internalized and externalized homophobia, from least to most satisfactory for psychological adjustment, are repression of desires, suppression of homosexual impulses, and acceptance and disclosure to others.[75] Although each is discussed below as a distinct coping strategy, it is rare that distinctions are so clear in real life. Instead, the behavior of each lesbian, gay, and bisexual adolescent evolves to best serve the individual and the immediate environment.

Few youths enter treatment to change their sexual orientation unless the family makes this demand. Most attempt home remedies, especially ones that deny same-sex attractions and emphasize heterosexual roles.[76]

Repression of Desires

By repressing unacceptable or disconcerting desires, the lesbian or gay teen attempts to prevent these desires from entering her or his consciousness. Unfortunately, this strategy offers the youth no opportunity to integrate sexual desires and sexual identity. Behavior and identity also become disconnected. Repressed or hidden feelings may work for a while but eventually emerge, often unexpectedly, resulting in panic, coping disruption, and disorganization. Some repressed teens may display acting out behavior.[77] The most common forms of repression are rationalization, relegation to insignificance, and compartmentalization.

Rationalization. The rationalization strategy uses the claim that the behavior was only for gratification and was a special case or situation.[78] Events are characterized as isolated incidents not to be repeated. Common rationalizations include:

> *We were both drunk.*
> *We just got high and. . . .*
> *It's just a phase; I'll grow out of it.*
> *I just needed some money.*
> *I was just lonely.*
> *All guys do it once.*

Relegation to insignificance. The insignificance strategy can be summarized as "No big deal."[79] Common types include:

> *It was just experimenting; so what.*
> *It was no big deal; we hardly touched.*
> *I was curious, that's all.*

It was just a favor for a friend, nothing more.
He's the one who gave me head.

Compartmentalization. In the compartmentalization strategy, sex and relationships become disconnected.[80] Sexual behavior is set aside as if it is unrelated to the person who engages in it. Common compartmentalization phrases include:

It just happened once.
It's just something that happened; I'm not like that.
I mess around; it don't mean nothing.
We're really good friends; that's it.
I love her, not all women.

Suppression of Homosexual Impulses

Unlike repression which tries to prevent same-sex desires, suppression tries to override them. The result is a moratorium on development that merely delays positive same-sex sexual identification until age thirty or forty but does not "cure" an individual.[81] Sexual orientation does not change. In general, the more heterosexual experience a person has had, the older the age at which she or he self-identifies as lesbian or gay.[82]

Youths employing this coping strategy are heavily invested in "the big lie" or "the big secret." Real fear of exposure and/or rejection exists. On the incorrect assumption that homosexuals possess the behavioral characteristics of the other sex, youth may attempt to remedy the situation by accentuating gender-typical behavior. This compensation can be noted in an accentuated male swagger or in male bodybuilding or female interest in clothing and cosmetics. Spontaneity may be suppressed as the youth attempts to control all behaviors and agonizes about all uncertainties.

A teen may become sexually active with the other sex, to the point of pregnancy in some extreme cases among women.[83] Meanwhile, fear may prevent same-sex experimentation, sexual maturation, and exploration of intimate relationships by a youth suppressing same-sex feeling. Peter, age seventeen, did not begin to question his sexuality until age sixteen and attempted to suppress his feelings, thus delaying identification of his true sexual feelings.[84] Withholding and suppressing personal information and interests in order to gain peer acceptance results in a false persona that is kept in place with vigilance and elaborate defenses.

As a result of delayed sexual identity, some individuals display adolescent-like behaviors when they finally come out even if well beyond adolescence. These might include intense but brief romantic involvements, frequent sexual experimentation, and over concern for one's own physical appearance.[85]

Withdrawal to celibacy or asexuality. Although relatively infrequent, a small percentage of gay male youths report that puberty was sexless and that they were deeply involved in masculine activities such as sports.[86] These teens may look and act like other males and participate in male activities. They may crave male friendships deeply, but terminate or avoid close relations because of the temptations encountered. Likewise, mas-turbation may be avoided because of same-sex erotic feelings and fantasies. Often these young adults deny that they had sexual feelings and attractions as children.

Tran, who lettered in three sports, believed he was too busy for sex. Carlton competed in high school track, gymnastics, and swimming but had to be cautious with the feelings he could not totally suppress.

> I felt like I had to be ultra-careful in the dressing room. I couldn't let my eyes wander; I couldn't let anyone suspect the slightest thing. I found myself putting up more of a front in sports than anywhere else. I felt like it was such a proving ground—proving my manhood to my father, to the other guys, to myself.[87]

Tom had his paper route, football, Boy Scouts, and the band.

Females may also choose to remain asexual under the guise of saving themselves for marriage or for just the right man. These individuals may even avoid information pertaining to sexuality. Those who choose to remain asexual, whether male or female, may delay awareness and gradual self-acceptance.[88]

In some cases, individuals, particularly those from strict religious backgrounds, may use crossdressing or transexualism in an attempt to confront their true feelings of homoeroticism. Sometimes this behavior disappears when individuals become exposed to a gay peer group.[89] In some ethnic groups, especially among Hispanics, cross-dressing behavior is more common among both lesbian and gay youths.

Overcoming obstructionism requires overwhelming alternative information or a traumatic event that forces the individual to be honest with her or his feelings. It is difficult to help a youth with sexual issues when for the youth there is no issue.

Denial and heterosexual dating and sex. "Passing" or "learning to hide" as a heterosexual is the most common adjustment.[90] Responding to peer and societal pressure, a teen may use heterosexual dating as an attempt to fit in or to change her or his sexual orientation. Approximately two-thirds of gay men and three-fourths of lesbians have engaged in heterosexual dating.[91] The increasing pressure on teens to date may have raised these values to 85 percent of today's youth.[92] These figures may be even higher in conservative areas, such as the South. Norma Jean, a poor, small town, Southern teen, felt she had no choice but to adopt a heterosexual persona. As for being an open lesbian, "It wasn't an option."[93] Vince, was muscular, played football, made fag jokes, had a regular girlfriend, attended a fundamentalist church, and sang in an evangelical choir. The outward signs were a perfect cover. He tried to be "The Best Heterosexual of the Year." Eric, a white twenty-one-year-old, recalls, "Hiding became an art."[94]

A youth may try to control any mannerisms or dress that might be perceived as gender inappropriate by peers. Lesbian and gay adolescents monitor themselves:

> *Is my voice too high?*
> *Did I appear too happy when she entered the room?*
> *Am I standing too close?*

Malcolm describes the process:

> I had to become more masculine. . . . I would make myself walk[,]. . . .
> I would make my voice sound[,]. . . . I would make myself sit a certain
> way. It was total insanity. I was not being me.[95]

Greg, a young African-American man, recalls, "Once when we were in Sunday school, the guys were ganging up on me about my eyelashes, saying they were entirely too long and beautiful for me to really be normal. I was so appalled . . . that I went home and cut my eyelashes off."[96] In addition to perpetuation of self-denial, this strategy can lead to problems of self-esteem because it fails to change sexual interests and desires.

Some teens attempt to cultivate a heterosexual role and to engage in antigay jokes and teasing. By teasing others suspected of similar feelings, a youth hopes to deflect suspicion from herself or himself.[97] In other words, the *best defense is a good offense.* Audrey told fag jokes and played pranks: "My social objective was to fit in," he explains, "and homosexuality definitely was not fitting in. I wanted to deny it in front of other people because I denied it to myself."[98] John, age sixteen, continues, "And the more nasty comments I made about gay people, the less gay I felt, like further and further away from this horrible thing."[99] "[O]nce I beat up a guy for being a faggot," confesses another young gay man. "No one suspected me [of being gay]," he adds, "because I did sports and had a girlfriend."[100]

Heterosexual girlfriends and boyfriends become a screen for hiding the true self and a wall between a youth and self-awareness. This wall enabled at least one gay youth to confide, "I guess I'm homosexual until I find the right woman."[101] Nathaniel, a middle-class African-American high schooler, explains, "When I got Delta [his girlfriend], it was like a cover. I was having sex with a man but for security I got a girlfriend. . . ."[102] As part of the cover, members of the other gender may be pursued as "sport" but with little serious intentions. Trying desperately to fit in, a young man explains, "It [pursuing women] gave me something to do to tell the other guys who were always bragging."[103] Monica acted "boy-crazy," although she had no sexual interest in boys. For Lee, a lesbian high schooler, the most difficult part was pretending when "I really didn't care."[104]

A lesbian or gay youth actually may believe that she or he is heterosexual but uncomfortable. Sex may feel unnatural, lacking an emotional component.[105] "I was just going through the motions," explains Kimberly. "It was expected of me, so I did it."[106] Drew reports that heterosexual dating anxiety results in nausea and diarrhea before each date.

Heterosexual relationships are often of short duration for gay and bisexual male youths but over half involve some sexual contact with young women.[107] Sex with one or two girls is often sufficient to satisfy curiosity. Gay and bisexual males express a preference for friendship over romance with females. As one adolescent explains, "I was disappointed because it [dating and sex] was such hard work—not physically, I mean, but emotionally."[108]

In similar fashion, lesbians may have two or three sexual contacts in the context of heterosexual dating. "I never really wanted to be intimate with any guy," explains Georgina, in a comment that echoes the sentiment of many lesbian teens. "I always wanted to be their best friend."[109]

Young women may engage in promiscuous heterosexual behavior in an attempt to make themselves heterosexual or to prove to themselves that they really are not lesbian.[110] Lisa, a young lesbian, states that she never enjoyed sex with boys but did it "to prove I wasn't gay."[111] This tactic can be summed up as *I can't be a lesbian; I have a boyfriend.*

The benefits of this coping strategy tend to be short-lived. A fourteen-year-old white gay male writes in his school paper,

> If there is anything I hate, it is having to be a fake. Unfortunately, I'm forced to do this every day of my life when I go to school.

"I fervently tried to take a more active interest in girls, "notes Paul, "but I could tell that it was contrived."[112] Although she strenuously tried to be heterosexual in high school, Bonnie, a twenty-one-year-old bisexual, remem-

bers, "I developed painful crushes on female teachers and straight girlfriends that left me feeling so pathetic and impotent."[113] Passing as a
heterosexual negates a lesbian or gay youth's feelings and ultimately herself or himself. John, age nineteen recalls,

> I used to stand around with the guys and try to look interested in all
> their gas about this girl and that. . . . All the time I'd be thinking
> about one or the other of them. It seemed like I didn't belong.[114]

Fear of exposure becomes very real. Jack, age twenty-two and described
as "straight-acting," recalls the panic at age thirteen or fourteen when "I
saw a Bloomingdale ad for Calvin Klein underwear that I could not take
my eyes off of."[115]

The overall result of this charade is psychological tension which may
lead to depression, shame, fear of disclosure, and anxiety, although her or
his surface demeanor may seem calm.[116] For example, covert gay college
men experience more psychological tension, social problems, and isolation than openly gay men.[117] In short, those in hiding "have the most
concern over self-esteem, self-acceptance, and status and feel the most
social isolation, powerlessness, normlessness, and personal incompe-
tence."[118] Paul, a gay college student, tried desperately as a teen to be
heterosexual. "From seventh grade to tenth grade," he recalls, "while
everyone's hormones were running rampant, I was attracted to no one;
emotionally I was numb. I hadn't a clue about what it meant to be sexually
attracted to someone."[119]

Healthy personalities develop when they are shared openly and honestly with others. Those in hiding have little opportunity to date or to
develop same-sex relationships in a socially sanctioned context similar to
that of heterosexual youth.

Redirection of energies into other areas (Compensation). Some queer
kids become too busy to bother with sex.[120] The student who is class
president, yearbook editor, school play lead, and tennis team captain is too
busy for any dating, heterosexual or otherwise. Although effeminate-
acting and disinterested in girls, Jacob, an African-American high school
overachiever, was never questioned by his family about his sexual orientation. "He don't have time for girls . . . " his family rationalized. "He's
doing his books."[121] A positive correlation of both delayed same-sex
erotic behavior and self-identification with better grades exists among gay
men.[122] In other words, those with later behavior and self-identification
have higher grades.

In similar fashion, in ninth grade, Malcolm, a young African-American
male, became a religious true-believer, an indefatigable "pioneer" in the

Jehovah's Witnesses. He would hide in his room for hours reading the Bible and proselytize door to door for over 100 hours a month. "If I prayed all the time and stayed active in the church," he reasoned, "maybe somehow I could appease God . . . and He wouldn't be so angry at me. . . ."[123] When this strategy failed, Malcolm devoted himself to his studies and became an honor student.

Self-Acceptance and Disclosure to Others ("Coming Out")

Accepting one's homosexuality is the optimal strategy.[124] Unfortunately, society encourages lesbian and gay teens to adopt a repressive or suppressive strategy. As a consequence, lesbian and gay youths become subject to psychological stresses that can affect their well-being.

Awareness of sexual orientation may encourage some adolescents to gain limited exposure to the larger lesbian, gay, and bisexual community. First steps may be very tentative, such as calling a hot line or attending a youth group. A teen may attempt to get to know another lesbian or gay youth or adult. For this youth, the goal is usually explorational, not sexual or relational.[125]

Accepting oneself need not always be a traumatic process. Michael, age sixteen, remarks:

> I can bring love and happiness to someone's life . . . Different is not bad. . . . [126]

Another teen, a cocky fourteen-year-old, adds that although the thought of being gay was frightening, the possible terror of living life as a "pseudo-heterosexual" was indescribable.

FIRST SEXUAL CONTACTS AND DATING

Same-sex erotic contact, such as body rubbing, manual genital contact, or oral genital contact, may begin around thirteen years for gay boys and fifteen for lesbian girls.[127] The mean age of first consensual orgasm is approximately sixteen years for today's young gay males, although some studies have placed the age much earlier.[128] Data vary with the definition of "first sexual contact" and with the age of both the subjects and the study itself. It is important to remember that many children, who, as adults, do not identify as lesbian or gay, engage in adolescent same-sex erotic behavior, and that such behavior is not a cause of homosexuality.

Frequently, the first same-sex kiss, whether sexual in nature or not, is significant. Nancy describes the "incredible feeling" when she and Connie brushed their lips together lightly for the first time. Neither Dan nor Steven, swim team buddies, said anything as they turned from their homework toward each other. "I remember thinking, oh God, don't let me be wrong; don't let me be wrong about this one thing in my entire life," Dan recalls.[129] The unplanned kiss was like a rush of air through his body. Others describe a feeling of "being home at last."

Both boys and girls engage in same-sex erotic behavior prior to self-identifying but the time between these two events differs greatly from about two-and-a-half years for males to four months on average for females.[130] Approximately two-thirds of gay male youths who reported that their sexuality felt natural very early welcomed puberty as a link between their attractions and sexual behavior. "Until then," reports a male student, "I had felt I could never fall in love, that I had no sexual feelings. . . . "[131] Often, there is an "ah-ha" or "eureka" when sexual arousal, imagery, fantasy, romantic notions, and sexual behavior come together. According to Linda, a young adult, she had "an undeniable feeling that this was . . . best for me."[132] A young gay man explains, "I didn't feel like I was cheating on Beth [his girlfriend] because the sex felt so different, so right."[133] John, a high school student continues, "I felt everything that I hadn't felt with a woman."[134] Although some lesbian, gay, and bisexual youths will still persist in their notion that they are similar sexually to others of their gender, they have great difficulty denying their attractions, and most explore and experiment with same-sex behaviors.

For some youths, same-sex erotic behavior is accompanied by shame and guilt. For example, although he had been engaging in sexual behavior for at least four years, Mike continued to promise not to transgress again and to ask God's help in making him stop. Those males with a history of rejection may begin to fear that such rejection will continue.[135] Same-sex sexual encounters are one more thing for which they may be ostracized by their peers. When Rob, age thirteen, agreed to perform oral sex on a very handsome athlete in his junior high, he had no idea that the ensuing "trap" would reveal his homosexuality to many of the boys in his scout troop and result in extreme embarrassment and isolation.

Lesbian and gay youths are more likely to engage in early sexual behavior of all types than are heterosexuals. As a group, lesbian and gay adults report earlier and more frequent same-sex contacts than do heterosexuals and more adolescent sexual behavior involving both sexes.[136] These trends are most evident among gay male youth.[137] Almost two-thirds of gay men masturbated with another boy before adolescence, more than double the figure reported by nongay men.[138]

In general, gay males behave sexually much like heterosexual males. Both are more likely than females to give in to sexual urges and to have serial partners. Unlike their heterosexual counterparts, however, gay males don't have socially sanctioned opportunities to learn a dating "script." Freed from the constraints that women place on male sexual assertiveness, however, gay males may experience a series of sexual encounters with little emotional attachment. In contrast, women, regardless of their sexual orientation, tend to value intimacy and attachment in their intimate relationships with others.

Sex role behaviors may become evident within same-sex relationships although they are not unique to lesbian and gay couples.[139] Male relationships may lack intimacy if both partners exhibit male sex role characteristics of competitiveness and independence. In contrast, female relationships may be very intimate while lacking individuality and autonomy. These tendencies can be counterbalanced over time with practice and patience.

As many as 70 percent of lesbian and gay teens may have had some *heterosexual* experience by adulthood.[140] In contrast, over 30 percent of self-identified lesbian and gay youths have no *same*-sex experience.[141] Heterosexual erotic behavior may continue despite a personal recognition of a lesbian, gay, or bisexual orientation by an individual. For some sexual-minority teens, heterosexual activity is part of their "cover."

In general, lesbians are more likely to continue to engage in heterosexual behaviors and relationships even after they come out to themselves. This difference reflects the positive relationship between self-worth and *success-with-boyfriends* found among junior and senior high school girls.

Emotionally vulnerable youth, especially males, may make sexual contact with other gay teens or adults under less than ideal conditions. Unfortunately, these furtive, solely sexual contacts may set a pattern for interactions with other gays. Dangerous settings, such as parks or rest areas after sunset, and the exploitive nature of the sexual encounters reinforce the worst gay stereotypes and may be internalized by a teen. For those queer kids still denying their feelings, such sexual encounters allow them to participate in sexual behavior devoid of an affectional component.

On the other hand, a naive youth may also misinterpret the intense feelings aroused by sex, the supportive environment, and physical affection as romantic love. Joseph, a gay student, concluded, "There's no simple answers; feelings are more important than sex."[142] Subsequent nonfulfillment of these feelings and the indifference of the other participant may convince the youth that love and intimacy are not possible within same-sex relationships.[143]

Other youths may welcome a mutual emotional commitment, nurture it, and develop mature feelings. Jacob, an African-American high school junior, met Warren, a senior, in a community choir. Jacob recalls,

> [W]e started to have sex. It started to be an emotional thing. He got to the point of telling me he loved me. That was the first time anybody ever said anything like that. It was kind of hard to believe that *even after sex* there are really feelings. We became good friends.[144]

For Christopher, age nineteen, expressing his sexual orientation for the first time confirmed and validated his feelings.

> Having repressed my sexuality for so long, it was an amazing experience to physically express it . . . It was . . . a giant step toward accepting who I am.[145]

For still others, sex and love may come together and be terrifying. "And that [emotion] scared the shit out of me . . . " confides a young gay man. "As I moved into eighth grade, it became more and more clear to me what it was all about, and it was sex, but with a twist, romance."[146] Still, it is important to remember that only 15 percent of self-identified lesbian teens and 25 percent of gay teens report negative feelings regarding their first same-sex erotic activity.[147]

Same-sex experiences are often the product of crushes, hero-worship and/or intimate friendships, especially for heterosexual youth.[148] Jeff's first experience at age twelve occurred at the urging of a high school neighbor. Another young man explains,

> Derek was my best friend. After soccer practice the fall of our junior year we celebrated both making the "A" team by getting really drunk. We were just fooling around and suddenly our pants were off. . . . I was so scared I stayed out of school for three days. . . .[149]

Beyond enjoyment, these erotic behaviors serve an information-gathering and comparison, reassurance, or experimentation function for queer kids.[150]

Among all males, the reported differences in the percentage of individuals engaging in same sex activity varies, especially with increasing age (Table 2.1). As would be expected, gay youths increasingly engage in same-sex sexual behavior while nongay youth demonstrate an opposite trend.[151]

TABLE 2.1. Percentage of Males Engaging in Same-Sex Experiences

Age level	Sexual orientation	
	Nongay	Gay
During childhood (ages 5-9 yrs.)	5	40
During preadolescence (ages 10-12 yrs.)	25	60
During adolescence (ages 13-17 yrs.)	15	70
During early adulthood (ages 18-24 yrs.)	5	95

Adapted from Savin-Williams and Lenhart, 1990.

Possibly as high as 60 percent of *all pre*pubescent males and 33 percent of *all pre*pubescent girls have some type of same-sex experience, while 33 percent and 17 percent respectively experience postpubescent orgasm with a same-sex partner.[152] Although other studies have reported lower percentages, the values are still higher than the percentage who will later identify as lesbian or gay.[153] Matthew, a student, observed, "Everyone is a bit gay, especially when you're young."[154] Only 2 percent of heterosexual men and almost no heterosexual women report predominantly homosexual activity as adolescents. In contrast 56 percent of gay men and 41 percent of adult lesbians had engaged in predominantly homosexual behavior.[155] The majority of heterosexual youth who engage in same-sex erotic behavior do not continue to do so in adulthood.

The quality of same-sex erotic behavior appears to differ among adolescents based on sexual orientation. Same-sex sexual activity by lesbians and gays may be more emotional, more planned, and less playful than same-sex activity among heterosexuals.[156] Lesbian and gay teens report a strong affectional component and feelings of love and desire. In contrast, the heterosexual activity by lesbian and gay youths may have an experimental quality.

Among gay and bisexual male youths, there is a positive relationship between the age of onset of puberty and the age of first same-sex erotic activity.[157] In contrast, the age of first heterosexual activity among the same youths is more closely related to chronological age. Heterosexual encounters seem to begin around age fifteen regardless of the age of onset of puberty.

Most lesbian and gay youths state that they want committed same-sex relationships.[158] The more a youth has engaged in same-sex erotic behavior, the more she or he desires a romantic relationship. In our culture, the process of dating and forming relationships is an important developmental experience through which we define ourselves and gain self-confidence. Falling in love and forming long-term romantic relationships is related to higher self-esteem and self-acceptance.

Although societal supports are nonexistent, 90 percent of lesbians and nearly 70 percent of gay youth between the ages of fourteen and twenty-three have been involved in at least one same-sex relationship. Unfortunately, these are often secretive, short-lived, and covert.[159] Social pressures make it difficult to form and maintain same-sex romantic relationships. "[L]ove of a woman," explains Diane, "was never a possibility that I even realized could be."[160] "[L]ove was something I watched other [heterosexual] people experience and enjoy," continues Lawrence. "I was expected to be part of a world with which I had nothing in common."[161] John, age sixteen, adds, "I've gone through my whole life not getting to know about relationships, not learning about any of this stuff."[162] Vic, a college-age lesbian, concludes,

> I think that whole straight ceremony of dating is not accessible to queer youth. Dating implies a certain amount of choice, the freedom to pick and choose. Well, pick and choose from who? A bunch of people who have to flash each other secret signals to be recognized.[163]

SELF-IDENTIFICATION

Self-identification usually occurs in late adolescence between the ages of sixteen and twenty-one.[164] The mean age for openly gay young adult males to self-identify is 16.2 years, although some self-identifying occurs as early as age 14.[165] As some segments of society become more open, self-identification is occurring even earlier,[166] especially in large urban areas. There is much individual variation. Self-identification does not imply self-acceptance which is dependent on many things, including romantic relationships and acceptance by others.

The relative lateness of sexual identification for lesbians and gays as compared to heterosexuals can be attributed to homophobia, discrimination, and societal prohibitions. No doubt, confusion and fear account for the lapse of time between first becoming aware of erotic feelings and labeling them. Sixteen-year-old Andy was caught between self-hatred for cowardly remaining in the closet and the threat of harassment should he come out.

Although Victor, a seventeen-year-old bisexual, reminds us that, "Bisexuals are *not* waiting to make up their minds about their sexual identity,"[167] for many *youths*, self-identification as bisexual is a rest stop on the way to claiming a lesbian or gay identity. Bisexuality seems more accepted and maintains a link to the heterosexual majority. More African Americans than European Americans choose this route because African-American communities seem to be more tolerant of bisexuality.[168] African-American teens may adopt a less heterosexual lifestyle than their white peers while being less willing to identify as lesbian or gay.

Initial feelings may gradually evolve into a sense of relief, of well-being, and "rightness." Naomi, age twenty, explains,

> [T]his feeling was so natural, I guess I trusted my own feelings enough not to believe anybody's negative ones. Because I felt that if what I'm doing is what they're saying is sick and bad, well they [the critics] must be sick and bad.[169]

This conscious recognition of sexuality is the beginning of self-acceptance.[170] A lesbian or gay teen may express self-anger at her or his earlier pattern of conformity.

Self-identification can be viewed as a two-step process in which a youth first accepts her or his sexual identity and then integrates that identity with her or his personality and self-concept. A twenty-year-old female student describes how it feels to be an integrated whole:

> I feel that I am the terrific person I am today because I'm a lesbian. I decided that I was gay when I was very young. After making that decision, which was the hardest thing I could ever face, I feel like I can do anything.[171]

Through acceptance, an adolescent begins to view the notion of "lesbianness," "gayness," or bisexuality in a positive way. "It's a real love and trust of women, and respect," states Brenda, age seventeen. "It's something inside me that I can't explain."[172] During this phase, a youth may make an initial disclosure or "come out" to a very trusted friend or family member. Disclosure seems very important for positive self-identification as lesbian or gay.[173]

Acceptance is followed by integration in which a young person identifies as lesbian or gay and proud. "My soul feels more comfortable," explains Shannon, age seventeen. "It feels right."[174] Integration and pride often are accompanied by a public self-disclosure known as "Coming out of the closet" or simply as "Coming out." Coming out is an adjusting between the real and the social self and as such, is a necessary process for healthy personality integration. Being known as lesbian or gay is an important step in identity formation.[175] Early self-disclosure seems to be related positively to high self-esteem. Michael, a student, explains the process:

> Contrary to . . . opinion, I didn't wake up one morning and say, "Gee, I think I'll be gay for the rest of my life. That'll be fun." Why would anyone choose a life filled with discrimination? The only choice I made was to come out of the closet.[176]

Coming out and the often accompanying anger and pride are important for identity stabilization.[177] Integration of sexual identity is a lifelong process.

Integration is enhanced through interaction with other lesbian and gay adults and involvement in the sexual-minority community.[178] Typically, youths come to prefer social interactions with other lesbians and/or gays. Self-identification with others becomes positive.

When compared to those still in sexual-identity turmoil, the well-integrated lesbian or gay male may have higher self-esteem and greater well-being, a greater capacity for and more confidence in love both in sexual relationships and in friendships, and increased productivity.[179] More energy is spent in living an open life and less on trying to hide it. Honest heterosexuals occasionally will express awe for the lesbian or gay adult who has come through this process and now knows who she or he is and faces the world confident and unafraid. The battle with homophobia and heterosexism and with their own internalized "demons" can leave the winners proud to proclaim "I am who I am!"

Unfortunately, not everyone can accept her or his own lesbian, gay, or bisexual identity. The road to a well-integrated, healthy, positive, cohesive identity is strewed with those who can not really accept themselves and continue to use all manner of subterfuge to hide their true identity.

CONCLUSION

Sexual self-identification is part of the larger process of adolescent development, a confusing, sometimes contradictory, process in itself. For many teens their sexuality is ambiguous and not clearly delineated. They may begin to understand their feelings but not to clarify them. All the while these processes are occurring within an atmosphere of adolescent conformity and burgeoning independence. The adolescent question "Who am I?" becomes entangled with a second question "What does it mean to be lesbian or gay?"[180]

Most homosexuals accept their sexual orientation and "lead successful, productive, nonneurotic lives as self-acknowledged gay men and lesbians."[181] More than half would not change their sexual orientation if such were possible, despite the negative attitudes of the larger society.[182] The process of becoming has its own rewards. Questioning and exploring can make an individual more sensitive to difference and more accepting of it. Every issue from coming out to having children is there to be explored, discussed, and decided. Erna, a young Navajo woman, concludes that, as a result, "[W]e are special, because we're able to deal with . . . life."[183]

Through the process of "becoming" lesbian, gay, or bisexual, the individual's range of possibilities increases, and the coping skills acquired to transcend adversity give an individual the ability to find fulfillment. "I have learned a lot more about myself," states Rachel, a sixteen-year-old Midwesterner. "If I had a choice, I wouldn't change my sexual orientation."[184]

Chapter 3

Coming Out of the Closet

Went out last night with a crowd of my friends,
Must've been women, 'cause I don't like no men.

Ma Rainey, "Prove It on Me Blues"

Coming out of the closet or simple *coming out* or *outing oneself* is a developmental process, a self-affirming rite, through which lesbian, gay, and bisexual individuals first recognize their sexual orientation and develop positive feelings about themselves and that orientation and then integrate this knowledge into their lives.[1] The process has cognitive, affective, and behavioral aspects. It is important to recognize that coming out is a *process*—not an outcome or single event—that occurs every time a lesbian, gay, or bisexual person shares the news of her or his sexuality with another person. With each new acquaintance, the process begins anew.

The act of coming out is as individualistic as the person involved. "[O]n Halloween, all of my close friends and I were gathered in one of our bedrooms counting out loot . . . I spoke up, 'Hey guys? What would you say if I told you I was gay?' Julia . . . shrugged and said, 'I'd say I was happy for you.' . . . Marion glared, 'Is that all? I've known that since 5th grade!!!'"[2] The extent of coming out is culturally based and the process is not universal.

Various studies have found that roughly 40 percent of lesbian and 63 percent of gay adults are open about their sexuality with their parents.[3] Most disclosed to their family members when they were financially independent and living on their own. Some individuals never come out.[4] In contrast to older lesbians, gays, and bisexuals, adolescents are being more open about their sexual orientation and demanding more community support. Most live at home and are not economically self-supporting. The process of disclosure can be perilous.

For many, coming out is a "rite of passage" into a well-adjusted adulthood. Although coming out can be social suicide in high school, more and

39

more adolescents view it as a badge of honor or courage and an expression of individuality. In the process, they are increasing the visibility of sexual minorities and making coming out easier for the next teen.

The most frequent reasons given for not self-disclosing are fear of hurt and rejection. Often individuals are afraid that parents will be disappointed or hurt and may reject them.[5] "I want so much for her [her mother] to be proud of me," explains Obie, a young middle-class African-American lesbian.

> I know there are certain things that won't make her proud. Being gay is one of them.[6]

In general, young lesbian adults seek support from their families first and then from male and female friends, while young gay men seek support from male friends first and then from families.[7] Fear of peer rejection also exists. Lew's college roommate moved out when he found out about Lew. Glen's basketball buddies stopped asking him to play. Sophie became a pariah in the high school band.

The lesbian and gay communities are so stigmatized that disclosure of same-sex orientation often marks a person as less than whole. Being lesbian or gay typically takes precedence for others over everything else and becomes the entire person.

The demographics on coming out are very interesting. As a group, upper- and middle-class young lesbian and gay adults are more likely than working-class young lesbian and gay adults to be open about their sexual orientation.[8] Among African Americans, middle-class families, who may be less secure in their status, seem to be less accepting than working-class families of their members who deviate from strict community "norms" or call negative attention to the family.[9] Metropolitan dwellers are more likely to be open than their country and small town cousins.[10] "In a small community," notes 'Lizabeth, a young lesbian, "people here have the ability to make life miserable for you."[11] As a group, men come out before women but women experience fewer mental health problems when coming out and are more open as adults.[12] The difference in age of coming out between men and women may be decreasing.[13] Religiosity seems to be negatively related to self-identification as a male homosexual but not as a lesbian or bisexual. This relationship may reflect the male-centered nature of biblical prohibitions and religious expectations.[14]

In general, those most likely to come out have the lowest levels of homophobia and/or the greatest degree of positive feelings about homosexuality in general.[15] Involvement in sexual-minority political and social organizations and having a supportive environment are positively associated with self-acceptance and coming out.[16] In addition, those most likely to come out have the most comfort with same-sex arousal and lifestyle, more same-sex erotic experiences, a more exclusively homosexual orientation and behavior, and the least fear of negative societal reactions.[17]

By all accounts, more and more youths are self-identifying as lesbian, gay, or bisexual at a younger age and remaining open as they get older. Studies from the early 1970s to the present record a steady decline in the mean age of coming out from nineteen to fifteen or sixteen years of age.[18] Some youth who self-identify early are coming out as early as age fourteen.[19] As a result, the challenges inherent in self-disclosure are now becoming associated with the problems of adolescence.

No rules exist for coming out, so each individual must improvise.[20] The decision to out oneself is a very personal one in which each person must consider the consequences for herself or himself and for her or his relationships with others. Success in coming out is related in part to the maturity of both the youth and the person to whom she or he is coming out.[21] Coming out is often a disorderly, highly individualized process, characterized by diversions and detours.[22]

The rationale for coming out is simple. Healthy personalities are those that are shared with others.[23] "If I . . . don't tell *anyone*, how long must I keep it all in?" reasons Philip, a gay high schooler with deafness. "What's the point of keeping it in?"[24] "It's been real bad for my parents," confides John. "I just lie to them more and more."[25] Dan, age nineteen, concurs, "Lying is the one thing that I've perfected over the years. . . ."[26] The sexual identification of a person and the social identification that is presented to the world must become consistent or the youth risks feelings of hypocrisy and falsehood that can lead to isolation.[27] Christopher, a young white gay man, explains:

> The hardest part about coming out is telling something that's so deep in your heart with the realization that at any point they could say, "You're immoral; you're wrong.". . . But what's wonderful is that finally you're not lying. You're being completely honest and they're sharing that joy with you.[28]

One of the results of coming out is a decrease in feelings of aloneness and guilt. "I've come out to almost all of my friends," states Michael, age sixteen. "Sometimes it was hell, but nothing compares to holding it inside."[29] Brent, age sixteen, explains further:

> I knew my coming out wouldn't allow me to have the same everyday existence heterosexuals did. I knew I'd have more people treating

me badly. But at least I wouldn't be treating myself badly. I'd rather be bashed by other people than by myself.[30]

When given an opportunity to renounce his former claim of homosexuality, Joseph Steffan, a high-ranking Annapolis midshipman, refused, responding, "Yes sir, I am." He recalls:

> It was a moment I will never forget, one of agony and intense Pride. In that one statement, I had given up my dreams, the goals I had spent the last four years of my life laboring to attain. But in exchange, I retained something far more valuable—my honor and my self-esteem.[31]

The benefits of coming out aside, most lesbian and gay individuals come out for reasons other than mental health. Rather, they feel compelled to self-disclose when denial can no longer be sustained, possibly accompanying a relationship or infatuation.

Self-esteem and the degree of openness, especially in a supportive environment, are directly related. More of one leads to more of the other.[32] Those who have been out the longest have the highest self-esteem.[33] Adolescents who have discussed their sexuality with parents feel more confirmed and less anxiety-ridden.[34] Individuals who have come out often report a sense of freedom, of not living a lie, and of genuine acceptance.[35] When Karen first came out in college, she proclaimed, "Finally, for the first time, I felt like who I was."[36]

Being out is also correlated with a positive queer identity.[37] With the fusing of sexuality and emotionality, open homosexuality becomes a preferred way of life.[38]

Although an open lesbian or gay youth may face harassment and hostility, she or he may avoid the negative aspects of nonidentity, including denial, repression, and/or suppression. Aaron Fricke, one of the first adolescents to take a same-sex date to his high school prom, saw his actions as a strong positive statement. He concluded, "I would be showing that my dignity and value as a human being were not affected by my sexual preference."[39] At one level, coming out can be seen as an attempt by the individual to redefine herself or himself rather than to accept the negative societal stereotypes.

Coming out can lead to nonsexual interactions with other lesbians, gays, and bisexuals. The lesbian and gay community can provide support for teens and is a source of friendship, romantic relations, role models, and social norms.[40] In general, it's more important to have someone to talk to than someone to socialize with.[41] The extent of this interaction varies with an individual's social and vocational needs and with the availability of other individuals.[42] Marshall and a friend made frequent trips of several hours length to a large city to explore gay bookstores and to attend gay film festivals and pride marches. Many lesbian, gay, and bisexual youth speak of the exhilaration of attending their first pride or rights march.

In general, coming out can be discussed as a three-step process of coming out to one's self, to others, and to all or "going public."[43] Individuals will vary in the degree of disclosure and degree to which each considers herself or himself to be out.[44] The degree of disclosure will vary with income, occupation, place of habitation, and the sexual orientation of one's friends.[45] At each stage of coming out, the act of disclosure redefines an individual's notion of self which, in turn, influences the process of disclosure.[46]

Although more information is available on lesbians and gays, anecdotal data suggest that the process for bisexuals is similar to that for homosexuals.[47] Gillian came out while driving around with his friend Josh.

> I said "Josh, I really need to talk to you about something. I think I might be bisexual. . . . " And he . . . turns to me and goes "I'm so glad you brought this up because I know that I'm gay. . . . " We gave each other the biggest hug for a long time, just because we knew we were there for each other.[48]

STAGES

As mentioned, coming out is a lifelong process not a one-time event. We can describe this process in three stages. Their importance for the individual, the difficulty or ease of each, and their length will vary across individuals.

Coming Out to Self

Coming out to one's self is part of becoming lesbian, gay, or bisexual. An individual passes from nonrecognition through a sense of difference to self-recognition and lesbian, gay, or bisexual affirmation.[49] Feeling different and the growing awareness of what that difference means can create inner tension and affect self-esteem. The realization can be frightening. "I said it to myself when I was fourteen, but I know that I clearly knew it before then; I just didn't admit it to myself," explains a young gay man: "I said to myself, 'I can't be.' I couldn't accept it."[50] Nonetheless, realization can provide a self-explanation and a context for self-examination.

Self-recognition and identity formation are based on more than the emergence of sexual feelings. Lesbian and gay teens and young adults cite other events that contribute to their self-realization.[51] For males, contact with other gay males or with lesbians is particularly important for self-realization. For females, falling in love is the most important event although contact with other lesbians and gay males is a strong second. "I realized that these women were feeling the same things that I felt," recalls a seventeen-year-old lesbian, "and what I'd been reading about lesbians was, in fact, what I am. That's when I started feeling really good."[52]

Self-acceptance and self-esteem are positively related.[53] In general, openness increases and/or is encouraged by self-esteem. Recalling his ordeal at Annapolis after coming out, exmidshipman Joseph Steffan stated, "By coming out to myself, I gained the strength that can come only from self-acceptance, and it was with that added strength that I had been able to persevere . . . "[54]

Gender differences exist in self-labeling.[55] Males define themselves as gay in the context of same-sex erotic behavior. In contrast, lesbians self-define in the context of romantic love and attachment.[56] In addition, self-labeling appears to be more threatening to males than to females.[57]

Healthy self-esteem is difficult for queer kids to attain in the face of society's negative messages. "I believed all the [negative] things I'd been told," recalls Robin, a sixteen-year-old lesbian. "So I hid from myself."[58] Pervasive negative feelings may make it difficult for a youth to feel good about anything she or he accomplishes. The attitude may become, "Yeah, I won the bowling trophy [received the scholarship, got straight A's, became an Eagle Scout, etc.] but I'm still a faggot [dyke, lezzie, queer, etc.]." With gay-positive feelings self-esteem is enhanced in other areas of life.

Usually, in this phase, sexual orientation is placed in perspective with personal identity so that the stereotypes of lesbians, gays and bisexuals do not overwhelm other aspects of personality. Sexual orientation becomes only one aspect of the person.

Coming Out to Others

Disclosure to others is best when the discloser has a strong self-image. Unnecessarily painful disclosure may result if a youth comes out while internalized homophobia is strong and issues of self-worth still unre-solved.[59] Christopher, age nineteen, tried to resolve these issues prior to coming out. It took him four years of dealing with his own internalized homophobia before he was ready. "Our society is so homophobic that it can take someone who is gay years before being able to say the words out loud."[60]

Initially, lesbians and gays are very cautious in selecting to whom and when to come out. The relationship with the other person and the expected reaction are considered carefully. Those who are generally supportive of an individual youth and can be described as warm, accepting, and nurturant are the most likely candidates.[61]

Recent studies have found a mean age of sixteen for first disclosure.[62] As a group, lesbian, gay, and bisexual teens usually self-disclose first to a friend, same-sex peer, sibling, or another lesbian or gay teen.[63] Queer kids risk less by telling friends rather than parents. Friends can reject an outed teen, but parents can withdraw financial support. Reportedly, most peers and friends respond favorably, possibly reflecting the selection of tolerant or homosexual confidants.[64] The even more positive responses reported in more current studies may reflect changing attitudes.

Over half of lesbian and gay teens consider their gay friends more important than their families. Of the remainder, 15 percent consider their families more important.[65] Terry, a gay teen, couldn't have wished for a response as positive as his sister's.

> Well, I have a friend who is that way. She's my best friend. I just want to let you know that if you need any help or need to talk, just come to me.[66]

Among parents, mothers usually are informed before fathers, possibly because they are perceived as the more accepting parent.[67] When Jim told his mother, her initial response was to cry and to curse and ridicule him. She later relented and became more accepting. When Marcus, age eighteen, told his father he was gay, his father's response shocked him:

> This isn't what I wish for you. It's not going to be an easy life for you. But I don't love you any less than if you were straight.[68]

Coming Out to All

Disclosure to others is an important step in positive self-identification. An individual slowly becomes fully aware of herself or himself as that self is revealed fully to others. Through the coming-out process, lesbian and gay youths develop a sense of self-control and self-respect and begin to heal from the burden of carrying a secret.[69] Without this openness, "the lie" can distort all relationships. The wall that protects the deception results in the youth's isolation. Distancing from others, including parents, becomes a survival technique.

One of the results of being an invisible minority of closeted individuals is that it is difficult for lesbian, gay, and bisexual teens to meet each other.

Slowly, in part because of the insistence of these teens themselves, a network of support groups and services is being established.

Those youth who successfully come out usually disclose themselves slowly to others considered to be safe and gradually build a support network. Coming out is a more positive experience if an adolescent gains support from family and friends.[70] Quality of supporters is more important than number of supporters for sixteen- to twenty-year-olds. Those supporters with whom a youth can talk honestly are the most important.[71]

Those young gay men who are out tend to be involved in more gay activities; to be more open about their sexual identity and in a more supportive environment; to describe themselves as accomplished, outgoing, and understanding of the feelings of others; older; better educated, earlier maturing; and from wealthier, more urban families.[72] In contrast, young out lesbian adults are more involved in lesbian and gay rights; have more lesbian and gay friends and family support; and have fewer, if any, sexual relations with men than do closeted lesbians.[73]

Coming out is not without risk, but the eventual results far outweigh the destructive psychological price of concealment.[74] The most frequent reasons for not coming out are fear of hurting or disappointing loved ones and fear of rejection. Family relationships are a major concern for teens. Disapproval and rejection are very possible reactions. The threat of expulsion from the home is all too real.

Although difficult, coming out to family members is extremely important for identity development.[75] Disclosure to parents, probably one of life's most fearful events, is accompanied by stress and anxiety, especially for a disclosing youth.[76] More than half of lesbian, gay, and bisexual teens and young adults fear disclosing their sexual orientation to their families.[77] "I haven't come out yet to my parents," confesses a young African-American lesbian. "I'm sure it'll be a problem when I do."[78]

Families, the primary socialization context in our society, are awash in heterosexism. Barbara, the mother of a gay son admits, "You realize that you have expectations for your children that you didn't know you had."[79] Thus, lesbian and gay youth often hide their sexuality from their parents and endure a litany of questions about dating and perspective boyfriends and girlfriends. The secretiveness comes at a cost as noted in the comments of an eighteen-year-old lesbian:

I was so frustrated from hiding that I just told her [her mother]. . . . But at that point I didn't care anymore.[80]

Not to come out is to surrender to fear and mistrust, to become alienated, and to stifle openness and spontaneity.[81] For some teens, running away is easier than continued deception.

Occasionally, parents will ask about sexual orientation before the youth is ready to come out and before the family and the teen are adequately prepared to discuss the issue maturely and calmly. Beth's mother asked her one Saturday while in the car. Luckily for Beth, her mother was very supportive. Julio's father quizzed him angrily and made verbal threats, but his mother was more reasonable, although she was also very upset.

Matt, an openly gay student in Newton, Massachusetts and three-time state gymnastics champion, was asked by his parents if he was gay when he was fourteen. Initially unsure, Matt had come out to the entire high school by his senior year and was organizing awareness training for students and faculty.

Some parents may not wish to know about their child's sexual orientation. Jacob, an African-American high schooler explains,

> Maybe they were afraid of me saying, "yes." I think that may have been why my parents never mentioned it to me.[82]

Confronting sexual issues may be too difficult for some parents.

The coming-out process will vary with the particular family member and the individual lesbian or gay youth.[83] Coming out to the family is especially difficult for males.[84] Siblings are perceived as potentially more accepting than parents. Elderly parents seem to be more negative than younger ones.[85] In general, more lesbian and gay youths are out to their parents than to other family members with mothers favored over fathers by a ratio of two to one. Mothers often serve a supportive role and negotiate relationships between their lesbian or gay child and other family members.

Travis came out to his mother as a high school junior but feared telling his stepfather, "who doesn't drink homogenized milk because it says 'homo' on the label!"[86] More youth may come out to their mothers because they rightly predict that mothers tend to respond more positively than fathers, who if not negative may just be very nonresponsive. Chris's father pronounced his son's coming out a death sentence.[87] The boyfriend of Thomas's mother scrawled "FAGGOT MAGGOTS" on Thomas's bedroom wall.[88] Mitch's father saw no need for his son to cause "problems" by telling everyone. Vince's father, a very religious man, told his son that he really believed Vince had no choice in his sexual orientation, then explained, "Your orientation is the result of some form of demonic possession."[89]

Young lesbian adults tend to tell siblings earlier and fathers later than do young gay men.[90] Often, the concerns and responses of siblings differ from those of parents. The shame and guilt that parents generally experience is replaced by feelings of embarrassment and betrayal. Siblings may feel that the stigma of homosexuality affects them in some way too.

Girls tend to be more open with either parent than boys. Although parental response does not seem to vary with the gender of the child, fathers seem to experience more difficulty accepting the news from their daughters, possibly because lesbian youth seem to be less influenced by prevailing gender roles than males.[91] According to Jennifer, her father "insisted that I was just being rebellious and trying to make him look like a bad father."[92] The greater openness of girls may reflect the more open conversational style of females in general or the less negative societal reaction to lesbians than to gay men. Overall, males receive more negative reactions from their families than do females. In addition, lesbians are more likely than men to view coming out as a political statement.

Approximately half of lesbian and gay youth report that they have lost friends or received negative reactions from family members.[93] "I have no friends that are guys," admits Mike, a white nineteen-year-old. Athletic and energetic, he likes football but has no friends with which to play. "They can't get past 'Mike the faggot'," he explains.[94] "I went from very popular to not having any friends," declares Alessandra. "Most people wouldn't talk *to* me but there was a lot of talk behind my back."[95]

Angela's mother found out about her teenage daughter's sexual orientation from reading Angela's diary. Angela now lives alone and is isolated from family members. Scott's parents, who are Jehovah's Witnesses, physically removed him from their home when he came out at age seventeen. No member of his former congregation, including his family, may interact with him.

The response of family members is influenced by such factors as conformity, religion, politics, ethnicity and race, discomfort with sexual matters, and attitudes about family cohesion.[96] Families that emphasize religion, marriage, and children are perceived by lesbian and gay teens as being disappointed at hearing a member's disclosure, although these types of beliefs do not seem to be a factor in whether or not to come out.[97]

Homophobia seems to be more prevalent in ethnic-minority communities, making coming out very difficult.[98] For a youth to come out may be to risk losing the extended family and bringing disgrace to all its members. Losing family support leaves a youth alone, jeopardizing her or his sense of self.[99]

It may be especially difficult to be open in the ethnic-minority community. Even parents who know a child's sexual orientation may not wish to embarrass the family or community by asking. The subject may be quarantined, a taboo topic, especially in Asian-American and Latino homes where sex is discussed rarely, if at all. In these two ethnic communities, approximately 80 percent of lesbian and gay young adults are out to a sister rather than to a parent.[100]

Sex role expectations vary with culture also. In Latino culture, for example, males are expected to exude *machismo*. In contrast, gay men are expected to be effeminate and passive, a *maricón*. Many gay men are not willing to take this "female" role. Lesbians who do not subscribe to this inferior role may be just as subversive. "Being a lesbian is by definition an act of treason against our cultural values," states a Latina lesbian.[101] Gay men who accept the Latino stereotype and lesbians who reject the Latina feminine role may be embarrassments to their families.[102]

For parents in many cultures, the love for their child may be in conflict with their internalized societal concept of lesbians and gays.[103] Duane's parents, unable to accept their son's gayness, were reluctant to talk about his sexuality and ignored his repeated requests for books and information. Parents may chose to respond with rejection, ostracism, and/or violence, or with acceptance.[104] Although Jeremy's mother has come to accept her son's sexual orientation, his older adult brother has isolated Jeremy from his son for the stated purpose of protecting his son from molestation by Jeremy. In contrast, Barbara's mother counseled her daughter to be happy with herself:

> We love you. We support you. And we'll defend you to the death.[105]

Parental reactions are as varied as youths' coping strategies.

Parents may be comforted by the notion that their son or daughter's sexual orientation is just a phase or a fluke, the result of hero worship or a close friendship. Such rationalizations are common. Travis, who came out to his mother as a high school junior, was originally frustrated by his mother's unwillingness to accept what he was telling her. In his diary, he recorded, ". . . for the last five years I have known that WITHOUT QUESTION I am gay."[106] Later, Travis' mother began to question his feelings:

> She tells me that I've never even tried dating . . . "You haven't even given heterosexuality a chance!" Oh, brother.[107]

"I think that you are bisexual," rationalized another mother, "because you have a strong need for love and affection." "[Y]ou need so much," she continued, "that you believe that you need it from both sexes."[108]

A second reaction is compartmentalization by which a parent attempts to separate the person from the orientation or the orientation from sex. "It is sex, pure and simple," concluded Michael's mother, "just physical."[109] In that one statement she has negated her son's feelings and probably alienated him.

From the first two reactions comes a third, the "simple solution," and its implication that the youth is weak. "Program your mind and then the emotions and physical attractions will follow," counsels one mother.[110] Michael's mother offers, "Don't allow yourself to get involved."[111] This is the *Just Say No* approach. Such advice is insulting in its giver's inability to comprehend what the youth is experiencing. The inherent insensitivity leaves a youth feeling frustrated, rejected or abandoned, and angry.

Unfortunately, a parental attitude that finds excuses for feelings or behavior while not confronting them causes great difficulties for a youth who is becoming aware of her or his sexual identity. Although there is no rush to establish a sexual identity, such attitudes only result in sexual confusion and may unnecessarily delay sexual identification.

The importance of parental acceptance cannot be overstressed. An accepting family can greatly facilitate the coming-out process.[112] Brent, age sixteen, recalls coming out to his mom:

> The words just wouldn't come out. . . . She kept guessing things and finally she got it. . . . She gave me a hug and told me she loved me. I didn't expect it to be that good.[113]

In general, a youth's perception of family attitudes is a very important factor in overall self-esteem.[114] The well-being of each lesbian and gay youth is closely related to her or his perceived or actual level of parental acceptance.[115] Parental attitudes are often incorporated into a child's self-perception. Barbara came out at age twelve:

> [M]y mother . . . said that since I was very young . . . I should wait a few months at least before deciding that this was an absolute fact. But if it turned out, indeed, that I was a lesbian, then that was fine.[116]

"I think my mother knew," recalls a young gay man. "She wanted me to be in therapy since seven or eight, not to change me but so that I could be happy and sure of my homosexuality."[117]

CONCLUSION

The process of coming out may involve guilt, self-hatred, self-pity, fear of nonacceptance, and denial. Successful navigation of each can lead to better understanding and self-acceptance. For those who are not successful, these feelings may impede progress. It is only the well-integrated person who can really share herself or himself with the world. In turn, clarifying oneself by self-disclosure can facilitate integration.

Coming out does not ensure success. Careful and thoughtful decisions must be made about when, to whom, and how to self-disclose, and the psychological costs must be weighed. Covert behavior and fear of disclosure can lead to psychological difficulties. The most closeted lesbian and gay adults have more personal conflict, more alienation and depression, and more negative self-esteem than their more open peers.[118] Some lesbian and gay youths, unable to cope with deception and isolation, may run away or engage in antisocial behavior, such as prostitution.

Nonetheless, the benefits of being open usually outweigh the drawbacks. "I lost several friends," laments Heather, age seventeen, "but the real friendships I've gained are worth so much more than the superficial friendships that I've lost."[119] My true friends supported me and became even better friends," concludes Salim, age sixteen; "the ones who didn't accept me were truly never my friends in the first place."[120] It has been reported that coming out may result in healthier psychological adjustment, fewer feelings of guilt and loneliness, less need for psychological counseling, more positive attitudes toward homosexuality and a positive lesbian or gay identity, and a greater fusion of sexuality and affect.[121] One fourteen-year-old male writes:

> I was on a roller coaster where my emotions began to collide.
> Should I live, or shall I die, went through my mind when I began to hide.
> Hide from the world and hide from my mom,
> I shall rinse that away, and let my life go on.
> Thy melted snow has seeped away,
> My boots are clean, and that is good,
> I am out of the closet, just as I should![122]

Chapter 4

Challenges for Queer Kids

> There is really nothing to fear from us
> except the pain that comes from your ignorance.
>
> Brett, age 19[1]

Although quite possibly the largest and most invisible minority group in our schools today, lesbian, gay, and bisexual youth are marginalized and isolated. Many heterosexual individuals believe that sexual minority youth simply do not exist. Queer kids look like other students and can "pass" for heterosexual, often masking the hurt, anger, fear, and isolation they experience.

Public discussion of homosexuality focuses almost exclusively on adults with most youths unable or unwilling to speak for themselves. Sexual orientation is considered to he an adult prerogative. When sexual-minority youths are discussed they are treated as "the problem." The accompanying question is "How do *we* deal with *them?*"

Although most lesbian, gay, and bisexual teens mature into healthy, happy, well-adjusted adults, many are fearful, frightened, and isolated and may have a sense of personal failure.[2] They are often the targets of harassment and discrimination. From a youth's perspective, explains pediatrician and lesbian, gay, and bisexual youth researcher Dr. Gary Remafedi, "Being gay is probably the worst thing . . . that can possibly happen. . . ."[3] Sexual-minority youths are subjected to ridicule and scorn and many occupy the sidelines of mainstream adolescent culture.

A youth who may already feel different in some way may face a "life crisis" when she or he attempts to define this difference as homosexuality or bisexuality. The ensuing identity struggle is summarized clearly by Scott, an Ohio youth:

> I was trying to define who I was, and there was absolutely no role models. The only gays I ever saw, like in pride parades, were real flamboyant. It really confused me, and I kept thinking, *That's not me.* Then the mass media kept feeding me constant images of murder and

AIDS. When you hear all the negative messages from your friends, your parents, and TV, you begin to think, *What is wrong with me?*[4]

In a society that expects and assumes everyone to be heterosexual, lesbian, gay, and bisexual youths are not prepared for their emerging sexual identity and have no context for understanding and acceptance.[5]

WHAT CHALLENGES?

Lesbian and gay youths must make decisions about sexuality and their degree of openness. These are decisions that they may not be mature enough to make. The process is made more difficult by the lack of guidance and the absence of role models. Individuals who are under stress are less likely to make good choices.

A youth may be in denial. In a quandary, a young male may wonder where male bonding ends and same-sex attractions begin? Thirteen, at the time, Sam, now age twenty, confesses, "I was attracted to males, but I dared not say this to anyone, including myself. . . ."[6]

The socialization process is explicitly and implicitly heterosexual. All the models, expectations, supports, and rewards are for establishing a healthy heterosexual identity, and they do not apply to lesbian or gay adolescents.

The antihomosexual environment of home, school, church, and society does not support the healthy psychological development of lesbian and gay youths. "It's a rare gay teenager who finds support in his or her high school—either from another gay student or an openly gay teacher."[7]

In early adolescence especially, the gender roles may be very stereotypic. Those students who do not conform are vulnerable to ridicule as the sissy, queer, or tomboy. Lesbian, gay, or bisexual youths may have an especially strong need to conform and to fit in. For example, an eighteen-year-old African-American male states, "When I refer to some person I like, I'll say 'she' or use different names. . . ."[8] Queer kids are caught between their families, school, church, peers, and the lesbian, gay, and bisexual community. All of these diverse groups tug at and challenge youths.

Societal, Political, and Religious Intolerance

Most Americans are embarrassed by frank sexual discussion. Playing to this uneasiness, religious conservatives have skewed the public sense of morality to equate interest in sex with shame and guilt.[9] It is assumed that an interest in such topics is abnormal or immoral. In entertainment, sadly, portrayals of a loving sexual encounter are censored while gratuitous violence is accepted for its thrill factor. If sex is shameful as the conventional wisdom purports, homosex is revolting and dangerous.

These conservatives, who supposedly are concerned with family values and family stability, attack anything that blurs sex roles and/or portrays sexual minorities in a favorable or even neutral manner. Both issues threaten the heterosexist assumptions of the majority society. When Lynn Johnston's comic strip *For Better or for Worse* ran a series about a young man coming out to his family, it was pulled from seventy newspapers nationwide. Justification for this censorship was that the strip provided a "bad male role model." Meanwhile, the likes of Hagar and Andy Capp remained.

Despite many indicators to the contrary, the American public continues to act as if all youth are innocent and sexless. As long as lesbian, gay, and bisexual teens remain invisible, the same assumptions are made about them. Once they become visible, however, they are damaged in some way and are cast aside as unclean or unworthy. It would seem that innocence and homosexuality are mutually exclusive.

The Committee on Adolescence of the American Academy of Pediatrics (1983) concluded the difficulties faced by lesbian and gay youths are the result of defects in the way society treats sexual minorities, not defects in these teens. Societal attitudes are slow to change, and the hostility toward lesbians, gays, and bisexuals is reflected in the value society places on sexual-minority adolescents. As a result, life can be difficult for a lesbian, gay, or bisexual adolescent. One gay student explains, ". . . growing up gay in my family is like being Jewish in a Nazi home."[10]

Societal support for developing as a heterosexual is pervasive and very strong. The mass media have been one of the major purveyors of heterosexism.[11] The hegemony of heterosexism has led one researcher to conclude that "The personal, social, and institutional support systems that assist the adolescent heterosexual minor are not available to the homosexual minor."[12] Phillip, a young urban gay man of twenty with a Southern Baptist upbringing recalls,

> In my hometown there was no one I could talk to and there were no role models. . . . Homosexuality is just something that's not talked about. It simply doesn't exist. There wasn't anything in the library except medical definitions. There was never anything pro-gay. I couldn't talk to my teachers. . . . [13]

Heterosexism formalizes a societal dichotomy of heterosexuality versus homosexuality with little room left for bisexuals.[14] Although all sexual minorities experience the pressures to become heterosexual, bisexuals receive the greatest amount.[15] With no room for a middle orientation, heterosexism attempts to force bisexuals into the heterosexual category.

The co-occurring antihomosexual message is equally strong. Paul Gibson, author of the 1989 Department of Health and Human Services report on lesbian and gay teen suicide, states emphatically that "The root of the problem is a society that stigmatizes homosexuals while failing to recognize that a substantial number of its youth are gay."[16] Families, churches, and mass entertainment support heterosexual values. Imprinting of these values begins before any child is even aware that there are alternatives.[17]

"Twenty years of upbringing—everything you've ever absorbed or been taught or heard," recalls Henry, a young gay man. "ALL that time you're taught that it's awful to be gay."[18] A seventeen-year-old continues:

> All that I ever knew about gay men at the time [age eleven] were the stereotypes and the lies that my parents taught me. My father was always telling me, "Walk like a man; stop sitting like a woman." My parents taught me that gay people were not people at all. They taught me that they don't deserve any respect at all. So how was I supposed to feel when I discovered that I was gay? How is someone supposed to feel when you know that your own family would never even accept you?[19]

Paul, a young gay man, summed up the situation: "[S]ociety still ruthlessly and relentlessly sends us the message: *'There is no place for you here'.*"[20] Thus, Florida entrepreneur Frank Flanagan saw nothing wrong with printing and selling T-shirts with the Kix rabbit logo and the words "Silly Faggot, Dix are for Chix."

From an early age, words such as *dyke, queer,* and *faggot* are bandied about the ballfield and the schoolyard. Although the reference is usually not sexual, the connotation is always extremely negative. These words become part of the societal "little red wagon" lesbian and gay adolescents and adults tow around behind them for a lifetime.

Each queer kid must wrestle with feelings that society traditionally has condemned as bad, sinful, pathetic, and criminal.[21] These teens have difficulty reconciling themselves with the prevailing attitudes and myths. While our political institutions give lip service to individuality and our religions preach tolerance of difference, no acceptance or tolerance exists for this type of individual diversity.

Homophobic attitudes are most prevalent among those individuals who describe themselves as "religious."[22] Placed in a Christian Boys' Home at age thirteen, Matthew, a sixteen-year-old prostitute, reports, "I was hassled for being gay," and concludes, "It was terrible."[23] Bobby, age sixteen, lamented,

> They've [his parents] said they hate gays, and even God hates gays, too. It really scares me . . . because they are talking about me. . . . Sometimes I feel like disappearing from the face of this earth.[24]

A few days short of his twentieth birthday, Bobby ended his own life. Betty, a young lesbian and a Catholic, continually asked God to help her change her sexual orientation.

The pressure to conform is especially strong in adolescence and places great stress on lesbian and gay teens. Rejection by peers is difficult to handle, and for adolescents, who often lack coping skills, it can be devastating.

Antihomosexual feelings may be particularly strong within racial-minority communities and when close personal individuals such as friends or offspring are identified.[25] These feelings are especially virulent among young males. Internalized antihomosexual feelings also may be very high in lesbian or gay youths, especially among the latter. Although Rich and Randy had formed a loving relationship in high school, Randy betrayed Rich whenever they were in the company of others. Rationalizing that he had to protect himself, Randy made antigay remarks and called Rich "faggot."

The intolerant attitude of the African-American community toward lesbian, gay, and bisexual individuals may reflect culture-based gender roles and the reaction of the white majority to these roles. African-American models of masculinity and femininity each include some elements of European-American femininity and masculinity, respectively.[26] These models can be confusing for European Americans who may question the masculinity or femininity of African-American individuals. This questioning can lead to defensiveness about gender roles by African Americans and to outwardly hostile antihomosexual attitudes even though grudging tolerance of lesbian, gay, and bisexual African-American individuals exists.[27]

"The enmity toward homosexuality has long been rampant in black life," comments Ann Shockley, an African-American author.[28] Some African Americans claim, despite considerable evidence to the contrary, that homosexuality is an import from European Americans and not found in African populations.[29] "Even though there are a lot of black homosexuals," explains Jacob, a young African-American male from a small Southern town, "a lot of blacks do not want to accept that fact." To them, a "homosexual thing is a white thing."[30] Many African-American youths are left to choose between their sexual orientation and their race. This situation can be summarized as follows:

> African-American gay men [and women] are treated as marginalized people . . . To be African, black, male [or female] and gay in America is to challenge the basic assumptions of society by simply existing.[31]

Change is occurring slowly with the emergence of strong, proud African-American lesbians and gays.

Youths are well aware of the lesbian, gay, and bisexual civil rights disputes, such as those involving same-sex "marriage" or the military ban on homosexuals and the rhetoric surrounding these issues. Homophobic remarks stigmatize sexual-minority teens and negatively affect their self-esteem. The highly publicized battle over the New York City School District's Rainbow Curriculum and the court battle over Colorado's Proposition 2 have not gone unnoticed by lesbian, gay, and bisexual youths. The proposed *Children of the Rainbow* curriculum was an attempt to teach children to celebrate diversity. Opponents used the very tiny portion on sexual minorities as an excuse for sabotaging the entire curriculum. Ballot Proposition 2 forbade any Colorado community from passing human rights protections for lesbians and gays and was eventually overturned by the Supreme Court as unconstitutional. After antigay Proposition 2 passed in Colorado, the high school drop-out rate among lesbian and gay teens doubled.[32] "Imagine how a sixteen-year-old teenager felt," explains Michael, a white gay student, "when Pat Buchanan attacked gays at the recent Republican National Convention. . . . "[33] The inaccurate and sometimes hateful remarks made in these discussions become the internalized homophobia of these youths. Vanessa, an eighteen-year-old, concludes,

> The government perpetuates homophobia. . . . The message that I get from the government is that it's OK to be homophobic and it's OK to gay-bash. It disturbs me. . . . I deserve to be respected and protected too.[34]

The message from society is that homosexuality and, by implication, the homosexual individual are despised, unnatural, and abnormal.

Few obvious role models exist from which lesbian, gay, and bisexual youth have a positive reference and thus find social validation. The lack of objective discussion of homosexuality at home and in school forces teens to rely on the mass media as sources of information. Henry, a gay upper-class Southern youth, explains:

> As far as I knew, homosexuality was unnatural, wrong, horrible, and barbaric. I assumed that the natural way was for men to be with

women. That was the way of my parents; that was the way of people on television; that was the way of all my friends' parents; that would be my way.[35]

Continuing adolescent characters on television are always heterosexual and the audience is assumed to be likewise.[36] It's as if a big sign hangs around adolescent television: "Heterosexuals only." High schools are portrayed as "homosexual free zones."[37] The resultant invisibility contributes to isolation and to internalization of society's negative messages. The not-so-subtle message is that only heterosexual teens and their coming-of-age rituals matter.

When lesbian, gay, or bisexual adolescents are portrayed, they are always angst-ridden over their sexuality, confused, guilty, and often suicidal. In contrast, heterosexual teens are never confused about their sexual orientation. Nor is homosexuality addressed directly; rather, it is the vehicle to explore confusion. Young lesbian, gay, or bisexual love is never addressed, only the topic of sexuality which reinforces the stereotype that sexual minorities care only about sexual behavior. Instead of portraying a lesbian, gay, or bisexual individual as a real person, mass media characterize these persons as unfortunate victims. Often, some extraordinary circumstance, such as a dysfunctional or abusive family, alcoholism, or drugs are involved. Taken together, the subliminal message is that events can cause sexual behavior, and that sexual orientation which is synonymous with behavior can be changed by modifying that behavior.[38]

The occasional positive character, if indeed, we can use the term *positive*, is usually asexual and with no connection to the lesbian, gay, and bisexual community. These characters are also clearly adult, not adolescent. Characterized as the "straight gay,"[39] these characters are portrayed as a heterosexual might imagine them to be. They are gay taken out of their gay context and are as valid as quotes without the surrounding text. Sexless, powerless, continually cheery, and uninvolved, these characters are no threat to the patriarchal heterosexual hegemony. Usually, they desire mainstream recognition desperately. "I always thought of homosexuals as old men who walked poodles on rhinestone leashes and wore makeup," explains James, a young gay man. "I never . . . realized that there were . . . homosexuals my age."[40]

In contrast to the harmless eccentric is a second image, that of the menacing pedophile or psychopathic killer, inciting hatred and revulsion. This character's homosexuality is evidence of the inner sickness or more often is a theatrical device that gives the audience permission to loath the character. "Through cultural heterosexism," concludes one researcher, "homosexuality is largely hidden in American society and, when publicly recognized, is usually condemned or stigmatized."[41]

Some lesbian, gay, and bisexual youths may find it difficult to relate to the sensationalist nature of sexual minorities presented on television talk shows. In addition, such shows may leave a negative impression because "balance" usually requires a rabidly homophobic antigay "opposition." If this is lacking, the audiences on these shows usually can be relied upon to make some outrageously homophobic comments.

The AIDS epidemic has heightened awareness of lesbians and gays, but news coverage also reflects prevailing attitudes. Gay men are often portrayed as AIDS "sufferers," accentuating the supposedly dreary unfulfilled lives of these individuals. There are other consequences, as Terry, a young gay man describes,

> AIDS has made growing up gay more difficult. There are so many people . . . who are still ignorant about AIDS and that believe homosexuals cause it. . . . Being gay in the South was never easy; with AIDS, it's just that much more difficult.[42]

For lesbian, gay, or bisexual youths, mainstream entertainment only heightens the feelings of isolation and of being a misfit. Searching for some answers, lesbian, gay, and bisexual teens, especially those who feel isolated and insecure, may be even more vulnerable to the media message than are adults.[43]

The relative invisibility and stereotyping of sexual minority youths in mass media is similar to that of other minorities in the past. Termed "symbolic annihilation,"[44] media invisibility is used by the majority to maintain the status quo for less powerful minorities. "When groups or perspectives do attain visibility, the manner of that representation will itself reflect the biases and interests of those elites who define the public agenda."[45]

The media are not the culprit. They merely reflect prevailing societal attitudes. In the cowardly role of follower rather than leader or challenger, however, the media perpetuate the societal stigmatization of sexual minorities.

Parental Assumption of Heterosexuality

Unless a child is abandoned or in a custody situation, parents have the right and the responsibility to determine the child's health, education, and moral upbringing. The overwhelming majority of parents are heterosexual. Their attitudes and those of their family most often reflect this fact and the prevailing social values. It is not surprising, therefore, that heterosexism is prevalent. "The grasping at straws by so many parents is significant. It demonstrates the still widely held belief that all young people are heterosexual and can only be corrupted into homosexuality by contact with homosexuals."[46] Matt, a college student, recalls, "When my sister announced her sexual preference, I hoped someday she would 'switch back.' Back to something she had never been."[47]

As a result of this assumption, parents and families are predisposed toward nonacceptance of homosexuality and of lesbian or gay or even bisexual offspring. Parents assume their children will fall in love with someone of the other gender, marry, and produce grandchildren. This assumption rings false for lesbian and gay youth. "When we noticed he was effeminate, it became a nightmare," laments the mother of a gay son.[48] Chrissy, a sixteen-year-old white lesbian, describes her mother's reaction, "She denies that I'm gay and believes someone talked me into it. She thinks I'm too young to know."[49]

Accompanying the assumption of heterosexuality may be negative parental comments about homosexuality which most lesbian and gay teens endure in silence. Derek, a minority student, remembers his father labeling some men as "being funny."[50] The connotation was negative. Terry, a young white gay Southerner, recalls his father ranting in response to a gay-related television news story, "I don't know what I'd do if any of my kids grew up to be a faggot." Kate, eighteen years old, lesbian, and homeless, recalls, "My father told me that if I ever came home and told him that I was gay, I wouldn't be welcome in the family anymore."[52] "Life is much tougher," summarizes a seventeen-year-old Chinese-American gay male, "when the environment prohibits your real identity."[53]

In general, the more gender inappropriate a youth's behavior, the more her or his parents express their anxiety through homophobic remarks.[54] These remarks usually are not part of a conscious effort to change the child's behavior. In any case, the effect on the child is the same. The teen becomes frightened of possible rejection, punishment, violence, and/or expulsion. The accompanying shame of a lesbian, gay, or bisexual teen can become internalized self-hate.

Inability to Accept Other Than Heterosexuality

A parent's inability to acknowledge an adolescent's sexual orientation places their relationship at risk. The result for the youth is isolation, confusion, marginalization, and alienation. Sometimes, the result is physical separation, substance abuse, or suicide.

Often isolated within their families, lesbian, gay, and bisexual adolescents, whether out or not, do not have the family support enjoyed by other minorities nor do they develop the coping strategies that come from this family support. Conflict within the family can contribute to an increased sense of isolation and can lower self-esteem. Conflict and stress may be particularly acute if a teen comes out during the formation of her or his sexual identity.[55] In contrast, a supportive family buffers a child's development of positive self-esteem against the assaults of a prejudicial society.[56] Coming out by a youth may result in a disruption of child-parent ties and a weakening of a child's support system.[57] Perceived or real family rejection or fear of rejection can be a major stress factor that contributes to adolescent suicide.[58] It is not surprising, therefore, that lesbian and gay teens rate self-disclosure and family relations as their most common problems.[59]

Ethnic-minority youth also may experience disruption of communal relationships as the family attempts to isolate them from cultural activities to avoid bringing shame upon the family.[60] "I have two marks against me because I am black and I am gay," explains Mark, a seventeen-year-old prostitute.[61] For Franklin, being black in a society that prefers white and being gay in a family that expected heterosexuality only increased his isolation.

> l was ready to fight when someone called me "nigger". . . . But I couldn't go home and tell my parents about being called "faggot." I just dealt with it. I felt real tied up inside.[62]

The often conservative religious practices of racial and ethnic minorities may further isolate the youth who is regarded as disrespectful of and disobedient to God. Mark, a prostitute mentioned previously, explains, "I started to feel bad about myself because . . . of my religion . . . "[63] Teens from blue-collar families may also experience more guilt than youth from white-collar families concerning their homoerotic feelings.[64]

The decision by a lesbian and gay youth to come out to parents is a mark of personal growth and an expression of trust, often after a long period of self-deceit and lying. This adolescent is in the uncomfortable position of desiring to be honest while knowing that the response may be very negative. Scott, who attempted suicide at age thirteen, explains:

> It's so much harder to come out as a teen knowing possibly your parents aren't going to accept you. . . . One year in high school I had my car headlights broken three times. How do you explain that to your parents? There were so many things to worry about.[65]

In general, those adolescents who have not come out to their parents fear the worst. An adolescent male explained, "My father would tear me apart if he found out I was gay."[66]

Even the most liberal of parents may not react positively when it's their own child:

> As open-minded, straight, mature adults, we [parents] can deal with
> the gay issue. . . . Just as long as it doesn't venture into our homes,
> touch our lives, and become part of our world.[67]

Parents may experience feelings of guilt, anger, shame, and/or hurt and are
often too preoccupied to consider their child's needs.[68] This preoccupa-
tion, in turn, may be interpreted by the youth as rejection.

Usually, acceptance is not immediate, and parents must go through a
process not unlike grieving for a dead loved one in which shock, denial,
guilt, and anger hopefully lead to acceptance.[69] Parents and families have
shared expectations for individuals and look forward to shared life events
within the family.[70] These expectations include weddings and grandchildren, future employment and success. Any unexpected event such as the
self-disclosure of a gay son or lesbian daughter sends shock waves beyond
the individual. The parental sense of security and accomplishment may be
seriously challenged.[71]

It may take time for parents to put their previous concept of a child and
the associated goals to rest and to grieve that loss. Along the way, parents
may feel helpless or guilty and perceive their child as a "stranger."[72] In
one support group study, 64 percent of parents and 75 percent of the
mothers reported that they experienced grieving and 44 percent experienced guilt.[73] It should be noted that these parents may be somewhat
predisposed to be more supportive of their children as evidenced by their
membership in a support group. The actual percentage of parents who
grieve and experience guilt may be higher.

For parents of an older youth, it may be difficult to alter their assumptions and expectations. In contrast, parents of younger adolescents may
dismiss their child's declared sexual identity as confusion or immaturity.
Unfortunately, some parents never get beyond denial. For them, their
child's sexual orientation does not exist.[74]

Some parents turn against their child or are unable to resolve the issue
of their son or daughter's sexuality.[75] The resultant bitterness of a lesbian
or gay teen can be heard in the following from a sixteen-year-old African-
American male:

> She [mom] sees me as her asexual child. She said, "You're too
> young to think anything one way or the other." . . . We never talk
> about it now.[76]

The consequences are often destructive to the family unit itself and the real
possibility exists that the parents will lose their relationship with their

child. An eighteen-year-old describes the "we don't talk about it" strategy of his parents and the result for himself:

> I tried to . . . talk to them, answer their questions, but they wouldn't hear of it. All my father said was, it made him want to puke . . . my mother just cried . . . When I realized that my own family couldn't accept me . . . , I thought why should I expect the rest of society to cut me any slack? I felt hopeless, disillusioned, and worthless. My own family . . . how could they do that to me, be so cold, so uncaring.[77]

Unresolved conflicts or hurtful words add to queer kids' feelings of isolation and rejection.

Parents often express a fear that younger family members may be "exposed" to homosexuality. Unreasoned fear of AIDS has further complicated this situation.[78]

> I never wanted to be gay. Now, with AIDS, I have even less reason to feel positive about that part of myself.[79]

The family pariah becomes a perceived carrier.

In some cases, the family will lose the child, to drugs, to alcohol, to homelessness, or to suicide. Tommy's family reaction was very destructive:

> After I told her [his mother], she got drunk and told me I was a faggot and she didn't want no queer in her house. My brother, he called me a sick fag. So I figured it was either stay and take their shit or leave. So here I am.[80]

Tommy is homeless; the family unit is destroyed.

At the dinner table shortly after his sixteenth birthday, Mike was asked by his parents if he was gay. "My heart leaped into my throat," he recalls. "I wasn't ready to deal with it."[81] As Mike began shaking and remained silent, his father repeatedly demanded an answer. Meanwhile his mother called the parents of Mike's best friend and told them Mike was gay and might have designs on their son. Mike was evicted that night. At age nineteen, he now lives with an older couple he found through an ad he posted in a local church. He calls them "Mom" and "Dad."

Some parents place unrealistic rules and unreasonable expectations on their child. Caught between her or his own feelings and the desires of parents, a youth may choose to lie, furthering the internalized isolation that she or he feels. "When I am older I will be able to be more myself," claims a male student. "Like I will not have to make up stories about where I am going and who I am with."[82] A fifteen-year-old white lesbian tells of family pressure to change her behavior and her appearance, and of verbal and physical abuse from her parents.

Many parents are unwilling to support counseling for their child unless the goal is changing the youth's sexual orientation to heterosexual.[83] "My mother. . . . took me to a psychiatrist," explains Elizabeth, age sixteen. "She wanted the doctor to 'fix' me."[84] Other parents may even resort to treatments for their child as radical as hormone therapy in the mistaken impression that lesbians and gay men are not truly women and men.

Adolescents who are harassed by their parents to change their sexual orientation are at their parents' mercy. In the last analysis, parents have a relatively free hand to do what they want to their children. As the past director of the Hetrick-Martin Institute, a service agency for lesbian and gay youth, explains,

> It is not uncommon when young people come out for their parents to try to "fix them," usually through psychiatric care. . . . If you are under eighteen, you are in a difficult position. You don't have a lot of choices.[85]

In its extreme forms, harassment or emotional abuse may come in the form of "change" therapies or even institutionalization.

The decision to authorize institutionalization is issued after an administrative hearing which denies a youth due process and legal representation.[86] Laura, a fifteen-year-old who was institutionalized by her parents, recalls a friend who had undergone aversive therapy to "cure" his homosexuality:

> He killed himself. He was a happy and healthy person before he went.[87]

Abducted herself by her family, Laura was spirited across the state line where the hometown courts and police had no jurisdiction. Placed in a Mormon-run institution, she later recalled hypnotic therapy, badgering, isolation and lockdown, and a heavy dose of "religious brainwashing." Lyn, who suffered a similar fate and now publishes a newsletter for former institutionalized individuals called *24-7: Notes from the Inside*, recalls, "When I was there about half the kids were in 'cause they were gay."[88] Luckily Lyn escaped, fled to San Francisco, "divorced" her mother who had institutionalized her, and had a lesbian couple appointed her guardians. Reportedly, Lyn's mother had taken her daughter to four experts before she could get a diagnosis that resulted in her daughter's institutionalization.

Although homosexuality is not considered a disorder by the American Psychiatric Association (APA), youths who are lesbian or gay may be classified as having gender identity disorder or borderline personality disorder in order to justify incarceration. "Treatments" may include drugs, hypnosis, and aversive therapy paired with the use of penile plethysmography in which a device attached to the penis measures arousal. Although strongly opposed to such measures, the APA has yet to label them unethical.

No laws exist to protect minors in these situations. In short, parents have a right to institutionalize adolescent children. Once incarcerated, a youth has few legal rights to contest events. Lyn, mentioned previously, was lucky to escape after six months in an institution where she was subjected to drugs and behavioral "therapy."[89]

The typical parental response is "It's just a phase" or "You're so young; how do you know?" An eighteen-year-old female relayed the remarks of her father who told her "[Y]ou just haven't found the right guy yet."[90] "My . . . mother . . . asked me questions like 'How can you know that you're gay when you've never had a sexual experience,'" relates Jennifer, age eighteen.[91]

Family members may punish or verbally or physically threaten lesbian or gay youth. Comments range from "It's disgusting" through "We can't accept it and won't talk about it" to "That's it; you're out of here." The response of Christi's mother to her daughter's disclosure of her lesbian orientation, while less negative, is nonetheless hurtful:

> When I came out to my mom, she said, "But you're so pretty!" Like I had to be ugly to be a lesbian.[92]

Stereotyping will influence the responses of parents.

Parental religious beliefs may hinder or aid acceptance of a child and her or his sexuality. Strict "Thou shalt not . . . " Judeo-Christian sects and Islam may emphasize condemnation and the need to "convert" a youth to heterosexuality. Some lesbian, gay, and bisexual teens face the difficult choice of denouncing their sexual being or suffering exclusion from their family's church. "I think it's loathsome of them [the church]," exclaims a pastor of the Metropolitan Community Church. "It cuts the kids off from stuff that's precious to them."[93] Many parents are desperate for any cure. Marcus's mother tried prayer, a twenty-one-day fast, and an exorcism to rid her son of the "crazy notion" that he was gay.[94] More liberal Judeo-Christian denominations and Eastern religions can provide comfort to parents by stressing the love, acceptance, and the celebration of life in all its forms.

It is sad to admit, but safe to say, that most parents will not accept the knowledge of their child's sexuality with joy. Parents are not immune to societal stereotypes of lesbians and gay men. A sense of alienation and of not "knowing" a child any longer may develop.[95] Luckily, change by parents is possible and damage to the parent-child relationship may be repaired. In one study, a majority of lesbian and gay youths reported that parents had made some positive change.[96] Males reported more positive changes for fathers, while females reported more negative changes and distancing by fathers. Distancing may result from women asserting their independence and rejecting traditional female roles.[97] In general, the older a youth, the more positive changes reported for parents. Within the transition, parents may move to the new role of confidant, advisor, and/or friend.

In the defense of parents, few educational opportunities exist for exploring the topic of sexual orientation. Parents are often in need of a crash course in sexual orientation upon disclosure by their child. Support groups, such as Parents and Friends of Lesbians and Gays (PFLAG) can help parents understand and accept their children.

The facts speak for themselves: A loving family results in a better self-image.[98] Parents who respond to their child's sexuality with caring and love, who attempt to learn all they can, and who are open and honest with their child, eventually come to accept and to celebrate their child. (See Chapter 10.) On the other hand, rejection by the family is a major factor in adolescent homelessness, substance abuse, and suicide.

Inability or Unwillingness of Lesbian, Gay, and Bisexual Adults to Provide Guidance

Unique among minorities, lesbian and gay teens do not share their status with their families. Lacking positive role models and community support, they may envision a life of loneliness and shame.[99] Knowing no one who was gay, Tara recalls,

> I just thought that gays were hated people. . . . I didn't want to be gay.[100]

Lacking role models, lesbian, gay, and bisexual teens must rely on the less than flattering portrayals of sexual-minority adults in the media.

Feelings of aloneness and guilt may be especially acute for lesbian, gay, and bisexual youth who are also members of a racial and ethnic minority. Dennis, a Chinese-American gay man, notes:

> I think there are a lot of gay images that emphasize the whiteness, the
> blue-eyedness, the blondness. . . . [T]he only way not to be second
> best is to start gaining support for being oneself.[101]

Rejected by their community, ethnic-minority youths also may be rejected
by the "mainline" adult lesbian, gay, and bisexual community which has a
disproportionately larger white membership. To be black and lesbian or
gay is to be not wholly accepted in either community.[102] Each identity is
downplayed in order to gain acceptance by the other.

The existence of an open and active lesbian, gay, and bisexual community does not ensure that queer kids will feel welcome or that they will take
the initiative to reach out to that community. Many teens have no contact
with sexual-minority adults, although those with positive self-images have
emphasized the importance of such interactions.[103] Terra, age seventeen,
concludes, "[W]e are left to fend for ourselves in a very . . . close-minded
society."[104]

Contact with other lesbians and gays has a number of benefits for
lesbian and gay teens. Most important of these is debunking myths and
stereotypes.[105] Adults can also serve as role models and mentors. "[T]he
biggest tragedy for me . . . ," states Amy, "is that I didn't meet role models
until *after* I was past the critical point of needing them. It wasn't until I
was in the gay community that I started meeting role models."[106]

The lesbian, gay, and bisexual community and the activities within are
decidedly adults-only. The subculture of lesbian and feminist music, art,
literature, and humor is not youth oriented, and the women's movement
usually does not directly address lesbian issues. Milieus such as sports also
have an adult focus. "I think lesbian and gay adults ignore us," stated a
young women, "because we remind them too much of their painful
youth."[107]

Ninety-five percent of the youths at the Institute for Protection of Lesbian and Gay Youth in New York City expressed a desire to talk to a
lesbian or gay adult in a nonsexual context.[108] Few safe, nonsexual locations exist in which queer kids can meet with sexual-minority adults.

Youths may use false identification to gain entry to lesbian and gay
bars, an atypical and inappropriate socialization atmosphere involving
alcohol and a sexual focus. The stark contrast between the "bar scene"
and the "home/school scene" may further fracture an adolescent's image
of who she or he is. Wendy, age eighteen, relates, "I felt like I was two
different people during the week and then on the weekend."[109] In addition, the secretiveness, late hours, and alcohol can create home and parental problems.

The modern convenience of phone sex lines offers little help. In addition to being expensive and for the use of those eighteen and older, phone sex is blatantly sexual in nature, thus inappropriate as a role-modeling medium. Although on-line computer services can be very useful, teens are vulnerable to the promises of friendship offered by some unscrupulous adults over the Internet. Teens in one youth group collectively expressed their fear of being "hit on" by adults on-line. Still, chat lines can provide a much-needed outlet for openness and support.

Personal ads are equally inappropriate and potentially exploitive. Although Dan, a tenth-grade suburbanite, used Tom, an older man, as a vehicle for entry into the city and found their sexual encounters "an easy way to get away from the pain," he was clearly being exploited by a more mature, more mobile, wealthier adult.[110]

For some male youths, prostitution serves as their opening to the gay community. Some report that they engage in prostitution for the money and to be around men. They may not know how to meet men in other settings. In one study, the only gay men some young prostitutes knew were their "tricks."[111]

Youth interpret the reticence of lesbian and gay adults to interact with them to be rejection or elitism. Kathy, age sixteen, explains,

> [P]eople will support you if they think you're nineteen. . . . They'll do anything. . . . They hear you're sixteen, and nothing.[112]

The result is an even stronger feeling of isolation and aloneness.

Contact by lesbian, gay, and bisexual adults is made more difficult by charges from the religious right and others that these adults are trying to "recruit" adolescents. In an August 9, 1989 letter to then-President Bush, then-Congressman and rabid homophobe William Dannemeyer (R-CA) claimed that "public school programs such as Project 10 [a lesbian, gay, and bisexual youth support program] simply add legitimacy to the heretofore crime of child molestation."

Certainly, the opportunity for sexual exploitation of sexual-minority youths exists. Although predators exist in the lesbian, gay, and bisexual community just as they do in the heterosexual community, the stereotype of the lesbian or gay adult molesting young children is a falsehood. Adult-child sexual relationships, whatever the orientation, are based on an imbalance of power which gives the adult an immense advantage. The exploitive or nonexploitive nature of such relationships varies with the two individuals regardless of their sexual orientation. Certainly, situations exist in which young adults and older adolescents form loving relationships.

Some of the blame for teen isolation must be shared by the sexual-minority community. For whatever reason, many lesbian, gay, and bisexual adults are unwilling to involve themselves with youth. The feeling of many queer kids may be summarized in a quote from Dr. Martin Luther King: "Silence is betrayal." Isolation from lesbian, gay, and bisexual adults may be especially acute for those youths who are most stereotypic and at the greatest risk of violence. It has been suggested that lesbian and gay adults may unconsciously avoid these youths so as not to reinforce the stereotype.[113] In their defense, however, many sexual-minority adults are not qualified to provide the guidance that many youths desire. Many lesbian, gay, and bisexual organizations lack the personnel, funds, and knowledge to reach out to sexual-minority youths.[114] These youths do not desire or need lesbian, gay, and bisexual adults to be peers. Rather, they need role models, especially ones in committed relationships who can reassure teens that life can be fulfilling and productive, containing love and happiness.

The isolation of bisexual youths may be even more acute than that of lesbian and gay youths. The role models are even rarer and may have blended into the heterosexual or homosexual communities.

Verbal Abuse and Physical Violence

"The most frequent victims of hate violence today," concludes a 1987 U.S. Justice Department report, "are blacks, Hispanics, Southeast Asians, Jews, and gays and lesbians." The report continues, "Homosexuals are probably the most frequent victims." The U.S. House of Representative Select Committee on Children, Youth, and Families reported in 1989 that adolescents are disproportionately the victims of violence, with minority youth at an even greater risk. Another study reports that 46 percent of all youth assaults were gay-related with a disproportionately higher incidence among African-American and Latino/a lesbian and gay youth.[115]

According to a 1995 report of the Governor's Task Force on Gay and Lesbian Minnesotans, lesbian and gay youth regularly face hostility, especially in rural areas. Abuse and violence are especially acute in educational environments or other locations in which there are high concentrations of youth. Adolescents are more likely than any other age group to commit premeditated acts of violence against sexual minorities.[116] The recollection of Malcolm, a young African-American man, is not uncommon:

> Every day I was called "fag" and "nigger." People would pick fights with me. . . . I would sit at the front [of the school bus] in a seat by myself because nobody wanted to sit next to me.[117]

In general, adolescent males are more homophobic than females, reflecting the adult population.[118]

Approximately 35 percent of lesbian and gay youth report physical assault while slightly over half report regular verbal abuse from their peers.[119] As Alston transitioned from elementary to junior high school, the epithets changed from *sissy* to *faggot* and *queer*. "It seemed like every class had their *one* homosexual, their *one* scapegoat, their *one* outcast. I was the one in our class," he explains. "I was picked on and harassed for it."[120] "I was teased and punched on," recalls Matthew, age sixteen. "I felt that if I was gay then I would end up being beaten up all my life."[121] "[P]eople throw stuff at you," explains Christi, a young lesbian. "It's not that they just yell stuff, but they get real mean."[122] Jaime, a young lesbian, offers a more graphic description:

> There were some frat boys . . . out looking for trouble . . . and I was walking with my girlfriend. And they had a baseball bat. They whacked me a good one and broke two ribs. And they broke her nose . . . with the butt of the bat . . .[123]

According to the Governor's Task Force on Bias-Related Violence, high school juniors and seniors in New York disapprove of gays and lesbians more than any other minority. The antigay remarks of other teens are described as "openly vicious."

Antigay violence in schools is very real and ever present. A survey of nearly 400 students in Boston's Lincoln-Sudbury High School found that 60 percent would be fearful if people thought they were gay. Ninety-seven percent had heard an antigay remark.[124] "Clearly schools are not safe for gay and lesbian students," concludes Beth Reis of the Safe Schools Anti-Violence Project.[125]

Other environments—homes, foster homes, youth centers, churches, and the like—may also become places where abuse occurs. At home, a lesbian, gay, or bisexual youth can become the center of the family's dysfunction, the target, blamed for all that is wrong in the family.

Even when the *target* of violence, lesbian, gay, and bisexual youth may be assumed to be at fault. The assumption may be that queer kids deserve whatever they get. When Brandon, an openly gay fourteen-year-old bit one of seven bullies who attacked him while on his paper route, the bullies were set free, but police held Brandon and forced him to have an HIV antibody test.[126] Although those who remain secretive may experience less abuse, the "closet" is no guarantor of safety.

Although it is not clear that lesbian, gay, and bisexual youths receive more abuse than other minority youth, they most certainly receive more abuse centered on sexuality and sex roles. The added stress of abuse and violence has an effect on its recipient.[127]

The constant barrage of insults—*faggot, dyke, pato, maricóna* [Spanish for *fag* and *dyke* respectively]—and injuries compound into questions of "Why me?" and "Why can't I be different?" The result for the individual may be a cautious, untrusting nature similar to the one a young gay man describes:

> [E]verywhere I go I think: Am I safe here? Is someone waiting to get me? So many people get bashed.[128]

It is very tiring to be constantly in a state of caution and to be checking one's behavior and speech for fear of ridicule or harm. "I shouldn't have to confront people just for being who I am," complained a sixteen-year-old lesbian. "I should get respect because I am a person, just like they are."[129]

It would be wrong to assume that all adolescents are raging homophobes. Brent, age sixteen, recalls being confronted by several other males in the locker room when an African-American student intervened.

> He looked over at me and said, "Hey, dude. Are you gay?" I said, "Yeah." And he said, "That's cool. Kind of like being black." The rest of the time in the class, he dressed for PE next to me. I really admired that.[130]

At School

As with all students, sexual-minority teens are required by law to attend school even though, for them, it is continuously dangerous and unsafe. In most school districts, no policies exist to ensure their safety. Nearly 60 percent of gay males and 30 percent of lesbians are verbally or physically harassed in school or on campus.[131]

Constant verbal abuse can become intolerable, making it all but impossible to succeed in the classroom. Gender nonconforming behavior is taken as a sign of sexual orientation. "I was getting beat up on the bus," recalls Vic, a lesbian college student, "just for having short hair and dressing like a boy."[132] Ed dropped out of school because of the unending teasing. He was refused entry to a private school because he was gay. Most males fear being labeled gay more than the potential physical risk that may accompany that label.[133] In fact, in schools, antigay epithets are the most frequent and most feared type of verbal harassment.[134]

The effect of verbal harassment varies with the target. In general, those who are secure in their identification and proud are less bothered by the teasing of others. Matt, a state high school gymnastics champion, has become immune. He comments, "It's like where I live—behind the subway: The subway goes by so often, I just don't hear it anymore."[135] In general, exceptionally popular or successful teens seem to suffer less harassment, although these same youths are often most anxious about possible exposure.[136]

For Daniel, a new kid in his Oklahoma school, junior high was a nightmare.[137] Nonconforming to the local macho behaviors, he was challenged daily to fistfights. Incidents such as being held under water for a prolonged time during water polo and being chosen as the target for tossed dissected animals in biology class left him angry and depressed. His grades faltered, and he became rebellious and argumentative at home. Of the constant name-calling, he recalled, "Their words hurt a lot worse because I knew they were true."[138]

Randy, a high school senior, reflects on his freshman year when it was rumored that he was gay:

I was spit on, pushed, and ridiculed. My school life was hell.[139]

"By the ninth grade," explains Brent, age sixteen, "I would be happy if I came home from a day in school and hadn't been called faggot or cocksucker once. That's a really sad standard for what makes you happy."[140] Dan, a white suburbanite, counts as many as twenty-four taunts in his school day. "It was constant," he explains. "It was everywhere."[141] Heckling was accompanied by destruction of his personal property and by pushing and tripping. Paul, a big, bleached-blond gay teen, was dragged into a bathroom stall by eight boys who called him faggot while bashing his head against the toilet and burning his arm with a lighter. Later, mowed down by a truckload of students while on his bike, he spent months in a body cast.[142]

Unfortunately, like the society as a whole, many school authorities assume that the lesbian, gay, or bisexual student owns the problem. As the source of ill will, which it is assumed the student brought on herself or himself, the student must be dealt with. For example, a lesbian couple at a local suburban high school was forbidden by administrators to hold hands on school property. All too often, the solution to abuse is to transfer the lesbian, gay, or bisexual student rather than deal with prejudice. Roger dropped off the swim team after only one practice when tormented for supposedly being a fag. The coach, within earshot of the taunts, did nothing.

Chris had attended four high schools. His former teachers described him as "nice," "sweet," and of average ability. In each school, he was harassed by students and subjected to innuendos and subtle remarks by teachers about his homosexuality. When he defended himself against other students, he was reprimanded repeatedly by the dean. In each case, the school responded by transferring Chris.[143]

Sexual-minority students report threats and beatings by self-appointed "fag patrols." As one young man relates, "I didn't like walking down the street because I was afraid someone was going to holler 'queer,' because it happened quite a bit." Kurt dashes for the relative safety of the school bus each day after school. Soon, a queer kid begins to believe that nowhere is safe.

In Athletics

Few areas of our culture are as blind or hostile toward lesbians and gays as athletics and sports.[144] School-based athletic classes and programs are of particular concern when attempting to make schools safe places for sexual minority students.

Athletics holds a strong grip on the national psyche, especially for males. Male athletes are given preferential treatment and rewarded handsomely for their efforts and revered as role models. Female athletes are usually treated as inferior by the male-dominated society, befitting their status as women. In addition, male adolescents with little power to attain status often rely on athletic prowess to advance themselves relative to other males. For all these reasons, athletics has taken on the qualities of religion for some male adherents.

In some ways, athletics helps to define our culture's concept of masculinity, and those that do not conform are punished. Sean, a white student, recalls,

> I always loved football but there was something about it that I didn't like. . . . I came to see that it was about proving yourself as a man. All the boys together, acting tough, bragging about sexual conquests, putting down women. . . . They had to keep telling each other that they were real men.[145]

Locker room banter is often filled with antifemale and antigay remarks.[146] The differentiation between male athletes and these two groups is part of a bonding ritual evidenced nationwide among most males. To be compared to a female or to a gay male is an insult. Adrian, a gay student, saw the obvious contradiction: "It's strange really because heterosexual men are supposed to be attracted to women, so you would think that they would respect them."[147]

Female athletes threaten the hegemony of males. To be a lesbian athlete is a double whammy, and thus the threat of this label is used to keep many women from excelling in sports.[148] The outcomes of participation in athletics may be very different for gay males and lesbians. Males may use sports to help reinforce their heterosexuality with peers and teachers. In contrast, young women may be presumed to be lesbian because of their sports affiliation. Caught in this situation, a young woman may feel a very strong need to "prove" her heterosexuality. Either situation is stressful for the young woman working through issues of sexuality and self-acceptance.[149]

A young woman may receive very negative messages, both explicitly and implicitly. For example, she may be warned not to attend certain schools or colleges or work with certain coaches because of the taint of homosexuality. Lesbian coaches may participate in this conspiracy by their silence, fearful of losing their jobs. In spite of the silence, many women establish peer support networks among other lesbian athletes.

This type of support is not as easy for gay men to find. One of the supposed characteristics of male athletes is heterosexuality. To many, the term *gay athlete* is an oxymoron. The myth of heterosexuality amidst the close physical bonding of athletes is maintained by the contempt shown for "faggots." Gay men self-identify at some risk, thus making the formation of support networks difficult.

Physical education class can be especially difficult for the gender-non-conforming male. The last to be chosen in team sports, he faces a continual stream of verbal epithets such as "sissy" and "faggot." The gym teacher may encourage participation in athletics by comparing the slackers to "fairies" and "pansies." "I can still hear my gym teacher making 'fag' jokes during class," a young gay man recalls. "It made me cringe inside. . . ."[150]

The locker room can offer even more terror. Tom a thin, fit young white adult, was physically abused and verbally harassed all through high school after he accidentally became aroused in the locker room shower. He always kept his eyes down for fear of repeating his indiscretion. Michael, a rural youth, always removed his glasses quickly when he entered the locker room to avoid being accused of staring. Thomas, an African-American student, recalls the gym teacher's stern warning that anyone caught glancing at others would be disciplined severely. Less evenhandedly, Jeff's instructor told the nongay students to "take care of it" because they supposedly knew what to do with that type of person.

In order to cope, some lesbian and gay athletes may abuse alcohol or drugs, withdraw, or become outwardly homophobic. Performance on the athletic field or in the classroom may suffer. Other lesbian and gay youths may push themselves to excel even more to compensate or to silence speculation.

On Campus

Across the country, suspected or openly lesbian, gay, and bisexual college students are facing an increase in verbal and physical harassment. What began for Libby as harassing telephone calls, escalated to a physical attack at her locker by two men who shouted "dyke" as they kicked and punched her, leaving her with a dislocated shoulder.[151] Harassing phone calls, destruction of personal property, physical attacks, verbal harassment, and isolation of sexual-minority students are common on college campuses. Commenting on violence, Joseph, a college student and sexual minority representative in the Cornell University Student Assembly, states, "That [harassment and violence] is a reality that gay students face every day."[152] In a 1989 University of Oregon poll, 61 percent of the schools lesbian, gay, and bisexual students said that they feared for their safety.[153]

Sexual-minority student groups have also had difficulty gaining recognition and funding, although the groups' members pay student activity fees which are supposed to support student organizations. Often, opposition is framed as religious conviction. On more conservative campuses, lesbian, gay, and bisexual student groups are nonexistent or secretive.

Housing in campus dormitories is a continuing issue. Some heterosexuals refuse to live with lesbian, gay, or bisexual students. Only a handful of campuses have proposed separate sexual-minority dorms. In addition, most campuses do not recognize domestic partners for placement of students in married student quarters.

At Home

Even home does not offer a refuge for some youths. Nancy, an honor student, had to leave home to avoid a father who became physically abusive when he confronted her about being a lesbian.[154] An article in the *Los Angeles Times* described parents "who battered their own son into insensibility" after finding homosexual literature in his room.[155] Approximately a third of respondents in a 1984 National Gay and Lesbian Task Force survey reported being verbally abused by family members while approximately 7 percent reported physical abuse. In one study of New York City teens seeking services, over 60 percent of those reporting violence indicated that it had occurred in their home.[156]

Rajinder, a student, observes, "We are the enemy within."[157] In short, lesbians, gays, and bisexuals are a threat to the system of male superiority and female devaluation found in many families and to heterosexual privilege. Joseph, another student explains, "If there are different ways of being men then . . . there are no set roles to justify why men must rule, are there?"[158] " . . . I don't think it's really about sex . . . " Rajinder continues, "It's mainly about power . . . "[159]

Violence begets violence. Rob had been an overachieving teenager with his own auto detailing business, a pizza delivery job, and a love of fast cars. His life changed forever shortly after high school graduation when his brother and Steve, his brother's friend, crashed a party attended by Rob and his gay friends. In the ensuing scuffle, Rob's nose was broken and his guests roughed up. Rob's brother repeatedly shocked Rob's neck and face with a stun gun. Subsequently, Steve disclosed Rob's sexual orientation to Rob's parents. In a confrontation a week later in which Rob attempted to force Steve to recant, he shot Steve ten times at close range, killing him.[160]

According to Teresa DeCrescendo, founder of Gay and Lesbian Adolescent Social Services (GLASS), sexual abuse within the family also may be more widespread among lesbian and gay youths than it is among heterosexual youths. "I think there's an identification within the family," she explains, "that this youngster is more vulnerable than other family members."[161] After Eddie's teacher informed his parents that their son was gay, Eddie was kept home from school for a year, chained to a radiator, and sexually abused. His father forced him to have sex with men for money.[162]

From the Lesbian, Gay, and Bisexual Community

Sad to say, queer kids also may experience violence at the hands of other lesbian, gay, and bisexual youths and adults. A 1987 study in the *Journal of Interpersonal Violence* and a 1989 study in *The Journal of Contemporary Social Work* reported that 65 to 70 percent of all college students and 35 to 50 percent of high school students have been in violent dating relationships. Many domestic violence counselors believe the level of violence to be even higher for lesbian and gay youths. The causes may be as varied as sexism, homophobia, the pressures on sexual minority youth, and the furtive nature of sexual contacts among some lesbian and gay teens. At age sixteen, Randy was raped by an older man but the matter was not pursued by the authorities when the man told police that he and Randy were dating.[163] Undoubtedly, many female heterosexual rape victims can empathize.

From age fifteen to twenty-one, Jim was "hit, slapped, beaten, and generally punched up" by the men he dated. "I was a kid, I came from a very tight-assed suburban neighborhood in New Jersey," he explains, "and I dated the guys I could find who were out." Jim assumed that physical abuse "was just what guys did together."[164] Luckily, he was able to break his cycle of abuse with counseling and through a relationship with a gentle, loving gay man. Other less fortunate youths become victimized.

Conclusion

"It is a time when dykes and faggots are knifed and bludgeoned, too often, with impunity . . . ," concludes writer and film director Marlon Riggs. "Yet in such savage attacks, the weight of the crime lies less on the teenaged bigot who wields the bat . . . than on the society whose values, laws, education—and religion—systematically sanction . . . hate motivated violence. " In many ways the stigma and shame of being different convince lesbian, gay and bisexual youths that they deserves this type of treatment.

Little Support for Relationships

All adolescents have a need to socialize with their peers. With the exclusively heterosexual orientation of adolescent activities, queer kids have an even greater need. Lesbian, gay, and bisexual youths are overtly denied an opportunity to explore such nonerotic socialization and often are forced to socialize with adults in sexual situations in which the power balance may result in demeaning or dangerous behavior. This situation is especially true for males.

Although potentially dangerous if exposed, same-sex relationships do occur in high school. The form may vary from purely sexual relationships with little or no emotional commitment through dating to "going steady" and monogamous coupling. In general, females are more likely than males to be in committed relationships.

One of the ironies of lesbian and gay relationships is that sexual contact receives more tacit societal support than dating and commitment. In part, this attitude reflects our culture's obsession with sexual behavior and its fear of intimacy and sexuality.[165] Lesbian and gay sex is excused as a phase or as exploration, but romantic attachments are seen as a more serious "problem"[166] Thus, while heterosexual teens are encouraged to date and form relationships, lesbian and gay teens are not. As a result, many lesbian and gay youths may doubt their own self-worth and believe that same-sex relationships are not possible. For others, the obvious double standard results in resentment, anger, and antisocial behavior. In either case, societal censure interferes with social and emotional development.

Steve, a gay high school student, had little difficulty with his same-sex attractions or with same-sex erotic behavior. Relational problems were more vexing, especially when he was unable to talk to teachers who knew of his sexual orientation but refused to acknowledge his relationships.

Positive relationships affirm each partner's self-concept and sexuality. Each partner is validated. For lesbian and gay teens, relationships also can ease the loneliness and end the isolation while providing emotional support. Relationships, by validating the person, can enhance the development of an individual's adult identity. Unfortunately, societal hostility discourages or punishes these relationships by lesbian and gay kids. The factors that make it difficult to establish and maintain lesbian and gay adolescent relationships include the lack of contact as a result of most teens being closeted, verbal and physical harassment, peer pressure, and the lack of public support.[167] Even simple expressions of affection may lead to harassment and violence.

The personal needs of many lesbian and gay teens may also place unrealistic demands upon relationships. Lesbian and gay youths may expect a relationship to end their isolation and destroy their pain.[168]

Professional Attitudes

Antihomosexual attitudes and treatment regimens continue to persist with a large number of professionals.[169] Both physicians and nurses are likely to have homophobic attitudes.[170] These attitudes may be harmful to the development of positive self-esteem by lesbian, gay, and bisexual youths and may interfere with counseling and health service delivery. In turn, these attitudes may result in lesbian, gay, or bisexual pediatricians, counselors, or other health care providers being fearful of revealing their sexual orientation to adolescents confronting issues of sexual orientation.

A local church in my midsized city held a weekend-long "Heal the Homosexual" retreat led by a prominent, if censured, psychologist. Such professionals attempt to gradually replace homosexual feelings with heterosexual ones as they pressure the youth to make a "choice" or change to be heterosexual.[171] Claims of success—for which no scientific or long-term results exist—are based on behavior change, thus demonstrating the lack of understanding of sexual orientation these practitioners possess.

The argument that "change" is preferable to the human right to choose, if indeed sexual orientation were a choice, is particularly odious. During electioneering for a recent statewide antigay referendum in Maine, the Coalition to End Special Rights ran an ad that trumpeted, "When I was a homosexual, if a law had passed giving me special rights I wouldn't be happily married today." The ad went on to explain how unhappy and trapped homosexuals are and that their only remedy is a continuation of discrimination that will force them to seek help to change. Luckily, Maine voters weren't that gullible!

Mike, whose parents placed him in a religious-based change therapy program, dropped out after a few months, because the program wasn't helping him feel good about himself.[172] Such religion-based programs can be extremely destructive. Since, in theory, God never fails, inability to change is the failing of the individual lesbian, gay, or bisexual teen. Like many questionable procedures, it is not the premise or the method that has failed, it is the client. As a result, this personal failure or unworthiness is added to other negative self-evaluative notions.

Despite the claims of success by some practitioners, the American Medical Association does not recognize change treatments as necessary or effective. If there is no illness, there can be no "cure."[173] Still, a large percentage of counselors persist in the notion that homosexuality is patho-logical.[174] Given that sexual orientation—hetero, bi, or homo—is a perva-sive, relatively fixed phenomenon, counseling that emphasizes individual adjustment to one's sexuality seems more appropriate.

Self-identified adolescent lesbians are concerned about the gentleness and gender of potential health care providers. Self-identified gay male teens are more concerned with a practitioner's sexual orientation regard-less of gender and with the potential for humiliation about being gay. Both males and females are desirous of receiving nonjudgmental care.[175]

Even counselors who do not consider themselves to be homophobic may be reluctant to mention the subject of homosexuality with youthful clients.[176] Jonathan's harassment by fellow students began in sixth grade. Subsequent therapy was a further frustration because the counselor would not discuss sexual orientation.

> I was obviously more effeminate than other people, so . . . it wouldn't take . . . a college degree to figure out, hey, we have somebody here who is struggling with their sexuality . . . [I]f this group of sixth graders could figure it out, then why can't a profes-sional counselor . . . ?[177]

The age of a youth and the nature of her or his concern may encourage counselors to discount a youth's feeling as immature or to dismiss same-sex erotic activity as an example of adolescent experimentation. Phrases such as "It's a phase" or "You'll outgrow it" are less common today but common enough for concern. Bill, age eighteen, finds such advice harmful.

> I told a couple of counselors. . . . One said it was just a phase I was going through and everybody has these feelings, and the other one said it was because I masturbated. So I really didn't deal with it, and they gave me an excuse to keep on deceiving myself.[178]

One young woman reported that her school counselor told her she was too small and feminine to be a lesbian. "I was told that something must be wrong with me," recalls another young lesbian, Julianna.[179] In general, lesbian, gay, and bisexual students perceive teachers and counselors to be ill-informed about homosexuality, unconcerned about them personally, and uncomfortable with sexual issues.[180]

CONCLUSION

Society would rather that lesbian, gay, and bisexual teens die than admit that they exist. Continued denial and stigmatization make the dead and wounded less significant and cause less guilt for the larger society. If these same kids become confused, frightened, isolated and/or suicidal along the way, so the reasoning goes, all the better—either it makes queer kids more vulnerable to repentance and change therapies or it eliminates the "problem" altogether.

Chapter 5

The Special Problem of Schools

If even one of my teachers had been openly gay and proud, maybe some of the trauma I experienced could have been avoided.

Tom Shepard[1]

For a queer kid, high school can be a lonely, inhospitable, and danger-ous place. Homophobia is "condoned or at least tolerated by many school authorities."[2] Ridicule, harassment, violence, and a lack of recognition and support make learning difficult at best. For some youths, learning is all but impossible. Institutionalized heterosexism and homophobia are psy-chologically damaging in the extreme.

When Leonard, a fourteen-year-old straight-A student from Ohio, came out to one of his teachers, he was told he had no reason to live.[3] Another teacher told him that he would prefer for one of his own children to have cancer than to be gay. After an unsuccessful suicide attempt by Leonard, his family moved to enable him to attend another high school where he remained closeted and graduated without further incident. Gary, a subur-ban youth, cautiously came out to selected teachers and counselors in the hope of obtaining some guidance. No useful advice was forthcoming. Gina, a young lesbian who went to the school administration after inces-sant verbal abuse, was not supported and was told that the school could not get involved in such issues. Julian, an effeminate teen, was harassed from kindergarten on and told by his teachers that his behavior was to blame for the tormenting. In high school he attempted suicide.[4] Matt Stickney, a Burlington, Vermont, transsexual teen, was suspended from school when he attempted to attend classes in a dress and makeup.[5]

Few lesbian and gay adults reminisce of high school days. High school was recalled as a time of lies and deceit in which they tried to appear heterosexual in a potentially hostile environment. Of those who recorded "best" memories of adolescence, most chose experiences outside of school, such as visiting a lesbian and gay bookstore for the first time.

Homosexuality is conspicuous by its absence in high school and middle school. "It's like in the sixties," states Arthur Lipkin of the Harvard School of Education, "when we were telling black kids that black is beautiful but leaving black culture and history out of the curriculum." He adds, "Kids can see through that."[6] Absence invalidates who these kids are.

The presence of sexual-minority youths in the school population is still denied by many educators, and many school counselors are unprepared to deal with the unique concerns of these students.[7] One researcher concludes, "Not only does the group [lesbian, gay, and bisexual students] remain invisible, the existence of and the problems associated with gay youth are largely denied by public school educators, particularly school administrators."[8] Anthony, age nineteen, explains, "Schools have a responsibility . . . even if school officials and parents refuse to acknowledge it."[9]

Few topics raise as much emotion among the self-anointed protectors of public morality as recognition by schools of lesbian, gay, and bisexual adolescents and their needs. One chief psychologist in a large urban, southwestern district states, "Oh, that's not an issue in OUR school," when asked to discuss the services for lesbian and gay students. The district does not recognize any sexual-minority teens. Such denial can have enormous consequences for both student well-being and for AIDS education and the spread of the HIV virus.

The heterosexism that subsumes education masks for many adults the fact that sexual orientation has long been an "issue" in public education. Strict enforcement of heterosexual orientation and privilege in curricular and extracurricular aspects of education is a conscious decision to raise the issue of "No queers allowed."

Acknowledgment of a student's sexual orientation or relationships may be even more difficult than general tolerance. Letitia, a high school senior from Los Alamitos, California, had her 5-by-6-foot acrylic painting of two bare-breasted women embracing covered with a cloth by an administrator of the Orange County High School for the Arts. Letitia's accompanying statement referring to "loving another woman" was changed to read "another person." The immediate threat of a lawsuit and a hastily organized protest resulted in the administration backing down.

The issue of positive portrayal of homosexuality in the public schools is complex and politically charged. Homosexuality is usually not mentioned in history, literature, science, or contemporary issues, and often not even in sex education. In fact, the topic is actively avoided, not only by teachers, but by counselors and administrators. This supposed act of decency prompted author Armistead Maupin to ask of administrators and school boards, "What earthly good is your discretion, when teenagers are still being murdered for the crime of effeminacy?"[10]

When the topic of homosexuality is mentioned in class it is often portrayed in a negative manner.[11] "Mr. Jensen . . . mainly talked about the wrongs of it [homosexuality] and how it was such a sin and that they should be condemned," reports Franklin, a rural African-American student. "I felt really bad."[12] Negative or stereotypic portrayal of lesbians and gays and the presence of violence in the schools prompted one gay teen to write,

> [G]ay bashing . . . makes me crawl back further into the closet that I am protected by. Young students need to learn about the diversity of life.[13]

In contrast, heterosexuality is presented as natural, normal, desirable, and universal.

Teachers may use negative, simplistic, and overly moralistic descriptions of lesbians, gays, and bisexuals that assume the superiority of heterosexuality. In this atmosphere, myths, stereotypes, and misinformation persist. Middle school sexual-minority youths are especially vulnerable. Sex is a forbidden topic and these teens receive even less support than older lesbian and gay high school students.[14]

It is no overstatement to observe that one of the largest challenges facing educators is the acknowledgment of lesbian, gay, and bisexual students. Numerous studies have demonstrated that schools and educators lack the awareness, sensitivity, knowledge, and skills appropriate for meeting the needs of sexual-minority teens. Rea Carey, coordinator of the National Advocacy Coalition on Youth and Sexual Orientation, an umbrella group of youth agencies, concludes, " . . . school systems are either passively or actively discriminating against gay and lesbian youth."[15] Virginia Uribe, founder of Project 10, a lesbian, gay, and bisexual support system in the Los Angeles public schools, adds,

> We are supposed to be affirming kids and giving them a good sense of who they are. And yet many gay and lesbian kids are told flat-out that they're sick perverts.[16]

In short, the schools are not a very *gay* place. Schools are a microcosm of the larger society. Institutionalized homophobia is very alive and very well.

Honest discussion of sexual issues or advocacy for queer kids is difficult under present circumstances. Our schools are under assault by conservative religious special interest groups that wish to perpetuate the naive notion that sex is solely for procreation within marriage, thus, adolescents must remain chaste.[17] There is no room in this model for "unnatural" or "abnormal" behavior such as homosexuality or bisexuality. In recent years, Congress has attempted repeatedly to pass laws denying funds to any school district that teaches acceptance of homosexuality or provides counseling or referral for lesbian and gay students. The message is a not-too-subtle one that sexual-minority teens are not welcome.

The absence of discussion or even the free access to information perpetuates prejudice and ignorance. Youths struggling with issues of sexual orientation can expect little support when special interests, such as religious fundamentalists, control their school boards.

Although educators say they are committed to proactive support of all students, their visible support of lesbian, gay, and bisexual students is negligible or nonexistent.[18] This lack of support is usually the result of personal prejudice or fear. To them, Brett, a gay high schooler responds, "There is really nothing to fear from us except the pain that comes from your ignorance!"[19]

One study of school counselors and prospective teachers in the southern United States found that two of three counselors and eight of ten prospective teachers had negative attitudes toward homosexuality.[20] Fully a third of the prospective teachers could be described as homophobic and 40 percent thought that a lesbian or gay student should be transferred at the request of a homophobic teacher.

SCHOOL PERSONNEL

For teens, the school experience is one of interaction with supposedly caring adults. Unfortunately for queer kids, most teachers' and counselors' concern does not extent to sexual minorities. These influential adults can greatly affect the self-acceptance of lesbian, gay, and bisexual teens.

Teachers

Teachers walk a very fine line in discussing sexual minorities in the classroom. Some justify inclusion by the importance of tolerance of diversity. Many more choose not to address the topic in any way or to make neutral or negative statements when the topic arises. When Penny Culliton, a high school English teacher, attempted to introduce *Maurice, The Education of Harriet Hatfield,* and *The Drowning of Stephan Jones* to counter the negative stereotypes in books such as *Catcher in the Rye,* she was fired by her school board in New Ipswich, New Hampshire.

Almost uniformly, lesbian and gay students perceive teachers and counselors to be detached, ill-informed, unconcerned, and insensitive. High school student Fawn tells of a teacher who "hated me because she knew I was gay." The teacher actively made life difficult for Fawn and used terms such as "people like you."[21] Less than one-third of lesbian and gay students believe teachers would provide useful guidance with their problems and concerns.[22] For whatever reason, these professionals are perceived to be unwilling to show concern or to express an opinion. As one young woman puts it, "I didn't want to kill myself; I just wanted to talk to someone who knew what they were talking about."[23] As reported by teens, most teachers don't inquire into their well-being. One young lesbian explains, "As long as you keep them happy, they think that you're well adjusted."[24]

Repeatedly, lesbian, gay, and bisexual youth complain about the unequal treatment given to prejudicial statements. Those made on the basis of sexual orientation go unchallenged by teachers who, on occasion, contributed their own antihomosexual comments or jokes, while those based on race, ethnicity, and religion are censured. "If there was a sexual slur, like 'fag,'" complains Franklin, an African-American student, "they would pay no attention to it. That told me they didn't feel homophobia was as important as racism."[25] Concerned Students of Des Moines report that 97 percent of Des Moines high school teachers do not respond when students make antigay remarks in their presence.[26]

Some teachers have an even more hurtful agenda. For example, the technology director and guidance counselor at the Byron Center, Michigan, high school used student addresses to distribute an antigay video.[27] Fortunately, he was suspended. He should have been fired.

Teachers are perceived by lesbian and gay students as tolerant of homophobia. "The problems are not always other students," cites Donna Fernum, a teacher at the Harvey Milk School, "but insensitive teachers and administrators."[28] Lesbian and gay teens report that teachers actively participate in verbal taunting. "I hear a minimum of three derogatory remarks a day," one fourteen-year-old gay male stated in his school paper. "This quota is often filled by teachers who do not refrain from making antigay remarks." One ethnic-minority student concluded, "I think that teachers feel more threatened by gays than by any other group."[29]

Although a majority of prospective teachers say they would intervene in harassment of a lesbian or gay student, far fewer are willing to take a proactive role in their teaching.[30] In general, the more knowledge a professional has, the less homophobia she or he expresses. Having had a lesbian or gay friend is also a very strong factor in decreasing homophobia.

Closeted lesbian, gay, and bisexual teachers may actively avoid students suspected of being lesbian, gay, or bisexual. Christi, a homeless youth, gives an example:

> This one English teacher . . . I *know* this guy is gay. . . . And he avoids me like the plague for two years. . . . He could have helped me. He could have talked to me. But no-o-o.[31]

The message sent is very negative and self-devaluing. These teachers are shirking their responsibilities as role models. Everetta, a lesbian student struggling with issues of sexuality, had been seeing a psychologist but felt that this professional did not really understand. In contrast, the physical education instructor, Ms. Hightower, seemed to understand but never approached Everetta on this topic. "It would have been nice to know someone older, like Ms. Hightower, who had struggled with this, too," recalls Everetta.[32]

In my own survey of eighty-nine school districts nationwide, over 75 percent report that they have no openly lesbian or gay teachers or staff. As expected, larger urban and suburban districts report more openness than rural districts.

The needs of most lesbian, gay, and bisexual students are unbelievably simple. Over and over youths have told me that they want to be treated like other kids, to be supported, and not to have negative comments made by teachers about sexual minorities. "Accept us for what we are," urges one teen, "a regular teenager . . . except our 'sexual preference' is different."[33] "Gays' sexual views might be different," concludes another, "but their hearts hurt like everyone else's."[34]

School Counselors

Comprehensive guidance programs found in many school districts are designed to handle large caseloads effectively and efficiently within a mental health model.[35] It is assumed that counselors have broad knowledge of developmental processes and needs. Counselors may lack knowledge on the differences among diverse populations within the student body.

Few mental health professionals are trained in sex therapy and even fewer are educated on sexual-minority youth issues.[36] The conclusions of a 1989 study in the journal *Pediatrics* are illustrative:

> Virtually no professionals in the country receive any kind of special training on homosexuality, let alone the issues surrounding adolescent homosexuality. . . . Many . . . professionals . . . are reluctant to refer gay and lesbian kids to social support groups. On one level they believe that by doing so, they might entrench the person's homosexual identity. They are worried about parents' reactions or what their supervisors might think.[37]

In general, lesbian, gay, and bisexual students characterize school counselors as poorly informed, unconcerned, and ill-at-ease.[38] When Chris went to a school counselor because he couldn't take the continual harassment in class any longer, he received the following response:

> She said, "You need to go to class or you're going to flunk. You aren't going to make it to college." I remember thinking to myself, "Honey, I'm not going to make it to the next day."[39]

Only 25 percent of all fourteen- to twenty-one-year-olds feel comfortable discussing sexuality with a school counselor.[40] An even smaller 15 percent of lesbian and gay students perceive school counselors as being helpful with their problems and concerns. Royce, a gay youth, offers,

> In my school, guidance counselors were there to offer career advice, hand out college catalogues, and do tests. I never considered going in and saying, "Look, I'm sleeping with Jason. What should I be doing about it?"[41]

"The counselor told me my homosexuality was all in my head," recalls Lea, a young lesbian, "and that if I went through therapy I would be all right."[42] Georgina, a young lesbian, sums up the feelings of many high school teens when she observes, "I just wanted to talk to someone who knew what they were talking about."[43]

Within my own survey of school districts, nearly 30 percent of counseling supervisors believed that sexual orientation was the result of conscious choice and/or a learned behavior. One director of pupil services in a large suburban district explained her nonparticipation in my survey by stating, "We do not become involved in any direct or formal way in addressing the issues of gay and lesbian adolescents."

When a student does come out or seek advice or support, she or he often becomes "the problem."[44] The solution becomes moving or changing the schedule of the sexual-minority student. It is classic "blame the victim" logic. The real problem is school systems that shirk their responsibility to provide a quality education for *all* students. Resultant acting-out behaviors and emotional difficulties often are attributed by counselors to an adolescent's homosexuality. Although Julian, a young gay man, suffered continual abuse ostensibly because of his effeminate behavior, he recalls, " . . . all the teachers and counselors could tell me was that it was *my* problem."[45]

In my own survey of eighty-nine school districts across the United States, most reported a variety of counseling approaches for lesbian and gay students with the most popular being education and the supplying of information, referral to other agencies, and in-house counseling designed to help the teen accept herself or himself. Self-acceptance counseling is not without its detractors, especially in the political arena. Utah State Senator Craig Taylor recently proclaimed "Encouraging . . . students who are confused about their sexual orientation to label themselves as homosexual causes psychological and emotional harm."[46] No districts surveyed recommend placement in a special classroom or school and less than 5 percent use in-house counseling to try to change sexual orientation. Most districts feel that even more varied therapeutic techniques should be available.

Among high school counselors, less than a third feel that administrators view lesbian and gay concerns as a legitimate topic for discussion with students and fewer than 20 percent of counselors have participated in any specific training.[47] As expected, counselors from rural areas express more negative attitudes and have less professional preparation.

In my own study, nearly half of the school districts reported that their counseling staffs had no education on lesbian and gay youth issues, while slightly over half felt that at least a workshop or conference was warranted as minimal training. Unfortunately, in nearly two-thirds of the districts, less than 10 percent of the counseling staff had even this minimal training. Only one-fourth of the districts reported that over half of their counseling staff had attained this minimal level of training that they deemed necessary. Even among counseling supervisors nearly four out of ten reported no direct experience with lesbian or gay students. Nearly 70 percent of the districts report no support organizations for sexual-minority students in the community. Where they do exist, over a third of counseling supervisors don't know the name of the agency.

Schools in rural areas are particularly difficult for lesbian, gay, and bisexual students. When Skye, age fourteen, confided in her school counselor in rural Idaho, he immediately called her parents. In desperation she ran away from home. "I felt I had no one to turn to," she recalls.[48] Ill-informed and insensitive, school counselors are often the only resource for rural sexual-minority youths and their parents, and their input can have disastrous outcomes.

Administrators and School Boards

Administrators and school board members are perceived as distant and uncaring as far as queer kids are concerned. When Joshua, a fourteen-year-old gay high school student in Allen Park, Michigan, complained of harassment in 1996, the school board passed two antiharassment policies. Neither mentioned sexual orientation.[49] When Jeremy, an eighteen-year-old senior at Huntington Beach High School in California claimed he had been physically attacked and verbally harassed by a high school football player, the principal defended the attacker as an "excellent" student and questioned whether the complaint was part of some gay agenda.[50]

CURRICULUM

A student has a right to know about homosexuality. Freedom of thought dictates that each student be exposed to diverse information and be able to make judgments based on factual information.[51] One recent high school graduate concludes, "[B]y trusting young people with honest information, . . . we empower them to make educated and nonbigoted choices. . . ."[52]

The unstated curriculum in high school is a heterosexual one. To a large extent, the curriculum reflects the heterosexist notion that everyone is essentially heterosexual and that only a contaminated environment, such as a curriculum that includes homosexuality, can disrupt this norm.[53] Any hint of homosexuality must be eradicated or the "disease" might spread. Texts, pictures, audiovisual aids, classroom topics, and extracurricular activities all have a heterosexual foundation. Homosexuality is perceived as a problem. Heterosexuality and antihomosexuality are enforced by teachers, school rules, and adolescent conformity. This lack of education on homosexuality surely contributes to homophobia.[54]

A course in sexual-minority studies probably is not practical given the current political climate. Lesbian, gay, and bisexual issues are relevant to many other topics, however, and could be presented objectively. Nearly 70 percent of the school districts in my own survey mention homosexuality within the curriculum, most frequently in current issues, biology, and sex education classes. The manner of presentation is even more important.

Teachers, often poorly informed on lesbian, gay, and bisexual issues, may feel the need to present sexual minorities in a negative light in the misguided belief that anything less is "advocacy." Upward of 50 percent of lesbian and gay teens claim that homosexuality is discussed in class only in a negative manner.[55]

Administrators often counter that the curriculum cannot be stretched to include sexuality. This issue, they contend, is better addressed at home. Ironically, for many lesbian, gay, and bisexual youths, home is one of their most difficult challenges. Parents are often in denial or outwardly hostile and usually ill-informed.

When the curriculum is "stretched" to include lesbians, gays, and bisexuals, it is a given that right-wing extremists will protest the decision. When California attempted to include the role of lesbian and gay parents and the suicides of lesbian and gay youth in a health curriculum, Lance Fortin of the Traditional Values Coalition clamored, "Telling kids who are wrestling with uncertainty imposed by puberty and today's society that they can find self-worth in a perverted behavior borders on child abuse."[56]

"This [educational programs that discusses homosexuality] is extremely destructive," intones John Hale, sometime legal adviser to the Archdiocese of New York. "In order to give comfort to that one out of one hundred who may ultimately choose a homosexual lifestyle, they are willing to put at risk the other ninety-nine by encouraging them to experiment in their formative stages of adolescence."[57] Debra Haffner, executive director of the Sex Information and Education Council of the United States (Siecus) counters, "[T]here is absolutely no evidence that orientation can be changed due to exposure to other people and educational messages."[58]

The result of right-wing pressure is evident in states such as South Carolina. By law, homosexuality is not to be mentioned in sex education for grades K-7. In the upper grades, homosexuality is confined to the context of sexually transmitted diseases.

In Elizabethtown, Pennsylvania, the school board passed a "pro-family" resolution on September 17, 1996 that stated that "Pro-homosexual concepts on sex and family will never be tolerated or accepted in this school." The resolution went on to describe the two-parent family as "the norm."

My own survey of eighty-nine school districts found that fewer than 25 percent use sexual-minority adults and service organizations as classroom resources or consultants. Those that do, employ these individuals and groups as staff trainers, classroom special presenters, and as resources. The most frequently cited reasons for not using these resources are that such outside aid is unnecessary and that use might raise vocal opposition in the community.

Sex and AIDS Education

Adolescents engage in sexual activity and are doing so at younger and younger ages. Although the majority of parents favor some form of sex education, a well-organized and vocal minority has, in some districts, severely restricted the message that all youths need to hear. As a result, sex education has been reduced to "plumbing and prevention" with little emphasis on the emotional dimension or the joy of sexuality.[59] The hetero-sexist bias only reinforces the notion among adolescent males that sex is about their satisfaction and everything else is "the girl's problem."[60] My own survey found that only 75 percent of school districts have a sex education curriculum for high school students. Over half of these are ten classes or less in length.

In sex education classes homosexuality often is ignored or given tangential status to the main discussion of heterosexuality. Summarizing his own high school "sex ed" experience, Anthony, nineteen and gay, recalls,

> I could have done better in an adult bookstore. I think I would have learned more. . . .[61]

David, an eighteen-year-old African-American gay musician, sculptor, and actor, is more specific.

> They don't teach anything in school except the man's on top, the woman's on the bottom. Well, sexuality is a lot wider than that. Kids are not taught anything at all about homosexuality.[62]

In my own survey, nearly half of the districts with a sex education curriculum did not include homosexuality as a part of that curriculum. Many sex education programs do not mention same-sex contacts without condemning such behavior. To do more according to the religious right would be to legitimize an immoral "lifestyle." The consequences for teens can be deadly.

> Some policymakers appear to believe that high-risk behavior can be prevented by stigmatizing those in high-risk groups. But the exclusion of . . . gay youth from the larger community prevents us from offering them education and counseling about the risks of unprotected sex.[63]

Restrictions also keep sex and sexuality from being mentioned in other classes, although sex is pervasive outside the classroom and in the media and culture in general. The rantings of the religious right to the contrary, there is uniformity in the commitment of school districts to heterosexism and traditional families and family roles.[64]

Lesbian, gay, and bisexual youth continue to be placed at risk for the AIDS virus because of the failure of the American educational system to adequately warn them about prevention. In short, "AIDS education continues to be impeded by the pervasive American reticence about discussing sexual behavior."[65] This reticence is exploited by religious fundamentalists and political conservatives in Congress, in state legislatures, and on local school boards who restrict funds or require that only abstinence be taught as a prevention measure.[66] The insistence that prevention education follow their narrow moral strictures is resulting in the needless deaths of our youth.

AIDS education may be limited to an abstinence-only message based on the premise that there is no "safe sex" outside the bonds of heterosexual marriage. In November 1995, Michael Moses, Texas Commissioner for Education, rejected a $1.35 million federal grant because of its requirement that the state drop its abstinence-based sex education curriculum. Under pressure, he later reversed himself. Although nearly all districts in my survey taught AIDS education, nearly a quarter taught abstinence-only. Commenting on abstinence-only approaches, Julian, a student, concludes, "It's all about making you feel guilty and making sure that you're not doing it. . . ."[67]

Unfortunately, in some communities, AIDS education has also become the forum for examining the supposed unhealthiness of homosexuality. This condemnation only reinforces the notion that AIDS is a gay—and by association, lesbian—disease. Actually, given the rate of adolescent sexual experimentation, sexual orientation may have little to do with same-sex behavior. The amount and type of sexual activity is more important than the sexual orientation of the participants. Teens may in fact be at a higher risk than adults because of the number engaging in sexual activity with both sexes. The adolescent unwillingness to confide in adults makes it difficult for educators to know which students need this information.[68]

An effective AIDS prevention program for lesbian, gay, and bisexual youths requires consideration of three areas:[69]

1. Nature of transmission
2. Sexual practices of lesbian and gay individuals
3. Risk factors related to being lesbian and gay in a hostile society

In my own survey of eighty-nine school districts, only two reported that they had conducted a survey of student sexual behavior. In most districts sexual surveys were not attempted because of administrative opposition, a belief that students would not be candid, and a fear of adverse publicity.

Educational Materials

Literature texts include lesbian and gay writers but rarely identify them as such, history texts ignore the gay civil rights movement, and health texts usually exclude lesbian and gay sexual development. Houghton-Mifflin Company's *Health* text reads:

> Some psychologists believe that homosexuality is caused by confusion about sex roles that develops early in childhood. Because homosexuality is not considered normal in our society, homosexuals often experience many difficulties.

In *Health: A Guide to Wellness*[70] by Glencoe/McGraw Hill, homosexuality is mentioned only in connection with AIDS. Homosexuality is neither defined nor explained. The association of homosexuality and disease serves to reinforce stereotypes. *Health America*[71] is more blatantly antigay and includes the incorrect statement "With AIDS it is usually sexual conduct with males of the same sex." At least three times, children are warned "Never have homosexual sex."

Textbook companies counter that homosexuality is too controversial. To continue to treat it as such perpetuates this status.

For a queer kid with no role models, no close lesbian, gay, or bisexual peer relationships, and/or little positive support, literature can facilitate positive ego development. Lesbian, gay, and bisexual-themed literature has experienced tremendous growth in the last decade. Unfortunately, this literature is not readily available to adolescents as a result, in large measure, of objections by religious ideologues.

Few books on sexual-minority issues exist in school libraries. "I went to the library to get some books on homosexuality and lesbianism," explains Elizabeth, age sixteen. "Talk about a major hassle[,] . . . they hide books like that behind their front desk in a little room."[72] Those books available are likely to be "censored, inaccurate, or blatantly homophobic."[73] Given the authority of the written word, such books are an assault on a teen's self-esteem.

HARASSMENT AND VIOLENCE

Schools are social molds where rigid expectations of conduct and behavior are reinforced. Conformity is tyrannical. The wrong clothes or the wrong comment can result in ostracism. Sexual conformity is enforced most rigidly. Those that do not conform are open to the physical, verbal, and mental bullying of the majority. Reports from lesbian and gay teens range from put-downs and "rude comments and jokes" through "profanities written on my locker" and threats to actual violence and physical abuse.[74] The overall result is loneliness, fear, and self-loathing. Believing she had no right to protest, Kelli explained away the outward signs of being physically attacked in gym class as a field hockey injury. "It still hurts to think about it," the high school senior recalls, her eyes moistening, "I hated myself so much for being gay."[75] High school coach and physical education teacher Dennis Slatterly observes, "[H]omosexual kids take a lot of guff around here."[76]

Willie, a gay sixteen-year-old from Arkansas, was finally hospitalized with injuries, the culmination of two years of name-calling, death threats, and broken windows in the family home. These are not isolated incidents. The 1996-1997 report of the Safe Schools Coalition of Washington State reports seventy-seven attacks against lesbian and gay students during that school year. Seven of the attacks were gang rapes.[77]

"We were . . . used as punching bags by our classmates," recalls Chris, a young gay man, "just for being different."[78] Continual verbal and physical harassment takes its toll on a young person.

> I wasn't accepted. I knew I was gay, and I knew everyone else knew because they told me I was a faggot every day. . . . I felt like something was exploding inside me.[79]

Concerned Students of Des Moines report that the average high school student hears approximately twenty-five antigay remarks in a typical school day.[80]

Most violence against lesbians and gay men is the work of young male bullies. It is not surprising, therefore, to learn that high schools are often the site of such violence. Zoe, a high school senior, recalls a particularly troubling incident:

> Two female students were standing in the hall with their arms around each other. Students began to encircle them and yell profanities until a group of about thirty kids surrounded them.[81]

In a 1984 survey by the National Gay and Lesbian Task Force, 45 percent of males and 25 percent of females reported having been harassed or attacked in school because they were believed to be gay or lesbian.

Those who are most open about their sexual orientation are most often targeted. After Carla, the senior class president came out, someone spray-painted "Carla will die" in big red letters on the school building.[82] Julian, a young gay suicide survivor, provides a list of the horrors at his school:

> people used to pee on me in the shower. . . . People were slamming me into lockers. . . . I would be standing at a urinal and someone would come up and kick me in the small of my back. . . . I got chased with a baseball bat . . . and had to hide in a stall in the bathroom. . . . I used to get punched a lot in the locker room.[83]

Sadly, he concludes, "I couldn't learn there."[84] Another gay teen concurs when he states that he has "No where to turn, no one I can trust."[85] The choice for many queer kids is often a simple one of joining the majority by pretending to be heterosexual or suffering in silence or isolation.

EXTRACURRICULAR ACTIVITIES

Curricular biases are extended to extracurricular activities. Few high schools allow gay/straight alliance organizations or gay support groups.

The high school prom can be either a "rite of passage" or a reminder of isolation and ridicule. Renee, a high school senior, protests, "We *should* be able to have a night just like heterosexual people do."[86] Many lesbian and gay adults remember prom night as a lonely dateless evening or as an uncomfortable charade.

The blackout surrounding homosexuality in the curriculum also extends to the school paper. Despite the free speech guarantees of the First Amendment to the Constitution, school administrators have been granted broad powers by the courts to censor the topics discussed in school newspapers.[87] A recent story in the Palmer, Colorado High School monthly describing the angst of lesbian and gay teens met with vehement criticism and calls for censorship from groups such as Colorado for Family Values despite a 1990 state law that guarantees high school students the right to publish stories on any topic as long as they are not considered obscene, libelous, false, or inflammatory.[88] According to People for the American Way, a political education organization, school censorship was more successful in 1995 than in any year since the group began collecting data thirteen years before. Objections to school newspaper articles perceived as "promoting" homosexuality rose 50 percent in the last year.[89] "Teenage suicide, alcoholism and homosexuality are topics that most [school newspaper] advisers tend to steer their newspapers from covering."[90] Yet, these issues can broaden student awareness and encourage sensitivity while teaching student reporters responsible, thorough journalism. Such stories are best when the staff agrees to tackle the issue rather than when the adviser imposes the topic. All too often, however, it is the adviser who nixes sexual orientation as a topic.

COLLEGE CAMPUSES

University and college environments are little better than high schools even though they are more open. Religious institutions practice blatant discrimination and the nature of dormitories and fraternities and sororities fosters enforcement of rigid heterosexist conformity. Just before final exams, Brandon, an openly gay student at a small Catholic college, was told to vacate his dorm room within twenty-four hours because, he was told, he "didn't care about building community; . . . didn't fit the image."[91]

Individual and institutional ignorance of and insensitivity to lesbian, gay, and bisexual students is widespread. By overlooking sexual-minority students, colleges send the message that there is a lack of concern and caring.

As with high schools, the situation is not all bleak. Over 800 gay, lesbian, and bisexual college student groups exist and many campuses are making efforts to be more welcoming. Some colleges have experimented with sexual-minority housing and a few fraternities for gay men exist. Courses in sexual behavior usually cover homosexuality but it is often treated as a tangential topic. Few courses exist nationwide that address gay, lesbian, and bisexual issues exclusively, although a handful of colleges have gay and lesbian studies programs.

CONCLUSION

While heterosexuality is woven throughout the typical high school curriculum and heterosexist assumptions are the basis for all interactions, homosexuality and bisexuality are determined to be private matters, unfit for the classroom. Teachers who overstep the bounds by discussing homosexuality freely and honestly or by coming out risk censure or worse.

In general, attending middle and high school is a barren experience for queer kids. A young gay male recalls,

> I don't know what they thought they were giving us, but it wasn't an education. My self-esteem has never been at such an extreme low. . . . My post–high school plans were very simple. I planned to either commit suicide, or become a prostitute . . .[92]

Sexual-minority teens are often isolated from each other and from many heterosexual peers. The dating rituals, the proms, and the parties are irrelevant, and few support services or groups designed for lesbian, gay, and bisexual teens exist. Students who are isolated are vulnerable to exploitive adults.[93] "It's . . . damaging when you don't see yourself reflected in any part of school life," concludes nineteen-year-old Phoebe.[94]

Even with the odds against them, most lesbian, gay, and bisexual youths are part of society. They cope as best they can with few observable difficulties. Studies, sports, and extracurricular activities, plus church and family, provide a screen behind which these teens hide their sexuality.

ACT UP or the AIDS Coalition To Unleash Power has a slogan "Silence = Death." These words aptly apply to educators' attitudes toward queer kids. By being silent, educators support heterosexism, homophobia, and oppression. By being silent, educators help to create an atmosphere of guilt and isolation, and ultimately, of fear. The burden of making our schools safe for queer kids can not be foisted onto their backs. It is not their responsibility. Many of them remain closeted. It is their only way to survive.

"Every student is deserving of a sense of respect and dignity," states Virginia Uribe, founder of Project 10. "And we have not given that to our gay and lesbian students."[95] David, a nineteen-year-old African-American gay man, concludes,

> It isn't about sexuality. It's about building . . . self-worth. . . . It's about saving lives.[96]

Chapter 6

Outcomes
for Sexual-Minority Youths

> . . . the most deadly of all possible sins
> is the mutilation of a child's spirit.
>
> Erik Erickson[1]

Adolescence is a time of complex change that can result in stress even for the most well-adjusted youth. For most healthy individuals, adolescence is a period in which they cope with developmental and maturational changes. Anatomically and physiologically, a young person's body changes rapidly with accompanying hormonal changes that can create unfamiliar feelings and extremes of emotion, bewildering both the youth and others. A young person is faced with the task of stabilizing her or his individual identity and enhancing self-esteem, emancipating from family, formulating vocational goals, and adopting an adult sex role.[2] For some adolescents, same-sex orientation is a part of their self-identity, complicating development and adjustment.[3]

Adolescence is also a time for learning to establish and maintain healthy relationships. This task is complicated for sexual-minority youths by a hidden sexuality and a hostile community. A heterosexual facade and reinforcement of heterosexual rituals, such as the prom, do little to aid learning about mature lesbian and gay relationships. It is not uncommon for lesbian and gay teens to withdraw from adolescent socialization. Social interacting with either gender may be too difficult, arousing strong sexual feelings or reminding a youth of her or his heterosexual failings. As a result, lesbian and gay teens may not experience the adolescent interpersonal experimentation common for most heterosexuals.

Queer kids share the constraints of other adolescents, plus additional constraints somewhat similar to those of ethnic-minority youths without these youths' familial and cultural support. The process is a double whammy. Vic, a college-age lesbian, explains,

> I don't think there's anyone more isolated than queer kids. You don't see yourself anywhere. At least racial minorities have their families. With queers, oftentimes families are who we're *most* alienated from.[4]

There are few guidebooks to sexual-minority adulthood. Lesbian, gay, and bisexual youth are raised by heterosexual families with heterosexual values and expectations, have heterosexual peers, and attend or are directly or indirectly influenced by heterosexual institutions, such as school and the media. Those who exercise control over teens assume that their charges are heterosexual. The fact that we know so little about the adjustment processes of lesbian, gay, and bisexual teens reflects their marginalization.

Queer kids lack positive role models, confidants, and information on sexual identity.[5] Fewer than one in five lesbian and gay adolescents can identify anyone who has been supportive.[6] The hostility and lack of support experienced by lesbian, gay, and bisexual teens hampers mature ego development and can be manifested in secondary social, physical, and psychological problems.

In some ways ethnic-minority youth who are lesbian, gay, or bisexual may have better coping skills. Dennis, a young Chinese-American man explains:

> You go through a lot of hurt when someone calls you a "Chinaman." And so, in one sense, you're more able to deal with someone calling you a "fag." And you can spring back more easily and say, "I'm a person. I am me."[7]

Gaining acceptance within ethnic-minority communities, however, may pose other problems. Sexual-minorities are considered a "white thing" in many African-American communities. The racially segregated nature of American society and the extremely limited contact of many African-American children with white adults ensures that those children who are lesbian, gay, and bisexual have a distinctly African-American outlook.[8]

The task of developing into an adult is complicated by the stigma attached to homosexuality and the confusion created by societal messages. As Hetrick and Martin (1987) observe, "[S]tigmatization creates situations and problems that must be resolved."[9] The degree of success encountered by a youth is influenced by many factors such as mental well-being, gender, age, race and ethnicity, socioeconomic status, urban-suburban-rural environment, and degree of support.[10] Social stigmatization is a major stressor that can result in lesbian and gay teens being vulnerable to psychological and adjustment problems.

The effects of internalized homophobia and negative stereotyping are difficult to overcome. We should not underestimate the damage to self-esteem from simply growing up gay in our society. Each teen must reconcile herself or himself with the notions that homosexuals are believed by many to be evil, sinful, and/or sick.

STATISTICS

Although lesbian and gay teens may be 10 percent or less of the adolescent population, they account for 30 percent of "successful" youth suicide.[11] From adult accounts, it is estimated that 20 to 40 percent of lesbian and gay youth have attempted suicide and over half have contemplated it.[12] These figures compare to 8.3 percent of all teens who have contemplated ending their own lives. In real numbers these percentages mean that approximately 1,500 lesbian and gay youth kill themselves annually. According to the *Journal of Pediatrics,* suicide is the leading cause of death for gay, lesbian, and bisexual youth.

In addition, lesbian and gay adolescents may account for 30 percent of teen drug and alcohol abuse. Among poor, urban, at-risk gay and bisexual males, as high as 50 percent may abuse substances.[13]

Homes are not always happy places for lesbian and gay teens. It is estimated that homosexual youths make up about 20 percent of the 50,000 youths forcibly institutionalized annually.[14] Twenty percent of lesbian and gay adolescents are thrown out of their homes by parents.[15] Among homeless youths 25 to 50 percent are likely to be lesbian, gay, or bisexual. This translates into 2,500 to 5,000 homeless sexual-minority kids in Los Angeles alone.

As horrendous as these figures are, they are only the tip of the iceberg. Many sexual minority youth face isolation, despair, violence, and depression daily.

Although many explanations have been offered for these frightening statistics, the cause of the problem is clearly not the lesbian or gay youths. On the one hand, a teen is told by society that she or he is inherently bad or undesirable, and on the other, that same teen has her or his own undeniable feelings and desires that contradict societal notions. A society that despises homosexuals has little desire to help lesbian and gay youths adjust in a healthy way to their sexual orientation. One leading researcher concludes,

> The personal, social, and institutional support systems that assist the adolescent heterosexual minor are not available to the homosexual minor. . . . The homosexual adolescent must either try to complete the developmental process in a hostile and psychologically impoverished heterosexual environment or must decide to seek peer support and social opportunities in the homosexual community.[16]

With the latter choice, when available, a youth may risk family alienation, homelessness, and a loss of educational and employment opportunities.

Impaired Self-Esteem and Emotional Growth

Self-concept is a composite of identities related to the performance of various situationally determined roles.[17] The value of the role and the desirability of mastering it are related. A hostile environment that stigmatizes some roles is reflected in self-appraisals that are obstacles to positive self-identification. Denial of accurate information makes the process of identity integration even more difficult.

Homophobia and heterosexism are two arrows aimed at the self-esteem of lesbian and gay youths. A teen may experience harassment and violence directly or witness others being victimized. Possibly more devastating for self-esteem are the effects of jokes and media portrayals of lesbians and gays. It is difficult to develop a positive self-image when one is a member of a stigmatized group. Trying to pass as a heterosexual may be doomed to failure which only serves to further injure self-esteem.

After repeated attempts to fall in love with a woman, Rick, a gay youth concludes that he "was incapable of human love."[18] The feeling of failure and the fear of disappointing parents and peers can be compounded by the guilt accompanying furtive same-sex erotic encounters. Void of romance, such clandestine sex handicaps the growth of healthy intimate same-sex relationships and the development of strong, positive self-esteem.

It is difficult for queer kids to find a successful strategy for balancing their psychological needs. Amy, a junior high student, chose to adopt more gender-neutral dress and as a result, was rejected by her peers. Reflecting later, she concluded, "I guess my friends ditched me because I was learning to be myself instead of who they wanted me to be."[19]

The asexual strategy also has its price. Dan, a white suburban youth, avoided crass sexual jokes and teasing only to find that "By seventh grade I was out of it, . . . nobody talked to me."[20] Uninterested in boys, Jen immerses herself in sports but drinks to avoid uncomfortable girl-boy social situations. Failure to suppress same-sex feelings may result in guilt, depression, and self-destructive behaviors.

Denial, coupled with passing as a heterosexual, is the most common adolescent coping strategy.[21] Kevin's dogged pursuing of "normalness" has its cost. He dated frantically and pushed his dates for sex. He concludes, "I hated myself, and this I couldn't escape from . . ."[22]

Bonnie, age twenty-one, lost her virginity at fourteen in a drunken stupor, convinced that it would make her feel in love with the boy and stop her fantasizing about women.[23] Lew's dates with girls feel hollow; he merely is going through the motions. Rachel began to experience physical pain and nausea every time she goes on a date with her "boyfriend." "I didn't like it," recalls Darla, who began having sex with males at age twelve, "but . . . I just kept on with the guys just trying to prove myself not being gay."[24]

The anxiety of living a lie can be great. The entire house of cards is in danger of collapse at any given moment. Spontaneity must be kept in check for fear that such behavior might reveal some hint of homosexuality. Even though others may be fooled, this strategy takes its toll on the youth who may become depressed, feel awkward, shameful, and hypocritical. "I tried going out with boys," confesses Lauren, a college student, "and when we'd start getting close it would feel really weird, and I'd freak out and tell them I couldn't see them anymore."[25] "I tried all this different stuff," recalls Matt, "to make myself straight, like going to dances with girls. But it really didn't work . . . because it made me feel depressed."[26] Katie found heterosexual dating intolerable without drinking. As the pressure to date increased, so did her alcoholism.

As sexual desire increases with puberty, more and more energy is required to maintain denial. Although "passing" protects a teen from the social consequences of being openly homosexual, it cannot protect a teen from the psychological effects of living a lie. "I was on guard and watching everyone," explains Richard.[27] Continual lying leads to a chronic sense of shame.[28] Unable to continue with his heterosexual sham, Bill, a college sophomore and former high school class president and star athlete, ended his life by hanging himself with a woman's slip.

Other manifestations may include emotional blockage and perfectionism. "I was constantly denying the feelings I had for other guys," states Devin, age seventeen. "In the process of hiding any feelings, I repressed all emotions."[29] The suppressed teen's development may be truncated while she or he attempts to overachieve in order to compensate for feelings of inadequacy and unacceptability.[30]

Repression of sexual desires also has a psychological cost. Compartmentalizing sexual desires leads to a moratorium on developmental tasks such as identity integration.[31] Other effects may include a restricted ability to relate intimately to others, loss of identity, and a disregard for one's own needs and for those of others.

Without the practice afforded heterosexuals, lesbian and gay teens may lack the intra- and interpersonal skills needed to be a functioning adult. Drew, a young white gay man, recalls,

> In junior high school you're . . . learning to be comfortable with yourself as a sexual person . . . and how to interact with people. I wasn't taught to be comfortable with myself. I was taught to hide that part of me rather than to develop it. As a gay person, I didn't learn to interact. I learned to hide and not let myself show at all.[32]

The result is a compartmentalization of self and a delay in integrating sexuality with other parts of self. Lesbian and gay youths may come to fear intimacy which may be eschewed in favor of anonymous sex.[33] Intimacy is too meaningful, too frightening. Jacob, a young African American, recalls the first time another man expressed his love for him, "It was kind of hard to believe that *even after sex* there are really feelings."[34]

Isolated as a misfit, lesbian and gay teens can suffer further loss of their self-esteem. Betrayal can be devastating. Grant had been having sex regularly with a star on his high school football team, but they barely acknowledged each other in school. "[S]ince it was rumored that I was gay," Grant explains, "he didn't want to get a close identity with me."[35]

A youth's concept of the lesbian and gay community and, by association, of herself or himself is formed from several encounters, both actual and secondhand. Adolescent gay males form their images of gay adults and of homosexual life primarily through sexual encounters, and less through the media, and word of mouth. In contrast, young lesbians rely more on the media than on word of mouth, and association with open or thought-to-be lesbians.[36] Regardless of the source, both gay males and lesbians develop societal stereotypic images, such as the effeminate nature of gay men and the masculine nature of lesbians.

Isolation and the Downward Spiral of Depression

As a youth reaches the realization that this is not a "phase" and that feelings and desires will not change, she or he often faces an identity crisis. Orientation and behavior might be homosexual but identity may be very different. More lesbian and gay adults than heterosexual adults report that as an adolescent they felt anxious, insecure, frustrated, and miserable.[37] Heterosexual behaviors seem unnatural but are espoused, while same-sex behaviors feel natural but are stigmatized. To add to this dilemma, parents, teachers, and preachers—those individuals trusted by youths—are the ones heralding the heterosexual standards. Although a lesbian or gay adolescent has strong feelings, there is no support in the schools, churches, or among peers for developing an identity.

Ethnic-minority youths may have a particularly difficult task because of the three communities they must balance.[38] Often, ethnic-minority lesbian, gay, and bisexual individuals try to keep the sexual-minority, ethnic-minority, and the majority communities separate in order to maintain the support each provides. The result is increased isolation and the fear of being separated from any of these communities.

Depression can lead to withdrawal or to a lack of interest in or excitement about people and events, and to irritability and moodiness. "I felt like there was a part of me [sexual orientation] that wasn't being acknowl-edged," explains Theresa, age nineteen. "That it didn't exist [as far as others were concerned], and it made me feel alone and depressed."[39] "Just imagine that you are a black American," explains Leilani, "who was . . . turned white . . . and then dropped right in the middle of a Ku Klux Klan meeting. This is how I feel most of the time," she adds. "As a lesbian, it's *painful* to sit and watch while my friends, classmates, and peers tell gay cracks right in front of me."[40]

Brian, a white gay teen, cuts classes incessantly and is truant. He spends much of his time alone. Christopher, age nineteen, began to withdraw emotionally from his family, not sharing his feelings for fear of what they would do.[41] Kenneth, now age seventeen, found life and school becoming more and more difficult. In his freshman year of high school, he became depressed and suicidal, and eventually dropped out. "All I did was stay in bed and ask God, 'Why me?'" he recalls. "I thought that because I was gay, I didn't deserve happiness."[42] Isolation, such as Brian's, Christoph-er's, and Kenneth's, prevents access to accurate information and may result in a youth operating on myths, stereotypes, and misinformation. Vanessa explains,

> I felt alienated from the rest of the world. I didn't really have friends that I could relate to. . . . What I wanted was attention.[43]

A queer kid may feel helpless, hopeless, and worthless. "I just began hating myself more and more," explains Steven, age eighteen, "as each year the hatred towards me grew and escalated. . . . "[44] "I was angry that I turned out this way," recalled Elizabeth, age sixteen. "Nothing has ever made me hate myself as much as being gay."[45] Tragically, her feelings, plus the physical harassment at school and parental nonacceptance led Elizabeth to take her own life.

Depression is cited by lesbian and gay youths as one of their most common problems.[46] It has been estimated that depression is four to five times as high among lesbian and gay teens as in the adolescent population in general.[47] As a consequence, a youth may experience a loss of peer relationships which, in turn, increases a feeling of isolation and a fear of rejection and leads to further depression.[48] "I wasn't having any harass-ment problems," recalls William, a high school senior, "but I was isolat-ing myself from the rest of the students." He adds, "I knew if I came out, there would be consequences, either verbal or physical, and I wasn't willing to do that."[49] Although he temporarily found joy in extracurricular theatrics, Stewart could not escape the belligerency of his classmates. Eventually, the hostility wore him down; he became depressed and lethargic. Some youth may retreat from same-sex social interactions for fear that these relationships may become too intimate and reveal true feelings. Ninety-five percent of the youths at the Institute for Protection of Lesbian and Gay Youth in New York City described feelings of aloneness, of being the only one, and of having no one to talk to about their feelings.[50]

Depression may be exhibited as a loss of pleasure and a feeling of overwhelming sadness, changes in appetite and sleeping, slower thought processes, lower self-esteem, and feelings of shame and failure. Feeling very alone, Danielle, a young lesbian, began to lose weight and to have trouble sleeping. In contrast, Todd takes refuge in food. By being obese, he removes himself from the sexual field, reasoning that no one—male or female—will find him attractive. Ken did the same thing. One study found the most frequent psychosocial problems of gay youth to be poor school performance, mental health problems, substance abuse, running away, and conflict with the law.[51] Henry, an upper-middle-class Southern youth, recalls,

> I felt isolated throughout high school. I didn't talk to anyone. I was just weird—just flat out warped. I went through a shoplifting period. I didn't have anybody to hang around so I'd go downtown and shoplift.[52]

Isolation and depression can also lead to thoughts of suicide.

Queer kids may fear their own homosexuality and its discovery. In order to keep her or his "deep, dark, shameful secret,"[53] a youth may try to limit damage by attempting to manage information and situations. The motto becomes: *Only give as much information as is necessary, lie sometimes, and be truthful when you can't.* When his best friend came out to him, Eric refused to speak to him for weeks, in part, for fear his own homosexuality would be revealed. Fear of discovery and inability to self-disclose increase a teen's emotional isolation. "I would do anything to escape school," David admits. "I was already comfortable with myself as a gay person; I just wasn't comfortable with what other people might do if they found out."[54] While heterosexual youths are learning their adult sexual roles, many lesbian, gay, and bisexual adolescents are learning to hide. As a result, the maturational development of adolescence may be postponed until adulthood. The plea of these youths is summed up by one of them, "Why can't we say where we are really hurting."[55]

The process can be terribly destructive for the individual.[56] Within the family, the youth may become secretive, less open and less honest, and in turn, less of a family member. Amy was so stoic at home that her unaware parents never guessed that she was being harassed at school by savage notes, such as "Do you have a penis, too?"[57] A teen with lesbian and gay friends may lie about even the most innocent of social activities for fear of self-incrimination. This pattern of deceit usually contrasts strongly with the openness teens desire in their relations with their parents.

The lack of friendly and open teachers and counselors may increase a youth's feeling of isolation and alienation. The isolation, especially from other lesbian, gay, and bisexual adolescents, may result in a youth failing to develop the coping strategies seen in other minority teens. Bill, age eighteen, explains,

> If anyone knew about me they would freak. I look straight and nobody would suspect. And you really can't talk to anybody about it or I'd be an outcast. . . . There's not a day goes by that I don't have these feelings for guys, . . . it's always there. So I'm always aware of being different, of not fitting in, of having to hide, of being unacceptable. You can't possibly know what that feels like. It's real lonely. . . .[58]

A lesbian or gay youth may be conflicted by same-sex desires and self-contempt. Most likely, she or he has incorporated familial, religious and societal judgments of homosexuals as sick, disgusting, and/or sinful. "Not only does society shout at me that I am evil," states Lee, "but an inner voice whispers it as well."[59] This internalized homophobia is most prevalent during adolescence, especially among males. These feelings can become externalized in the form of anger toward lesbians, gays, and bisexuals in general. Linda, a young lesbian, began to hate others she perceived to be lesbian or gay. This inner conflict may be expressed in rebellion, acting out, and/or careless sexual behavior. Anonymous sex, which separates sex from other aspects of self, can intensify feelings of shame, guilt, and worthlessness while promoting deception.[60] Negative attitudes about a part of one's self can become generalized to include the entire person. An individual may begin to think of herself or himself as bad, evil, undeserving, or inferior.

Manifestations may include abuse of alcohol or drugs and voluntary homelessness.[61] Other more subtle effects of self-depreciation may include abandonment of educational goals, acceptance of discrimination and abuse, and sabotaging of one's own successes. Failures become further proof of unworthiness.

Individual youths may also express feelings of rage and frustration. Tommy, a gay student, proclaims, "Our parents hate us, our teachers hate us, straight kids hate us, adults hate us. . . . "[62] When Deborah, a young lesbian, could contain her anger no longer, she channeled the rage into violent gang activity.[63] Wayne became a skinhead. These feelings may be based on ceaseless encounters with daily homophobia or on the lack of affirming activities and attitudes.

School Difficulties

According to the 1989 U.S. Department of Health and Human Services report on teen suicide, "The shame of ridicule and fear of attacks make school a fearful place [for lesbian and gay students]." The consequences of abuse and violence in school and the lack of openness with counselors and teachers are, all too often, poor academic performance, truancy, and dropping out.[64] "I was so afraid," relates one student, "that I would do almost anything not to have to go to school."[65] As a consequence, according the U.S. Department of Health and Human Services, 28 percent of lesbian and gay teens drop out of high school. "I decided to leave school," Randy, age eighteen, explains, "because I couldn't handle it [ridicule and physical abuse]."[66] In one study, 80 percent of lesbian and gay adolescents reported experiencing deteriorating school performance that they attributed to issues surrounding sexual orientation.[67]

Brent, age sixteen, describes an especially traumatizing event that destroyed his will to succeed in school:

> I was in the locker room, and this guy who didn't like me starts going, "Brent sucks dick, Brent sucks dick," and soon the whole locker room was full of guys shouting this for . . . three minutes. And I had to pretend I didn't give a shit . . . , but really I wanted to kill myself. That's when I started to cut school. I had a 4.0 grade average, and within months I went to Ds and Fs.[68]

Schoolwork has taken a backseat to his other dilemma. "I'm lying to myself and to the world every day that I'm in school," he claims. "And there's no way I can be out in school without being totally ostracized, without violence."[69]

It is a societal disgrace that some lesbian, gay, and bisexual youths must forfeit their education in order to avoid harassment and abuse. Queer kids who rebel or fight back risk being labeled severely emotionally disturbed (SED), a label that can lead to forced institutionalization in some states.

Substance Abuse and Chemical Dependence

Chemical dependence is a symptom of stigmatization and oppression.[70] It is estimated that 20 to 50 percent of gay youths abuse drugs or alcohol.[71]

Percentages are highest for poor and ethnic-minority youths and those who are homeless. Kathy, a cheerleader and high school athlete, abused alcohol and had to be admitted to a hospital for depression. Jesus goes to school drunk and/or stoned. Gene, a sixteen-year-old gay youth, becomes more and more involved in prostitution to support his drug habit. He has become depressed and suicidal and has tried to slash his wrists.

Substance abuse can mediate the anxiety of concealing sexual identity, help to discharge sexual impulses more comfortably, temporarily decrease depression, provide a feeling of power and self-worth, and offer a sense of identity or wholeness.[72] For some, the abuse of drugs and alcohol erases temporarily their feeling of being different or the hurt of nonacceptance or rejection by their family and/or friends. Drugs dull the pain or can be a form of revenge. "There was absolutely no way that I wanted to feel different," explains Sarah, age twenty, "and I felt very different from everyone and I didn't want that. So I didn't feel normal unless I had alcohol or drugs in me."[73] Bonnie, a twenty-one-year-old bisexual from California, continues, "The drugs helped to take away the pain of being with men, an experience that left me feeling incompetent and unsatisfied."[74] As with many of their heterosexual peers, sexual-minority teens are also susceptible to peer pressure and hedonism.

For aimless or street youths, lesbian and gay bars may reinforce substance abuse. In addition, lesbian and gay homeless youth are exposed to crack, a central part of street life.[75] Crack is inexpensive, easy to obtain, and highly addictive. Drugs may also be an integral part of prostitution with drug abuse possibly as high as 75 percent among homeless youths who engage in survival sex.[76]

Foster Care, Group Care, and Homelessness

After she was unable to have her twelve-year-old son Michael institutionalized for his homosexuality, Michael's mother placed him in the foster care system citing her inability to accept his sexual orientation because of her religious beliefs.[77] At age fourteen, Paul was placed in a group home for three years and forced to attend a sexual offenders group because he had attempted to touch the penis of a younger boy in his mother's foster care.[78] In such settings, a lesbian or gay teen may act out by cross-dressing or violate curfew in order to test the limits.[79]

Residential treatment centers make few provisions for lesbian or gay teens, operating instead under the assumption that these adolescents should be able to "fit into" existing programs.[80] Youths in such centers may be dealing with several sexual identity issues relative to previous sexual abuse or to sexual orientation. Lesbian and gay teens are overrepresented at residential facilities.[81] The limited access to private masturbation and to opposite-sex peers and the close same-sex living quarters, and emphasis on openness and sharing may heighten concerns about sexual orientation among the staff.

In these facilities, an open exploration of one's sexual identity risks rejection from both staff and peers. Many human services workers have been shown to be homophobic or ignorant of lesbian and gay concerns.[82] Some religious institutions are openly homophobic, expelling lesbian and gay teens for no other reason than a youth's honest admission of her or his sexual orientation.

In addition, staff too often react to acting out behaviors while ignoring the causes. As a result, queer kids may have to endure harassment and physical violence from both the staff and other youths. Those who resist may be labeled "provocative" or "aggressive," further stigmatizing them for future placement which may be difficult in any case given the high number of religious-affiliated facilities. Often the needs of lesbian and gay teens are shunted aside as agencies try to avoid the perception of being too accepting of homosexuality. The result: Equal access to services is denied.

Many lesbian, gay, and bisexual teens who have been rejected by their families face a foster care system ill-equipped to meet their needs effectively. Discrimination may continue with an accompanying increase in the teen's feelings of isolation and rejection.

After years of familial harassment and forced institutionalization because of her lesbianism, Everetta was desperate to escape her bondage. At age fifteen, she made a calculated entrance into a short-lived marriage, thus establishing her independence from her parents.[83]

Estimates of the total number of homeless adolescents vary widely from 500,000 to just over one million. The percentage of these youths who are lesbian, gay, or bisexual is estimated at a range of 25 to 50 percent with 30 to 40 percent representing a more accurate figure. Although only 6 percent of runaways nationwide self-identify as lesbian and gay, this gross undercounting, attributable to fear and lack of trust, is not confirmed by studies in specific cities.[84] The Seattle Commission on Children and Youth in a 1988 report estimated that approximately 40 percent of the city's homeless belonged to sexual-minorities. Los Angeles estimates are slightly lower at 30 to 40 percent.[85] Whatever the percentage, lesbian and gay youths are overrepresented.

While approximately 25 percent of gay males are forced to leave home because of their sexual orientation, not all become homeless. Mitch moved in with a high school friend who had very accepting parents. Danny was thrown out by his mother when he was only twelve. After six months of living on the streets, Danny was able to find his way to the foster care system. Now eighteen, Danny ponders,

> I end up asking myself, . . . Am I really loved? Am I not? I don't know. I get really emotional because I want to be with my family. But my mother doesn't want that.[86]

At age sixteen, Troix was removed forcibly from his parents' home at their request by police.[87]

Homeless lesbian and gay teens often congregate in large cities with sizeable lesbian and gay populations. Usually, they are under the illusion that they will find acceptance and nurturing within the adult sexual-minority community. Instead, they must rely on their own survival skills and the support of their street family. The bonding with that family may be so strong that a teen is reluctant to leave the streets even when better opportunities appear.

Despite the need, no federal or state funds for homeless teens specifically target sexual-minority teens. Teresa DeCrescendo, founder of Gay and Lesbian Adolescent Social Services (GLASS), states, "The scope of the problem is enormous . . . "[88]

Homelessness is compounded by lack of both education and employment. Life on the streets can be brutal. "I've been raped . . . robbed . . . held at knifepoint and at gunpoint," recalls red-haired Alex. "And one time I was picked up by a police officer, and he took me someplace up in the Hills, and he shoved a billy club as far as he could up my anus."[89]

Despite the realities of life on the street, some youths find such a life preferable to the violent and abusive home life they escaped. "I think that very often, running away from home is an adaptive move, not a maladaptive one," explains DeCrescendo. "It's an attempt to save yourself."[90]

All too often, it is an attempt to escape abuse. "The statistics are staggering," States Francis Kunreuther of the Hetrick-Martin Institute, "in terms of the relationship between physical and sexual abuse and street youth."[91]

Desperate to survive, many homeless youth turn to drugs, petty crime and/or prostitution. It has been estimated by youth workers that the average amount of time from a teen's becoming homeless to becoming a prostitute is about two weeks. Usually, hustling results from economic need.

Prostitution and Survival Sex

Prostitution and survival sex occur among all youths, especially the homeless. Although males tend to engage in same-sex prostitution, females do not, possibly reflecting the predominance of male clientele.[92]

Many young male prostitutes are homeless, have dropped out of school, are from dysfunctional or rejecting families, and are from lower socioeconomic groups.[93] Many are also sexual victims for whom their first associations with the sexual predators of the gay underworld have become the norm and the defining feature of their sexual identification. As teens, they are extremely vulnerable, often in dire economic straits, immature, and in need of a caring, loving environment.

Jeremy began hustling for the money. In one six-month period, he claims, he had sex for pay with over two hundred people. He boasts, "You could make three hundred dollars a day, if you work at it."[94]

Nikki, a seventeen-year-old runaway from Nebraska, panhandles along Hollywood Boulevard by day and sells his only commodity, his body, by night. Like many youth before they run away, he had no idea what it would be like to be homeless and on the streets. "I used to think that if I walked up and down Hollywood Boulevard all day I would get seen and get an agent."[95] Unfortunately, movie agents don't cruise the streets or bus depots looking for potential Hollywood stars, but the "Johns" do.

Approximately 70 percent of male prostitutes are gay or bisexual although the actual sexual orientation of many prostitutes is difficult to determine.[96] Most same-sex male prostitutes are adolescents, while most other-sex male prostitutes are adults.

Male prostitutes can be roughly divided into call boys/kept boys and street hustlers/bar boys. The former are usually middle class and have accepted their sexual orientation. In contrast, the latter, usually from working class or lower socioeconomic groups, often have difficulty accepting their sexual orientation. Homeless teens usually find themselves in the street hustler group. Levels of activity, measured by frequency, range from the occasional "trick" to continuous professional prostitution.

The average age of juvenile male prostitutes is sixteen to seventeen years. The first sex-for-pay experience usually occurs around age fourteen with more active hustling beginning within a year.[97] As many as 25 percent may have begun having sex prior to puberty.[98] As high as 75 percent may be homeless youth who ran away or were thrown out, often after years of abuse. The average age for leaving home is fifteen, often precipitated by the issue of sexual orientation.[99]

Most prostitutes have low self-esteem and state that they would like to quit.[100] Those factors that shape the self-concepts of other lesbians, gays, and bisexuals also contribute to the self-concepts of male prostitutes. Religion, law, medicine, and societal expectations relay the message that gay or bisexual male youths are sinful, criminal, mentally ill, and dysfunctional, effeminate males. At best, homosexuality is undesirable. One young man expresses this very well when he confides, "I was more worried about being found a homosexual than a prostitute."[101] Young prostitutes are well aware of the message. Some believe these restrictions, prohibitions, and condemnation created intolerable conditions that resulted in the need for prostituting one's self.

Many young male prostitutes have internalized societal attitudes toward homosexuals. As one states, "I feel guilty about having sex with men."[102] Guilt can lead to the downward spiral of depression, and the accompanying pursuit of acceptance may leave a youth open to victimization. Devan explains,

> I'd already had so much hurt I decided I wasn't going to feel anymore. I didn't feel anything—good, bad, or indifferent. I turned off the emotions.[103]

Most prostitution is very dissimilar to Julia Robert's life in the film *Pretty Woman*. While only 12 percent of heterosexual and homosexual males report negative sexual experiences, 87 percent of young gay male prostitutes do so. Approximately 42 percent of young gay male prostitutes report being raped, most prior to beginning prostitution, but more than half by customers, and 36 percent report molestation as a child. Most rape goes unreported because, as Luke, a young gay prostitute, notes, " . . . it wouldn't do any good because I am gay."[104] Rapes that are reported often are not taken seriously by the authorities.[105] Ironically, young males often run away to escape molestation only to experience it at the hands of their tricks.

Molestation doesn't cause homosexuality, but it is closely related to prostitution and continued victimization. Most prostitutes, two-thirds by some estimates, had their first sexual experience with a much older male, often under coercive conditions.[106] Eddie, a young gay male prostitute who was sexually abused as a child, relates, "I was always sad . . . when I was younger."[107] Alex, age seventeen and sexually abused as a child, relates, "I thought being a hooker was all I was good for."[108] A teen who doesn't feel in control may try to reassert control by reclamation through sex.[109] Possibly a youth who has been abused, more than one who has not, recognizes that a market for sex exists. Sex can be used to fulfill nonsexual needs.

Nearly 70 percent of prostitutes engage in sex solely for the money.[110] Most perceive their need for money as temporary. For homeless youths or those addicted to drugs, prostitution offers easy money with few skills required. Twenty to forty percent of prostitutes also use drugs. Sex for sale offers a quick way to earn drug money.

For some, the thrill of hustling itself becomes addictive. Sex is reportedly the motivation for at least one-third of the male prostitutes in one survey.[111]

"I crave it sometimes," Jeremy, a young prostitute, explains, "I kind of enjoy that kind of danger."[112] He lists the possible dangers as AIDS and other sexually transmitted diseases, physical abuse, rape, and death.

Mark, age seventeen, states, "prostitution is addicting because you can get the money so fast."[113] The gratification, in the form of money, is almost instantaneous. Other compensations might include food, shelter, drugs, or cigarettes. In addition, fulfillment may include a need to flee a bad home environment, to find someone to provide nurturance, to deal with sexual identity, to obtain male affection, and/or to experience the excitement.[114]

Prostitution may provide an identity and decrease the loneliness of some gay teens. Mark wanted companionship and often fell in love with his tricks. "In the beginning prostitution was easy," he concludes, "It was sort of romantic."[115] Inevitably, his tricks disappoint him, leaving him unfulfilled and feeling unlovable.

A young hustler may have difficulty with intimacy also. Fears of closeness may be related to a promiscuous past and/or a dislike of restriction.[116] Gay teens also have little opportunity to explore intimate relationships.

Prostitution provides some comraderie. Unlike female prostitutes, young male prostitutes may congregate together on the street.[117] For a lonely, homeless teen, these groups may be his only family.

For some gay teens, prostitution is a vehicle for exploring and experimenting with their sexual identity. In a society that offers little support for establishing a gay identity, prostitution offers one avenue for some youths. Being desired can also prop up a sagging self-esteem and provide some thrill.

Some teens may attempt unconsciously through prostitution to fulfill the negative stereotypes of gay men held by society. Within prostitution, a youth can live an exaggerated version of male sexuality and become the star, the desired one. Over time, however, a teen can not escape the stigma of prostitution or the compartmentalization of feelings and actions. Luke describes,

> I never really enjoyed sex with the tricks. I just lay there, whatever they want they get. . . . I am quite capable of turning my feelings off and on. . . . [118]

With a seemingly tougher hide still, Tom declares, "Ultimately I don't care about them and they don't care about me, so that's all it was, not caring."[119]

AIDS and STDs

For many queer kids, the threat of AIDS has become another stumbling block in establishing a positive gay identity.[120] Denial of one's sexual orientation is easier for some than dealing with the possibility of contracting a terminal illness. At the same time, other gay youths seem to believe that they are invulnerable and that AIDS only infects older gay men.

Adolescents of all sexual orientations are sexually active. Although this behavior is not officially sanctioned by society, popular entertainment portrays and glorifies the maturity of and the gratification inherent in sexual activity. While accumulating these messages, lesbian or gay teens receive almost no information on healthy and fulfilling same-sex sexual behavior and intimate relationships.

In general, all youths are ill-informed about STDs, AIDS, and safe sex practices. Unfortunately, those with the least knowledge of AIDS seem most likely to engage in risky sexual behavior and least likely to seek AIDS information.[121] AIDS education and even data collection have become highly politically charged. The effort to identify high-risk teens by surveying adolescent sexual behavior has become mired in a debate which demonstrates the worst effects of denial, homophobia, and misinformation by the Religious Right. It is safe to say that only the bravest of school administrators or school board members would propose teaching junior high and high school students how to have safe sex.

Recently, adolescent sexual behavior has resulted in an increase in all sexually transmitted diseases or STDs. A 1992 congressional report on HIV, the virus that causes AIDS, concluded that HIV infection is unchecked among adolescents in all economic brackets. The steady increase in the number of individuals in their twenties with AIDS and the long incubation period suggest that many were originally exposed during adolescence. "I've been HIV positive for seven years," declares Luna, a twenty-year-old Latino. "I'm still healthy, but it's been hard."[122]

The hostile environment experienced by a lesbian or gay youth may serve as an impetus to engage even more in high-risk sexual behavior that increases the chance of STDs. As many as two-thirds of gay and bisexual youths below the age of twenty-two may be at "extreme risk" of HIV exposure, mostly from unprotected sexual behavior and needle sharing.[123] Stress, the use of alcohol and drugs, and contracting other sexually transmitted diseases may suppress the immune system and make it more vulnerable to and less able to retaliate against the HIV virus. The incidence of alcohol and drug abuse is high among prostitutes, especially while hustling.[124] It is estimated that 50 percent of young gay and bisexual prostitutes have STDs.[125]

In addition, coming out may result in a disregard for all previous sexual inhibitions. For many gay males, few means exist beyond sexual encounters for exploration of their sexuality. The "scripts" that guide heterosexual teens are absent. Casual, anonymous sex may be perceived to fill a need for closeness, acceptance, support, and physical intimacy.[126] Gay boys are more likely than lesbian girls to seek out same-sex erotic encounters.[127] Nearly 25 percent of gay and bisexual African-American and Hispanic males in one survey in New York City reported bartering sex for drugs or money.[128] Such behavior increases the likelihood of transmission of the HIV virus.

Even those teens who "limit" unprotected sexual contact to their own immediate group of gay friends may be at risk if one member of that group is HIV positive.[129] The rationale for this behavior is that the youths know each other and none are older men, the perceived infected population. An equally alarming trend is for teens to only engage in sexual behavior with those who "look healthy." The long incubation period for AIDS makes such distinctions meaningless.

Given the brevity of most adolescent relationships, monogamy offers little protection. Those youths in "steady" relationships may be at risk also, because of repeated exposure to a partner who may be HIV positive. Often, shortly after deciding that they are in love, a couple will dispense with safe sex practices. The approximate six-month delay between infection and the presence of HIV antibodies highlights the danger inherent in this practice.

A lesbian or gay youth who denies her or his sexual orientation but engages in furtive sexual activity may also be at risk. She or he may translate denial into a rationalization for unsafe behavior: "Since I'm not gay, I can't get AIDS" the reasoning goes.

In similar fashion, gay youths may engage in unsafe sex in the mistaken belief that acquiring AIDS is inevitable. William, a senior at the Harvey Milk School, claims that his closest gay friends have all told him, "I'm going to get AIDS anyway so it doesn't matter."[130]

Homeless teens, runaways, or "throwaways" are also at risk through street prostitution. With only limited means of support, these youth may turn to prostitution to survive. They may be particularly vulnerable for two reasons. First, young people often are not skilled in asserting sexual boundaries—learning to say "No!" Second, there is a real demand in the "trade" for unsafe sex. In other words, unsafe sex pays.

In short, gay male youth are a high-risk group for contracting the AIDS virus. They engage in more unprotected sex with serial partners who are often older than do their heterosexual counterparts.[131]

The risk to lesbian teens is unknown. The relative ease with which females, in contrast to males, contract HIV during heterosexual intercourse and the amount of heterosexual experimentation engaged in by lesbian youths suggest that the threat of HIV infection is very real.

Minority youths may be especially at risk. Although Hispanics make up approximately 8 percent of the U.S. population, they account for 15 percent of the AIDS population.[132] Gay teens and young gay men, especially those with little education, may lack information and hold many misconceptions about the spread of HIV. Fully 60 percent of Hispanic adolescents in a 1990 joint Boston University-Center for Disease Control study did not know how HIV was transmitted. Educational efforts in these communities may be ineffectual, especially among those who do not speak English. For example, 35 percent of Hispanic youths in one study believed that there was a cure for AIDS, the same percentage as participated in unprotected sexual behavior.[133] Among young Hispanic gay men the percentage who engaged in unprotected behavior was an even higher 66 percent.

Even many knowledgeable lesbian and gay youths and street-smart runaways engage in high-risk behaviors with very little, if any, protection.[134] In part, this failing reflects adolescent bravado and feelings of immortality. Ironically, testing HIV negative may increase the feeling of invincibility. In contrast, the fatalistic youth may assume "I'm young, I'm gay, I'm going to get it sooner or later."

Although the incidence of AIDS among adolescents is still small, these figures do not give comfort. The low number of reported cases may reflect both the low rate of testing among adolescents and the long incubation period.[135] Some individuals infected as adolescents are later reported as young adult AIDS cases.

Although numerous reports and studies have recommended vigorous and aggressive educational programs for adolescents, the implementation of these recommendations, especially for lesbian, gay, and bisexual students has been opposed by the same conservative forces that oppose rights for lesbian, gay, and bisexual adults. Even where AIDS education programs are in place, sexual minority issues often are ignored, treated tangentially, and/or discussed in such a cursory manner as to be virtually useless.

Self-Destructive Behaviors/Suicide

Approximately five thousand children, teens, and young adults kill themselves annually in the United States. It is estimated that 30 percent of these are lesbians and gays struggling with issues of sexual orientation. This translates into approximately 1,500 young lesbians and gays taking their lives each year. Surveys of young lesbian and gay adults indicate that approximately 20 to 40 percent have attempted suicide.[136] Figures may be even higher among teens who have not self-identified as lesbian and gay and among those who have suffered violence because of their sexual orientation. White lesbian and gay teens attempt suicide at nearly twice the rate of their African-American lesbian and gay peers who, in turn, are twelve times more likely to attempt suicide than white heterosexual youths.[137]

After a long struggle with self-acceptance and conservative religious beliefs, Bobby, a northern California youth, jumped from an overpass into the path of an oncoming eighteen wheeler. Mark, a gay eighteen-year-old from Seattle, committed suicide by shooting himself on the altar of his church after being less than honorably discharged from the Marines and counseling with his minister. Mark's mother concludes, "I think that the message these kids get from society is that they don't deserve to live."[138]

Factors that contribute to suicide among all youth, including lesbians, gays, and bisexuals, are a family history of alcoholism associated with physical abuse; a perceived social rejection based on race, ethnicity, or sexual orientation; lack of religious affiliation; and stress such as that involved with coming out.[139] Self-hatred, low self-esteem, and intense feelings of aloneness are typical of suicidal individuals. Bobby, mentioned above, confided in his diary,

> Sometimes I sense that my life is very fragile. . . . I get this feeling deep within my bones, and I just want someone to protect me.[140]

For lesbian and gay youths, fear and feelings of rejection, especially by their family, are the most common reasons given for attempted suicide not an inability to accept one's own sexual orientation.[141] Brian, age eighteen, lost his best friend Shane to suicide at age fifteen. "I was so worried about my own standing that I forgot what to do, be his best friend. And tell him that I loved him and it was OK to be gay, because I was also."[142] "A wonderful child, with an incredible mind, is gone," laments a mother, "because our society can't accept people who are 'different'. . . . "[143] Even family caring and support can not moderate the effects of extreme victimization.[144]

As a group, those who attempt suicide exhibit more gender inappropriate behavior, become aware and self-identify earlier, have had earlier same-sex relationships, have experienced more sexual abuse, use more drugs, and are from more dysfunctional families than those who do not.[145] In short, the younger age at which a teen becomes aware of same-sex attractions and the greater the problems faced, particularly gay-related stress from others, the more likely she or he is to contemplate and attempt suicide.[146] In addition to their lack of physical and emotional maturity, younger self-identified teens usually lack a peer group with which to identify, have little life experience, and are dependent on their parents who may be hostile or unsupportive.[147] Steven, age eighteen, explains,

> I felt as though I was the only gay person my age. . . . Throughout eighth grade I went to bed every night praying that I would not be able to wake up. . . . And so finally I decided that if I was going to die, it would have to be at my own hands.[148]

Homeless gay youths are also at a higher risk. Possibly these teens suffer extremely low self-esteem, imagining themselves as only good for prostitution.[149]

The extreme aloneness experienced by many queer kids may also be an important factor.[150] Many do not belong to organized religion which is a source of conflicting feelings for lesbian and gay teens. A suicidal youth may cling all the more doggedly to the limited supports available and react more strongly when this dependency is threatened with rejection.[151] Royce, an upper-middle-class white gay teen from a small Appalachian community, clung to his relationship with Jason for whom their relationship was purely sexual.

> It hurt having him come over and having a physical thing and telling him, "I love you," and then him leaving to go out with a girl. . . . I got to the point of . . . suicide. . . . I kept it all bottled up inside.[152]

The period between the first same-sex sexual experience or the first self-indication and self-identification as gay and lesbian is extremely difficult emotionally, and most of those who attempt suicide have not yet established a positive sexual identity.[153] Nearly a third of lesbian and gay teens who attempt suicide do so around age fifteen.[154] Contrary to popular misconception, most suicide attempts by lesbian and gay youths do not result from romantic breakups. Although loss of a love interest is often a precipitating factor, low self-esteem and self-worth are the real causes of suicide. Suicide is most likely related to depression. Eighteen-year-old John attempted suicide because he could no longer continue with the sham of heterosexual dating. Jeremy, a young gay prostitute, offers some insight into his earlier attempts at suicide with "It's better to feel the physical . . . pain than to feel the emotional pain, because the physical pain is easier to deal with."[155]

Lesbian, gay, and bisexual youth face a government bureaucracy that is increasingly under the control of right-wing fundamentalists. For this group, their right-wing agenda is more important than the lives of the estimated 1,500 sexual minority youth who commit suicide annually. Likewise, school boards and teachers' associations have placed public image above the lives of young people. It is difficult to argue with the following conclusion:

A society that forces a gay person into suicide by making life unbearable and ugly, by attempting to show to us that we are sick and evil and unworthy of life, and conspires to eliminate all of us from the world—by our own hands if necessary—is a society that engages in mass coercive murder. Suicide in the gay community. . . . is the most pernicious strategy yet developed to achieve a genocidal end.[156]

THE PLUSES

Until recently, growing up lesbian or gay meant years of self-loathing and isolation. Even today many teens repress their sexual feelings and pretend to be heterosexual. Other teens, feeling peer pressure to experiment sexually, are exploring their feelings and confronting questions previously left until adulthood. In the process, they are learning about themselves, expressing feelings, and testing alternatives. Rajindar, a student, explains,

> . . . I think that one of the main reasons that male straights hate us is because they really know that emotionally we are more worked out than them. We can talk about and express our feelings, our emotions in a positive way.[157]

In the process of self-exploration, queer kids conclude such as did a sixteen-year-old African-American gay male who had been a prostitute for two years, "I learned I was a *nice* gay person."[158]

The important thing is, as Emma, an eighteen-year-old lesbian, advises, "don't give up!"[159] The stories of teens who stand firm are truly inspirational. In her junior year at Los Gatos High School, Gina Gutierrez came out to the entire student body by performing a monologue about a young lesbian who comes out to her Orthodox Jewish parents. Gina had previously come out to her mother, a school counselor, and a teacher. At each step she received support and strengthened her conviction that she was OK. Within a week of telling her stepfather, she and her entire family were attending Parents, Families and Friends of Lesbians and Gays (PFLAG) meetings. Gina later took a female date to her prom.

Gina was awarded a prize at graduation in honor of a young gay man, Bobby Griffith, who had committed suicide. After graduation she went on to pursue higher education. Her story is one of success because she had the love, acceptance, and support she needed to identify and strengthen herself as a person, a woman, and a lesbian.[160]

Chapter 7

Addressing the Needs of Queer Kids

> While the problems faced by lesbian, gay, and bisexual youth seem
> overwhelming, they are also one of the easiest groups of young
> people to help. Once they gain a positive understanding of their
> sexual orientation, acceptance from others, and support in dealing
> with the conflicts they face from others, many of their problems are
> greatly diminished. Most importantly, . . . they recognize they have a
> life that is worth living.[1]

> —Paul Gibson, author of 1989 DHHS
> Report on Adolescent Suicide

In the 1992 swearing-in ceremony for the Massachusetts' Governor's
Commission on Gay and Lesbian Youth, then-Governor William Weld
pledged,

> We must abolish the prejudice and isolation faced by gay and lesbian
> youth. We need to help them stay at home and stay in school so they
> can have healthy and productive lives.

Unfortunately, most states are not as enlightened as Massachusetts and
most governors not as committed to human rights.

At their best, even enlightened policies and services for queer kids are
stopgap measures needed until as a society, we are ready to accept full
responsibility for our collective heterosexist and homophobic assumptions
and to reverse centuries of unfounded prejudice and discrimination. In the
immediate past, educational institutions and agencies have been more
willing to provide separate services for lesbian, gay, and bisexual teens
than to address the basic inadequacies of the services that necessitate such
adjuncts and more important, the societal attitudes that necessitate the
services in the first place.

Consistent contact with a nurturing adult whether through the home,
school, youth organizations, or the lesbian, gay, and bisexual community

is essential for sexual-minority teens. Stacey had tried unsuccessfully to commit suicide several times during adolescence:

> Society told me that as a lesbian I was expendable. I was at the point where even a [lesbian/gay-friendly] public-service announcement would have given me the right to live. One person coming out would have really helped.[2]

Where is the help and why isn't it available?

Developing appropriate and effective policies and services for lesbian, gay, and bisexual youths is complicated by our somewhat limited knowledge of human sexuality development and our lack of will to change.[3] Most adults and teens lack accurate, unbiased information about homosexuality. It is sad but all too true that it takes less effort to continue to function with our old prejudices than it does to learn other ways of thinking.

In this chapter, we shall explore some of the solutions for the challenges faced by lesbian, gay, and bisexual teens. These include changing societal attitudes, providing more role models, educating families, eliminating untenable school conditions, monitoring juvenile courts, establishing special education programs and schools, opening all youth programs, involving the lesbian, gay, and bisexual community, training more knowledgeable and unbiased professionals, and organizing college students.

CHANGE SOCIETAL ATTITUDES

Societal attitudes are at the root of the difficulties encountered by queer kids. Attitudes can be very difficult to change. Changing societal attitudes through openness "feels like a privilege," stated a young Haitian-American lesbian attending the 1993 March on Washington after just coming out to her family, "But it is really a duty. Because that's how we'll make change."[4]

In part, society's negative attitudes toward sexual minorities reflects support for traditional gender roles and the patriarchal hierarchy found in many religious institutions, sexual behavior, and conventional morality.[5] Although societal conditions and statutes may change, personal attitudes are not so malleable.

Religious leaders must shoulder much of the blame for the current atmosphere of nonacceptance and be responsible for some of the healing. "Even if a religious institution is not favorable toward homosexuality," declares Rabbi Alan Katz, "it should be there to comfort and help the psychological healing of any of their members."[6] The Reverend Jim Callan, a Catholic priest, expresses an attitude that is all too scarce in organized religion: "[W]e're sorry that out of our ignorance we condemned you."[7]

The first step is consciousness raising. Parents of a lesbian daughter and a gay son conclude, "The more understanding people have, the better."[8] In Washington state, Scott Thiemann of the Spokane-based Outreach to Rural Youth and Jenie Hall of the gay, lesbian, and bisexual youth program of the American Friends Service Committee, a Quaker organization, have promoted awareness and visibility for sexual-minority youths by walking across the state raising money and consciousness. Along the way, they and others accompanying them stop at high schools, such as Wilson Creek, population 330, to meet school personnel, parents, and students.

The biggest obstacles to change are silence and invisibility. Lesbian, gay, and bisexual youths and their allies should write news releases and letters to the editor, call talk shows, publicize events, organize groups, and attend gay pride rallies. Visibility ends invisibility. Sexual-minority teens have been aided in their struggle to be noticed by a number of magazine articles, after-school specials, and even a comic strip segment. In 1993, Lynn Johnston used her *For Better or for Worse* family-oriented strip for five weeks to tell the coming-out story of seventeen-year-old Lawrence. The National Gay and Lesbian Awareness Project has promoted visibility with ads in both *Time* and *People* magazines with a picture of a diverse group of people and the caption "WE'RE YOUR FAMILY, NEIGHBORS, AND FRIENDS . . . AND WE'RE GAY."

Where society or the lesbian, gay, and bisexual community have failed them, often youths have taken the initiative. Queer kids have been instrumental in helping to organize the over 600 programs for sexual-minority youths nationwide. In addition, over 800 college groups exist. Many more are needed. Each summer lesbian, gay, bisexual, and transgender youth gather for a worldwide Young, Loud, and Proud Conference. The 1997 meeting in San Francisco drew 450 teen participants. Since 1995, California lesbian, gay, and bisexual teens have been able to participate in Youth Lobby Day. The event consists of educational activities for the state legislature.

PROVIDE MORE ROLE MODELS

Youth and adult role models are needed at all levels of society.[9] Learning to be a sexual-minority adult occurs, in part, from interacting with these role models. Although caring and empathic heterosexuals can serve some function, lesbian, gay, and bisexual youths and adults are the critical missing link. Luna is a young gay Latino peer counselor at the Hetrick-Martin Institute. Reflecting on his own role and on the model his teacher at the Harvey Milk School set, he states, "He made me feel good about myself, and I believe I do that for a lot of young people that come here."[10] After Jonathan's cousin came out, he became a role model for Jonathan. It transformed Jonathan's life.

> Whereas before I didn't want to get up in the morning, now I couldn't wait to get up. Because every day . . . was one day closer to . . . getting to where I could find my place in the gay community.[11]

Mass media is particularly important as a source of information and self-identity because of the isolation of most lesbian, gay, and bisexual youths.[12] Most teens watch twenty-one to twenty-two hours of television per week and identify it as an important source of information about sex.[13] The nonexistent lesbian, gay, or bisexual or the confused and troubled sexual-minority youth has earned a well-deserved retirement and replacement with a teen who is gay, out, and proud.

EDUCATE FAMILIES

Pediatricians, psychologists, clergy, and educators must educate families in the need for acceptance, love, and support of their lesbian, gay, and bisexual kids. Ideally, such education would begin in school so that adolescents will mature into nurturing parents. Once a youth comes out to her or his family, it is difficult for that family to adopt positive attitudes where none existed previously.

Parents need to view homosexuality and bisexuality as healthy forms of sexual orientation, not unlike heterosexuality. They need to know that sexual orientation is not determined by the home environment, but that environment can be extremely important in building strong character and positive self-esteem. All children need love and support. To that end, professionals need to work to reduce conflict within families around issues of sexual orientation.

Parents can also serve as allies and advocates. All parents whether gay or nongay can make a difference for all children. By not tolerating intolerance they can send a message. Emily, a "soccer mom" and league board member, sidelined a team when the coach did nothing to stop them from taunting another team with the epithet "faggots." When parents complained, Emily responded that if they were not going to take the responsibility for teaching tolerance and acceptable behavior then she would have to do it. More soccer moms—and hockey moms, and little league coaches—need to be outspoken.

Lesbian and gay parents can help all children by not remaining in the closet. Registering a child as having two mothers sends a message that the school had better be aware of and tolerant of difference.

ELIMINATE UNTENABLE SCHOOL CONDITIONS

"With more and more gay and lesbian students coming out, it's been very hard for school districts to completely deny their existence," says Kevin Cranston, director of the HIV/AIDS Program at the Massachusetts Department of Health.[14] It is well beyond the time for schools to break the silence that surrounds homosexuality and bisexuality and to affirm diversity.[15] We can no longer deny the existence of sexual-minority teens when against all odds they are self-identifying in increasing numbers.

Making our schools safe and affirming for all students, especially those who are lesbian, gay, and bisexual, requires the support of all personnel and a thorough evaluation of all curricula, programs, and policies. In 1993, the State of Massachusetts passed a law protecting sexual-minority students from harassment, violence, and discrimination. Much of the impetus for the law came from a grassroots campaign among high school students. In Rutland, Vermont, 200 students signed a petition to administrators requesting that something be done to end harassment of sexual-minority peers. The Massachusetts' Governor's Commission on Gay and Lesbian Youth recommended crisis intervention and violence prevention training for teachers, counselors, and school staff; school-based gay-straight support groups; informative lesbian and gay library holdings; and inclusion of lesbian and gay issues in the curriculum.

Our schools must be made to serve the needs of all their students. No child should be denied the *right* to an education because of harassment and violence. Public education must serve to educate the public citizen, to help the individual learn to think critically, to consider alternative viewpoints, and to separate fact from fiction. Instead, our schools have become political turf in which warring sides attempt to wrestle the curriculum from each other.

Clearly, those most responsible for the ill health of American education are those in the political and religious right who do not wish to weaken dissenting views but to silence them. With regard to homosexuality, their stated goal is to limit all reference to negative reference. In a moment of overblown oratory, Stephanie Cecil of the Eagle Forum, a radical right-wing group, called for school boards to be stripped of their power to select curriculum materials lest educators have students "calling homosexual hot lines and assembling genitalia puzzles on the classroom floor."[16]

The struggle to protect and to nurture all students is not for the faint-hearted. Change is never without conflict. Rightwing antigay crusades have resulted in power, privilege, and in some cases, wealth for their leaders. These perks are not surrendered easily. Maintenance of the *status quo* heterosexual privilege, however, is killing and maiming queer kids. "If not for the support that I found . . . at a homo-affirmative high school," explains Sharon, an eighteen-year-old student, "I would be dead today."[17] Possibly someday all schools will have an atmosphere in which the class valedictorian can proclaim at graduation, "I was proud to be a member of Brookline [MA] High School when I heard that thirty of my classmates went to the March in Washington [for lesbian, gay, and bisexual rights] under the Brookline High School Banner."[18]

Election of lesbian, gay, and bisexual or other friendly school board members is essential. The need to elect tolerant individuals is illustrated graphically by the hostile remarks of Robert Drummond, a psychologist and president of the Olathe, Kansas, board of education. He proclaimed in a hearing, "Homosexuality is a mental disorder similar to schizophrenia or depression."[19] These types of attitudes are chilling for adults and can be damaging to children.

If gay-friendly individuals do not staff school boards, someone else will. Ralph Reed formerly of the Christian Coalition has stated repeatedly that in an election he'd rather win 100 school boards than the presidency.

Protection from Abuse and Discrimination

At the very least, a school system should enact policies that protect lesbian, gay, and bisexual youth and faculty from discrimination and harassment. In Rochester, New York, the category of sexual orientation was quietly slipped into the student handbook paragraph on school district nondiscrimination policies regarding students. A young gay man offers the following advice:

> [T]he most important thing a school can do is make it known that harassment will not be tolerated under any circumstances. . . . [I]n most cases schools turn their backs. This in my opinion is the biggest mistake a school can make. It sends the message that gays and lesbians deserve abuse.[20]

When necessary, legislation may be required to ensure school district compliance. When State Representative Sheila Kuehl introduced a bill banning antigay discrimination in California schools in early 1997, some 500 lesbian and gay youth assembled at the state capital in support.

Schools that do not protect all their students should find themselves being sued, as Jamie Nabozny sued his Ashland, Wisconsin, school district. From seventh to eleventh grade when he dropped out of school and moved to a foster home in Milwaukee, Jamie was beaten repeatedly, punched, kicked, and urinated on. In one incident when no teacher was present, he was held down by fellow students who performed a mock rape while shouting, "You know you want it."[21] One attack required surgery for internal bleeding. Jamie now suffers from, and has been hospitalized for, post-traumatic stress disorder. His school's response at the time it was presented with Jamie's repeated complaints was "Boys will be boys." According to Jamie, the principal told him that "[I]f I was going to be 'openly gay,' I had to expect that kind of stuff."[22] Now a college student, Jamie was awarded one million dollars for damages in federal court which found his school district liable for failing to protect him from harassment and abuse.[23]

In Pacifica, California, Ethan, a twelve-year-old boy, is suing his former school district for alledgedly refusing to intervene in his years of harassment. The American Civil Liberties Union is suing the Kent, Washington, school district on behalf of a gay teen allegedly brutally attacked by eight youths. According to 1997 guidelines by the U.S. Department of Education, antigay harassment that is sexual in nature, such as mock rapes and kissing noises, are prohibited by Title IX, a federal sexual harassment statute.[24] Patricia Logue of the Lambda Legal Defense and Education Fund contends, "[N]o teenager should have to endure abuse to get an education."[25] When schools fail to protect our children they should be held responsible.

Human rights legislation for lesbians and gays usually does not apply to adolescents. Teachers and staff would be more likely to combat homophobia and abuse if school policy protected sexual-minority teens from harassment and discrimination. Without such support, teachers may be reluctant to intervene.

Harassment of sexual-minority students and teachers should not be tolerated regardless of the perpetrator's status. The bottom line according to Logue is that "Gay and lesbian students have that right [to a safe education] no matter what you think about homosexuals."[26] The well-worn slogan "Make our schools safe for our children" must be inclusive of all children, not just heterosexual ones.

Policy protections for lesbian, gay, and bisexual youth should extend to safety at social events. Several court decisions have upheld the rights of same-sex couples to attend social events in a nondisruptive manner. Administrators who fear repercussions need to reflect on the source of potential disruptions before assigning blame to a sexual-minority student.

Tolerance for diversity and for different types of diversity should be specifically targeted. The Toronto, Ontario, schools have attempted to decrease intolerance, homophobia, and violence through related topics in sex education classes, although this venue tends to emphasize sexual behavior differences only.

School policies condemning antihomosexual jokes, graffiti, and violence should clearly state the consequences of such behavior. Outlawing certain words is shortsighted and alone will not result in long-term behavior change for the offenders. Such policies must be enacted against a backdrop of acceptance of diversity and valuing the individual. Teachers need to be trained in techniques for interrupting homophobic remarks and confronting perpetrators in a manner that results in behavior and attitudinal change. With understanding and zero tolerance of homophobia, incidents of harassment of lesbians, gays, and bisexuals decrease. The two go hand in hand. Schools cannot punish students into tolerance. Attitudes change with education, understanding, and interaction.

Educated Faculty, Staff, Students, and Parents

"I've spent more than one lonely night sobbing . . . ," explains Devin, age seventeen, "and I've planned out my suicide more than once." He continues,

> Fortunately I was not alone. There were gay students and gay faculty to whom I could turn for help.[27]

The support of school personnel and peers can ease the pain of societal hostility.

Faculty and Staff

A "gay-friendly" and adequately trained teaching and counseling staff is essential. As adults, teachers set the acceptable school standards for attitudes and behaviors through the explicit and implicit messages they send to students.

Any attempt at faculty training must allow adequate time for teachers and staff to overcome their own feelings of uneasiness or discomfort. An uptight teacher will be of little help for students struggling with the same feelings. In addition, a teacher's uneasy feelings or cavalier or nonaccepting attitude can be passed along to students easily.

Changes in the nature and nurture of the educational system are never easy to obtain, especially when imposed from the top down. It is best if the call for reform comes from students, parents, and teachers. In Massachusetts, the Governor's Commission on Lesbian and Gay Youth has quietly encouraged districts to adopt its recommendations rather than requiring them by decree. This strategy was adopted in the hope of avoiding conservative backlash. Although curricular change is difficult in the present political climate, it is hoped that as teachers become more sensitive, lesbian, gay, and bisexual issues will be raised in class. Change may be best when it occurs in small doses, one person at a time. If individuals come to own the changes, they make them their own.

A school district might begin by offering a workshop on diversity, acceptance, and becoming allies for change. The National Coalition Building Institute, B'nai B'rith, and the American Friends Service Committee all offer excellent workshops on these and related topics. This introduction could be followed by faculty and staff in-service training such as "This is homosexuality and bisexuality" and progress to more specific issues that address the needs of lesbian and gay youth. In Massachusetts, under the auspices of the Governor's Commission on Lesbian and Gay Youth, the State Department of Health has offered statewide seminars on sexual-minority students for teachers and administrators. Ongoing training can address a number of lesbian and gay topics.

Local lesbian, gay, and bisexual organizations may have speakers or trainers who can assist in the planning and implementation of such training. Sexual-minority students also offer a valuable resource. With the help of Matt, a 5' 3" state gymnastic champion, his high school focused on sexual minorities for an entire year. The goal was to raise the awareness of both teachers and students. As Matt summarizes, "I can help the faculty understand what teenagers like myself go through."[28]

Faculty notorious for their homophobia may be helped individually. It is extremely effective to confront such teachers with the results of their behavior. I had the good fortune of having a gay father complain to a hotline about antigay comments made by his daughter's teacher. When confronted by the student, her father, and myself as a representative of the lesbian, gay, and bisexual community and offered the choice of making changes at his level or at the principal's level, the offending teacher was very open to suggestions for providing a more welcoming atmosphere is his classroom. He honestly had believed that making homophobic remarks would ingratiate him with his students and would not be perceived as offensive.

Helpful changes would include use of inclusive, stigma-free language in the classroom, such as "partners" instead of "husbands and wives," posting of pictures of famous lesbians, gays, and bisexuals, and the mentioning of sexuality where appropriate. Sexual minorities should be discussed in the same manner as other topics, avoiding the hoopla that surrounds extraordinary topics. I once was scheduled to present an introductory discussion on lesbian and gay issues to a local high school class. It came complete with media coverage, pickets, cancellation of all senior classes so all could attend, rescheduling in an auditorium, and an ex-gay minister flown in from 300 miles away accompanied by a rabidly antigay physician to "balance" the presentation which had since become a debate. My message of tolerance was lost in the atmosphere of carnival.

By demonstrating an accepting attitude, teachers can send a strong message to students and create a tolerant environment within the classroom. Issues of tolerance and acceptance can be explored separately or under the umbrella of diversity. One young lesbian gives the following advice:

> You don't have to understand. . . . You don't have to agree with it [homosexuality]. You do as a professional HAVE TO STOP ANY AND ALL PREJUDICE going on around you in the hall[,] in the class and on the street.[29]

Acceptance alone is insufficient, however, and faculty must also be knowledgeable. A teacher, when ignorant of the facts, is likely to pass along to students the shopworn myths of the past.

Teachers may wish to create "safe zones" for lesbian, gay, and bisexual youth. Symbols, such as those distributed by the Bridges Project of the National Youth Advocacy Coalition (NYAC), can be prominently displayed for all students to see. As noted on the NYAC sticker "A person displaying this symbol is one who will be understanding, supportive, and trustworthy if a gay, lesbian, bisexual, or transsexual youth needs help, advice, or just someone with whom they can talk."

Teachers should be prepared to answer questions about sexuality openly and honestly. Likenesses and differences across the sexual continuum and across minority groups should also be explored. Teachers should anticipate questions concerning their own sexuality, because students may assume that a gay-friendly faculty member is lesbian, gay, or bisexual.

Teachers and administrators must also be trained in interrupting acts of harassment and in counseling both the victimizer and the victim. Discipline for vicitmizers should be strong and swift and in line with a well-crafted policy of nondiscrimination and nonharassment.

Ongoing continuing education can occur through confrontation of homophobic or insensitive remarks by faculty and administrators. Teachers should be empowered with the strategies needed to confront these possibly hostile colleagues.[30]

Finally, teachers who are lesbian, gay, and bisexual should be encouraged to be open about their sexuality and be offered support and employment protection. An openly gay or lesbian teacher can affect the atmosphere in the entire school. "If not for the support I found in openly gay teachers at my high school," recalls Sharon, age eighteen, "I would be dead today. I hope to God that future teachers have the courage to come out for their students."[31] As Jessica explains, "The guidance counselor is an out gay man, and that just sets a tone where you know it's OK to be whoever you are."[32]

The importance of good lesbian, gay, and bisexual role models cannot be overstressed. Recalling two lesbian teachers who helped her with issues of self-esteem, Fawn, a young lesbian, notes, "They were good role models for me in the sense that it's okay to have feelings toward other people if you really do love them."[33]

Openly lesbian, gay, and bisexual teachers challenge stereotypes and myths for all students. Connie Burns, a Buffalo high school teacher, came out at the 1993 March on Washington. The effects have been overwhelmingly positive and she feels that she's making a difference.

> I feel I have to get information to kids that they're not now getting. . . .
> [T]hey need information that they're not alone; that they can grow up to be successful, happy, productive adults not condemned to horrible lives of doom and gloom. . . . But more than that, straight kids have to understand all that stuff, too.[34]

"I want to be there," continues Garry Stack, a Connecticut school principal, "so when people know me, and know I'm gay they have to weigh me against any other stereotypes and beliefs they may have heard. That's my whole purpose for being out."[35]

Commenting on the effect of having an openly gay teacher, Devin, age seventeen, states, "Through him, I learned that being gay is not the horrible and disgusting thing society makes it out to be, but instead, a normal and natural part of me."[36] A young lesbian summarized, "If the students know you're gay you're a living example."[37]

Teachers should confer with their administrators to ensure that they have some backing prior to coming out. The discussion should be within the framework of student needs. When a student sued the Brookline, Massachusetts, school district for $350,000 claiming she had been deprived a public education and had to transfer schools because her social studies teacher was a lesbian, the school district backed the teacher. The superin-

tendent lauded the teacher's decision to come out to the class saying it was
handled "sensitively and thoughtfully."[38]

In contrast, Wendy Weaver, a seventeen-year tenured teacher and vol-
leyball coach in the Nebo, Utah, school district was dismissed because she
shared her sexual orientation with students. Her free speech, privacy, equal
protection, and tenured position were disregarded.

Prospective Teachers

Massachusetts is again leading the way with innovative teacher education programs that address sexual orientation. Through a personnel certifi-
cation program associated with the Project for the Integration of Gay and
Lesbian Youth Issues in School and funded by the state department of
education, students, parents, and teachers are attempting to influence
teacher education programs by training professors and students.[39]

Students

More than anything else, queer kids require accepting peers and friends
who can help to break the cycle of isolation. One presentation or class
period is not enough to combat years of homophobia and heterosexism.
Yet, in some school districts, even one presentation or the use of the word
homosexual is out of the question.

Students would benefit from peer training led by young lesbian, gay,
and bisexual adults with student assistance. Such training presented by the
Hetrick-Martin Institute (HMI), a nonprofit organization dedicated to the
special needs of lesbian and gay youths, can serve as a model. In addition
to ending invisibility, these sessions can dispel myths and stereotypes.
"[K]ids . . . never expect a homeboy like me . . . to be gay," comments
David of HMI.[40]

Nongay students can also be instrumental in forming support groups.
Catherine, a sixteen-year-old student, started a group in her Ithaca, New
York, high school to change the attitudes of teens toward lesbians and gays.

Parents

Beyond the mechanics, parents often lack even rudimentary knowledge
of sexual development, sexual orientation, and sexual behavior. Often, it is
easier to imagine teens as asexual than to confront reality. Parents may
resist education in these areas believing that it is irrelevant for them and
for their children. The topic of sexual minorities can be introduced to

parent groups in two ways. First, they never know what may happen with their child. Second, their child may have friends who are or will be lesbian, gay, or bisexual. Few parents would knowingly harm a child. With this introduction, the stage is set for parent education to begin.

Grievance Procedures and Legal Redress

All students must have access to higher authority in cases of discriminatory actions against them. Schools, districts, and state departments of education should establish grievance procedures to enable students and teachers to complain about harassment or abuse by others in the school setting.

In addition, lesbian, gay, and bisexual students must be made aware of their legal rights. When Robert wore a button reading "I like men," the principal asked him to remove it despite the fact that other students wore tee shirts and buttons with comparable heterosexual messages. A few days later when the principal attempted to suspend him for continuing to sport the pin, Robert responded with his attorney's card. The principal wisely decided not to pursue the issue.[41]

Curricular Modifications

Relegating homosexuality and bisexuality to sex education classes only truncates the discussion and focuses attention on sexual behavior solely. Lesbian, gay, and bisexual topics should be a natural part of the curriculum, including an exploration of homophobia and the contributions of lesbian, gay, and bisexual individuals. Tolerant inclusion serves to validate lesbian, gay, and bisexual teens and those students with sexual-minority relatives and friends.

This "controversial issue" is sure to raise the hackles of religious demagogues in their continuous effort to silence all voices they do not wish to recognize. It should not be controversial to discuss individuals who are among the population of the country and the school. Controversy should surround attempts to deny students access to this information.[42]

Education and tolerance training can begin as early as first grade. Students need only become acquainted with diversity and learn that some children have one parent, some two, and a few three or more and that all-male, all-female, and mixed-gender parents are possible.

In upper grades, lesbians, gays, and bisexuals can be discussed in history, anthropology, sociology, psychology, biology, and literature courses. The human rights struggle of sexual minorities is a valid topic for contemporary issues courses. The Stonewall riots and their aftermath can offer a microcosm of change within a democratic state. Even discussions of the family in home economics can include a section on alternative families.

At some point in each youth's self-identification, a teen compares herself or himself with what she or he knows about homosexuality.[43] Inaccurate or limited information increases the difficulty of this task. Homophobic input may cause a fearful reaction. In contrast, honest portrayal and discussion of lesbians, gay men, and bisexuals and issues of sexuality have the potential to enhance the development of a positive self-image.

Too often, sexual-minority issues are presented from a white majority perspective. The experiences of African Americans, Hispanics, Asians, Muslims, and Jews, to name a few, may be very different. At the very least, each group experiences a special set of cultural challenges around lesbian and gay issues. A multicultural exploration is essential if all children are going to feel represented and the diversity of the lesbian, gay, and bisexual community conveyed. Books by and about minorities and sexual orientation are presented in Table 7.1.

Discussion of sexual orientation should not be introduced to titillate students, as one might whisper about Benjamin Franklin's prodigious sex life or John Kennedy's dalliances. Instead, sexuality should be introduced when it helps to explain behavior or offers another perspective. Lesbian and gay students may be helped by the mere mention of sexual minorities with little fanfare. There is no need for classroom presentation to be sexually explicit.

Frank discussion of sexual minorities also can aid heterosexual students. Hate is debilitating; therefore, any topic that reduces bigotry opens students' minds and fosters education.[44] In the process, all students will come to understand their own sexuality and sex roles better.

Each school district should have a policy stating that teachers have a right to present relevant topics in a balanced and factual manner. Likewise, students have a right to be exposed to evenhanded discussion of many topics in order to become thinking, contributing members of society. All complaints, including those from religious conservatives, should be submitted in writing, clearly stating the specific complaint.[45] Administrators can then review the complaint in a calm manner.

Even gay-neutral curricula result in hysterical responses from the religious right. They frame the argument that such curricula teach children how to be homosexual. Their position is based on the fallacy that sexual orientation is a choice or a learned behavior. The current movement by any small but vocal group of parents to forbid schools to teach anything objectionable threatens to erode any strides already made. If this proposition

TABLE 7.1. Curricular Materials for the Inclusion of Lesbian, Gay, and Bisexual Minorities

SUBJECT AREA	THEME	SUGGESTED TOPICS, AUTHORS, AND BOOKS
African Americans		
Literature	Harlem Renaissance	Cullen, C., Hughes, L., and Lock, A. Baldwin, *Giovanni's Room* (1956) Lorde, *Another Counter* (1962) *The Black Unicorn* (1978) *Zami: A New Spelling of My Name* (1982)
Contemporary issues	Gays in the military	Watkins, *Sin: The Perry Watkins Story*
	African-American women	Walker, *The Color Purple* (1982) Morrison, *Tar Baby* (1981)
	Sexual minorities	Clarke, *Living as a Lesbian* (1986) Hemphill, *Brother to Brother* (1991) Silvera, *Pieces of My Heart* (1991)
Music	Blues	Recordings of Bessie Smith and Ma Rainey
History	Civil rights	Mention Bayard Rustin and G. W. Carver Duberman, *Lives of Notable Gay Men and Lesbians*
	African civilization	Mention differing attitudes toward sex roles and homosexuality (wide diversity)
English	Literature	Baker, *Long Goodbyes* (1993) Delaney, *Tales of Neveryone* (1979) *Return to Neveryone* (1994) Gomez, *The Gilda Stories* (1991) Guy, *Ruby* (1977) Lefcourt, *The Dreyfus Affair* (1993) Sinclair, *A Coffee Will Make You Black* (1994)
Hispanic Americans		
Contemporary issues	Sexual minorities	Anzaldua, *Haciendo Caras* (1990) Ramos, *Companeras* (1987) Trujillo, *Chicana Lesbians* (1991)
Native Americans		
History	Customs	Mention female warriors and male wives Mention revered position of winktes or berdaches in spiritual life as shamans
	Sexual minorities	Fife, *Color of Resistance* (1993) Roscoe, *Gay Spirit* (1987) Sears, *Simple Songs* (1990) Williams, *Spirit and the Flesh* (1986)

Source: Adapted from Sears (1995).

becomes state law, curriculum, texts, and even library holdings could change drastically.

Student and parent activism should be encouraged. When the Elizabethtown, Pennsylvania, school board adopted a "pro-family" curricular resolution that was antigay and anti–single parent family, nearly one-quarter of the middle and high school students walked out of classes. "Why should gays be less important?" asked Dave Fritz, a sophomore.[46]

Accurate Sex Education

Sex education courses should help students realize that each of us has a sexual orientation. For the lesbian, gay, or bisexual individual, recognition of this orientation is only the first step in the journey to self-celebration. The stumbling blocks and coping strategies need to be discussed in order for heterosexual youth to understand the difficulties faced by some queer kids. Pedro Zamora, a Cuban-American gay youth with AIDS, was widely used as an educational resource by south Florida schools. He was constantly frustrated by the lack of accurate sexual knowledge. Many young people know him from his later role in the MTV show *Real Life.*

Most lesbian and gay teens become aware of their sexual orientation before they engage in same-sex erotic behavior. Fear of AIDS may confuse the issue of self-acceptance and adjustment:

> It would certainly be psychologically damaging to the gay individual if his fear of AIDS prevents him from normal homosexual development during his teenage years. On the other hand, the message that sex between males should be practiced safely . . . urgently needs to reach all gay and bisexual teenagers.[47]

Opposing sex education in general and homosexuality specifically, the religious right is using the issue of sex education to organize and fundraise. A study by People for the American Way, a civil rights group, estimates that attacks on curricula involving gay issues doubled from 1990 to 1994. By whipping voters to a frenzy with unfounded fears, the right is able to capture school board seats. Lesbian, gay, and bisexual adults must build coalitions with concerned citizen groups to return some measure of balance or even advocacy back into local school boards.

Right-wing backlash to even the smallest gains has been swift. In Chesterton, Indiana, a teacher was challenged by parents for hanging a gay-themed poster in the classroom. School boards are especially vulnerable. A Gaston, North Carolina, board member elected on a conservative Christian platform regularly takes board time to deliver antigay diatribes. In

Fremont, California, a board member compared lesbian and gay adults helping school officials draft an antiharassment policy to foxes in a henhouse.[48] Under pressure from conservative Christians, the Wayne-Westland school district in Michigan reversed its eight-month policy of protection from antigay discrimination and harassment for students and faculty.

Effective AIDS education begins with awareness training at the elementary school level. Most beneficial would be a factual discussion of the disease, free of the sex-negative scare tactics used in some religious circles.

Clearly, the adolescent population that would derive the most benefit from AIDS prevention training is gay males. Presumably, best results would be obtained if such training reached sexually inexperienced youths in whom high-risk sexual behavior had not become entrenched.

AIDS information should be presented in a manner that is acceptable, realistic, clear, nonjudgmental, culturally sensitive, and positive. Schools should promulgate AIDS prevention information in coordination with youth groups and center, health clinics, youth shelters, STD and mental health clinics, and bars. Given the situations of many lesbian and gay teens, effective training should be coupled with programs that foster self-esteem, positive identity, and community.[49]

Teens who frequently engage in high-risk sexual behaviors have additional educational needs. Knowledge alone is insufficient. Most have high AIDS knowledge but continue to take risks.[50] Their beliefs and their behavior belie their knowledge. Many express a belief that they have little control in high-risk situations.

Extracurricular Changes

Curricular changes alone are insufficient as long as the not-so-subtle message from extracurricular activities is "HETEROS ONLY." Heterosexual rights of passage, such as athletics and the prom, need to be open and welcoming to all students. Most important, queer kids need support and recreational groups of their peers.

Support and Recreation Groups

The needs of lesbian, gay, and bisexual youths for peer support vary with the individual. Self-identified teens may attend meetings to become more assertive, while more secretive youths may need caring and nurturing and the knowledge that they are not alone.[51] As harassment from fellow students and other teens increased, Chuck relied more on the support he received from a small group of lesbian and gay students. He credited this support with keeping him from exploring self-destructive coping options. Clearly in the more assertive group, Jan, age seventeen, declared, "We need some sort of hang-out-in-the-mall atmosphere. . . ."[52] Dean, a suburban teen, found that in a group of lesbian, gay, and bisexual peers, he could discuss openly and comfortably his frustrations with home and school around the issue of sexual orientation.

Interactions with peers offer lesbian and gay teens opportunities to establish relationships, learn social skills, and experiment sexually.[53] Such experiences help to decrease feelings of alienation and aloneness. Positive interactions increase lesbian-affirming and gay-affirming feelings.

Organizations for lesbian, gay, and bisexual students vary greatly and may include support and/or recreational/social groups or Gay/Straight Alliances as in Massachusetts. The goals of these organizations also range from support to advocacy and the elimination of homophobia. Membership varies with the purpose. Sexual-minority youth groups can help reduce social isolation and enhance positive development. Sarah, age twenty, explains,

> When you find friends who are supportive, not only supportive but in the same boat as you. . . . Then you think, "Gee, it's okay."[54]

Very slowly, school districts, one-by-one, are organizing support organizations for lesbian, gay, and bisexual students. "I don't see any reason why there couldn't be a Queer Club at high school like there's a Latin-American culture club or a math club," states Karina, age nineteen.[55] Students need to demand the formation of such clubs despite administrative resistance.

Pride USA, the first national organization to unite lesbian, gay, and bisexual high school clubs, was founded in Chicago in 1996 by seventeen-year-old Miguel Ayala. His goal is to help students form clubs and to link them through the Internet.[56]

The state attorney general's office in Utah recently sided with sexual-minority students at East High School in Salt Lake City, citing the district's obligation to accommodate all students under the federal Equal Access Act of 1984. In response, the state legislature banned all activities that "involve human sexuality." The Salt Lake City school district, in a separate action, cancelled all extracurricular activities. Student Kelli Peterson, a gay-straight alliance leader has vowed to fight all the way to the Supreme Court. Before a crowd assembled at the state capital, the high schooler declared, "I would like the legislators to know that I did not start this group to advocate homosexuality. . . . I started this group to end the misery and isolation of being gay in high school."[57]

The need for social and support groups exists because in the words of one youth, "the schools have failed us." The establishment of support groups for lesbian, gay, and bisexual students is only half the answer. These groups do not absolve the school of the responsibility to educate all students in diversity and tolerance.

Athletics

As mentioned, few areas of our culture are as hostile toward lesbians and gays as youth athletics. Any attempt to make schools safe places for sexual-minority students must consider school-based athletic classes and programs.

At the very least, schools should establish nondiscrimination and anti-harassment policies for all teams. Local, regional, and state athletic leagues and associations should adopt similar policies. More proactive policies can also be enacted to train coaches to combat their own homophobia and that of their athletes. Table 7.2 has additional suggestions for coaches and parents.[57]

Contemporary, Honest, Factual Library Books

Libraries often become safe havens for queer kids, a place to explore. Even a gay-themed novel can help to alleviate the feeling of isolation.

School and public libraries should provide a selection of both fiction and nonfiction books. The list presented in the Resources Appendix might provide some suggestions. Libraries need not provide sensationalized treatises praising or condemning. Balanced, thoughtful, supportive literature is more valuable for teens who are desperate for knowledge. Lesbian, gay, and bisexual adults and their supporters can make contributions of selected books to school, public, and college libraries.

Advocacy

As in the San Francisco city schools, one teacher in each middle and high school should be designated as a "gay/lesbian sensitive adult." This paid staff member serves as a confidential resource for students, someone with whom they can discuss issues pertaining to sexual orientation. The value of this position is reinforced by one young women who noted, "I think that if someone would have stood up for me and said, 'It's not OK to make fun of gays and lesbians,' it would have helped a lot."[58]

TABLE 7.2. Combating Homophobia in School Athletics

Physical education teachers and coaches can . . .

- Educate themselves about homophobia in athletics.
- Educate themselves about the needs of lesbian, gay, and bisexual youth.
- Monitor their own behavior for incidents that encourage hostility or condone antigay actions of others.
- Discuss homophobia and sports with students.
- Invite students to discuss issues of sexuality or homophobia.
- Serve as a referral source for students with questions concerning sexuality.
- Be open about their own sexuality if lesbian, gay, or bisexual, or support other coaches who are open about their sexuality.

Physical education teachers can . . .

- Recognize that no one sport is right for everyone and offer a varied athletic program from which everyone can benefit.
- Lessen emphasis on competition and foster more cooperative sports and personal excellence, thus indirectly decreasing competitiveness that can lead to homophobic put-downs.

Coaches can . . .

- Stop assuming that all athletes are heterosexual.
- Discuss homophobia with athletes.
- Invite students to discuss issues of sexuality or homophobia.
- Pressure coaches' associations to offer programs on homophobia.

Athletes can . . .

- Stop making homophobic remarks and harassing those suspected of being lesbian, gay, or bisexual.
- Act as role models and befriend teammates who disclose their lesbian, gay, or bisexual identity.
- Recognize the fear and prejudice expressed by homophobic comments or harassment.
- Seek advice and support from teachers, counselors, and/or peers if they are questioning their own sexual orientation.

Parents can . . .

- Challenge their own prejudices and monitor their own behavior for homophobic remarks and/or actions.
- Support antidiscrimination, antiharassment, and antihomophobic education by the school system.
- Demand that coaches not use homophobic remarks to motivate athletes.
- Understand that a coach or athlete's sexual orientation is personal and does not affect a person's ability to perform.
- Encourage open discussion about sexual orientation and prejudice among young people.

Source: Adapted from Griffin (1995).

Sometimes advocacy must come from outside the school. As part of the Boston chapter of Queer Nation's Save OUR Children campaign, volunteers at targeted high schools distribute gay-positive reading lists, leaflets, and condoms. In addition, students were encouraged to sign pledge cards promising to support openly gay and lesbian students and if lesbian or gay, to come out with a vengeance.

Restoration of Positive Self-Worth

Ask teachers what they teach and most reply with subject matter—history, English, physics, math—but beyond this response is the notion that *we teach children*. How can a teacher be concerned for the learning of math while disregarding the learner who may be distracted by teasing, fearful of physical violence, and in need of an open, accepting adult with whom to talk.

Positive messages from teachers have positive effects on students. Mary, the mother of a gay son who committed suicide, concludes, "When they [lesbian, gay, and bisexual youth] can sit there and learn with the other kids that their life is positive in the same way that their nongay peers life is positive, then I think it can make a big difference."[59] Jessica, with the support of family and friends, found the courage to invite another woman to be her date to the prom. Kevin, a college student, was able to come out when a respected professor helped him take charge of his life and take pride in all parts of himself including sexual orientation.[60]

Self-worth is built upon repeated success. It is the responsibility of schools to provide an environment in which every child has an opportunity to succeed in some way. Rigid adherence to traditional male-focused achievement can devastate the self-image of girls and gender nonconforming boys.[61] Girl athletes and boy cheerleaders, female science whizzes and male dancers should be as recognized as the male football captain.

Self-worth is enhanced also by interaction with other lesbian, gay, and bisexual teens. "When I learned there were other people like me," explains Mike, a nineteen-year-old who went through a very angst-ridden adolescence, "I learned not to hate me."[62] Events such as the Massachusetts' Annual Gay/Straight Youth Pride Fest empower students to take charge of their lives and to resist discrimination.

Conclusion

There is a lack of educational leadership on the issue of sexual-minority teens. Welcoming environments do not evolve in a hostile or neutral atmosphere. Dr. John Anderson, a Connecticut teacher, concludes that in the final analysis,

> We don't need directives, curriculum, policy; all we need is an environment, and that costs nothing at all. That's where there's a leadership vacuum.[63]

Although students should not be expected to exert all the pressure for change, grassroots student tactics are often effective. Lesbian, gay, and bisexual students can demand the same educational experiences as heterosexual teens. As mentioned, students in Salt Lake City demanded gay student support groups in the face of school district threats to end all extracurricular activities.

When school or public officials fail to respond to basic student needs for education and protection, students should file lawsuits to force compliance. A former student of Chicago's Riverside-Brookfield High School filed a suit in 1996 claiming that he was forced to drop out of school because of continuous harassment and name-calling that the administration failed to stop.[64] Jamie, age twenty, who sued his school district for failing to protect him from abuse by other students, claims, "I'm protected in the workforce . . . against discrimination, but when it comes to a public high school, I'm not. I think that's insane."[65] In effect, Jamie's suit alleged he was denied his constitutional right to equal protection, due process, and a public education.

"Gay youths are finally saying they have had enough," notes Rea Carey, Director of the National Advocacy Coalition on Youth and Sexual Orientation. "In many ways we're looking at the results of what we've been trying to achieve for years—the empowerment of gay youth."[66]

Students are advised to record by date and time all incidences of discrimination and to submit all complaints in written form with copies sent to local media. Meetings with school officials, as well as classroom presentations by hostile faculty, should be tape recorded openly. Such documentation is essential for future legal proceedings. Often, the knowledge that these data are being collected is sufficient to gain compliance by teachers and administrators.

Any positive step taken by a school district is guaranteed to fuel opposition. School administrators and board members need to be proactive. Representative community members should help draft curricular and policy changes; others, such as clergy and mental health professionals, should be consulted. Once invested, these individuals and local lesbian, gay, and bisexual adults can form a core support group. Community support is crucial.

MONITOR JUVENILE COURTS

In all but the most egregious cases, the goal of juvenile courts is to reunite the family. For a queer kid experiencing harassment for sexual orientation from family members, court-ordered family counseling for homophobia and heterosexism should be a mandatory first step. All too often the youth and her or his sexual orientation are treated as the problem, ignoring the larger acceptance issue. "Rehabilitation" may focus on a youth's behavior, such as running away, with little concern for the conditions that resulted in this behavior. Runaway teens may be returned to the home without identifying the reasons for their behavior.

Appropriate services are lacking and should be established. Intake workers must overcome any discomfort about sexual orientation in order to be able to ask appropriate, specific questions. Professional discomfort results in youth stigmatization.

Homeless teens are often in severe economic distress. The income avenues most readily available—prostitution, drugs, and other illegal activities—brand them as youthful "criminals." Society forces sexual-minority youths to take desperate measures and then labels these measures criminal.[67] To focus only on the criminalized behavior is to do a huge disservice to homeless lesbian, gay, and bisexual youths who have been motivated by a need to survive. For some teens, stigmatization as a criminal is the only alternative to harassment and abuse at home and in school.

Placement of homeless youth "offenders" is extremely important if the cycle of harassment and abuse is to be broken. The special stresses these teens encounter must be considered. Counseling must include a life skills component and incorporate the lesbian, gay, and bisexual community as an integral part.

ESTABLISH SPECIAL PROGRAMS AND SCHOOLS

Special programs, such as Project 10 in Los Angeles and The Triangle Program in Toronto, or special schools, such as the Harvey Milk High School in New York City and the Eagle Center in Los Angeles, may be necessary when youth are continually harassed. In the ideal world, the offenders—not their lesbian and gay targets—would be removed to a special school, but we do not live in such a world.

Taking its name from the ten percent of population that Kinsey found to be homosexual, Project 10 began in the Los Angeles Unified School District in 1984 as a lunchtime discussion between a counselor and lesbian and gay high schoolers. The impetus for creating the program was the high drop-out rate among these students. The program has expanded to include a large percentage of the approximately fifty high schools in the Los Angeles Unified School District and is open to lesbian, gay, bisexual, transgender, and sexually questioning students, although membership criteria are not strict. It is not the program's philosophy to label students based on sexual orientation.[68]

Components of the Project 10 model are listed in Table 7.3. At this time, Project 10 has four aspects: education, school safety, drop-out prevention, and counseling. Education is accomplished by library materials in each school and by a lesbian and gay youth speakers bureau that provides consciousness-raising for faculty and staff. One goal is the dissemination of accurate AIDS information. Safety is the responsibility of school authorities who are to report and respond to all incidents of antigay violence or harassment. Drop-out prevention and counseling includes informal discussion groups, drop-in individual counseling, and peer counseling with the goal of improving self-esteem and providing affirmation of sexual minorities. Community services are also used in support of Project 10 and include youth groups; hotlines; sensitivity training for professionals serving teens; and homeless shelters, group homes, and foster placement.

Information about Project 10 is spread by word-of-mouth, referral, and signs in the counseling office. Participation is voluntary and confidential, although Dr. Uribe, who started the program, worries that those who lack the courage to avail themselves may not receive vital services they need. Each school has one male and one female facilitator who provide counseling on sexual orientation, substance abuse, high-risk sexual behavior, stay-

TABLE 7.3. Components of Project 10 Model

- District resource center
- Paid program coordinator
- Ongoing inservice training on institutional homophobia and the special needs of lesbian and gay youth presented to teachers, counselors, and staff
- Trained on-site teams who provide information and support to students
- Fiction and nonfiction materials on lesbian and gay subjects accumulated with the assistance of school librarians
- Enforcement of nondiscrimination policies and codes of behavior with regard to harassment and abuse of lesbian and gay students
- Advocacy for lesbian and gay student rights through commission and task force reports, and PTA and community outreach program efforts
- Network and coalition building with community agencies, parents, educational organizations, and teachers' unions

ing in school, and choosing employment and higher education. Support groups meet weekly after school, at lunch, or during the school day. "I'm not saying that the entire school system should be mobilized to help gay and lesbian kids," explains Dr. Uribe, "But there are kids out there who are struggling and certainly need some attention."[69]

Two important issues must be addressed in the initial stages of organizing such programs. First, sexual-minority students must be identified and alerted. This can be accomplished by referral and by publicity in local and school newspapers and by pamphlets left with youth agencies. Second, funding must be procured. School districts may be reluctant to provide funds without a demonstrated need. Seed money may be obtained from local lesbian, gay, and bisexual organizations or from charitable-giving organizations. Incorporation of the group as a nonprofit corporation can aid receipt of grant money. Some organizations will not grant funds to public institutions such as schools.

Although similar models have been adopted by San Francisco and Cambridge, Massachusetts, schools, these programs are not without their detractors. Predictably, such programs are charged with "recruiting" and "promoting" homosexuality. It is also claimed that sexual orientation is not an appropriate topic for schools. Even in Los Angeles periodic protests are presented to the Board of Education. Dr. Uribe reserves her harshest criticism for "spineless, cowardly, gutless" school board members "who at the slightest criticism fall apart at the seams." "If they could just get it into their heads that public education serves all children, then they'd want to protect all children."[70]

Detractors can be handled calmly by asking them to state their objections in writing. Responses should note that lesbian, gay, and bisexual adults and the parents of lesbian, gay, and bisexual students are taxpayers and that the program has been undertaken after careful consideration and discussion. For those concerned that such programs weaken the educational curriculum, responses should note that student groups meet at non-academic times, thus the curriculum is not impaired in anyway.

It is a real act of courage for some individuals to attend their first meeting of a Project 10 or similar group. A youth may be unable to muster such resources again unless she or he is given some reason to return. All new members should be greeted warmly and integrated into the group quickly. It is best if first-time attendees are given something to take with them as a reminder, such as a local resource guide.

The Harvey Milk High School, an offspring of the Hetrick-Martin Institute, opened in 1985 and is a truly unique school that attempts to offer a successful educational experience to those lesbian and gay teens who had difficulty in school because of their sexual orientation. Named for slain gay San Francisco Supervisor Harvey Milk and designed as a transitional program, the school attempts to help students cope with trauma, acquire survival skills, and build positive self-esteem within a regular high school curriculum. In short, the Harvey Milk School offers a safe place for learning and personal healing.

The school is fully accredited by the New York City Board of Education and administered by its alternative high schools and programs division. As in other NYC alternative schools, the student body is small, averaging about two dozen fourteen- to twenty-one-year-olds.

The school has an open classroom format befitting the attendance pattern of its students. Students who disappear for a while can resume when they return. No violence is allowed and certain offensive epithets are prohibited, but otherwise, few restrictions exist. Still, students must complete the same number of courses as other high school students and pass the Regents Competency Test. As might be expected with kids in crisis, the successes often are nonacademic, such as restoration of positive self-worth. "Sometimes it's enough of an achievement just to keep kids coming and safe," attests teacher Fred Goldhaber.[71]

As might be imagined, the Harvey Milk School is not without its detractors. Those on the political right level the old charge of recruitment, while those on the left call it segregation.

The opinions of individual students are less divided. David is typical. Unable to cope with the verbal harassment at his high school, David convinced his mother to enroll him at Harvey Milk secretly to avoid confrontation with his father. David describes the experience:

> Harvey Milk was a true learning experience for me. I got support from my teachers. The fact that I was different was no longer a challenge for me. . . . I realized that I was many other things in addition to being gay. I was friendly and outgoing, and to my surprise I actually liked to be around people. . . . I actually grew to love school. . . . I learned that being gay was no barrier to my success.[72]

Unfortunately, such successes mask the larger failure of the school system itself to address homophobia and heterosexism districtwide. Until these issues are addressed, it will be necessary to establish more schools on the Harvey Milk model. Three teachers in Dallas, Texas, are planning to open a private school for lesbian and gay teens called the Walt Whitman Community School. The school's purposes will be to create an atmosphere of tolerance, to accept differing sexualities, and to promote personal growth.[73]

If school districts realistically address issues of homophobia and hetero-sexism, the need for a school such as Harvey Milk will vanish. "The goal of Harvey Milk School," explains teacher Fred Goldhaber, "is to create a world in which a Harvey Milk School is not necessary, but short of that. . . ."[74]

OPEN ALL YOUTH PROGRAMS
TO LESBIAN AND GAY YOUTH

Youth organizations, such as the Boy Scouts of America, cannot be allowed to discriminate against sexual-minority youths. In a recent case in New Jersey, Eagle Scout James Dale was dismissed by the Monmouth Council because he is gay. Although Dale had never behaved improperly, Judge Patrick McGann, a state supreme court justice, concluded "the moral law as espoused by the major religions continues to declare the *act* [my italics] of sodomy to be a serious wrong."[75]

Organizations who have been given a public trust to socialize our children have shown themselves to be neither public not trustworthy. They cannot be allowed to enforce a heterosexual standard by banning homosexuality and bisexuality. Most youths will not discover their sexual orientation until they are already members. The exclusionary policy is as reprehensible as "whites only" private clubs. Organizations that discriminate should not be allowed to meet in public buildings that are supported by taxpayer dollars.

Even the phalanx of discrimination that is the Boy Scouts of America may be starting to break ranks. In a confidential memo, the San Francisco Bay area council reportedly has forbidden scout leaders to question the sexual orientation of members.[76] This modest "Don't ask, don't tell" policy resulted from the proactive efforts of community groups who were successful in having scout troops expelled from school district premises and in slashing United Way funding by half a million dollars.

INVOLVE THE LESBIAN, GAY,
AND BISEXUAL COMMUNITY

The lesbian, gay, and bisexual community can be a sanctuary and a source of comfort and information for queer kids. "[I]t isn't enough to open only my own closet door," states writer James Earl Hardy, "I must make sure others know they can too, especially the next generation."[77] Within a support network, especially one consisting of other teens, individual internal conflicts can subside and a youth can begin to heal. Self-esteem can be rebuilt. Jennifer, age eighteen, declares, "I feel pride when I see one of 'my people' in Congress; honor when I see them battling discrimination in the military; respect when my friends risk arrest to fight AIDS; and dignity when I speak to a high school group. . . . "[78]

Slowly, as more lesbian, gay, and bisexual youths come out, a framework of support systems and resources is being established. Roughly 170 agencies in the United States and Canada provide services from hotlines to hot meals. The majority culture is beginning to recognize that queer kids exist. The variety of resources available includes teen centers, helplines, social programs, pen pal networks, and computer on-line services. Meeting places include schools, churches, social agencies, youth centers, college campuses, and computer monitors and phone lines. If the mushrooming size of the population being served is any indication, a huge need and a large potential service population exist.

One such agency is the Hetrick-Martin Institute, a nonprofit social service, education, and advocacy organization dedicated to meeting the needs of lesbian, gay, and bisexual teens and to educating society. It is hoped that sexual-minority youths can overcome the difficulties they face and lead happy and productive lives. Located in New York City, HMI serves more than 7,000 adolescents directly, provides outreach to more than 5,000 homeless youths, and touches almost 10,000 youths through educational programs. Founded in 1979 by Emery Hetrick, MD, and Damien Martin, EdD, HMI consists of six core programs staffed by more than forty professionals and scores of volunteers. "I came to HMI . . . because of the way I feel inside," states Marcos. "It boosts the way I look at myself and makes me feel better."[79]

Social services include an after school drop-in center that provides a safe, casual place for lesbian, gay, and bisexual teens to meet; individual and family counseling; and Project First Step that provides street outreach, hot meals, clothing, showers, and a safe social environment for homeless youths. One of the many innovative outreach and educational projects is the *Tales of the Closet,* a comic book format series addressing issues such as isolation, family, violence, health, pregnancy, religion, stress, love, and pride. A legal services "walk-in" clinic provides assistance with immigration, housing, police abuse, public assistance, and the like. Carmen, age sixteen and homeless, was helped to secure public assistance so she could complete high school and have a place to live.[80] As might be expected, those who attend programs at HMI reflect the racial and ethnic mix of a large urban area: approximately 45 percent African American, 35 percent

Latino, 15 percent white non-Latino, and 5 percent Asian and Native American.

Educational services include training and resource programs for professionals and the Harvey Milk School, an alternative high school for lesbian and gay students. HMI's Foster Care and Youth Service Project trains employees of foster care agencies to be cognizant of and sensitive to the needs of lesbian and gay youths.

Advocacy is accomplished through the National Advocacy Coalition of Youth and Sexual Orientation (NACYSO). NACYSO attempts to raise awareness of the existence and needs of lesbian and gay youths nationwide through professionals and peer leadership and education programs that reach out to other teens.

Project First Step (PFS) operates from a storefront in lower Manhattan where homeless youths can receive food, condoms and safe sex information, a shower, and clothing. More important, reports Luis, "The staff always encourages me to reach my goals."[81] Counseling and assistance with entitlements, medical care, job seeking, and education meet less immediate, but ultimately, more gratifying needs. PFS also provides outreach to other street youths to let them know of the services available.

To get the attention of lesbian and gay teens, the Illinois Gay and Lesbian Task Force used posters on buses and subways in Chicago depicting a school locker spray-painted with "Die faggot." Beneath the picture was the caption "Don't get scared. Get help" and the phone number for a youth hotline. Other agencies should be as equally aggressive.

It is not too much to ask that lesbian, gay, and bisexual adults provide services for queer kids while serving as role models. Attorneys who belong to sexual minorities can provide legal counsel to youth groups and to individual youths, especially those in the juvenile justice system. Social workers who are lesbian, gay, or bisexual can also track the justice system and work closely with sexual-minority youths who are homeless or in need of other youth services. Teachers who are lesbian, gay, or bisexual and open about their sexuality can be excellent role models for students. As citizens, lesbian, gay, and bisexual adults can pressure local school districts to establish youth groups and libraries to order accurate books and gay-themed novels. Adults can become foster parents and/or speakers for youth at local churches, professional organizations, and service clubs. A big brother/big sister or mentor program would help to combat the lack of positive lesbian, gay, and bisexual images in the media.[82] Just as it is important for African-American children to see African-American adults, it is important for queer kids to see themselves reflected in all aspects of the adult population. These adults represent the possibilities for sexual-minority youths.

Indirectly, lesbian, gay, and bisexual adults can facilitate the restoration of positive self-worth and decrease the victim mentality evidenced in much of the lesbian and gay community.[83] Chance Claar, who at age fourteen cofounded Atlanta's Out Youth, states the need very clearly:

> Until the larger community becomes involved in making provisions for and helping queer youth, we won't have the type of support we need to grow and contribute to that community. . . . All members of the community share the responsibility for developing better ways for queer youth to enter the lesbian and gay community.[84]

In the last analysis, lesbian, gay, and bisexual teens still must overcome the extremely large hurdle of taking the initial contact steps. For a teen struggling with her or his sexuality and still uncomfortable, this move takes a great deal of courage. Yet, it is when the internal struggle is most difficult that sexual-minority youths need contact with loving, caring lesbian, gay, and bisexual adults. "[W]e can't count on our government and society to reach out to them [lesbian, gay, and bisexual youths]," concludes Chris Gonzalez of the Indianapolis Youth Group, "so we as gay and lesbian adults have to rise to the occasion."[85]

By resisting the call to aid queer kids, the lesbian, gay, and bisexual community silently acquiesces to the stereotype of the homosexual pederast. Could it be that homosexual adults do not trust themselves around lesbian and gay teens? There is but one solution to this dilemma and it is to do what lesbian, gay, and bisexual adults are accused of every day. Recruit! Receruit! Recruit! By this I mean detractors be damned! If homosexual and bisexual adults are going to be accused of recruiting anyway, why not reach out to lesbian, gay, and bisexual teens?

Hot 'Zines and Hotlines

Several new magazines have targeted the sexual-minority teen market. With titles such as *X Y, InsideOut* and *OUT*, many are glossy and flashy, geared to appeal to young readers. It has been charged the photos, ads, long story format, and high price suggest that some of the magazines really are pandering to the interests of men who are attracted to teens. While the bra ads in *Teen* and *Sassy* are acceptable, the underwear ads in magazines such as *X Y* have been accused of being exploitive and sensationalized. In fact, only 25 percent of *X Y*'s readers are between the ages of fourteen and twenty. At the same time, a fifteen-year-old writes,

> Please don't ever stop producing *X Y;* it's about the only thing I have to let me know that there are other gay youth out there. . . . I live in

Kansas and as far as I know, there isn't any place to meet other people like myself.[86]

In the last analysis, however, it takes a brave adolescent to subscribe to or purchase a lesbian, gay, or bisexual magazine.

Hot lines or help lines are a godsend but many more are needed, especially in rural areas. "We get many kids who call from areas with no support," states Chris Gonzalez of the Indianapolis Youth Group. "Kids in rural America basically have zero opportunity other than . . . driving four or five hours to a metropolitan area."[87] Many lesbian, gay, and bisexual youths call to talk to anyone other than the school counselor. Most calls are about loneliness. The need is so acute that when Out Youth Austin (Texas) opened a national toll-free number it was swamped with enough calls to override its budget.

It may not be very easy for lesbian, gay, and bisexual youths to get help-line numbers from school counselors. The Denver school board was blasted by the Christian Right for counselors displaying a gay hot-line phone number in a prominent location. The Christian Right and its allies have it both ways. Their efforts have, in part, created many of the problems for queer kids and their continuing efforts restrict access to potential solutions. More publicity for help-line services is needed.

Given the potential of helplines and hotlines and their high usage, it is surprising that such a small percentage of lesbian and gay youth use this resource.[88] This situation may result either from a lack of access or from the lack of specifically targeted information for lesbian, gay, and bisexual youths.

Funding for hotlines and for publicity may be obtained through grants or appeals to the sexual-minority community. Proposals must stress the critical need for such services.

Internet

The personal computer offers unprecedented opportunities for queer kids to connect with others through the Internet, to declare their sexual orientation, to ask for advice, and to seek support. Gone are the fears of discovery by the librarian, the operator, or the accidental meeting with your sister at the entrance to a meeting. With anonymity, lesbian, gay, and bisexual youths can gain information about sexuality and lesbian, gay, and bisexual resources, swap coming out stories, discuss feelings, and seek advice.

"One of the beauties of the Internet is that nobody knows you're fifteen and live in Montana and are gay," says Reid Fisher, age nineteen, the founder of the Youth Assistance Organization, an Internet site.[89] David, a midwestern teen, recalls that through America Online "I was able to talk to people that have gone through or are going through the same thing I did."[90]

In addition, the Internet can be a nonthreatening venue for coming out or for just observing the postings of others. A variety of choices for participation exist, including bulletin boards, "chat" rooms, and multimedia sites. The National Coalition of Gay, Lesbian, and Bisexual Youth offers resource guides and youth support "start-up" kits on-line. The Youth Assistance Organization has an electronic pamphlet called "I think I might be gay (Now what do I do?)."

"When you see people around the world writing the same things you're feeling, you get the feeling you're not alone," explains a teen. "You may be no closer than a modem, but you go 'Oh, my God, that's exactly how I feel.'"

When Ryan, age seventeen, typed in "Does anyone else feel like you're the only gay guy on the planet or at least in Arlington, Texas?" he never dreamed he would receive over 100 supportive e-mail letters. Subsequently, with the advice of other teens, he was able to come out to his mother. He concludes, "The fact that all these guys are secure with themselves gave me courage."[91]

Drawbacks to on-line services do exist. Vulnerable teens may be susceptible to the "friendship" offered by older individuals stalking for sex. Several well-publicized cases should serve to admonish the lesbian, gay, and bisexual teen to be wary of anyone who is too friendly and too eager to meet. It may be best to remain anonymous at first.

It is also best not to rely totally on the Internet. It is no substitute for face-to-face interactions. In addition, depression or life-threatening issues may require more direct action. Nor is the Internet's access guaranteed. Groups honestly wishing to protect children from pornography may play into the hands of right-wing zealots who consider any mention of homosexuality to be obscene and therefore inappropriate for anyone under eighteen. All access to lesbian, gay, and bisexual chat or information lines could end for queer kids if these bigots have their way.

Youth Centers and Groups

It is ironic that a sex-negative society such as the United States offers few choices to lesbian and gay teens except sex. By limiting the social venues for lesbian and gay teens, stigmatizing lesbian and gay youth, and offering little support for same-sex relationships, society encourages secretive, furtive sexual encounters.

Youth centers for queer kids can fulfill a sanctuary and a social function unavailable through support groups. The nonthreatening atmosphere offers an opportunity for lesbian, gay, and bisexual youths to explore same-sex interactions and to form friendships. Teens are free to socialize, goof-off, dance, hold hands, kiss, or just talk, all part of the adolescent socialization process. The first center for sexual-minority teens was Seattle's Lambert House founded in 1991. A handful of centers, such as District 202, located in a storefront in Minneapolis, offer a place for students to relax and socialize. Center events at District 202 include dances and video nights for youths under age twenty-one. Commenting on the Seattle center, Jenie, a twenty-one-year-old lesbian, gushes, "For me the center is a dream come true."[92] Where no youth center exists, services may be offered at lesbian, gay, and bisexual community centers.

Youth groups are also needed outside of the educational setting. One of the oldest, the Boston Alliance of Gay and Lesbian Youth (BAGLY), begun in 1981, offers a model. Youth have power within the organization and run most events. Adults act as consultants. In addition to a wide range of support services, BAGLY has a speaker service and sponsors dances, trips, outings, and other social events. At a minimum, support groups or centers should offer a welcoming atmosphere free of racist and sexist language with a program targeted for queer kids and advised by trained adult and peer staff.

Peer support groups are especially important. "Being accepted by a group of age-mates with whom one can share existence and establish intimate relationships," explains Dennis Anderson, a rap group advisor, "is paramount to the early adolescent."[93] When many teens realize their sexual orientation, this self-discovery is accompanied by intense anxiety.

Peer support groups are often the only place where lesbian and gay teens can be open, be themselves, and talk freely. Atlanta's "Out Youth," founded by a sixteen-year-old lesbian, has become a vital resource for some young people. "[I learned] I was not the only young, black, gay person . . . " claims Maurice, age twenty-one. "It's been the cornerstone of my psychological health."[94] Commenting on another youth group, Greg, a young African-American male, states, "[T]he group helped us a lot. Not only to introduce us to other people, but to acknowledge that we weren't weird."[95] Renee, a sixteen-year-old African-American female, adds, "For the first time in my life I had something to talk about with people my age." "I felt like a normal teenager," she adds. "And the greatest part was I could be whoever I wanted to be."[96] Chris, a young gay man, states simply, "For the first time I wasn't alone."[97]

Unfortunately, there can be the downside too. "Now I have to go back for a week where I won't be with anyone gay," complained a seventeen-year old white male at the end of one meeting. "I have to think about how I talk and walk and what I say every minute of every day until I come back here."[98]

The main impediments to availing one's self of youth centers and groups are lack of transportation, fear of disclosure, and knowledge of such groups.[99] Often, word is spread from one youth to another.

Initial membership may come from youth known by the group's founders. Membership can be solicited from counselors and by advertisements in sexual-minority publications. School venues are also possible, although counselors and school newspapers often are reluctant to advertise lesbian, gay, and bisexual youth groups.

Support is only one function of such groups. Peer interactions should be encouraged and fostered. "I didn't want a support group," claims Vic, a twenty-year-old lesbian. "I wanted *friends.*"[100] Indeed, friends, especially those in lesbian and gay support groups, are a primary source of advice and guidance.[101]

Bisexual students may feel excluded from lesbian and gay support groups and every effort must be made to ensure that these groups are inclusive. Marilyn was open about her bisexuality but the topic rarely surfaced. When she began to date a man, she felt excluded and unwelcome.

Safe Shelters and Residential Treatment Centers

The Gay and Lesbian Adolescent Social Services (GLASS) center in Los Angeles provides the country's only licensed long-term residential program solely for lesbian and gay minors in trouble. The center operates four community residences for adolescents. Most teens served have no other home and are wards of the court or the Los Angeles County probation department. Usually, they have been removed from their homes because they were abused.

Lesbian and gay youths have a difficult time using many other youth service centers. Most centers are inherently heterosexual. Maria was asked to leave a youth center because she is a lesbian. Nathan was told he could stay but "you can't act gay."[102] Lesbian or gay relationships may be grounds for either expulsion or cessation of services, especially in residential programs. Ann, an abuse victim and suicide survivor, recalls her first day at GLASS when a counselor, referring to Ann's sexual orientation said, "You can be you now." "I was overwhelmed."[103] For a lot of the youths served by GLASS, according to Danielle Morris, a staff member, "This is the only positive family experience that they've ever had."[104]

Nathan, recently molested by an older man, is alternately angry and severely depressed. "Most of the things we deal with here," explains Sharon Kidd, the program director, "are those things that come up around abuse: self-esteem, depression, suicidality, and a lot of acting-out behavior from anger around abuse."[105] Consequently, there are rules against self-destructive behaviors.

GLASS has space for thirty kids. While in GLASS's care, teens attend school, participate in group activities, and do chores. Placement is provided until age nineteen. Other services at GLASS include a foster care program that places children with lesbian or gay foster families, case management for HIV-positive and at-risk youth ages twelve to twenty-one, and a lesbian and gay "big sibling" program.

In the end, the plight of homeless lesbian and gay youths may be the result of what Rea Carey of the National Advocacy Coalition on Youth and Sexual Orientation calls "dual denial." Youth service agencies do not want to acknowledge sexual-minority youths and lesbian, gay, and bisexual adults don't want to admit that queer kids are on the street.[106]

Obviously, many more centers for lesbian, gay, and bisexual youths are desperately needed. Other youth centers must make all youths, regardless of sexual orientation, feel welcome and safe. Posters can extend a welcome to all, and policies of nondiscrimination can soothe misgivings. Each center should have a policy to discourage racist, homophobic, and sexist remarks. In addition, the presence of openly lesbian and gay staff members can encourage teens to be more open and to discuss their feelings. A home atmosphere seems to work best with teens sharing responsibilities in a supportive, caring environment.

Lesbian and gay youths may attempt to test the limits of any setting in which they fear that they may be unwelcome. Sensing staff and resident discomfort, a queer kid may use her or his homosexuality to create crises that result in rejection. Staff should react to the underlying pain and self-hatred, not to the behavior.[107] It is also important to avoid scapegoating. A youth's gayness should not become the focus of treatment.

Some teens require residential treatment. In these settings, it is essential that staff be trained to discuss sexual issues and to debunk myths and stereotypes surrounding homosexuality, that sex education, including homosexuality, be taught, and that appropriate policies and procedures addressing sexual orientation exist.[108] In addition, sexual orientation should be added to an agency's list of categories for nondiscrimination. Harassment and physical violence should not be tolerated. Derisive terms such as *faggot* should be dealt with in the same manner as racial and ethnic epithets. Agency libraries should contain lesbian and gay literature.

Agency policies must recognize the sexual behavior of adolescents while setting limits and procedures for those who exceed them. Residential facilities should distinguish clearly between normal, healthy, and harmful, exploitive sexual behavior regardless of the gender or orientation of the youths involved. Staff can be trained to respond therapeutically to sexual behavior among residents and to respond in the same manner to all participants.[109] Within Child Protective Services guidelines, youths should be allowed privacy and dignity regarding sexuality. Discrete times and places should be provided to allow for private masturbation.

Working with homeless lesbian and gay adolescents is not easy. "A lot of these kids come from horrific backgrounds and have no social skills," states Daena Petersen of the Los Angeles Gay and Lesbian Community Services Center. "I was really violent with everyone if they tried to get close to me, emotion-wise," recalls Alex, age seventeen. "Everyone here [at GLASS]—no matter how mean I am and how much of a bitch I am—they still care about me and they still love me.[110]

Long-Term Family Alternatives

The legal options for all youths are extremely limited. They are dependent upon and legally bound to adults. The uneven power of the adult-child relationship and the heterosexism and homophobia of society combine with often brutal results for lesbian, gay, and bisexual teens. The queer kid who is banished from her or his family has the limited legal options of guardianship, adoption, or emancipation.[111] Other alternatives include foster care, moving in with a friend who has sympathetic parents, and homelessness.

In general, the appointment of a nonparental guardian requires that a court find parental custody detrimental and an alternative arrangement in the best interest of the youth. Where animosity exists between the parents and the child, as is often the case with sexual-minority teens, parents may refuse to consent to guardianship or may contest such decisions based on parental "right." If the proposed guardians are lesbian or gay, parents may contest on the basis of fitness. Youth workers are advised to propose several potential guardians in anticipation of such a challenge. Older teens may be given more latitude by the courts in naming potential guardians, especially when these teens refuse to return to a negative family situation.

Guardianship also may be contested by parents based on the supposed mental health problems of their child. Teens who have been forced into change therapies may have a mental health history on paper. In these cases, child advocates will need to provide countering mental health information in the form of unbiased evaluations.[112]

Although a youth may desire a lesbian or gay guardian, the state may specifically prohibit this arrangement. Courts may use so-called sodomy laws to disallow lesbian or gay guardianship.

Adoption is an even less likely alternative for lesbian and gay teens except in cases of extreme abuse, neglect, and/or abandonment. Unlike guardianship, adoption requires termination of parental rights and a more long-term commitment beyond age eighteen by the adoptive parent(s).

Emancipation is a legal procedure by which adolescents can be freed of parental custody and control before age eighteen. The burden of support is placed on the youth. This responsibility may place an undue burden on the lesbian or gay teen at a time when she or he is wrestling with other weighty issues of self-identity while relieving an uncaring and/or hostile family of all responsibility. If emancipation is to work effectively for sexual-minority youths, the lesbian, gay, and bisexual community must provide support in the form of stable housing, schooling, and self-support.[113]

Volunteer "foster" homes for lesbian, gay, and bisexual youths offer another long-term alternative to living with hostile families. Such a system can be entirely separate from the more hostile officially sanctioned system. Derek, an African-American teen, was evicted by his parents. Just weeks prior to his high school graduation, Derek was placed in the home of a gay couple by the leader of the Minneapolis Lesbian and Gay Youth Together support group. Derek had his own room and was able to live there rent-free until he was more financially sound.[114]

In all of these alternatives, a large supportive extended family of lesbian, gay, and bisexual adults and peers can ease an adolescent's transition. It is absolutely essential that queer kids be placed in self-affirming environments. Where none exist they must be created by the sexual-minority community.

Conclusion

Queer kids cannot be expected to successfully navigate their challenges alone. Nor can the lesbian, gay, and bisexual community expect that addressing adult concerns will necessarily benefit sexual-minority teens. The challenges of lesbian, gay, and bisexual teens must be faced directly by both adolescents and adults. These challenges include not only homophobia, heterosexism, violence, homelessness, suicide, and AIDS, but also hopelessness and a belief in a negative future. The sexual-minority community should make no mistake, for the religious right understands, that this is a battle for the souls and lives of our children. Scott, age twenty-one, concludes, "We need . . . to reach every gay person we can and let them know that being gay is all right and that they are good people, no matter what others might say."[115]

TRAIN MORE KNOWLEDGEABLE
AND UNBIASED PROFESSIONALS

Pediatricians, psychiatrists, psychologists, counselors must become aware of the special needs of and resources for queer kids. Lesbian and gay adolescents have the following suggestions for health care providers:[116]

1. Do not assume all adolescents are heterosexual.
2. Make sure peer support groups are available.
3. Have more openly lesbian and gay role models.
4. Make more materials and personal resources available to answer teens' questions.
5. Provide a supportive environment so lesbian and gay teens can discuss their feelings and fears related to school, home, and family.

Effective interaction with queer kids begins with self-analysis and soul-searching by a professional to discover her or his own prejudices and stereotypes. Next, a professional must educate herself or himself on same-sex orientation, behavior, and identity and recognize a youth's right to confidentiality. Sexual orientation is a very personal matter.

The lack of services for queer kids is justified by a circular argument—No services are available so there must be no need. This lack of services sends a message that the problems of lesbian, gay, and bisexual youths are unimportant.

Schools and communities must provide adequate counseling services to aid lesbian, gay, and bisexual teens. Special training for counselors in schools is required and should be financed by school districts.

The goal of counseling needs to be defined clearly as assisting positive self-image development. It is important that the focus be restoration of positive self-worth. Local and national professional counseling organizations should have the courage to denounce "change therapies" for the sham they most surely are. In the wake of their timidity to do so, sexual-minority adults should demand that such methodologies also be available to heterosexual youths who are struggling with sexual issues.

An NEA training manual offers guidance for teaching and counseling lesbian and gay students. Counseling suggestions are also given in the next chapter.

ORGANIZE COLLEGE STUDENTS

At present, over 800 organized lesbian and gay groups exist on college campuses in the United States. Many sponsor speakers and rallies, hold special events, such as Lesbian and Gay Pride Week, and offer alternative social functions. Often the goal is to increase visibility.

The issues faced by lesbian, gay, and bisexual students vary with each campus and student groups reflect these differences. Small, rural schools often have tight close-knit organizations, one of the few safe havens in such an environment. Larger urban schools often have more diverse student populations, and sexual-minority groups may be splintered along ethnic or gender lines. The newsletter *Out on Campus,* available from the Standing Committee for Lesbian, Gay, and Bisexual Awareness of the American College Personnel Association, addresses sexual-minority concerns nationwide.

More organizations are needed, especially on smaller, rural, or church-affiliated campuses. Whether support-oriented or social in nature, organizational funding and space should be provided by the institution or by student government. Sexual-minority groups should also have a representative on student government to reflect the concerns of sexual-minority students.

Membership in sexual-minority student groups may vary widely over time. On my own campus, a rural upstate public college of 5,000 students, initial membership struggled to break the twenty-member limit for several years. Some dozen years later, there are approximately 150 members.

Initially, membership may be very limited or may coalesce around a small group of friends. Visibility and publicity are essential, and college administrators should aid these early group efforts, although individual initiative is to be encouraged. Jeff McCarley organized the Association for the Needs of Gay and Lesbian Students (ANGLS) by blanketing East Texas State University in Commerce, population 8,000, with 300 fliers.[117]

Student activism can end invisibility and lesbian, gay, and bisexual students are encouraged to be vocal and visible. Carlos Vizcarra, president of the Gay and Lesbian Association (GALA) at California State University in Los Angeles, organized the school's first gay pride week, initiated a weekly newspaper column, spoke in sociology classes, and increased visibility by becoming the school's first openly gay homecoming king.[118] Students can host lesbian, gay, and bisexual pride weeks or coming-out days, work for positive social and political change on the campus, local, or statewide level and conduct civil disobedience, such as protesting the presence of ROTC because of the military ban on lesbians and gays which violates academic freedom and equal opportunity and access.

University administrations should also be pressured by students, faculty, staff, and alumni to establish a nondiscriminatory policy based on sexual orientation, an office of coordinator of services for sexual-minority students, and a grievance procedure for lesbian, gay, and bisexual students. For example, the University of Minnesota has an office for lesbian and gay concerns. Smaller campuses might house this function within the Office of Multicultural Affairs. Grievances should be handled promptly and efficiently to send a message that intolerance is unacceptable. In one incident, a teaching assistant at the University of Alabama who used a homophobic example in class was disciplined within thirty-six hours. At the same institution, a trace was put on the phone of individuals receiving harassing phone calls. The perpetrator was caught and disciplined.[119]

Tolerance on campus can be fostered by the inclusion of sexual orientation issues in staff training and student orientation and the inclusion of sexual minorities in the curriculum where appropriate. Faculty members can exert subtle pressure on their peers to modify classroom presentations to be more inclusive.

When desired by sexual-minority students, separate dormitories may also be a campus option. As with other minorities, lesbian, gay, and bisexual students often prefer to socialize and live with their peers. It is important that the impetus for such an arrangement be in response to sexual-minority student desires and not in response to intolerance by others.

Finally, college policies must ensure that responsive college health service delivery exists. The cumulative effects of heterosexism and homophobia may be seen in the reluctance of many lesbian and gay college students to be open with health care providers for fear of discrimination.[120] College students must be made to feel welcome.[121] This is accomplished by (1) representation on college health care committees; (2) regular campuswide programs for lesbian, gay, and bisexual students; (3) literature and posters with same-sex couples and addressing of health concerns, such as suicide, substance abuse, and safe sex; (4) health education programs that address these concerns; (5) no reference to sexual orientation on health care records; and (6) lesbian, gay, and bisexual health care staff. In addition, staff should be sensitive to and comfortable with sexual minority health concerns.

The Massachusetts Governor's Commission on Gay and Lesbian Youth contains a summary titled *Making colleges and universities safe for gay, lesbian, bisexual, and transgender students and staff.* This excellent resource contains many useful suggestions affecting policies, services, curriculum, employees, and community.

CONCLUSION: WHO OWNS THE PROBLEM?

Although many positive changes for queer kids have occurred, much need still exists. "There may be more places to go," explains Troix Bettencourt, a member of the Massachusetts' Governor's Commission on Gay and Lesbian Youth, "but at a point in time when you realize that you're gay and actually seeking support, nothing's changed."[122] At best, services are piecemeal and national organization and leadership are needed. National fundraising efforts require an organized approach and a more holistic vision. It is especially important that services be extended to rural and small town youths.

In a final analysis, we must face squarely the "problem" of homosexuality and bisexuality and its owner. It is a problem for lesbians, gays, and bisexuals only so far as they must deal with societal nonacceptance and hostility. "It's discouraging to be a lesbian," states nineteen-year-old DeMelon, "because of all the homophobia."[123] Alston, a young gay man, continues,

> If there had not been such a taboo . . . , if people had not ridiculed me . . . it would have been easier. *In dealing with myself there was no problem.* [My italics][124]

Even against these great odds, most lesbian, gay, and bisexual individuals lead happy, healthy, and productive lives. Deep within many, however, seethes the anger that accompanies the knowledge that it is society that is responsible for the guilt, the isolation, and the self-hatred.

It is our society that clearly owns this problem, not lesbians, gays, and bisexuals. Our society is unwilling to tell the truth about sexual minorities and to counter the myths and stereotypes, unwilling to confront the hatred in the form of moral condemnation, unwilling to end discrimination, and unwilling to extend equal rights to all its members. Society is unwilling because sexual minorities are different and therefore perceived as a threat.

Are families threatened? Is society being destroyed? Not by sexual minorities. Gay men and lesbians do threaten the basic assumptions of patriarchy but so do the women's movement and children's rights advocates. Homosexuality also challenges heterosexism and heterosexual privilege, a notion that one group of individuals, the majority, is inherently better than another, the minority.

Even academic research tends to study homosexuality in a clinical manner as one might report on a disorder. Sexual orientation is discussed only with regard to sexual minorities as if the notion of orientation is also disordered. Heterosexuals are heterosexuals but others have an orientation. How often does the popular press report that some researcher has found the cause for homosexuality, never the cause of heterosexuality?

We need a healthier societal attitude that encourages evolution of sexuality as a natural process for all humans regardless of their sexual orientation. This attitude would encourage appropriate experimentation, acceptance, and the development of positive feeling among sexual minorities.[125] It goes without saying that this most beneficial of changes for all individuals will be the most difficult to achieve. Acknowledgment of responsibility for past transgressions is the first step.

Some individuals are as rigid in their hatred of sexual minorities as the staunch segregationist were in their hatred of African Americans. Advocates for queer kids must expect resistance from the religious and political right as a given. Their strategies should be anticipated and, where possible, thwarted. The mean-spiritedness of their attacks must be exposed to fair-minded citizens. In the final analysis, these modern day bigots will be as vilified as the Bull Connors or as repentant as the George Wallaces of the last generation.

The final demise of homophobia and heterosexism, however, is not enough. Society must provide active support for lesbians, gays, and bisexuals, celebrate their difference, and acknowledge the contributions of all humans. Only this attitude will enable future lesbian, gay, or bisexual youths to grow and to mature without the baseless societal stigma with which youth are burdened today. Refuges, such as the Harvey Milk School offer temporary solutions for a minuscule number of queer kids. These teens should be able to attend regular high school, and it is those schools that must change to accommodate them. "We should be changing the system to accept them," concludes Francis Kunreuther, HMI's executive director, "not pulling them out of the system for their own school."[126] Lesbian, gay, and bisexual kids do not need special treatment, they need equal, fair, and unbiased treatment.

Chapter 8

Counseling

Before I built a wall, I'd ask to know what I was walling in or out, . . .
Something there is that doesn't love a wall, that wants it down.

Robert Frost, *The Mending Wall*

Amazingly, many queer kids and their families navigate the issue of sexual orientation with little need of outside assistance. These are typically not the individuals seen by counselors. For those who do seek professional assistance, the personal importance of this service and their need for it can not be overstated.

Each school counselor must answer the question "For whom do I work?" If the answer is "the school board," then counselors are free to push the school board's agenda. If, on the other hand, the answer is "youth in need of my counseling," then the approach becomes very different.[1] Nor do counselors need to focus exclusively on sexual issues. It is important for counselors to help lesbian, gay, and bisexual teens cope with the daily stresses in their lives and with the effects of homophobia.[2] This requires a holistic approach that integrates all aspects of the person in a nonjudgmental manner.

Sexual-minority teens need a welcoming person to listen to their stories. Karii, a lesbian adolescent, explains,

> When I started talking to a counselor at HMI [Hetrick-Martin Institute] I was able to let out my anger, frustrations, and fears. Someone was finally listening to me. Someone who didn't judge me. Someone was there to give me support my family and friends could not give me. Gradually I became more comfortable with my sexuality and a sense of pride came over me.[3]

It was a long journey for Karii, an equally long one for her counselor, and a learning experience for both.

DIFFICULTIES IN SERVING QUEER KIDS

Any counseling with youths may be complicated by the secretiveness of many adolescents and their unwillingness to confide in adults. It may be especially difficult for some lesbian, gay, and bisexual youths to discuss very intense, personal, sexual feelings, that they may not fully understand themselves, and the accompanying shame and guilt. Cultural differences and the stage of coming out influence attitudes in varying ways.

Misunderstood Feelings

Adolescence is a time for testing and clarifying one's identity. As with other youths, lesbian, gay, and bisexual adolescents have conflicting needs to separate from their families and claim their individuality while still needing nurturing and guidance from these same families.

Conflicting needs can result in conflicting, often contradictory, behavior. Mood swings are not uncommon. Writer James Earl Hardy describes the real young man beneath the tough exterior of Sydney, a hip-hop-loving, droopy-jean-wearing B-boy (Bad boy), "Sometimes . . . he'd just cry on my shoulder—which he'd never do in front of his homies—because of the confusion he felt about his sexual orientation."[4]

Intensely Personal Feelings

In many families discussion of sex is difficult at best. Homosexuality may be a forbidden subject. Add to this situation the normal adolescent secretiveness and unwillingness to confide in adults, especially surrounding sexual issues. Finally, the pervasiveness of homophobia may make lesbian, gay, and bisexual youths hesitant to discuss their feelings and risk ridicule or punishment. "I never talked about sexuality . . . ," confessed Renee, a sixteen-year-old African-American bisexual female. "I'd pushed it all inside."[5]

Many lesbian, gay, and bisexual teens feel a need to hide "it" from their families, especially their parents. The secrecy comes from a fear that their parents will reject them. A nineteen-year-old white male explains,

> I don't think my mom is very accepting of gay people at all. It is not so much gay people as it is anyone who's different. I don't feel that she would reject me, but she would have a hard time accepting it if I told her.[6]

Queer kids crave acceptance. A young lesbian recorded the following in her diary:

> Please help me. . . . I have to talk to someone. . . . I have to tell someone, ask someone. WHO? . . . Would someone please help me? Someone, anyone. Help me. I'm going to kill myself if they don't.[7]

The well-being of these adolescents often is linked to perceived parental acceptance. Isolation and withdrawal restrict the access to information and support for lesbian, gay, and bisexual teens.

Lack of acceptance may lead to withdrawal, but it can also lead to anger. It can be especially infuriating for the lesbian, gay, or bisexual youth whose sexual orientation is well established and personally accepted. As eighteen-year-old Kyle states, "[B]eing attracted to the same sex is as natural to me as being attracted to the opposite sex is for heterosexuals."[8] Anger can take many forms. Alston, a young gay, refused to cooperate with school counselors as a form of punishment.

> I wouldn't talk to her. I didn't trust her. I didn't want to share it with anyone in school because they had treated me like an outcast. I didn't feel they deserved to know that part of my life.[9]

Christopher punished his parents for their supposed nonacceptance before he even told them. "I desperately wanted parents . . ." he explains, "but I had emotionally divorced myself from them."[10]

Adolescent Need to Conform

Adolescence is not a time of self-affirmation, especially when what is being affirmed is a difference. Affirming a positive lesbian, gay, or bisexual identity is particularly difficult and consumes a lot of energy. "Kids can't even wear different blue jeans from the kid next to them," observes Kitty Moran, a psychologist and cofounder of Lesbian and Gay Youth of Rochester, New York. "You think they'd choose to be so different?"[11] "[W]hen you're dealing with young people," continues David, age nineteen, "different means not cool."[12]

Queer kids must endure a forced heterosexual socialization. The guidelines for behavior, ideals, and family expectations are all heterosexual. Imprinting begins early and with a co-occurring antihomosexual message. In contrast, no societal sanctions or opportunities exist to develop healthy sexual/intimate relations.

Fearing disclosure, closeted lesbian and gay teens may monitor their personal behavior, dress, and actions and not stand too close to or be too enthusiastic about same-sex peers.[13] Secretly eroticized friendships may be terminated, and other friendships may be monitored apprehensively to ensure that they are not misunderstood by others.[14] Heterosexual dating may be pursued with the resultant feeling of being a phony or a fake. The price is one's authenticity.[15]

Those who do not conform to the supposed standard are harassed or injured. Majority assumptions overrule individual rights. As Tommy explains, "When I was about . . . fifteen . . . people at school . . . just started calling me faggot this and faggot that, and all of a sudden I don't have any friends anymore."[16]

Reluctance to Use Mainstream Counseling Services

Counselors may be perceived by queer kids to be heterosexist and homophobic. The antihomosexual bias of some professionals may cause them to view a youth as immature with emotional problems concerning sexuality. The common "Oh, it's just a phase" diagnosis reflects this bias as does the prescription for "change" therapies.

In contrast, lesbian and gay services are perceived as more lesbian and gay affirming. Some teens may prefer to confide in peers. As one professional observed, "Although self-chosen peer contacts may seem safe, knowledge by adults carries the threat of labeling and exposure beyond the boundaries desired by the young person."[17] Unfortunately, peers may lack the appropriate knowledge to serve as effective counselors.

Culturally Inculcated Shame, Guilt, and Self-Contempt

Teens are very vulnerable to societal expectations. James Earl Hardy describes Sydney, a tough-acting, black, street kid: "He is a sweet, sensitive young man who, like most gay men, was brainwashed into believing he should be ashamed of who he is."[18] Mike, a white student, explains further,

> No one can fathom what gays, lesbians, and bisexuals face every day of their lives. . . . Imagine how a sixteen-year-old gay teen felt when Pat Buchanan attacked gays at the recent Republican National Convention or when people every day debate the causes of homosexuality.[19]

At every encounter, including counseling, a youth must take into account possible rejection.

Brandon, a young gay Southerner, is caught between the strong sense of family, tradition, and inheritance of family pride and his sexual being, between his Bible-based Baptist upbringing and his sexual desires, and between the societal code of silence and his need to confide and to find support.

I never told them [his parents) what was wrong. . . . I couldn't put them through it. They would be too hurt. It would be embarrassing for them and bring shame on the family.[20]

The result for Brandon is a compartmentalized life of family and church on the one hand and bar friends and anonymous sex on the other.

Cultural Differences

The adolescent process of self-acceptance and self-celebration can be complicated for a queer youth whose racial/ethnic/cultural identity is at odds with being lesbian, gay, or bisexual.[21] A youth may fear that acknowledgment of her or his sexual orientation may result in loss of support from the ethnic-minority community. Quang, a young Vietnamese-American gay man, took strength from his community until his coming out resulted in a rupturing of that bond. "I think that's something people of color encounter a lot," he muses, "the struggle against racism conflicting with the struggle against homophobia."[22] To identify with both ethnic-minority and sexual-minority groups may seem impossible to a youth, thus forcing a choice. Either choice may result in isolation from the other. "Our already tenuous position as Black men [and women] in white America," explains Joseph Beam, African-American author, "is exacerbated because we are gay. We are even more susceptible to the despair, alienation, and delusion that threatens to engulf the entire Black community."[23] In one study, 60 percent of African-American gay men identified principally as black and 40 percent identified as gay.[24] This division has life consequences that go well beyond the labels.

Racist attitudes in the lesbian, gay, and bisexual community are as persistent as homophobia is in some ethnic-minority communities. "In the gay community, I feel that the majority of the white women are prejudiced," states a young African-American lesbian, "just as much as they are in the straight world."[25]

The teen's inner conflict often goes unrecognized. Many ethnic-minority youths feel that they are expected to assimilate into a white gay culture.[26] To be African American, Latino, or Asian American and queer is to straddle a chasm. As a young Asian-American gay male explains, "Caucasian gays don't like gay Chinese, and the Chinese don't like the gays."[27]

Special Needs of Teen Prostitutes

One group of queer kids, teen prostitutes, has special needs. A prerequisite to effective counseling is that it meet their basic and educational needs and provide consistent contact with a nurturing adult.[28] In order to get these teens into counseling, professionals must provide more and effective outreach programs for street hustlers. The goal of restoration of positive self-worth can be accomplished by helping youths clarify their sexual orientation and offering healthy opportunities for ego-enhancing socialization and the development of trust and intimacy skills.

Many street prostitutes have learned not to trust anyone and have become accustomed to sex without intimacy. It may take an especially lengthy period of interaction in order to build trust between a prostitute and a counselor.

EDUCATION OF THE COUNSELOR

Most youth counselors possess a genuine desire to help young people but have little experience helping youth with lesbian, gay, and bisexual issues.[29] Good counselors for sexual-minority youths are comfortable enough with their own sexual feelings not to feel threatened, at ease discussing intimate sexual issues, and truly unbiased.[30] If knowledge truly is power, then counselors can increase their own power for doing good by utilizing the resources of the lesbian, gay, and bisexual community, national organizations, hotlines, and helplines.

Inexperienced counselors may be confused by the novelty of the topic of sexual orientation, by the belief that ignoring "it" will make it go away, and by fear.[31] A counselor must explore her or his own homophobia and educate herself or himself about homosexuality.[32] Each counselor must come to accept those with different sexual orientations before she or he can try to help lesbian, gay, and bisexual youths.[33] Awareness and knowledge are needed before a counselor can develop the skills required for establishing trust with teens.

Although 83 percent of school counselors believe special training is needed to work with sexual minority youths, no training is required.[34] Even liberal, accepting, and well-intentioned counselors are often poorly prepared.[35]

The would-be counselor for queer kids must first acknowledge that this population exists despite official pronouncements to the contrary. The entire human population is not heterosexual and neither is the adolescent population. Not only do sexual-minority youths exist, but they may be sexually active and may identify with the larger lesbian, gay, and bisexual community of which most heterosexual counselors know very little. Acknowledging differences is not enough, however, and a counselor cannot assume that either the developmental patterns or psychological needs for different sexual orientations will be similar.

Counselors who work with lesbian, gay, and bisexual teens must be sensitive to these youth's needs and have explored their own attitudes and biases.[36] The greatest danger exists for queer kids when a counselor is unaware of her or his own personal prejudices. One school psychologist claims that most of the "sexual confused" students he has seen "tend to *even out and get back"* [my italics] to heterosexuality with maturity.[37] The not-so-subtle prejudice is all too evident.

Even a mildly homophobic counselor may be inclined to attempt "change" therapies to help a teen overcome her or his homosexuality. In general, those with less education and less counseling experience are more likely than those with more of both to recommend these regimens.[38] African-American counselors are also more likely to recommend "change" therapies than white counselors. Given the failure of change therapies, such a recommendation is a clear violation of professional ethics and borders on the criminal.

The prospective counselor needs to know about myths and realities surrounding homosexuality, causal theories of sexual orientation, legal implications, the coming-out process, attractions, experiences, self-identification, male and female experiential differences, significant relationship characteristics, disclosure to significant nongays and the need to do so, positive identification as lesbian or gay, vulnerability of lesbian and gay adolescents at the point of disclosure, and high-risk sex and HIV transmission.[39] It is not the lesbian, gay, or bisexual youth who is responsible for educating the counselor; the lines of responsibility clearly run in the other direction. Issues will differ with the individual, race or ethnicity, and the stage of sexual identification. Education might include attending a lesbian, gay, or bisexual event such as a community picnic or fundraiser and meeting sexual-minority adults. It is appropriate for a counselor to question sexual-minority adults in order to develop empathy. Discussions of life experiences, discrimination, and coming out may help a counselor understand the challenges faced by lesbian and gay teens. Initial counseling sessions with lesbian, gay, or bisexual youths might be attended by another counselor or supervisor who has worked successfully in the past and can provide critical feedback.

Obviously, one relatively brief training session for professionals is inadequate.[40] Short exposure may either increase or decrease negative attitudes and homophobia.[41] Resultant changes in attitude are often small and temporary. Effective training should be more extensive and include films, readings, discussion, and role-play. Lesbian, gay, and bisexual youth and adults should be included in such training because of the positive effects for participants of interacting with someone who is lesbian, gay, or bisexual. The most effective training seems to be one that addresses myths, stereotypes, fears and discomfort.[42] Lesbian, gay, and bisexual topics also should be included within discussion of other issues of professional training, such as suicide, homelessness, adolescence, alcoholism, and drug abuse.

The title of counselor or psychologist does not confer objectivity. It is often difficult to step away from societal influences. Exploration of biases includes examining one's knowledge, attitudes, and feelings, and professional preparation. Professionals who are not aware of their own biases and prejudices run the risk of providing less than optimal care when they are face-to-face with a real lesbian, gay or bisexual teen. Such professionals may fix or perseverate on sexual orientation even when that is not a concern for the youth. A counselor may display pity or deny that an adolescent can be lesbian, gay, or bisexual.

Data on prejudice and bias among professionals is often conflicting and difficult to obtain. In some studies, male counselors are more homophobic than females, and in others they are less. As a group, however, psychologists rate lesbians and gay men as less well adjusted than heterosexuals despite the fact that no study has ever found a deficit. Yet, among the helping professions, psychologists are the least prejudiced toward lesbians and gays while social workers are the most prejudiced.[43]

GETTING 'EM IN THE DOOR

There may be a reluctance by sexual-minority students to talk with teachers or counselors. Such students may be unwilling to initiate discussion or to trust the confidentiality of that discussion. "I thought 'I can't trust anyone with this information,'" explained Kimberly, a lesbian student. "You know, teachers talk."[44] Students also worry about teacher or counselor reaction and are especially fearful that their confidences will be shared with their parents.

The prospective counselor or teacher-counselor must "advertise" her or his availability to lesbian, gay, and bisexual students. This can be accomplished if a counselor maintains an attitude of openness toward, acceptance of, and support for diversity and unpopular causes and decisions. In conversations with students and in the classroom, a teacher or counselor can be supportive of women and racial, ethnic, and sexual-minorities and express offense at humor based on stereotypes. Posters that celebrate diversity can be prominently displayed for students to see. "Safe zone" stickers, mentioned previously, can be prominently displayed on doors to classrooms and offices. Reading lists and handouts distributed to students can include some entries on sexual orientation and lesbian, gay, and bisexual issues.[45] These actions will signal students that a person is accepting of differences.[46]

Students also need to know that adults are approachable. Carlton, a gay high schooler lamented, "If she'd [teacher] only have said, 'If you want to talk about anything, you can'—but she didn't."[47] Schenectady, New York High School counselor Christine Augione has a pink triangle on her office wall with the word *ALLY* printed on it."[48]

If all else fails, the prospective counselor might approach students who seem to be experiencing some personal difficulty. Students who are harassed can be invited for a chat. Obviously, soliciting students in this way can be very risky unless a counselor is extremely careful and indirect. Direct confrontation can lead to denial. Conversations might begin with any of the following:

- Your schoolwork seems to be slipping and you haven't been participating in class. Is anything wrong?
- I noticed that some of the other students seem to be getting on your case. Want to talk about it?
- You seem a little out of sorts. I'm always here if you want to talk.
- Is something bothering you that we could talk about? I hope I'm not the problem. You know you can talk to me anytime you want to.
- You look kind of bummed. Being a young adult isn't always so great, but I'm here to listen if you need to talk about it.

Sometimes, all the posters and posturing possible are not enough because a student is just waiting to be asked. As one student put it, "It has to be easier for you to ask than for me to just come out and tell you."[49] Open discussion of relationships and intimacy may signal a teen that it's okay to introduce sexuality.

KEEPING 'EM THERE

Once a student demonstrates a willingness to discuss personal challenges and problems, a counselor must make every effort to enhance the experience and to make it a fruitful one. Counselors must remember the goal of support, set the tone, use nonjudgmental language, use the opportunity to educate, ensure strict confidentiality, appreciate the sexuality of adolescence, foster coping and self-esteem, aid the teen with the process of coming out, and act as a referral source and advocate. In short, counselor and client need to build a mutual relationship.

Keep One Goal Foremost

Stated succinctly, the overall goal of counseling with queer kids is "To provide corrective experiences to ameliorate the consequences of biased socialization."[50] A counselor's task is to help teens decrease internalized homophobia before self-defeating patterns become ingrained.[51]

Counseling should focus on three aspects of the corrective task:[52] (1) facilitating social experimentation, (2) facilitating understanding, and (3) facilitating self-acceptance and formation of a healthy and positive sexual identity. Through social experimentation, a counselor and teen focus on relationships with peers and with family. A counselor guides a teen's decision on how, when, and to whom to disclose her or his sexual identity, and how to cope with the consequences. Understanding is fostered by helping a youth gradually explore her or his sexuality and self-awareness and the advantages and disadvantages of various life decisions. Finally, self-acceptance and a healthy and positive sexual identity are fostered by providing clarity and sense of security, helping a teen avoid feelings of suppression and repression, and by helping her or him cope with societal homophobia and with shame, guilt, and self-contempt. Bill, age eighteen, expresses the ambivalence of many young people:

> I've been having these feelings for other guys for at least twelve years and sometimes I'm OK with them and I feel good about myself. And then other times, well, . . . I hope they'll go away and I deceive myself for awhile but they don't go away. I think about what Mom and Dad would say if they knew. They'd be so hurt and I've already hurt them a lot.[53]

Effective intervention must be based on "becoming." A counselor can help a teen redefine her or his own homosexuality free of narrow, societal constrictions and of self-destructive attitudes.

Set Tone at Onset

Counselors should be comforting *and* comfortable and provide a sense of security. A youth may be reluctant to trust a counselor and may use a smoke screen of nonissues as a test. A counselor will need to be patient and gently move the conversation along with "Did you want to talk about anything in particular today?"

Some youths may need help in establishing and clarifying their concerns. Terms such as *homo* and *lezzie* or *dyke* are tossed off casually by adolescents and it is helpful to explore a teen's understanding of those terms. It is helpful for a youth to be able to see her or his sexuality within the larger context of other interactions and concerns.

It is essential that a counselor ensure confidentiality and state this policy at the onset. A queer kid's concerns about sexuality are not to be shared with parents. A teen has the right to determine when and to whom she or he will disclose sexual orientation.

Counselors should avoid being cavalier. Phrases such as "Doesn't matter to me" convey that sexuality is of little difference. It matters to the youth. A nonchalant attitude by a counselor minimizes a youth's struggle and feelings. For a teen desirous of not confronting her or his sexuality, a cavalier counselor provides an "out." "So I really didn't deal with it," explained Bill, age eighteen. "They gave me an excuse to keep on deceiving myself."[54] Likewise, phrases such as "politically correct," "trendy," or "rebellious" also dismiss the youth's feeling.

Counselors really must listen and resist the temptation to dismiss a youth's feelings as "a phase" or "something that everyone experiences." To deny the validity of an adolescent's feelings is to deny the adolescent as well.[55] Julian, a student, challenged a teacher's assumptions:

> I went to a teacher and told him that I thought I might be gay. He said, no . . . it was just a phase all boys went through. So I asked him if his own children were going through it and he went white and mumbled. . . . So I asked him if he or any of the other teachers remembered going through it and he said he hadn't. . . . So I asked him if all the boys in our class were going through it and he was so embarrassed. I felt sorry for him. But I deliberately pushed him because it was important to me not to be lied to about how I felt about myself.[56]

Although it may seem reassuring to a counselor to say that same-sex attractions are common and temporary ("Oh, everybody feels that way sometimes; it'll pass."), it may create more anxiety for a queer kid who feels otherwise.[57]

It is appropriate for a counselor to explore the way in which a teen decided that she or he is lesbian or gay. It is totally inappropriate for a counselor to question that decision. If a youth is confused, she or he will share this information at the appropriate time. The counselor must not rush in assuming her or his own discomfort to be the adolescent's. Several behaviors may be indicative of a youth's internal struggle and confusion:[58]

1. Stereotypic clothing, mannerisms, and affectations
2. Heterosexual promiscuity
3. Unusually strong interest in sexuality and an often demonstrated misunderstanding
4. References to homosexual experiences of others or to personal experiences in the distant past
5. Distancing from parents with whom the youth was previously close; secretiveness
6. Loss of interest in the other gender by a previously outgoing youth

None of these indicators alone or collectively can be used to identify sexual orientation. They do indicate possible internal struggle about this issue. Other acting out behaviors may also signal a conflict. The cause of such conflict may or may not be sexual orientation and it may be best to let the teen identify the source of conflict.

All too often counselors minimize a teen's same-sex feelings. It is important for counselors to appreciate the great difficulty a youth experiences in even voicing such a concern. Even a heterosexual youth who expresses some concern about same-sex erotic behavior or feelings must display great courage to do so. To dismiss such concerns may serve only to increase anxiety.[59]

An effective counselor is empathic and conveys an acceptance of both the individual teen and of human sexualities.[60] It is important to remember that, most likely, the youth has internalized the negative attitudes of society and will be looking for signs of disapproval in the counselor's behavior.[61] A counselor should discuss sexual orientation within a "developmentally nonpejorative perspective."[62]

It is important to distinguish between abusive or predatory relationships and healthy or beneficial ones. The gender of the partners in a relationship is irrelevant. Caring, loving, respectful relationships are not hurtful. Selfish, violent, exploitive, and impersonal relationships are, regardless of the gender of the partners.

Counselors should meet lesbian, gay, and bisexual teens where they find them psychologically. Individual needs will vary with the process of becoming a self-identified lesbian, gay, or bisexual person. Each teen needs to be reassured that it is okay to be lesbian, gay, or bisexual or to be confused. Tentative exploration and questioning should be encouraged and supported.

Each counselor must be sensitive for internalization of negative attitudes and challenge assumptions and stereotypes about sexuality.[63] Queer kids have many of the same homophobic attitudes as their heterosexual peers.

Finally, an appreciation of adolescent sexuality including experimentation with both sexes is a must for any youth counselor. Counselors should be clear about their definition of homosexuality.[64] All same-sex contact—hugging, kissing, sleeping together, even some erotic behavior—is not homosexual, even among sexual-minority teens. A friend of mine who is a lesbian wants to get a sweatshirt that says "This is NOT a sexual moment" to wear when she is hugging or kissing friends, so that nongay individuals will not jump to conclusions. It is as important not to overemphasize homosexuality as it is not to minimize it.

Use Nonjudgmental Language

Working with sexual-minority youths is not for those unwilling to take risks. Seventy-nine percent of counselors in one study reported working with teens that they thought were lesbian or gay, although most said they would not ask about sexual orientation.[65] In another study, over 60 percent of nonlesbian and nongay professionals working with youths feared a negative reaction to openly addressing the same-sex concerns of these teens.[66] Among lesbian, gay, and bisexual counselors there is a fear that discussion of sexuality would lead to charges of recruiting.

Counselors may be uneasy initially. Such feelings may arise from the novelty of the situation and a counselor's lack of experience and knowledge, from a feeling of helplessness and a desire not to get involved, and/or from an overall fear of sexual issues.[67] Uneasiness should not show and the discussion should be nonjudgmental in nature.[68]

Counselors who attempt to educate queer kids and other students can expect to be challenged. Many adults will feel that such intervention is inappropriate. School board policies may even preclude such intervention, stating that only "change" therapies may be attempted. A counselor's own sexuality may be questioned.[69]

Counselors must become aware of the power of language. It may be helpful to practice saying the words "lesbian," "gay," and "bisexual" so the words do not sound strained or unacceptable.[70] Any hint of discomfort by a counselor will be sensed immediately by a lesbian, gay, or bisexual teen.

Counselors should encourage openness by being matter-of-fact. In this way each student is free to explore her or his feelings and unique experiences free of evaluation.

It is best if counselors make no assumptions about a youth's sexual orientation. A neutral stance may be beneficial until students disclose that they are heterosexual, homosexual, or bisexual. This information will be forthcoming if students are allowed to speak freely. Similarly, counselors can provide a rationale for the questions to be asked and let a teen know that no assumptions are being made about her or him. A series of questions such as the following may be beneficial:

> Have you had sex? With a male? With a female?

Counselors should avoid tag questions that seek agreement and express an opinion, such as "You aren't gay, are you?", or that express a heterosexist bias, such as (to a female) "Do you have a boyfriend?" Questions that overlook sexual orientation imply a lack of concern or caring. For example, a question about birth control methods to a group of students implies that they are engaged in heterosexual behavior. Counselors can inquire about sexual orientation in a "permission giving" manner, as in the following:[71]

> Often young men and women your age are worried about feelings for others of the same sex. Have you ever had these feelings or attractions or worried about them?

This type of question lets the student know that she or he is not alone and that it is acceptable to talk to the counselor about sexuality. Open-ended questions are better than those that couch an answer.[72]

Use the Opportunity to Educate

By being factual and avoiding or correcting stereotypes, a counselor can provide clarity and perspective.[73] A youth's confusion often signals a lack of information. Counselors can help a teen to develop positive qualities through knowledge and to clarify her or his feelings.[74] In turn, this knowledge can be shared with family and friends to correct misinformation.

Although same-sex and other-sex desires are not necessarily good indicators of sexual orientation or later sexual identity, it is also true that sexual orientation is established by puberty for most individuals.[75] Helping a youth distinguish between orientation, behavior, and identity may be a first step toward positive self-identification and celebration. A youth needs to realize that sexual orientation is not a choice, a character flaw, or an illness.

Sexual identity confusion may be explored by gently probing questions. This procedure can help to locate the cause of a teen's concern. It is important that a counselor be comfortable with the questions if she or he hopes to get honest answers and an open discussion. Probing questions might include the following topics:[76]

- Self-perception and self-identity as opposed to labeling by others.
- Amount of discomfort surrounding homophobic jokes and pressure to date the other gender and/or elation surrounding lesbians, gays, or bisexuals in the news and mass culture.
- Ability to separate myth and stereotypes from reality.
- Degree of sexual arousal by both sexes, including masturbation fantasies.
- Extent of initiation and enjoyment of same-sex sexual activity. Sexual behavior and pleasure alone do not signify sexual orientation.
- Frequency of sexual activity with both sexes, and the gender of choice. It is important to remember that adolescents engage in sexual experimentation with both genders.
- Intensity and length of same-sex relationships.
- Future expectations and fantasies about relationships.
- Types of support systems available.

These topics are not definitive and no one topic or combination can be used to signify sexual orientation.

Sexual orientation is very complex and is not determined by having slept with one or even a few members of the same or other sex. By the same token, same-sex erotic behavior is not a prerequisite for sexual identity. Many lesbian and gay youth have no sexual experience but know that their orientation is same-sex.

Helping professionals should create an environment that affirms a youth's identity and fosters identity integration.[77] Integration is facilitated by helping each teen shape her or his own agenda based on individual needs and interests. The approach should be overwhelmingly affirmative. Queer kids need to be helped to explore prejudice and homophobia and to foster an adaptability and resilience to counter the effects of that prejudice. In the process, a professional provides a corrective alternative to homophobia and heterosexism.

A counselor can help a youth avoid premature self-labeling.[78] It is important not to pigeonhole, because attempts at early labeling may actually be at variance with a teen's still-emerging sexuality.[79] Premature labeling superficially resolves identity questions but may increase the youth's anxiety. Labels are just names and do not define who we really are. Letitia, an eighteen-year-old high school senior and accomplished artist, explains,

> First, I'm a person. . . . Second, I'm an artist. And third, . . . I'm a lesbian. But I really don't have any labels for myself. I'm extremely uncomfortable with labels.[80]

There is no need to accept even a self-label unless it fits and only if the owner wants to claim it.

Many youths will want to know, somewhat impetuously, "Am I or am I not." There is no need to rush into an answer. In helping a teen take the long view, a counselor can explain that all of life is full of questions and that along the way many sexual decisions will need to be made.[81] It is all right to wait and to explore one's sexuality slowly.

An adolescent must come to share some of the counselor's accepting and affirming attitudes before she or he can develop a positive self-identity. Counselors might focus on interpersonal relationships and coping skills while gradually exploring aspects of sexuality.[82]

The decision about a label is only one of many. A counselor can help by exploring other decisions, such as establishing and/or maintaining a relationship, moving beyond friendship, expressing love, beginning a sexual relationship, and so on.

A lesbian, gay, or bisexual teen should not self-identify before being ready to own the label. Each youth must determine her or his individual definition of that label. Victor, a bisexual young man, explains, "Self-definition must be respected, because once you let other people start defining who you are and what you are, that's when the game starts being played against you."[83]

Teens who have chosen to self-identify should not be challenged automatically. A counselor would do well to recall that most teens self-identify as heterosexual with no challenge at all from knowing adults.

Similarly, some teens will not resolve their internal conflict over sexual orientation. Resolution may need to wait until a youth is more mature or more independent. Coping, decision-making, and communication skills can be addressed in counseling as future internal conflict resolution tools.[84]

Just providing general coping skills is inadequate. The counselor must help the youth cope with homophobia and stigmatization.[85] The youth may need to overcome victimization, to explore and manage feelings of hurt and anger, and to examine and identify efficient self-protection behaviors to deal with conflict, depression, and peer pressure.[86] Self-esteem and life skills may also be targeted.

Counselors should be extremely honest about high-risk sex. They can provide information on safety and on the importance of privacy. It is best not to try to prohibit same-sex sexual activity, because such prohibition might spark an unintended reaction.

Homosexuality should be discussed in an interesting and informative way, with openness and honesty. Youths will be helped by sexual-minority books in public and school libraries.[87] Counselors can take a lead in ordering or recommending these books.

It may be beneficial for a counselor to explore religious beliefs with a youth. Even if this issue is of little importance to a teen, it may be paramount for the family or become so. Possible avenues of inquiry include:[88]

- Does the youth see herself or himself as a sinner?
- Does the youth feel unacceptable to God?
- Has the youth developed a self-perception as a bad person?

Religious strictures must be viewed in context. Counselors would do well to consult some of the books recommended in the resources chapter. If necessary, counselors can help the teen and family locate accepting and caring religious leaders.

Ensure Strict Confidentiality

The counseling relationship must be based on trust and respect.[89] Standards of confidentiality must be strictly observed in contrast to the disturbing violation of Terry's trust that follows. At age fourteen, Terry told a school counselor that she thought she might be a lesbian. In a panic, the counselor relayed the information to Terry's mother, a friend. The family's response was horrendous and all trust for the counselor by the student was destroyed. The counselor justified her actions with scripture and the desire to save Terry from sin.

Appreciate the Sexuality of Adolescents

Counselors should help youths explore their sexuality. Emphasis should be on feelings, emotions, attitudes, and behaviors, not labels. It is best for counselors to remind themselves that there is a great variety of sexual practices among teens.[90] It may also be helpful for counselors to recall the orientation-behavior-identity paradigm discussed in Chapter 1.

Counselors should provide a rationale and framework for certain feelings, thoughts and fantasies of teens. It is good to remember that although a youth may discuss tolerantly the sexual orientation of others, she or he may be very intolerant of her or his own sexual orientation.[91]

AIDS needs to be discussed openly and candidly. Counselors and teens should discuss potential partners, their selection, and safe-sex procedures. A youth must be impressed with the seriousness of the risk and of ways to reduce it. It is best if a counselor is matter-of-fact in this discussion and thus conveys a nonjudgmental posture. Forthrightness may relieve some of the embarrassment for both participants.

Right or wrong, some gay male youths' self-esteem seems to be related to a large number of sexual relations.[92] Counselors need to recognize this factor and to be certain that sexual relations and safe-sex techniques are explored thoroughly. There is no room for the squeamish here.

Foster Coping and Self-Esteem

In general, demographic factors, such as age, education, and community size, have little effect on self-esteem for lesbians and gay men.[93] Those with the highest self-esteem are involved in the lesbian, gay, and bisexual community, committed to and accepting of homosexuality, and enjoy the support of family and friends.[94] Contrary to conventional wisdom, the status of most teens' same-sex love relationships does not seem to affect self-esteem.[95] Teens do not need love interests to prop up self-esteem but they do need support and contact with others who care.

Among lesbian and gay youths, demographic factors also account for little variation in self-esteem.[96] Positive, confirming attitudes and activism within the lesbian, gay, and bisexual community seemed to result in the highest levels of self-esteem. Those with high self-esteem state that they would not give up their homosexuality even if they had the chance to do so.[97] A positive sense of self-worth and a positive attitude about sexual orientation are linked to good mental health.[98] It is important that counseling emphasize self-acceptance.

Some factors differentiate gay and lesbian youths on self-esteem.[99] Male youth with the highest self-esteem claim to be exclusively homosexual and do not try to pass as heterosexual, although no similar factor is noted among lesbian youth. In contrast, early self-definition as lesbian has a positive effect on self-esteem, while no similar effect is seen among men. Counseling that facilitates denial or emphasizes "change" therapies may have a negative effect on a youth's self-esteem.

Becoming lesbian, gay, or bisexual consists of many small and a few large steps or transitions. Developmental transitions are smoothest when the individual has adaptive skills congruent with the demands of the transition. To delay transition may delay development; to transition prematurely may place an individual at risk.

Labeling can be very frightening. The teen who prematurely identifies as lesbian, gay, or bisexual in a context with few positive role models may adopt stereotypic behaviors as the only available identity. Flamboyancy may evoke a reaction from family and peers. Those without the strength to endure the reaction may be forced to withdraw into themselves. Other teens may react with anger and an in-your-face effrontery. In the first situation, the withdrawn teen needs the support of a caring professional as she or he learns to be more self-reliant and independent and to seek out peer support. In contrast, the angry teen can be helped to channel her or his rage into self-affirming strategies.

The most effective way to aid the development of self-esteem is to interact with the whole person, the whole youth.[100] Youth resent being treated as "the problem" or as someone who needs to be helped or healed. Counselors should avoid pity. Not all of a teen's problems will be related to her or his sexuality.[101] Sexual-minority youths have many of the problems of other adolescents and for many of the same reasons.

The counselor who is lesbian, gay, or bisexual and open about sexual orientation can be especially important as a role model. In contrast, the closeted counselor must decide if and when to disclose her or his sexual orientation to a student in counseling. It is important to consider the mixed message of being closeted while attempting to instill self-acceptance and pride in lesbian, gay, and bisexual youth. A note of caution is needed here: Counselors should avoid social interaction with their clients outside of the therapy situation.

Help Client Prepare for Coming Out

Counselors should proceed cautiously with teens who wish to disclose their orientation.[102] A thorough discussion of the risks and rewards is warranted, including options in case the family expels the teen. Each youth should be helped to explore her or his own reasons for wanting to come out and the possible consequences of that act. The next chapter discusses counseling relevant to the coming-out process.

During coming out, a youth is on an emotional roller coaster of fear, anxiety, euphoria, and possibly despair or release. Each youth will need to decide when and to whom to disclose. It is a very selective, individualistic decision. A youth will need to be supported gently throughout this process.

Act as a Referral Source

A competent counselor is also a referral source when necessary or when unable or unprepared to cope with a situation.[103] The judgmental counselor should refer a queer kid to someone else. After careful research, a counselor can refer a lesbian, gay, or bisexual youth to supportive, caring, knowledgeable, nonjudgmental professionals, including other counselors, psychologists and psychiatrists, and clergy.

It is also appropriate to refer a teen to lesbian, gay, and bisexual organizations, such as youth groups, support groups, and groups with religious affiliations.[104] College student groups can also serve a valuable support function.[105] In general, groups within the sexual-minority community do not focus on psychological adjustment specifically but offer a welcoming environment for self-exploration. Several organizations are listed in the resources chapter.

Be an Advocate

It is not enough to counsel queer kids with problems. Counselors must become proactive in order to forestall the development of these problems before they arise. Thus, counselors can advise the school board on policy decisions, help effect curricular change, and educate faculty and staff on homosexuality and on lesbian, gay, and bisexual youths and their challenges.[106] It is important that faculty training not focus on homosexuality or bisexuality as a "problem" but as a part of development. Mere tolerance is not sufficient; faculty must support and affirm lesbian, gay, and bisexual students if true change is to occur.[107]

Counselors also must confront examples of homophobia personally in the school and community, and in so doing, provide a role model for lesbian, gay, and bisexual youth. On one level, counselors can let it be known that they do not tolerate homophobic remarks. On another, counselors can help homophobic faculty and students explore the basis of their irrational fears and possibly reach an understanding and acceptance of lesbian and gay individuals.

As professionals, school counselors can write to ask professional organizations to which they belong to lobby the APA to delete gender identity disorder (GID) or supposed gender confusion from its list of mental illnesses. Gender-atypical teenagers still are being forced legally to undergo psychiatric treatment and incarceration for GID.

COUNSELING BEYOND THE INDIVIDUAL TEEN

It is appropriate and highly desirable at times to work with others in a youth's environment. These may include the family or a partner. When a youth's problem stems from relational disruption, little progress can be made in counseling without addressing the relationship.

Work with the Family Unit

Most lesbian, gay, and bisexual youths come from heterosexual families. Parents are a powerful influence on self-acceptance. In addition, family involvement in counseling is crucial to a youth's recovery from chemical dependence.[108]

Family support is especially important for the self-esteem of gay youths and slightly less so for lesbian youths.[109] Acceptance by the mother is an important factor for many young males. The number of heterosexual and bisexual friends is also important.

Counselors should work with the family unit if at all possible when counseling sexual-minority youths.[110] Changes in a youth's behavior can result in chaos for the family and provoke resistance. Family preservation therapy is less costly than social services for runaway or homeless lesbian, gay, and bisexual youth.

No counselor should take it upon herself or himself to contact a youth's parents. Parents and siblings should only be welcomed to participate at the invitation of the lesbian, gay, or bisexual teen. Counselors can suggest strongly that parents and siblings be involved but must wait for the sexual-minority teen to agree.

The experience of the parents of lesbian, gay, and bisexual teens may not have prepared them to play a supportive role for their child. Most parents' opinions will reflect the prevailing societal attitudes of nonacceptance. Parental homophobia must be assessed prior to any attempt to have parents take a supportive role in their child's development and reformulate their concept of their child to include a lesbian, gay, or bisexual orientation.

Counselors would do well to accept cautiously—with however many grains of salt—the youth's and family's description of each other's behavior. Both may exaggerate in order to justify their own behavior.

Parents may need to "compartmentalize" as they adjust to and accept their child.[111] In this process, each parent identifies those aspects of their child that still receive immediate approval. Gradually, through counseling, other aspects are discussed and receive approval. Parents are helped to see that their child is no different from before disclosure and to identify those aspects of their child which still receive unconditional approval.

Most parents will panic at the mention of sexual behavior. Initially, it might be best to work on relationships within the family. If there is some precipitating sexual event, counselors do best not to focus on it. For example, Walt's parents seemed to fixate on their intrusion upon him and his best friend making love. Up to that time they claim to have no suspicions about Walt's sexual orientation. His mother would cry and his father become angry when referring to this event, which they did whenever the topic of homosexuality was discussed. When the dust has settled, the "event" can be placed in perspective, although its importance should not be minimized. For a counselor to minimize the event is to discount the feelings of family members.[112]

Family responses will cover a range from shock, through denial, anger, resistance, and grieving, occasionally followed by guilt. Through counseling, families should arrive eventually at acceptance and restructuring of parental expectations. Parents must deal with the dissonance between parental love and responsibility versus societal values. Naturally, there is concern for the happiness and well-being of their child.

Counselors and youths must be prepared for nonacceptance. Not every parent accepts a sexual-minority offspring. Some parents report a sense of alienation from their child and from their previous life. Other options should be explored in the event that a family expels their queer kid.

Acceptance begins when parents begin to come out too. Parents can be referred to support groups, such as PFLAG. Often, the best "cure" is for parents to meet sexual-minority adults and other parents of lesbian, gay, and bisexual teens and adults.

Help Couples Adjust

The loving relationships of queer kids are no more inherently stable or unstable than those of heterosexual couples. On the other hand, the societal pressures on lesbian and gay couples may be enormous. Same-sex couples may also have less experience with relationships and be less socially mature. The nature of loving and the mutual aspects of coupling must be explored by the two individuals with the aid of a counselor.

In addition, sex role behaviors may influence the quality of lesbian and gay relationships. Although sex role behaviors influence all relationships, they may be more intense and more obvious in same-sex relationships. The autonomy, independence, and competitiveness of males may lead to difficulties. The sexual aspects of the relationship may predominate with self-esteem related to perceived sexual performance. Intimacy and mutual cooperation may be sacrificed.

In contrast, the tendency of women to be more intimate may lead to rapid coupling and a loss of autonomy. Dependency may become very strong with little individual independence.

Although sex role behaviors may be overcome, and fulfilling relationships maintained, lesbian and gay youths may need some help overcoming the effects of sex role learning. Lesbian and gay teens can be helped to understand and to appreciate the effect of sex role socialization.[113]

HELPING SUICIDAL LESBIAN, GAY, AND BISEXUAL YOUTHS

Suicidal adolescents are often in crisis. It is important in the initial session to establish a constructive relationship, to encourage a youth to express painful feelings, to discuss the precipitating event(s), to assess and evaluate the extent of impairment and the prognosis, to formulate an explanation of the factors that have prevented resolution of the problem, and to restore cognitive control by helping a youth interpret her or his response.[114] A counselor should demonstrate regard, respect, and an eagerness to help. It is important to avoid embarrassing the teen, shaming her or him, or blaming her or him for the situation. Sufficient time should be allotted for venting painful feelings and discussing the event that prompted the teen to seek help. Through assessment, formulation of a dynamic explanation, and restoration of cognitive functioning, a youth can gain control by understanding her or his response and can begin to identify alternative coping strategies for the future.

Planning and implementing treatment will occur over several counseling sessions. It is important that a queer kid learn coping skills for later use.

CONCLUSION

Research and clinical experience demonstrates that queer kids benefit from two types of information.[115] First, they need accurate and complete information on human sexuality. Second, they need to hear a consistent message of support and of their worth as an individual.

Sexual orientation is only one facet of personality and does not determine value as a person. Unfortunately, the constant drumbeat of condemnation and ridicule regarding sexual orientation can have a very negative effect on one's feelings of self-worth. Proud, young, lesbian, gay, and bisexual women and men, who have explored who they are and have come to a realization of the truly unique and wonderful individuals they are, walk a little taller and speak more confidently. All they need to accomplish this transformation is the support of someone who cares.

Chapter 9

Counseling for Coming Out

I can be honest with the people around me because I'm honest with myself.

Eric, age 21[1]

As mentioned previously, coming out is a process, not a event. In some ways, it is a never-ending process. It is a context in which an individual defines who she or he is, learns coping skills, and matures. Hopefully, each queer kid will be able to self-disclose at her or his own comfortable pace.

When coming out, an adolescent is extremely vulnerable. The situation can be summarized as follows:

> In general, a large part of the problem that adolescents face in coming out can be attributed to their status as minors. They have no mobility, poor access to information, no rights in the matter of sexual preference; and they are also surrounded by peers who are struggling with their own sexuality and enmeshed in the super-conformist and highly antigay world of adolescence. Being minors, they cannot be actively helped by adult gays, which means that one of the major sources of support for gays is not available to them.[2]

In a society that actively despises sexual minorities, coming out is not without its perils. The reaction of others can have important consequences for the development of their self-acceptance.[3] In short, while coming out, a teen is on an "emotional roller coaster" of euphoria, anxiety, and despair.[4] Of particular importance are the reactions of close friends and family. If, when and to whom a youth will disclose are very personal and individual decisions.

A negative reaction can delay the self-acceptance and coming-out process, make it more difficult, or derail it completely.[5] Both self-esteem and sexual behavior may be affected. Teens are extremely vulnerable and still need love and support from their families as they struggle to establish their own identities. In general, the best indicator of individual adjustment is a youth's general mental health prior to coming out.[6] It is crucial, therefore, that other issues of self-identity, self-acceptance, and celebration be addressed prior to discussing coming out.

Counselors can help a youth select to whom she or he will disclose sexual orientation to ensure success. Teens often can predict accurately an individual's response, so a counselor and youth can explore the options and the rationale for selecting certain individuals before disclosure actually occurs. In general, as a youth acquires more positive reactions, she or he is less disturbed by the negative ones.

Recognition of the steps in coming out is helpful to its understanding. Roughly, these steps—explained previously—include self-awareness, same-sex experiences, self-recognition, significant same-sex relationship, disclosure to significant nonlesbians or nongays, and positive self-identification. Counselors should expect individual differences while keeping the larger process in mind. Identity formation, of which coming out is a part, is a lifelong procedure for each individual. In addition to her or his concern for the queer kid, a counselor may also need to provide support and aid to family and friends.

CHALLENGES TO COMING OUT

The daunting task of coming out is made all the more difficult when it begins in adolescence. In addition to the challenges of the coming-out process, teens have several other constraints on their behavior.[7] These include the following:

- Other aspects of identity are also being clarified at this time
- Dependence on families for financial and emotional support
- Lack of good information about sexuality
- Little mobility
- No legal rights or protections for teens who are members of sexual minorities

Counselors must address these constraints while focusing on a youth's coming out.

The overall goal of counseling for a teen who is coming out is the establishment of independence, while keeping close ties to family and friends. In some ways, the struggle for independence is similar to that of other teens, although the sexual-minority adolescent lacks the societal support received by other teens. This deficit, in turn, increases the need for close friends and family.

In order to be successful, an adolescent must possess a "clarity of communication that is deeply rooted in self-esteem and self-awareness."[8] This may be difficult to achieve when a youth is struggling with other issues of self-identity and independence. Counselors and youths should remain mindful of the goal and the challenges as they address issues such as motivation, when and to whom to disclose, options and supports, and the need for patience.

Examining Motivation

It is appropriate for a counselor to begin the coming-out discussion by describing the possible ramifications and by examining with a youth her or his personal motivation for desiring to self-disclose.[9] Honesty is not always the best policy, and each queer kid must weigh the consequences of a partial lie versus possible rejection. Occasionally, a sexual-minority teen will be reluctant to come out to parents for fear of "hurting" them. Counselors can help a youth understand that most parents would prefer the pain of knowledge to deception and a unauthentic relationship. Ultimately, a youth must be true to self.

Some adolescents will be motivated to come out in order to strengthen their self-acceptance. This can be self-defeating and destructive. Self-acceptance should not be contingent on parental approval or approval by others. A teen who is coming out must be operating from a position of strength, not weakness. The teen who is not is apt to begin her or his coming-out disclosure with "Mom and Dad, I have something terrible to tell you."[10]

In a similar fashion, coming out is not a weapon to be used in anger. Coming out is not a way to settle the score, to embarrass, or to tease. Some queer kids will be angry at their families for having raised them as a heterosexual offspring. A youth may feel that her or his entire upbringing was an inherent demand to be what she or he is not. All such anger should be resolved before coming out to the affected individuals.

A healthy coming out is motivated by caring and by a desire to be open.[11] It is a motivation grounded in strength, not weakness. The resultant coming-out statement might sound something like "Mom and Dad, I want to share something very significant because I care about you and you're important to me."

Assessing to Whom, How, and When

At the Hetrick-Martin Institute, counselors try to help teens realistically appraise the risks in coming out. "There are a lot of young people who are closeted in our community," explains Frances Kunreuther, executive director, "and we don't necessarily encourage them to come out if that's the way they need to survive."[12] Instead, counselors complete a danger assessment to determine whether it is safe for teens to come out. In addition to discussing motivation, such an assessment should target individuals to whom a youth desires to come out and estimate their likely reaction. A realistic discussion should be forthcoming and include exploration of possible harassment and physical violence, alternative living arrangements, available support, future plans, and revision of the teen's plan.

Individual parents should not be told unless the youth is secure with her or his sexual identity and has a good relationship with that parent.[13] All families are not alike and will not respond in the same manner. A teen must be helped to appraise her or his family realistically and to avoid self-blame for creating this "problem." A counselor can probe and facilitate discussion by asking some of the following questions:[14]

- Do your parents (friends, siblings) want to know? Are they intimately involved in your life?
- Do your parents (friends, siblings) need to know? Is it better to keep it to yourself for the time being?
- Are your parents (friends, siblings) asking? If so, how?
- Are your parents actively avoiding any possibility that you have same-sex attractions?
- Have they ignored all of your hints so far?
- Do you need to tell both parents? If not, which one should you tell first? Should you tell your parents (friends, siblings) separately or together? Who should you tell first?
- Are you aware that acceptance may change over time? Although your parents (friends, siblings) may not be too accepting at first, this situation may change for the better if we work at it.
- What are the best ways to tell your parents (friend, sibling)? Is there a best time? A youth should be helped in assessing and predicting the reactions of others.

A rule of thumb is that the better the relationship between a youth and the other person, the better the reaction by that person. Families that possess good communication skills and are loving, nurturing, and supportive should respond in kind. Always open and supportive, Jen's parents cried when she came out, but through their tears they said they loved her and were proud of her.

A family's or friend's overall attitude toward sexual minorities is also an important factor in gauging their possible reaction. If unsure, a teen can introduce the topic into conversation in a general way. The topic can be initiated by referring to a talk show, TV or movie character, magazine article, or current event.

Some teens will need a strong dose of reality when assessing relationships, especially among friends. It may be best for a teen to proceed cautiously if a friend or sibling is very conforming or a sibling too immature, or a parent excessively demanding, intolerant, rigid, neglectful, status conscious, sexually repressive, or critical.

Good coming outs do not just happen. They take planning and practice. A counselor should help a youth prepare and rehearse coming out and be ready for the questions that will follow disclosure.

Most queer kids will also need to be helped to appreciate the feelings of others to whom they intend to self-disclose.[15] The revelation may be a shock to many potential targets and it is important that a teen express herself or himself without causing further discord. Through role-playing, a teen can learn to come out while avoiding sarcasm, flippancy, and/or angry remarks. A counselor can help a youth stress the positive aspects of being lesbian, gay, or bisexual and of coming out. A lesbian, gay, or bisexual adolescent needs to come out in a manner that is sensitive to the feelings of the listener. Coming out is not an "Oh, by the way, . . . " phenomenon and a youth should be prepared to discuss the topic and to answer questions. Role-playing can put a youth in charge, changing the coming-out process to a proactive rather than reactive experience. Potential scenarios and questions should be discussed and rehearsed. A counselor can help a teen decide the comfort level of certain types of questions, which ones to answer, and which ones to decline.

The *when* of coming out is just as important as the *to whom* and the *what*. In general, it is best to disclose in private when sufficient time exists for questions and discussion. Counselors can help teens identify the best times for each particular relationship in which they wish to come out.

Some queer kids will be "outed" by others, either through direct confrontation or rumor. For example, parents may learn about their child's sexual orientation from other sources. If so, a family breach may result. When outed, a teen may find it very difficult to discuss her or his sexual orientation because the family may be very emotional or embarrassed about hearing this information from someone else and the lesbian, gay, or bisexual teen may be unprepared to discuss the subject in a confrontative manner. A good counselor can help diffuse emotions and explore options by working with family members individually and collectively.

Exploring Options

Any counselor who does not explore the worst possible scenario with a queer kid is doing that kid a disservice. A teen needs to be helped to examine the worst possible reaction of each individual and to discuss possible ways in which to deal with that reaction. Being disowned when one is a financially dependent high schooler could be devastating. Nick was told in the morning to be gone when his parents returned from work. Jeff was handed his coat and a few dollars by his stepfather and told to leave immediately. His mother remained in the background and said nothing.

Accompanying each worst-case scenario must be a alternative plan. A counselor should help a lesbian, gay, or bisexual teen identify other means of financial support, support groups and other sexual-minority teens, and alternative housing arrangements. Maria's counselor helped her realize that her grandmother could provide an alternative living arrangement.

Most parents, friends, and siblings will not respond catastrophically. For most, there will be a reaction of mild shock or recognition followed by a period of adjustment during which most individuals will accept the new information either grudgingly or willfully. Unfortunately, some individuals will not be able to reconcile their image of their child, friend, or sibling with this new information. Perhaps Aaron Fricke, one of the first high schoolers to take a same-sex date to his prom, offers some consolation: "if they [his parents] rejected me merely because I was gay, then I would . . . realiz[e] that my parents were good people but were horribly misled."[16]

Most teens will need counseling in order to cope with all forms of rejection. Negative responses may come in many forms. Table 9.1 includes some common negative responses and possible replies. In addition to learning various replies, a teen will need support to cope with the effects of these and other remarks and actions.

Some families will practice scapegoating. Occasionally, parents and siblings, and even the sexual-minority youth, will hold homosexuality responsible for all other family problems. In counseling, it is important to distinguish sexual orientation problems from family or parent-teen problems.[17] It is not fair or healthy for the queer kid to have an internalized notion that she or he has caused "the problem."

Exploring Supports

Youth support groups are especially important when coming out, especially when coming out to parents. The potential hazards of coming out to parents can be offset by a peer support group.[18] Each counselor should have a readily available resource list of such groups, along with supportive clergy, temporary "shelters," and phone and on-line services.

Counseling Patience

Although a queer kid may be bursting to come out and to share herself or himself, it may be best to counsel patience. The odds against success

TABLE 9.1. Responses to Common Negative Reactions to Coming Out

---

How do you know? You're so young. You haven't even had sex yet, have you?

> You're right. I'm just a teenager, but didn't you know you were *hetero*sexual when you were a teenager? You don't have to have sex to know who you're attracted to.

Are you sure?

> I've known for some time that I am a lesbian. I have been attracted to women since I was _____ years old. I've wanted to discuss it with you for a long time. I've thought about it a lot, and yes, I'm sure.

It's just a phase. You're not gay!

> I've known I'm gay for a long time. It's not a phase. Heterosexuals do not go through a phase when they believe they are homosexuals. I'm gay.

You're just doing this for attention (or to get even with us)!

> There are lots of ways to get attention other than being bisexual. Besides, I told you I was sharing this information with you because I love you and want you to be part of my life.

Where did we go wrong?

> You didn't go wrong because *there is no wrong*. You can't make someone gay. I've been gay for as long as I can remember.

How could you do this to the family? It'll kill your grandfather!

> I didn't do anything to hurt anyone. I'm sharing a very personal part of who I am, not what I did. There is no reason for Gramps to know unless you want me to tell him.

This is so embarrassing!

> It's not embarrassing to me and it *is* about me. It's who I am.

You're ruining your life. You'll be alone and unhappy.

> Being *hetero*sexual does not ensure happiness or fulfillment. Neither does being gay. If I want to have a full life I'll have to work at it like everybody else. Having a loving, supportive family can be a first step.

Did that _____ (Jones boy/girl, queer teacher, new neighbor) do this to you?

> No one can make you a lesbian. It's who you are.

We'll get counseling to change you!

> I don't need to change. I'm perfectly happy as I am. Besides, change therapies have never been clinically proven to work. We might all go to counseling to talk about our feelings.

Call the priest; he'll know what to do.

> I don't wish to get into a religious argument, although I'd like to discuss religion and sexual orientation at another time. I am as God made me.

I saw it on the TV. It's dirty and disgusting! Besides, it's a sin.

> It is only a sin if you take Bible verses out of context. I'd be glad to share some books with you if you're interested in the topic.

---

may be too high. Gary has decided to wait until after college because he believes that his parents might withdraw all financial support.

Patience may also be needed with parents and others who may need time to accept the new knowledge that an individual is lesbian, gay, or bisexual. Erna, a young Navajo woman who is lesbian, cautions, "[A] lot of young Indian girls . . . expect . . . changes in a short period of time, and you can't . . . , especially of your family."[19] She adds that patience is the most important thing. A well-prepared and self-assured youth can help others through the process.

In addition to counseling patience, counselors can educate a sexual-minority teen in the acceptance process that accompanies the coming-out process. Each queer kid should realize that there may be pain for others and a period of adjustment. Both the teen and her or his family need to grieve the loss of the old identity—even if it was false—before they can celebrate the new one. For the individual lesbian, gay, or bisexual youth this is a two-step process of self-acceptance followed by grieving the loss of the old self.[20] Many of the losses are attributable to society: the potential loss of friends, job security, legal protections, and the privileges of heterosexual married couples. When an individual has dealt with these losses and understands the practical problems associated with adopting a lesbian, gay, or bisexual identity, then she or he is able to come out and interact with others from a position of strength.

COUNSELING OTHERS

Coming out can be a very positive and self-affirming process. Success is not guaranteed and is highly dependent on the responses of others. When a youth comes out, the parents, siblings, and friends must do the same by yielding all their previously held expectations of heterosexuality. The acceptance process, discussed more fully in the next chapter progresses from disbelief and denial through anger and guilt to acceptance.

Those with whom a youth shares should feel honored that they are respected and trusted enough by the youth. Julio, who came out to his mother in high school, explains,

> [N]ot being out made my interaction with her [his mother] very hard because I couldn't be honest. She was the person I'd always gone to. She's my best friend. So I thought, if I want to communicate with her, I have to come out.[21]

Counselors can help others to see the esteem in which they are held by the queer kid who has come out to them. Table 9.2 lists some reminders for the

TABLE 9.2. Things to Remember When Someone Comes Out

- Thank the outed person for being so trusting and honest with such personal information.
- Congratulate the outed person for knowing herself or himself so well.
- State that the relationship will not change.
- Reassure that you still feel as close to the outed person as before.
- If uncomfortable, say so, and ask for time to adjust.
- Get informed.
- If you can't accept the fact that this person is lesbian, gay, or bisexual, at least be mature enough to recognize that it's your problem for which you need help and to state this.
- Confront homophobic comments and jokes by others.

---

person to whom a queer kid comes out. Shawn, a sixteen-year-old white female, had very negative feelings about homosexuals until her best friend, a gay teen, came out to her and helped her realize that her discrimination was based on ignorance. She concludes that "We reject that which we do not understand . . ."[22]

Self-disclosure is an indication of the importance of the relationship for a lesbian, gay, or bisexual youth. It is a courageous act from a teen who may be terrified at the thought of losing the love and support of the person to whom she or he is disclosing.

Denial and nonacceptance can alienate a queer kid. Parents can destroy the bond with their child. If angered, an alienated youth may go off to solve the dilemma alone, a process she or he may be too immature to accomplish.

Acceptance by parents may be especially difficult because they may consider their children to be an extension of themselves.[23] Poor communication, parental grief and/or anger, and other unresolved family issues can complicate a situation already made difficult by religious beliefs, homophobia, misinformation, and/or stereotyping. Parents may view sexual orientation as the source of all family problems and focus their anger on it.

Parents and other family members and friends must be helped by counselors to acknowledge their anger. Without such recognition, they may be closed to information and insights that can foster realistic and genuine understanding.[24]

Parents and siblings also must shed their prejudices and apprehensions about homosexuality. They must learn to deal with realities, not react to stereotypes. They can be educated by reading gay-related materials, such as those published by PFLAG. It may be best to avoid bar publications or explicit novels. The goal is not to shock but to educate. Suggested readings are presented in resources chapter.

Some parents report that they have real fears for their child in a hostile world. This fear must be acknowledged, discussed and placed in perspective while the process of understanding and acceptance continues. All of life has risks, but it must still go forward.

Finally, acceptance by parents, friends, and siblings can not be selective. Parents, friends and siblings can not accept only a part of an individual while denying another. Philip, a young gay male, has the following advice for his mother: " . . . if she wants to be part of my life, she has to be part of all of it, not just the parts *she* likes."[25]

CONCLUSION

Counselors should be careful not to push a youth to disclose until she or he is ready. Coming out is an ongoing process in which the individual must decide when the appropriate comfort level for disclosure to others has been reached. A teen does not need to share with everyone.

Coming out can be liberating for the individual and for her or his family. As the family members change their perceptions and begin to understand, they come to know a lesbian, gay, or bisexual teen better and to share more fully her or his life.

Chapter 10

Parental Acceptance

But the greatest of these is love.

I Corinthians, 13:13

For many parents, the acceptance of a lesbian, gay, or bisexual child is an act of unconditional love. For others, it is a fatalist acceptance of the way things are. For still other parents, it is a celebration of their child whose sexual orientation is but one facet of her or his individuality. Unfortunately, all too often through nonacceptance, parents lose the special bond they have with their child. Without a doubt, the first three options—really knowing and understanding one's child—seem difficult at first but they are the most rewarding.

It is important for the parents of queer kids to know that they are not alone. It is estimated that there are 20 million parents of lesbians and gay men, even more if we count the parents of bisexuals.[1] Books, support groups, and counselors can offer advice and help.

Once parents become aware of their child's sexual orientation, most require some period of adjustment. Even a very liberal, loving, accepting professional and friend admitted to me that there was some sadness, fear, and a short period of recrimination before she accepted her son's gayness. She was sad because her son would be hated for his sexual orientation and fearful that he might encounter hostility. To her credit, two months after his coming out to her she attended her first gay pride march with my partner and me.

Parents may become so absorbed by their own feelings initially that they neglect to communicate their continuing love to their lesbian, gay, or bisexual child. It is imperative that parents convey this love and express their feelings honestly. Parents should be open, especially if their child's sexual orientation makes them uncomfortable. It is okay to ask for time to adjust. It is not necessary for parents to rush their acceptance, although any delay should be of reasonable length and should allow for continued growth. Silent "holding patterns" convey nonacceptance. As mentioned in Chapter 9, parents may experience a type of grieving. They must remember, however, that their child is still the same person as before, only now as parents, they know their child even better.

Several authors have offered suggestions to foster parental acceptance of a lesbian, gay, or bisexual child and a potential partner or lover and to aid parents with disclosure to others.[2] These will be presented in the following sections. A short version is presented in Table 10.1.

ACCEPTANCE OF A LESBIAN, GAY, OR BISEXUAL CHILD

To some extent, we all need the approval of others. Consistent, unqualified acceptance by others is important for self-validation and self-approval. For the child who is stigmatized by peers and by society, parental acceptance becomes especially important. Family support and self-acceptance help to moderate the effects of victimization.[3] In contrast, parental rejection leaves a teen that much more vulnerable.

Unfortunately, damage to a child's self-worth may begin well before she or he becomes aware of sexual feelings. Negative comments about sexual minorities by parents or other adults are stored away and become part of the psychological baggage of lesbian, gay, and bisexual teens. It can only be hoped that parents will avoid reproachful comments, and if they do not, that they will cease to do so when they suspect that their child may be lesbian, gay, or bisexual. Although *fag, dyke,* and *lezzie* may have little meaning for a young child, explains Mitzi Henderson of the Federation of Parents, Families, and Friends of Lesbians and Gays (PFLAG), "When they discover what it means and that they indeed might be gay, it is very threatening."[4] Children who hear hate speech directed at ethnic and racial minorities learn to hate those groups. Queer kids who hear hate speech directed at sexual minorities learn to hate themselves.

Once a youth's lesbianism, gayness, or bisexuality is known, she or he will be less likely to develop emotional or behavioral problems if the family is supportive. The healthiest attitude for the parent of a lesbian or gay youth can be stated as follows:

> There is nothing to accept. You are my child. This is who you are and I love you.

The story of Rachel, age sixteen, and her mother is illustrative. As she began to disclose to her mother and fearing the worst, Rachel began to cry. The more she tried to speak, the more she wailed.

TABLE 10.1. The *Do's* and *Don'ts* of Parental Acceptance

Do . . .
• Give consistent, unqualified acceptance.
• Practice saying, "There is nothing to accept. You are my child. This is who you are and I love you."

• Have a welcoming home well before children even consider sexual orientation.
  Positive or neutral comments about lesbians, gays, or bisexuals.
  An established home atmosphere of tolerance.
  Speaking out against intolerance for all minorities.

• Congratulate the child on her or his honesty and trust.
• Respect individual privacy.
• Recognize that sexual orientation is NOT a choice or a lifestyle any more than handedness is.
• Focus on the reality and the future rather than on the past and what might have been.
• Talk honestly to, not at, a lesbian, gay, or bisexual child.
• Leave discussions of sexual behavior for calm, comfortable sessions, free of emotion. Let the teen decide how much to disclose.
• Use the terminology that the teen prefers. Practice saying the words so they don't stick in the throat and denote discomfort.
• Keep sexual orientation and sexual behavior in perspective.
• Educate yourself in order to counter stereotypes and to allay fears of the unknown.
• Talk to professionals.
• Offer professional counseling for the teen if she or he desires it.
• Seek out tolerant religious organizations, groups, or denominations.
• Read books and pamphlets on homosexuality and bisexuality.
• Contact Parents and Friends of Lesbians and Gays (PFLAG).
• Call lesbian, gay, and bisexual hotlines with questions.
• Grow and learn.
• Celebrate the child's sexual orientation.

TABLE 10.1 (*continued*)

Avoid . . .
• Reproachful comments and terms such as *fag, dyke,* and *lezzie.*
• Snooping for proof.
• Overreacting and responding with physical assaults or expulsion from the home.
• Denial that belittles a child.
• Comments such as—
"It's just a phase," "You'll outgrow it," or "What about all those girl-friends?"—that devalue a youth's sense of self.
"Oh, you're just trying to be different" or "What is this, the new cool thing to be?"—that devalue the child's experience.
"How do you know if you haven't even had sex yet?"—that may lead to unsafe sexual practices.
"You were always such a good boy" or "You were always such a loving girl"—that may backfire or cause a reaction.
"Why can't you just be yourself?"
"I know you'll have a lonely, miserable life."
• The "Blame Game."
• Shifting the responsibility for adjusting to the revelation of having a lesbian, gay, or bisexual child to the child.
• Punishment or abandonment that can alienate a teen and damage the child-parent relationship.
• Asking leading questions about sexual behavior.
• Placing unrealistic and/or punitive restriction on the youth for her or his "own good" or "best interest."
• Counseling by professionals or religious leaders who offer the unrealistic promise of change in the child's sexual orientation.

"Mom?"

"Yes, Rachel. Go ahead. You can tell me anything."

"Mom." Tears rolled down my face. "Mom, I'm . . . "

"Go ahead, honey; it's okay."

"Mom . . ." I took a deep breath and decided this was it. "I'm a . . . a . . . a . . . lesbian. " I cried again.

"Go ahead, honey. Tell me the rest. You can trust me."

"Mom, that's it. I'm a lesbian."

"So why are you so upset?"

"I thought you would be upset. . . . "

Mom began to chuckle as she surrounded me with a hug. "I'm so proud of you." A tear rolled down her cheek. "You're my daughter and I love you. I will always love you, no matter what you are. . . . As long as you're happy, I'm happy."[5]

Few parents respond in this manner on first learning that their child is lesbian or gay, but they could. Hopefully, parents will arrive at this place after searching their own feelings and talking openly with their child. "Of course she [her mother] has had to do some growing and information gathering on the subject," explained a young woman, "but she has never hesitated in her support and love for me."[6] The first reaction is often parental shock at the realization that they don't know their child as well as they previously believed. For most parents, acceptance and support will add new understanding to their meaning of unconditional love.

A queer kid needs to feel that she or he will be welcomed by parents. When Trent came out to his mom, she surprised him with her response: "That's nice; at least you can be comfortable with yourself now."[7] A welcoming home is not difficult to establish. Positive or neutral comments made by parents following news stories or features about lesbians, gays, or bisexuals can help establish an environment for safe disclosure. An established home atmosphere of tolerance and speaking out against intolerance for all minorities is also important. Finally, all family members need to experience the three words "I love you" frequently.

Several methods of disclosure exist for a lesbian, gay, or bisexual youth but it is important that she or he feel empowered by the process, not humiliated or distressed. When a teen has become secretive and aloof, parents, suspecting the worst, usually become concerned and often are relieved to find out what is bothering their child.

Some parents sense that their child is "different" before she or he comes out to them. In this situation, parents should avoid snooping for proof but should offer an open environment in which disclosure is possible. For one fifteen-year-old female, parent-child trust was damaged before she had a chance to tell her parents about her feelings. As she relates, "I overheard my Mom tell my Dad that she thought I was a lesbian because of what she read in my diary."[8] All family members, especially adolescents, need to feel that their privacy is respected and that they, in return, are to respect the privacy of others.

It is not uncommon for a parent to have varied emotional responses when learning of a child's same-sex attractions. Initial parental responses vary from disbelief to anger, denial, and grief. Most parents are heterosexual and operate from a heterosexist point of reference. They may become angry, sad, or depressed, or may deny the veracity of their child's statements. "I felt a little sad when she did tell me," confesses one mother. "I felt it could cause her pain and grief as time went on."[9]

When parents first learn of their child's homosexuality, they may respond with shock and disbelief. If the goal is to maintain family ties, then parents must do what is best for their child. Parents must be careful not to overreact and respond with physical assaults or expulsion from the home. "I came out to my parents just after high school," explains Tristan, age nineteen. "I was supposed to go to this great Ivy League school but they pulled [the] funding.[10] Danny's mother slapped him repeatedly for refusing to recant his admission of homosexuality. When he raised his hands to defend himself, his father mistook Danny's actions as aggressive and ordered him out of the house. He lived with a friend's family until he finished high school. Blake was evicted from his home at age sixteen when his father found a gay-oriented magazine in his room. Homeless and in need of money, he began to hustle which, in turn, led to crack use and auto theft. "If my family had been different about it [his sexual orientation] . . . ," he explained, "I wouldn't have gone through all the bad things I've gone through."[11] Even nonviolent but overly emotional responses may overwhelm a teen with fear and humiliation, resulting in leaving the home or in self-destructive behavior.

Within hours or days, shock and disbelief usually coalesce into denial. Believing that their child's homosexuality is temporary or an aberration, parents may respond in a number of ways. They may insist that the whole event is entirely normal development or just a phase, pray for change, have their child attempt change therapy, demand that their child put such notions out of her or his head, and/or restrict their child's interactions with the supposed saboteurs of heterosexuality. After a stormy coming out to her mom, Lee, a lesbian high school junior, pronounces her mother "way out there in mother denial land."[12] Some teens will recant or go along with parental denial in an ill-fated effort to protect the parents. This action only prolongs denial. Parents must be careful not to coerce such self-denials from their children. It is pointless and demeaning to a teen for parents to attempt to interest her or him in members of the other sex. The "Oh, I met the most handsome boy from your school today" routine will probably result in angering the daughter to whom it is directed. Homosexual exploration by heterosexuals does not result in them "changing" to homosexual. Why should the reverse be true?

Comments such as "It's just a phase," "You'll outgrow it," or "What about all those girlfriends?" should also be avoided. These phrases devalue a youth's sense of self. Many gay and lesbian teens "experiment" with other-sex erotic behaviors. Having had a girlfriend does not prove that a young man was once heterosexual.

Parents also are advised to avoid the "Oh, you're just trying to be different" or "What is this, the new cool thing to be?" Being homosexual is not chic in America's high school today. No one consciously decides to belong to a stigmatized group.

Given the lack of knowledge of most adults concerning sex, parents may confuse sexual orientation with sexual behavior. This confusion leads to questions such as "How do you know if you haven't even had sex yet?" This type of challenge can lead some teens to become less cautious and to engage in unsafe sexual practices just to prove that they are lesbian or gay. To please their parents, other teens will engage in equally risky heterosexual behavior that can lead to pregnancy or to sexually transmitted diseases.

Rigid parents may remain in denial but usually it gives way to anger and guilt as they attempt to find a cause for the persistent homosexuality. Potential targets of parental wrath may include friends, teachers, the media, and support groups. Often, in an attempt to deny the depth and longevity of their child's sexual orientation, parents will use anger to cover their own guilt for not recognizing the truth earlier and trying to counteract it. The fact that sexual orientation is not caused by others is usually lost on parents. Anger and blame may be directed by one parent at the other and at supposed failings. In the end, blame, in the form of "I told you you should have . . . " or "Why didn't you listen to me when I said to . . . " is destructive for all involved.

Parents should avoid the "Blame Game." It is counterproductive and can damage other family relationships. Parents often focus the blame on themselves, their child's friends, other adults, or their child. "I did some self-examining when I first found out," explains one father. "I thought about what really did happen, what was it I did that might have had an effect on this."[13] Sandra Bayne, mother of a gay son, continues, "We began to ask ourselves the guilt-based question, 'What did I do wrong?' Clearly we had failed and he was some how defective."[14] No one makes someone lesbian, gay, or bisexual. Certainly, parenting practices do not cause homosexuality. Still, as Barbara, the mother of a lesbian adolescent, explains, "I did have this feeling that somehow I'd failed my kids, there was something I hadn't done that maybe I could have."[15] The result may be wild swings in parental practices as parents attempt to correct their supposed failings. Joe's mother began serving more meat and his father kept inviting him to "shoot some hoops." Stacey's family—previously casual churchgoers—began forced weekly attendance.

Trying to place blame is a vestige of the old myth that sexual orientation is a choice. Its use as a calculated lie by the religious right and its pairing with the term *lifestyle* serves only to confuse and does a huge disservice to lesbian and gay teens and their families as they struggle to accept revelations of a homosexual identity. What "family value" is served here?

It is especially important that parents not blame their child for being lesbian or gay. People are as they were created. While some guilt over causality may linger, the guilt from a parent's negative response to their lesbian, gay, or bisexual youth is reportedly even stronger and more long lasting.[16]

Likewise, it is best to avoid comments such as "You were always such a good boy" or "You were always such a loving girl." The unspoken part of this statement is " . . . and now you're not." It is quite possible that the youth recognized early that she or he was different and compensated in other ways, such as becoming the perfect child. Stigmatized by society, some lesbian, gay, and bisexual kids become "ideal" children for fear of parental rejection.[17] Reaping scholarship after scholarship, Eric, age twenty-one, did whatever possible to please his parents and "to balance out the . . . horror of being gay."[18] Even if this is not the case, the child has not changed, she or he is still "good," still "loving." As the clergyman father of a gay son observed, "He was still the same child we had loved all along."[19] All that has changed is a teen's increased desire to be more honest.

A similar bit of parental advice is "Why can't you just be yourself?," as if a queer kid is acting gay for the sake of being different or is acting some part. This advice can be confusing both for the youth who truly feels lesbian, gay, or bisexual and for the one who feels very ambivalent. "I didn't know how to be myself," recalls Julian, a young gay man, "I didn't know what that was."[20] Heterosexual programming and a homosexual orientation can be difficult to reconcile.

Upon learning any previously unknown truth about an offspring, it is natural for parents to feel a sense of loss and an undermining of their dreams and aspirations. Barbara, the mother of a young lesbian, explained,

> I felt real estranged, like, Who is this person? I thought I knew her. And obviously I didn't know her at all.[21]

A common feeling of loss surrounds the issue of grandchildren. "[D]id this mean that she would give me no grandchildren?," asks a father. "My egocentric feelings seemed to come out first."[22] The idealized heterosexual family headed by the parents has been lost. Loss is often followed by a grieving for what is no more. It is helpful for parents to remind themselves that there are no guarantees in life that any child will fulfill a parent's dream. In addition, parents need to remind themselves that their hopes and dreams are not dead, just modified. Parents must make a choice to focus either on the reality and the future or on the past and what might have been. The latter can never lead to a happy, healthy adjustment.

Anger, guilt, and the futile search for the cause of a child's sexual orientation follow in the wake of heterosexism. Everyone is not heterosexual until adulthood when a few are corrupted into homosexuality. Sexual orientation of all types—hetero, bi, and homo—probably begins in the womb and is formed in the early years of infancy and toddlerhood.

Anger may become projected as a parental concern for the supposed dismal future that a child will face. Even expressions of genuine concern can result from displaced anger, guilt, or loss. Often parents state that they " . . . only want my son [daughter) to be happy and not alone." The underlying assumption is that lesbian and gay adults are neither. This is not true. Most lesbians and gay men lead happy, fulfilling lives with family and friends and are very content with their sexual orientation. When problems arise, they are frequently the result of societal reactions external to the individual. One mother sensed this when she explained:

> I was concerned for his happiness. . . . We knew about the criticisms, discrimination, and harassment of gay men. We didn't want that for our child.[23]

Karl's mother worried that his life might be doubly difficult because he was African American and gay. He assured her that he had inherited survival skills from the family. She is one of his best friends, he admits, and ". . . she understands some of the oppression that I . . . face in being twice a minority (and twice blessed)."[24]

For parents who get beyond anger and guilt, acceptance usually follows. Acceptance does not equate with celebration, and some parents, especially those with fundamentalist Christian beliefs, may continue to view their child as sick or immoral and extremely unhappy. Parental support may be withheld. That they are the main contributors to their child's unhappiness is lost on them. Given the generally negative attitudes of society toward lesbians and gays, parental love, acceptance, and support are all the more important in ensuring happiness. In general, parents who are more knowledgeable of homosexuality, obtain more accurate information, and trust their own understanding of their child, are better able to reestablish family relationships.[25]

The stigma and accompanying guilt that a teen may experience can also be experienced by parents. "Even though . . . I knew that's the way it was, that she was a lesbian, I felt guilty," a mother confessed. "I felt other people weren't going to love her because of what she was."[26]

The responsibility for adjusting to the revelation of having a lesbian, gay, or bisexual child must not be shifted to the youth. "I would change my sexuality if I could," states eighteen-year-old Kyle reflectively, "because I don't like hurting people I love."[27] The burden is misplaced squarely on Kyle's shoulders. Parents must educate themselves and begin the process of acceptance.

Punishment or abandonment does nothing but alienate a teen and damage the child-parent relationship. For Derek, the hostility at home became unbearable, culminating in his eviction. Reflecting, he remarks, "At the time I needed my parents the most, they were very distant and unwilling to help."[28] Mike, a handsome, athletic nineteen-year-old who was thrown out by his parents, jogs to their house to see his younger brothers and sisters. His parents, avid churchgoers, will not acknowledge him and absent themselves when he arrives.[29]

Some parents will feel a need to strike back because their child has disappointed or hurt them in some way. Although difficult, a parent's struggle to accept pales in comparison to the process their child is completing. Parents do well to remember who is the child and who is the adult. Our children need our love, support, and guidance. They are not little automatons who do a parent's every bidding.

Once calm enough to listen, parents need to talk honestly with, not at, their child. It is important to listen to the answers asked for, even if these answers are not what a parent wants to hear. Discussions of sexual behavior are best left for later, more comfortable sessions. Concentration on sexual behavior tends to negate the many other facets of a teen. Parents need to remember that this is still their own very special child who just happens to be lesbian, gay, or bisexual.

It is best if parents use the terminology that their child prefers. Parents should become familiar with *lesbian, gay, homosexual,* and even *queer.* It is recommended that parents practice saying the words so they don't stick in the throat and denote discomfort. Parents should avoid derisive terms or phrases such as "your problem."

As mentioned earlier, parents also should avoid asking leading questions about sexual behavior as that is a very personal area regardless of the sexual orientation of the respondent. Nevertheless, sexual discussion should not be totally ignored. It is always appropriate for parents to discuss health and safety issues with their children. Just as parents explain the "facts of life" to their heterosexual offspring, they now need to discuss AIDS frankly and to explain safe sex practices carefully or find someone who can.

Sexual orientation and sexual behavior need to be placed in perspective. They are a part of each of us, not the only part. Peter, a gay adolescent complains, "When I say, Mom, Dad, I can't solve this math equation, they answer, 'Well, if you weren't gay . . .'"[30] Vanessa, who came out to her parents at age eleven, recalls that whenever she mentioned anything lesbian or gay, her parents would reply, "Is that all you can talk about."[31]

Parents should resist placing unrealistic and/or punitive restriction on the youth for her or his "own good" or "best interest." Such restrictions imply disapproval and nonacceptance, and may be interpreted as rejection or mistrust, further damaging the parent-child relationship.[32] Reggie, a suburban, gay, African-American youth, suspected his parents of reading his mail and eavesdropping on his phone conversations. When confronted by her father, Olivia confessed that she and her friends were lesbian.

> That was a mistake. He declared, "We're not allowing you to talk to any of these people any more. You're not going to write . . . or speak to them again." I go, "What do you mean? I'm twenty years old. You can't do that." He said, "Yes, we can. If you decide to continue living like that we will no longer support you [in college]". . . . They changed our phone number. I was not allowed to go out of town.[33]

Chad, a diminutive fourteen-year-old, was escorted to the school bus and back again by his parents every day and confined to the house at all other times with no telephone privileges in order to keep him from "them," his lesbian and gay friends. Travis, a gay high school student, cautions that parents should not restrict talking on the phone to other gay teens. He adds, "[I]t's safe, and it's probably the only support they get."[34] After some soul-searching, parents are often more realistic in their expectations and behavior controls.[35] It is hoped that the reversal does not come too late to prevent damage to the child-parent relationship.

Education can counter stereotypes and allay many fears of the unknown. In the process, a reversal of roles can occur in which the child can become the teacher, and the parents the students. The transition may be difficult but can benefit the parent-child relationship as parents learn more about their teen and the lesbian, gay, and bisexual community. "My son is very masculine, so it was hard to believe he was gay," confesses a parent, who quickly adds: "Since then I've gotten quite an education."[36]

By talking to others, especially professionals or other parents in support groups such as PFLAG, parents can air their feelings and concerns and keep from feeling isolated and/or depressed. The mother of a lesbian youth explains, " . . . the hardest thing was feeling like I was keeping a secret, and there was nobody really to talk to about it."[37] Ideally, the professional is qualified and licensed to counsel and is someone with whom the parents can comfortably discuss sexual matters. It is best if a counselor is nonjudgmental and does not espouse outmoded or rigid methods.[38] Local lesbian and gay hotlines can offer advice and may have a list of approved counselors.

Religion can be an obstacle to acceptance but is not inherently so. Parents need to realize that homosexuality is not a sin in many religions and that some Christian denominations are reanalyzing their position on sexual orientation. In general, the more fundamentalist a sect, the more prejudice of all kinds among its members, and homosexual prejudice is no exception. The important thing is for parents to go slowly and to continue to love and to express love for their child even if they do not fully understand.[39] Insecure and vulnerable at first, a teen may interpret negative remarks as rejection. Reflecting on her own son's suicide and religion, Arlene muses, " . . . when they [the religious] say you're a worse sinner than anyone else, how do you [a queer kid] face up to all that?"[40]

Parents are encouraged to read books and pamphlets, contact Parents, Families, and Friends of Lesbians and Gays (PFLAG), and call lesbian, gay, and bisexual hot lines with questions. Several good resources are listed in Chapter 12. Lesbian, gay, and/or bisexual friends of the child, who, initially, may be viewed as part of "The Problem," can be a valuable resource for meeting other parents or adult lesbians, gays, or bisexuals.

PFLAG was formed in 1982 to support loving family relationships, to educate society about homosexuality, and to advocate for lesbian and gay rights. Membership now exceeds 35,000 households and 350 chapters in the United States and Canada.

It is unrealistic for anyone to expect parents to accept a child's same-sex orientation without some hesitation or questioning. James Genasci states, "Society had ill-prepared me to be the father of a gay son. To be brought up in this society is to be brought up homophobic."[41] Even those parents who are open, positive, and affirming will experience the occasional twinge of anxiety. On those occasions, it is helpful for parents to focus on their uniquely beautiful child. None of us can change or even second-guess the past.

Just as a lesbian, gay, or bisexual youth must be patient and give family members a chance to adjust to her or his coming out, so parents must be patient with their child. Lesbian, gay, and bisexual teens often harbor feelings of anger and resentment because parents have not helped them learn to become sexual-minority adults. Teens may lash out as they try to explore and to search for information. They will test their independence and try to push the real or imagined confinement the family offers. In this way, the lesbian, gay, or bisexual youth is similar to a heterosexual teen, except that few role models of mature lesbian, gay, or bisexual adults are available readily.

No truly loving parent wants to harm her or his own child, but nonacceptance can do just that. Queer kids must face discrimination and the threat of violence every day and need the love and support of family members and close friends. Although it is hoped that parents will be accepting and supportive, this attitude may take some time to evolve, but the process of learning acceptance should not disrupt the parent-child relationship. A nineteen year-old male explains this continuing love as follows:

> I think she [his mother] may have realized that when I came out I would need her most. . . . I don't know what she thinks about gays. . . . You see, *my mother doesn't treat me as an issue. She regards me as her son who is gay and not her gay son.* [My italics][42]

The grandmother of a young lesbian observed, "We need to support young people who have the courage to change society."[43] A lesbian, gay, or bisexual teen still needs a parent's love and guidance for the challenges and decisions to be faced daily. Nonacceptance by parents conveys rejection, and the result is denial of the very support needed to ensure their child's success and happiness.

Hopefully, every life experience helps us grow and teaches us more. The experience of celebrating a lesbian, gay, or bisexual child offers such an opportunity, as one mother realizes:

> It's made me grow. . . . I'm a lot more sensitive to people's needs than before. I'm much more aware of all kinds of people.[44]

For a parent, acceptance and the road to celebration starts when that parent begins the coming-out process herself or himself. This means silencing a co-workers' speculation about a son's girlfriends and potential marriage by explaining that he is in a very loving relationship with another man. It means wearing an AIDS ribbon. It includes joining the speakers bureau at a local lesbian, gay, and bisexual community center. Ideally every parent will arrive at the truly loving spot occupied by Elise, who has a lesbian daughter:

> She cannot be reduced to statistics, polls, stereotypes, nicknames, prejudice, opinion.
>
>   She is my child.

I still have the same dreams. The details may have changed, but the dreams are the same: of happiness, love, home, family, meaningful work.

Because, you see, she is my child.

She's not some monster to be feared, some pervert to be sneered at, some child molester or converter of adolescents.

She is my child.

She is warm and caring and sensitive and vulnerable and angry and sad, funny and human.

Yes, she is my child.

She didn't drop from another planet to cause destruction and mayhem. She came from love between her father and me.

Yes, she is my child.

You will not harm her if I can prevent it. You will not hurt her.

She is my child.

I join with every black mother, every Jewish mother, every Native American mother, every Hispanic mother, every Asian mother, every disabled child's mother, and every mother whose child has known hatred and prejudice.

And I say they are our children, our very special, precious children.[45]

Finding a Counselor for a Queer Kid When Needed

Part of counseling for parents may be acknowledging the need for assistance for their child. A queer kid may benefit from counseling, but the motivation to do so must come from within. Parents should avoid forcing an adolescent to go to counseling and should have realistic expectations when a youth does request such services. It is inappropriate to expect that a counselor will "talk some sense into you" or "straighten you out." With this attitude, someone is going to be disappointed, injured, or worse.

On the advice of a counselor, Daniel's mother moved to the suburban San Francisco area to escape the harassment her son had experienced in Oklahoma. In Castro Valley, Daniel found the high school very tolerant of differences. When Daniel came out at age fifteen to his mother, she resisted an urge to berate him. Instead, she became supportive and found a counseling and support group for lesbian and gay teens.

Less than 10 percent of lesbian and gay students perceive religious counselors as providing adequate guidance.[46] It is best to avoid professionals or religious leaders who offer the unrealistic promise of change in the child's sexual orientation. One ex-gay minister, a spokesman for the change movement, confided in me that with parental and societal acceptance his own personal "conversion" would have been unnecessary. Ex-gays are usually self-deluded persons who are dysfunctional individuals in any sexual orientation and many spend their lives searching for their true identity.

Repairing the Parent-Child Bond

If the bond between parents and child has been broken, undoubtedly, hurt, anger, and pain exist. It is not the child's responsibility to repair the rift. Although parents may feel hurt or helpless, they can not give up or await an apology in anger. Sulking is nonproductive.

Parents are in a position of authority within the family and are the ones who must accept and celebrate. They own the problem of nonacceptance, not their child. Parents must extend their hands and hearts first. This requires recognizing that they have been wrong. Acceptance of their child must be wholehearted and inclusive. It will not do to say, "I accept you but this gay thing, I can never accept it." This ostrich (head-in-the-sand) strategy is also nonproductive. It guarantees that every mention of sexual orientation in the future will be an issue.

As unpalatable as it may seem at first, the only repair with long-lasting results is total acceptance and more. A child, including her or his sexual orientation, must be celebrated just as heterosexual orientation is celebrated in weddings, births, anniversaries, and the like. An "Oh, I accept your orientation; now let's not discuss it again" is just a variation on the ostrich strategy. Children want to share their lives with their families and not to be able to do so is hurtful. Parents must become artful in the following:

> Ann, are you seeing anyone? Is she a student too? How did you meet? She sounds really nice. Why don't you bring her to dinner? We'd love to meet her.

It may seem awkward at first but it is essential if parents and their children are to remain close.

ACCEPTANCE OF A PARTNER OR LOVER

Although a lesbian or gay youth's friends may be difficult for a parent to accept, a lover or partner may be even more so. Parents who are anxious need to remember that even potential heterosexual partners are often greeted initially by parents with some skepticism. Offspring are very special and almost all parents are uneasy about their children's welfare within committed intimate relationships.

Parents should set the goal of becoming comfortable with their child's same-sex lover or partner. Of importance is slow and steady progress toward acceptance. Parents can begin by asking what the lover likes to be called and asking for a description of her or his likes and dislikes. A negative tone of voice and pronouns such as *Him!* or *Her!* or use of *that person* should be avoided.

Likewise, parents should inquire as to the terms used in the relationship. Several terms, such as *lover, partner, significant other, girlfriend or boyfriend,* or *spouse,* may be used. It is best if parents avoid the terms *friend* or *roommate* unless these are used by their child.

The usual joy of initially meeting individuals important to their child may be replaced with parental anger and hostility when that person is a child's same-sex lover or partner. It may be best if such meetings are postponed until parents are more accepting and ready. These feelings need to be conveyed to their child in a calm and honest manner. In addition, postponement can not be indefinite. Nonacceptance of a lover or partner by parents conveys the message of nonacceptance of their child also.

Parents should talk with their child prior to meeting their child's lover or partner and should establish realistic expectations.[47] It may be best to meet in neutral territory, such as a restaurant. Holidays with all their attendant stress might be avoided for a first meeting. Initially, it may be best to keep the encounter short and pleasant.

It is important for parents to remember that they are not the only ones in a meeting situation. Their child and her or his partner will also be anxious. It is helpful if all parties are honest about their feelings and open-minded about the encounter. Preconceptions should be left at home. All individuals in any meeting desire to be welcomed as special persons.

Visits to the parents' home can also be tension producing. Most lesbian and gay offspring only want to be treated fairly. Although Joannie's mother claims to have accepted her daughter's sexual orientation, she has placed unrealistic demands on any future visit by a potential girlfriend— demands she would not make on a heterosexual child. The two may not hold hands or kiss. The groundwork for the next family disagreement is already in place. Parents need to consider and discuss how they will react to each of these situations and compare their potential reaction to that accompanying similar situations with heterosexual offspring. It would be extremely helpful to discuss these situations with a lesbian, gay, or bisexual child prior to the first meeting.

Once meetings and a few short visits have occurred and gone well, longer stays can be attempted. As with any new relationship, a period of adjustment is necessary.

If the youth is living independently, visits by parents of a long duration can be either a joy or a disaster depending on how they are handled. Parents should be mindful that their child and her or his partner will want to be treated as the parents would treat any other couple. "We shared Christmas together," exclaims Paul, a young gay man. "You don't know how much that meant to me."[48]

SHARING WITH OTHERS

Parents often feel a need to share their knowledge of a child's same-sex attractions with others, usually for support. They usually talk with other family members, friends, counselors, or religious leaders. It is important that parents get a youth's permission before sharing her or his personal life. Such sharing must not be accomplished in a punitive fashion, such as "Just wait until I tell your father; then you'll get it!" or "Oh, your grandmother will be so disappointed when I tell her." Parents also should avoid forcing a teen to tell other family members.

Once a youth has come out to a parent, she or he and that parent might elect to tell other family members together. From the onset, this method conveys support and caring for all.

Parents should not be surprised if they learn upon disclosure that their other children already know. It is common for lesbian and gay youths to come out to their siblings before they come out to anyone else (see Chapter 3).

Sibling reactions will vary with their age, experience, and relationship to their lesbian sister or gay brother. Younger siblings often receive the information better than older, married siblings who are vested in heterosexism.[49] Adolescents who are confronting their own sexuality may respond in various ways. Seemingly difficult or resistant adolescent siblings may be questioning "What about me; am I one too?" Parents who have done their homework can reassure such children that same-sex attractions are not learned from brothers or sisters.

Most children, including siblings, have heard the terms *lesbian, gay,* and/or *homosexual,* although usually in some derogatory usage. Parents who practice should be able to use these words without discomfort or a hint of disapproval. It is best for parents to keep any initial discussion with other offspring simple, honest, and to the point in order to dispel any misconceptions.

John, I want to share something with you. We've talked before about your brother's behavior. He seems angry a lot. Well, he has a lot on his mind. He's been struggling with quite a bit lately, wanting to tell us but also protect us. He and I just has a long talk and he wanted me to share it with you. Niko is gay. I know that this will raise more questions than it answers. The important thing is for us to let him know that we still love and support him just as we do you and your sister. I hope that if you have any questions, and I suspect you will, that we can discuss them together.

What parents say is not as important as the loving, accepting message that they convey.[50] This message will offer important reassurance to the sibling who is hearing about her or his brother or sister for the first time.

Siblings should also be allowed to ask questions or to air concerns. They should be left with the clear understanding that the parent and their brother or sister is open to discussing this topic at any convenient time.

Parents also may desire to share their feelings with close friends who know and care for their child. These individuals can be a source of comfort and understanding if chosen selectively. Not everyone needs to know. Again, it is best if parents consult with their child before sharing information on their sexual orientation with others.

Discussion with their child can also help parents examine the purpose of such sharing. It would be hoped that parents would deal with any of their own negative feelings first and use the occasion of sharing with friends for affirming their son's or daughter's sexual orientation and their own support of their child.[51]

CONCLUSION

In some ways, we are not as enlightened at the turn of the twenty-first century as we might believe. Paul Phillips came out to his parents around 1920 and their response, perhaps colored by the oppression they had experienced as African Americans, is instructive. His father responded:

> [F]ind yourself a friend that you can trust. And bring him home. I don't want you . . . on the streets. . . . Bring him home. What you do in your room is your business.[52]

Withholding parental love will not make a child heterosexual, but it will make a child angry, hostile, sad, disappointed, and alienated.

Parents are a part of the lesbian, gay, and bisexual human rights movement whether they choose to be or not. By withholding their support or being hostile, they support violence and discrimination against their son or daughter. By being supportive, they help their child survive in a hostile environment and help create a more accepting society. The mother of two sons, one gay and one not, makes a very strong case: "Both my sons deserve the opportunity to live in a safe environment, to be treated as full and equal members of our society, and to have their human rights respected."[53]

Chapter 11

Letter to a Queer Kid

Being gay is no rebellion, gaining a gay identity is. . . .

R. Lockwood, *Gay on Gay*

Congratulations!

You are lesbian, gay, bisexual, or questioning and you had the courage to open this book. It may have been your first step toward self-discovery and self-identification. Sometimes, it is difficult to be who you are. Be brave. Sometimes it feels as if life is very confining and you want to know who you will be and what you will do. You want to burst out. Be patient.

Being different requires one thing above all else. It requires courage. Just remember, *there's nothing wrong with you.* There *is* something wrong with a society that makes people feel guilty for loving each other. You are not to blame for most of the challenges you face. Heterosexism and homophobia are to blame. Let's forget about pointing fingers for just a moment and talk about you, your future, and who you can become.

WHO ARE YOU?

Life can be so confusing when you are a teenager. Your body keeps changing and the rules keep changing. People tell you to act like an adult and then they treat you like a child. Sometimes it gets extremely difficult. And being attracted to people of the same sex or to both sexes does not make it any easier. It is easy to be conflicted by your own feelings and your family's and society's expectations.

First and foremost, be truthful with yourself. Honesty is definitely the best policy. It takes courage, but self-celebration begins with self-acceptance and that requires honesty. Ask yourself, "How do I feel? What do I want? What is best for me?" Chrissy, age sixteen, continued to date males although she was not interested in them. She recalls, "I was trying to please everyone but myself."[1] With that realization, she began to change her life. Being true to yourself can be very fulfilling and positive. Listen to your feelings. Do not be afraid of yourself. Matt describes how, feeling uncomfortable and inadequate, he made a decision.

> I pretended to be someone else for long enough. I don't want to do it anymore. I'd like to have some integrity.[2]

"It felt wonderful," recalls Kris, age nineteen, "to finally know who I was—a lesbian. I felt like a great weight had been lifted off me."[3]

Second, trust your own reactions, not those of others. Do not allow other people to tell you how you feel or who you are. Define yourself. It may be a very different person from what others now perceive. The important thing is that you be comfortable with yourself. Calvin, a young college student, is thankful "I didn't listen to all those people who told me I could only be what . . . the world would let me be."[4]

Sometimes listening to yourself is as contradictory as listening to a whole group of other people. That is OK. It takes time to get to know someone really well, and it will take time for you to get to know the person you are becoming.

Sexuality does not just happen. Sexual orientation and sexual behavior are not synonymous. You may be a virgin or be heterosexually active but know inside that you are attracted to others of your own sex. You may have a crush on a friend or have had sex with someone of your own gender, but even that does not mean you are homosexual or bisexual. Orientation or attraction may be very different from behavior or experience. Some adolescents do a lot of sexual experimenting. Behavior does not determine your orientation. Not everyone is sure of her or his sexual orientation, especially during adolescence. It is okay to be confused. You do not need to self-label until you are ready to do so and want to. Often, sexual orientation slowly unfolds like a flower. It may not all be clear just yet. Remember, you are receiving many messages from different places— the media, school friends, teachers, church, your parents, and most important, from yourself.

Third, make a positive change when needed. If you spend a lot of time wishing your life was different, it is time to begin to change it. The results will not change unless you make an effort to change what precedes those results. There's a saying: *If you keep doin' what you been doin', you're gonna keep gettin' what you been gettin'.* You cannot change the past. Automobiles are made with a large front windshield and a tiny rearview mirror. You drive looking forward with the occasional glance rearward. Life should be the same way. Take charge of today and tomorrow. Leave yesterday behind. Chris, a gay man, could not live a lie any longer. He recalls, "I stopped pretending and let myself feel my true feeling." Derek, a young gay

African-American male, turned homelessness into the beginnings of a career with help from a lesbian and gay support center. "We all have to play the cards we're dealt," he advises, "It does no good to lie to yourself."[5] Invest time and effort into who you can be rather than reinvesting in who you were in the past. You deserve the very best you can attain.

Being you is the most important thing. You are a tall, short, thin, fat, or average-sized male or female African, Native, European, or Asian American or Latino/a, basketball player, computer whiz, budding artist, guitar picker, or concert pianist, who happens to be lesbian, gay, or bisexual. It is only a part of you. "Being lesbian is not the most interesting thing about me," claims Julianna, a college sophomore.[6]

BEING DIFFERENT

Being different is an opportunity, if you are courageous enough to take it. Once she had dealt with her attraction to women, Shula, a white seventeen-year-old, saw her next step as a choice: "Would I try to ignore it . . . or would I be strong enough to overcome the homophobia around me and simply let myself be what I instinctively knew I was?"[7] You can define who you are.

Being lesbian, gay, or bisexual is a part of *who* you are, a unique way of viewing and responding to the world around you. Do not forget that you are still more like other teens than you are different. Iris, a young lesbian explains,

> Some people think that we're different from other kids. We're special, but we're a lot like everyone else. We think about Nintendo, acne, and dating.[8]

Although sexual orientation seems to have a biological basis, it does not really matter how you became gay. You just are; accept it, and take pride in it. "I can be me or I can hide and lie to everyone—*that's* my choice," proclaims Lauren, a lesbian student.[9] You are unique. Many people are heterosexual. You are different; you are special!

You are different, but you are not alone. Lesbians, gays, and bisexuals, including teens, are literally everywhere. You are not the first young person to have the sexual feelings that you do. What is new, however, is that more and more teens are being open about these feelings.

For some individuals, accepting their own difference means reconciling it with their religion. Many Western religions have prohibitions against same-sex erotic behavior. You will have to make some choices that range from rejecting your religion to rejecting yourself. Most lesbians, gays, and bisexuals are in the middle.

I can make a pretty convincing case for the contention that supposed prohibitions in the Bible regarding homosexual behavior are misinterpretations and/or mistranslations, but that would take an entire chapter. Several good books on this topic are included in the resources chapter.

No one—even those fundamentalists who claim otherwise—follows every word of the Bible. Almost all Christians, Jews, and Muslims *selectively* follow biblical teaching. So can you. Choose to emphasize love. If we all love one another, all the prescriptions for good living found in the Bible naturally follow. "If God is love and God created me," reasons Daphne, "than it must be fine to love whoever I am."[10] Stated another way, Yevette decided, "that God would love me for who I am because I was created that way."[11] Find a congregation, such as Unitarian Universalist, Metropolitan Community Church, Quaker, Reform Jewish, or Buddhist, that will nurture and celebrate the special person that is you. "[Y]ou don't have to give up your Christianity for your homosexuality," advises Suzanne, age eighteen, ". . . God . . . loves you because you are her child."[12]

Self-acceptance is a feeling of inner peace. Positive self-regard begins small and grows slowly. 'Lizabeth came out when she was eighteen.

> I have a sense of peace about me that I've never had. I don't have to play any games. I don't have to pretend that I'm straight when I'm not. It's like a weight had been lifted off my shoulders. . . . My mother keeps telling me that the heterosexual norm would be so much easier . . . But, I had to live that way for eighteen years and it wasn't easier. It was screwing me up in my head.[13]

The important thing is to be yourself, whoever that is. Be comfortable with yourself. You do not need to fulfill anybody's stereotype, or act a certain way in order to advertise your sexual orientation. After all, there is no one official way to be lesbian, gay, or bisexual. Be yourself. Use your experiences to make you strong. Mickie explains,

> I'm a woman. I'm a lesbian. I'm a Latina. I get trouble from everyone. . . . Having these things to deal with has made me a stronger person.[14]

Accepting your sexual orientation will not erase your problems; it just changes your possibilities.

TAKE PRIDE IN YOURSELF

You do not have to be perfect in everything else in order to cover your supposed *one big imperfection.* You do not need to compensate for being lesbian, gay, or bisexual. You do not have to excel to make up for something. If you do excel, that is wonderful, but it is not required. Being *you* is the most important part. The best way to begin feeling good about yourself is to decide to feel good about yourself. Let your self like its self.

You have an enemy, but it is not yourself or your orientation or your parents or even the political right. The enemy is homophobia, and for centuries it has taught us to hate ourselves; it has demoralized us; it has held us down. You can defy it. You can be proud. You can demand your rights and your rightful place in society. It takes courage.

Withdrawal is not the answer. Kimberly, a young African-American lesbian, describes the consequences of withdrawal and isolation,

> You begin to doubt yourself. You begin to doubt your feelings. Are they really authentic? . . . A person that could be a really beautiful person becomes a real sour person. They don't experience the joys of life.[15]

Keep active. Continue to enjoy whatever gives you pleasure—horseback riding, bowling, reading, softball, painting, writing poetry, hiking, roller blading, and the like.

Surround yourself with people who love you and support you. Attend or establish a support/social group, seek out lesbian, gay, or bisexual students and adults or those who are gay-friendly, obtain a pen pal, or go on-line. "For the first time I wasn't alone," claims Chris, describing his first support group meeting. "I didn't have to bottle everything up." He continues, "I don't know where the concept of 'it's a lonely life if you're gay' came from, because that certainly has not been my experience. It hasn't been lonely at all."[16]

Unfortunately, a note of caution is in order here. When you talk with adults or older teens, be careful. Sexual predators are found in all sexual orientations. Some individuals, no matter how trusted their position, may try to befriend you to advance their own sexual agenda. Let trust grow slowly and do not do anything that is uncomfortable. Use another name on-line and be extremely cautious about face-to-face meetings. You do not deserve to be exploited by anyone regardless of one's sexual orientation.

"People do not choose their sexual orientation—but gay and lesbian people *can* choose to take pride in who they are, to respect themselves, and to end the isolation and solitude that come with invisibility."[17] Shula, mentioned earlier, recalls, "A gay teacher . . . said, "I don't choose whether I'm gay. I can choose whether or not I'm going to be miserable about it."[18] George Stambolian, an African-American gay author wrote in *A Black Man* (1984),

I am here, I am human, I have dignity, and therefore I will not allow
you to destroy me or change me. You must deal with me as I am, not
as you prefer me to be.[19]

"[D]on't panic if you are still unsure [of your sexual orientation]," writes
Sloan Chase Wiesen, a white gay high schooler and editor of the *Montclair
Kimberly Academy News.* "But never be afraid or ashamed to explore who
you are and to be yourself. The only road to certain unhappiness is to
pretend to be who you are not."[20] Likewise, you can choose how to
express your feelings and how to live your life.

"I was the little role model for teenagers," Marion, a young lesbian,
recalls,

> I did not smoke or drink. I played athletics, worked hard, and wore a
> dress to church every Sunday. But I didn't know myself. I didn't
> have any individual identity. I was somebody that someone else
> created. . . . I knew the rules and I followed them.[21]

Brent, age sixteen, explains,

> I grew up learning that what I felt was wrong, and there was a lot of
> shame involved. Now that I've come out, I'm expected to suddenly
> forget all about that. It took me a while to get to this point [of accepting
> the heterosexist message], and it'll take me a while to get out of it.[22]

You can reclaim the "self" that a hostile society has tried to take from you.
Jessie, a bisexual fifteen-year-old, proclaims, "I know that it is the way I
was born, and I am proud of what I am."[23] Reclaim yourself.

"Coming out to myself made things inside my head a whole lot easier,"
comments Tristan, age nineteen.[24] "No matter what people say or think,"
proclaims a seventeen-year-old rural lesbian, "I know that I am who I am
and I am not wrong or vulgar or unnatural. I AM ME." [My capitaliza-
tion][25] Susan, age sixteen, adds, "Don't compromise who you are. Be
honest with yourself. . . . "[26]

Hostility toward lesbians, gays, and bisexuals often makes us angry.
What we do with that anger is important. You can turn it on yourself with
self-deprecating comments and self-destructive behavior, or you can use
its energy to build a better life for yourself and a better world for your
lesbian, gay, and bisexual peers. Above all else, stay alive, stay healthy,
and do not harm yourself through unsafe sexual practices, drugs and
alcohol, or acts of desperation. Sex, drugs, and alcohol may seem to offer
a "quick fix" for erasing pain, but they are never the solution and can even

worsen problems. Believe in yourself. Life is worth living even when the road is bumpy. And life will get easier and more enjoyable as you become older and more independent.

There is a saying that "Living well is the best revenge" and it certainly applies here. You have a right to a satisfying, fulfilling life and to the satisfaction of being a whole person who is honest, open, and self-celebratory.

Turn your anger and despair into action. If you have been abusing drugs and alcohol, seek help. Begin today to plan your new life. Plan to get a job and your own apartment; plan to move from your homophobic town, or plan to attend a gay-friendly college. Jen attempted suicide when she realized she was a lesbian. Luckily, she failed. Now, comfortable in her foster home with a lesbian couple, she plans to attend college next year and become a marine biologist. How sad it would be if we had lost all she has to offer.

If you are experiencing verbal and physical harassment, take positive steps to stop it. One method is to confront the harassers, although this tactic is stressful and can be dangerous. Do not attempt this if the harassers are in a group. In this situation, they will feed off each other's remarks. Confront them individually. Do not act defensively. Simply state that you do not like it and that you do not judge them and would appreciate the same in return. Corey, age eighteen, came out in his junior year of high school. He offers the following advice:

> It's how you present yourself. Even if you're not totally secure with yourself, if you present yourself as secure it makes a big impact on other people. I found myself standing up more and more for myself, for the gay community, for anything I didn't like.[27]

You can also insulate yourself by being strong and self-confident. From a position of strength, you can use logic or humor—but not sarcasm—to defuse confrontation.

If all else fails, lodge a complaint with the faculty and administration. This may require you to be open about your sexuality with those who can help. If you are being abused at home by your parents, it is illegal and steps can be taken. Anyone, including yourself, can anonymously report your situation to your county's Child Protective Services.

If school officials fail to act, threaten them with legal action. My experience has taught me that if a lawyer calls or if you begin collecting data for a lawsuit—taking notes, taping meetings—you get a quick response. Take your tape recorder with you when you go to see the principal. As the meeting begins, excuse yourself long enough to state the time, date, and participants on the tape, then resume the meeting. Watch 'em sweat!

The Lambda Legal Defense and Education Fund publishes a sixteen-page guide called *Stopping Antigay Abuse of Students in Public Schools: A Legal Perspective.* The following guidelines are suggested:

> Get safe first.
>
> Report abuse to the school principal. Determine who counts as a legally liable school official.
>
> Document all incidents in writing and provide copies to the appropriate school officials. Record who, what, when, and where and collect witnesses' statements. Collect proof, such as a secretary's signature, that copies were given to the principal.
>
> Move up the ladder above the principal if satisfactory action is not forthcoming.
>
> Follow your school's complaint procedure.
>
> Keep a list of all unfair actions, verbal and physical abuse, and all official meetings.
>
> Be ready with solutions should you be asked. The resources listed in this book may be a good educational resource.

In a similar way, you should resist "change therapies." They do not work in the long term, and practitioners always blame their failure on the patient—you. Religious-based "change therapies" are particularly onerous because, according to the logic, "God never fails." That leaves you to accept the blame for not changing. Why would God want to change you from the way in which you were created by God in the first place? Resist enrollment in these dangerous therapies and if enrolled, resist their methods. They guarantee only unhappiness and delusion.

For yourself, remember that homophobia is an illness just as much as claustrophobia is. "[T]he harassment made me feel powerful," declares Brent, age sixteen. "They were reacting out of fear of me whereas before, when I was in the closet, I was reacting out of fear of them."[28]

In a study of self-esteem, the best predictors of high self-esteem among a group of young lesbian and gay adult college students were self-descriptors such as ambitious, aggressive, forceful, outgoing, and self-sufficient. These are strong qualities. Being lesbian, gay, or bisexual and being proud is being strong. Self-esteem is enhanced by taking a stand and by being more open and honest.

After much soul-searching, one young man concluded:

> . . . gays are just ordinary people living boring lives. . . . I'm just a kid who wants a man not a woman to share life with. The only way I differ . . . from straights is by my sexual needs.[29]

"Then I thought," recalls Henry, remembering his anguished soul-searching, "that some people are gay and seem to be happy and quite normal. That was a revelation."[30] With the feelings of victimization comes powerlessness. You are not a victim, pummeled by society with no will to resist, no will to assert yourself, dependent on others for gratification and nourishment. Decide today to love yourself. *Self-love cannot be based on the love you receive from others. It comes from within.*

COMING OUT

Coming out is a common, shared experience of lesbians, gays, and bisexuals, but it is a unique and singular experience for each of us, an experience that never ends.

> When we do [come out], our lives become irretrievably altered—so altered, in fact, that we can't stop telling everyone we can find about it. . . . For every individual, "coming out" is a singular experience: . . . a choice that is personal, sometimes public, and always political. . . . it is a beginning to making the world whole. It is the first step in claiming our place.[31]

What is the motivation for coming out? Perhaps Anais Nin, a bisexual, early feminist author, said it better than many.

> And the day came when the risk it took to remain closed in a bud became more painful than the risk it took to blossom.

Ann Bancroft, polar explorer and member of the National Women's Hall of Fame in Seneca Falls, New York, summarizes:

> Even if it's a struggle, it's worth it, because I become a better person by being out. Being in the closet is so debilitating. It doesn't allow you to live up to your potential.[32]

Coming out in a safe, supportive environment is a step in self-affirmation. It is not a prop or a support for who you are. Your validity as a person is not dependent on acceptance of you by others. You are you—with or without "their" support. By the same token, you need to find others who love, appreciate, and accept you. The affirming messages of others buoy you up.

By staying closeted, Kevin concludes, he was consenting to his own "inferiority."[33] The closeted lesbian, gay, or bisexual is acting as if something is wrong with herself or himself that she or he must hide from view. "It's worse to stay in the closet—it's a bad thing to do to yourself," Corey, age eighteen, explains. "I felt bad about . . . not standing up for myself."[34] At the April 25, 1993 National March on Washington for Lesbian, Gay, and Bisexual Equal Rights, Martina Navratilova, international tennis champion, cautioned against remaining in the closet:

> If we want the world to give us respect, not to look at us with shame, we must first be willing to give ourselves respect. We must be proud of who we are and we cannot do that while we hide.

The first step in coming out is being out to yourself. You are still the same person; you just know yourself better now. Self-acceptance is healthy psychologically and related to positive self-esteem. Once you accept who you are, you are ready to take pride in yourself and to make being lesbian, gay, or bisexual part of yourself.

You may be fearful of being honest with others regarding your sexual orientation or you may be experiencing ridicule and harassment because others know or suspect that you are lesbian, gay, or bisexual. Take strength from your endurance. You do not own this problem. "If people can't deal with me for who I am," states Matt, "it's their problem, not mine."[35] The judgments and actions of others tell us more about them than about you. I have a T-shirt that says "Are you sick?" On the reverse, it answers, "Racism is an illness." It could just as easily read, "Homophobia is an illness."

When you come out, you take a step in reducing the shame that accompanies victimization. You begin the healing process. "I've learned to associate these words [faggot, dyke, queer] with things I don't like," explains Robin, age sixteen. "It'll take time to erase all that conditioning."[36] Practice saying "I'm lesbian (gay or bisexual)" so that it doesn't sound like an apology. Say it with pride. Nathan, age eighteen, knew he was gay when he was fourteen, but it took him four years to share that knowledge with others. "[W]hen you are finally honest," he states, "[i]t is such a great feeling."[37]

Coming out is an extremely personal and individual decision. No one should tell you when to do it or with whom. You must decide. "I think there is a huge amount of political pressure to come out," explains Allyson; "And in a way it's good. But it makes a lot of people feel guilty and that's no good. . . . "[38] Come out when you're ready. "I'm certainly not advocating coming out all over the place," continues Roy, age nineteen. "Do it only when you are ready, and only to people you think you can trust."[39] "We do what we can to survive," cautions Heather, age seventeen, "and the closet is often a necessary part of survival. If you decide to come out, make sure you are strong enough to handle it."[40] Be sure you can trust the person to whom you're disclosing. Can they keep a secret? Few can. Are they too judgmental, insecure, or insincere? There are risks, as one teen notes,

> My school is liberal and it was still tough coming out. Come out where you feel safe.[41]

Beth came out in high school with some good results and some bad. Overall, she summarizes, "I've been honest . . ., and my true friends are still my friends."[42]

Coming out can also have long-term benefit for you. Mary, a courageous seventeen-year-old lesbian, speaks eloquently:

> I refuse to be afraid. And I do this out of an obligation not to the community but to myself. . . . Nobody should have a say in who I am.[43]

Each time you come out it gets easier. Believe it or not, you'll reach a point where being out is just you and announcing that you're lesbian, gay, or bisexual will be like giving your address.

> Hi, I'm Ted. I live down the street with my partner Rob and our son Mike, who's off at camp this week. Welcome to the neighborhood.

If you feel celebratory about your sexual orientation and you can safely come out, do so, but only when you're ready. Linda, a young adult, practically gushes when she proclaims:

> I feel so much more genuine for having accepted my lesbianism, and for sharing the strength and warmth that comes with having done that. . . . I know how it feels to have my sexuality out in the open, and . . . to enjoy the acceptance of the people I love the most—including myself.[44]

"It is good to know that there are other teens with the courage to stand up and be counted," states Samuel, age seventeen, editor of *The Triangle*.[45]

The results of coming out may be unforeseen. Within a year of admitting to himself that he was gay, sixteen-year-old Trey lost one set of friends and gained another, started a support group, fell in love, wore a

pink triangle pin to his Southern Baptist church, was placed in unsuccessful psychotherapy by his parents, and was harassed by teachers and students. He concludes,

> I have made better friends than I knew were possible, friends who
> care about who I am, not what I am. . . . My self-esteem and my
> happiness have increased a hundredfold. . . . I like who I am.[46]

David, a nineteen-year-old African American, had a less positive experience but remains defiant.

> Well, I can say it's not easy. . . . [But] there's too much at stake. . . .
> I demand respect.[47]

All of us must demand respect but it takes courage to be open and to make
that demand. Patrick concludes, "[I]f someone rejects me it doesn't mean
I'm a bad person. . . . it just means maybe they're an idiot. . . . "[48]

Weigh your options carefully. By coming out, you are taking a risk for
those who cannot. In the long term, this single act will be good for all
lesbians, gays, and bisexuals. A lesbian high school senior adds, "I think
that [coming out] helped everyone a lot, to know someone they were close
with was a lesbian."[49] When she came out, Aimee, a high school student,
found support at Metropolitan Community Church (MCC), a Bible-based,
gay-friendly denomination. MCC helped her face the everyday challenges of
being out. Aimee comments, "[T]he more visible I am, the less scary it might
feel to some kid in school who is struggling with her [or his] sexuality. . . ."[50]

A RELATIONSHIP: THAT SPECIAL SOMEONE

Most likely, you'll fall in and out of love many times during your life.
The crushes of early adolescence give way to long-term committed relationships as you mature. The isolation of early adolescence gives way to a
social network of lesbian, gay, and bisexual individuals as you get older.
Meeting other sexual-minority individuals—and possible partners—gets
easier. You can increase your chances of meeting someone by going to
youth events, such as band camp and gymnastics camp, to support groups,
and to lesbian, gay, and bisexual community events, such as picnics and
pride marches.

Do not expect everyone you date to love you instantly or at all. It is
easy, especially if you have not had much same-sex experience, to misread

interpersonal "signs." Do not be discouraged if your love is not returned. Use each experience to learn more for the next one.

Fall in love slowly. Do not confuse sex with love. Either one can exist separately. Sex alone feels good for the moment but vanishes. Sex within a loving relationship can enhance the feelings of love. Michael, a twenty-four-year-old, explains,

> Sex is always better with someone you really care about and respect. . . . it's better to allow the emotional and the physical to progress together so that the sexuality is complementing the emotional buildup. . . . [I]t's OK to move slowly.[51]

Do not allow others to have sex with you against your will. You deserve to be treated with respect, tenderness, and caring. Making love is not about getting all you can for yourself while exploiting someone else. Nor is it about being exploited.

Sometimes we try to use sex to entice someone into loving us. That practice can lead to getting hurt and to being abused. When Betty realized that sex was not love, she was "crushed" and felt "worthless." Domenic felt "cheap and used."

When a mutual, loving relationship exists, you will know it. Aaron Fricke, former adolescent activist, recalls his high school relationship:

> His strengths were my strengths. . . . I realized that my feelings for him were unlike anything I had ever felt before. The sense of comraderie was familiar from other friendships; the deep spiritual love I felt for Paul was new. So was the openness, the sense of communication with another. . . . It was the first time either of us had been in love like this and we spent much of our time just figuring out what it meant to us.[52]

Olivia began a sexual relationship with Kris at age fifteen.

> We were both enjoying it very much. I had never felt anything like it before. It was so special.[53]

Long-term relationships do not just happen. They take lots of work and commitment. Good relationships have much in common. They are built on mutual support and respect, a balance of dependence and independence, and good communication. Almost always, the partners share a common interest in some enjoyable pursuit, such as biking, hiking, going to the movies, cooking, making or listening to music, or playing sports. If your relationship is a crutch to prevent loneliness you may find it difficult to grow as an individual and as a couple.

Your relationship belongs to you. Claim it as your own and celebrate it. The two of you are not dependent on others to sanction your love. Love comes from within the relationship; it is not imposed from outside.

GENDER NEEDS

Women and men often bring different expectations to a relationship. They seem to have different needs and skills.

Women

In our society, women are usually defined in terms of their relationship to men, their father, husband, or boyfriend. Socially sanctioned sex roles and behaviors have been ingrained. You are not dependent upon men for your self-worth or for love or sex gratification. Beyond your immediate partner, you will have a whole sisterhood of other lesbians and access to women's culture, the feminist movement, and the lesbian community including art, music, politics, and humor.

In an old joke told in lesbian circles, the correct response to the question "What does a lesbian take on her second date?" is "A moving van." The joke is meant to chide women for a rapidness with which they fall in love and form relationships. There is nothing wrong with rapid romance but there is the danger of losing yourself in the process. Be sure to keep a balance between independence and dependence.

Men

Many men have the opposite problem, a lack of commitment. Men in our society are aculturated to be independent. This can make intimacy between two men difficult.

Many men also come from the "stick-it-in, pull-it-out" school of instant sexual gratification. This lack of intimacy does not provide enough of the needed warmth to maintain a mature relationship. Making love is not masturbating inside someone else. Take time to learn to love and to communicate that love.

CHOOSING A COUNSELOR

Most individuals carefully consider large purchases such as a house or automobile. Potential health care providers should be scrutinized thoroughly as well. Be especially wary given the bias and lack of training on sexual issues found in many school counselors. Several types of behavior signal potential counselors to be avoided at all costs. Do not begin or remain in therapy with counselors who make intolerant jokes, engage in stereotyping ("But you're not a man hater like other lesbians."), exaggerate or minimize indicators ("Everybody has those feelings."), repeatedly reschedule or are repeatedly late for the appointment, attempt "cure" therapies, deny their own occasional same-sex feelings or dreams, or give a general feeling of uneasiness.

LIVING WITH PARENTS

Coming out to your parents is not the great "cure-all," nor is it the end of the world as you know it. If nothing else, at least you are being honest with them. The best measure of their potential reaction is the type of relationship you have with them before you come out. If it is open, loving, caring, and trusting, they will probably be very accepting. There are a few other factors to consider:

- Your parents' attitude toward lesbians, gays, and bisexuals. Your family religion and your parents' adherence. Is your religion steeped in condemnation or is it open and accepting of difference? Are your parents diehard believers or casual followers?
- Your parents' reactions to other family crises, such as an auto accident, loss of a purse or wallet, missed appointment, unfinished chores and the like. Do they get angry and try to fix blame? Do they continue to treat others in the family with love and caring?
- The differing reactions of either parent.

When you decide to come out to your parents, you should do it carefully and with some forethought. Here are some points to ponder:

Have a plan. Decide when and how to tell your parents. Choose a time that is advantageous to you and comfortable for both you and your parents. It should not be an "Oh, by the way . . . " process but not too angst-ridden either. Be at ease and your parents will be too.

Have a place to go to live for a while, if necessary. Just in case your parents respond catastrophically, make prior arrangements with a friend or relative for short- or long-term shelter. You do not want to be on the street.

Try to anticipate questions and have well-thought-out answers. Do some research prior to coming out. Not all questions can be answered from your own perspective. Your parents may have questions about the sexual-minority community or about relationships or sexual behavior that you have not experienced yet. Knowledge is strength. By the same token, you do not have to have all the answers. It is okay to admit that you do not know, that this is new for you too.

Be confident. If you are not, they will sense your discomfort and conclude that you do not really understand yourself or the impact of being lesbian, gay, or bisexual.

Pick the right time and place to come out. The worst time is after a family squabble. Remember, coming out is not a weapon to be used in anger.

Be prepared for shock and disbelief. A conversation between two lovers, Eliot and Philip, in David Leavitt's *The Lost Language of Cranes* might be instructive. Philip has decided to come out to his parents and is convinced they will take the news in stride. Eliot cautions:

> It's hard for you to realize how new this thing is going to be for them because you've lived with it all your life. But they haven't. . . . I'm just saying that you should think about it very carefully before you do anything rash.[54]

Be patient. You need to remember that your parents will need to have time to work through many of the issues that you have. They may need your help to remember that you are the same person. They may also need to be reminded that being lesbian, gay, or bisexual does not mean that you now participate in one long endless orgy. Responsible people act responsibly whatever their sexual orientation, but you may need to regain your parents' trust for them to realize this fact. Be patient. To Linda, a young lesbian adult, it seemed as if she and her mom were always going to have that "same tense eyebrow" when they looked at each other.[55]

Reassure your parents. They need to know that they did not cause your homosexuality, but if they had you would be appreciative.

Be knowledgeable. You might want to learn a little about lesbians, gays, and bisexuals before you come out to others. This book is a start. Many excellent books are included in the resource chapter.

Have someone else to lean on for support. You may need additional support if your parents respond negatively. Arrange this ahead of time with a trusted friend or family member. Keep them informed so they can be available when you might need them.

CELEBRATE YOURSELF

You will be stronger from your experience of self-discovery. Michael, age sixteen, has discovered a lot about himself and others. He adds, "The bottom line is that it doesn't matter that I'm gay."[56]

Dan, an athlete in Gay Games 94/Stonewall, twenty-five, recalls the closing ceremony, "[W]e were being celebrated for being athletes and for being gay and for being strong enough to be both."[57]

The rewards of self-discovery and self-celebration are many. "I love the unique outlook on life I have as a seventeen-year-old lesbian," states Shula. "I've met many wonderful, supportive gay people."[58] Jonathan adds, "So many of my positive traits—like learning not to judge others by outside appearances—were formed when I was the brunt of so much teasing."[59]

Your future can be as bright and happy as you can make it. "[B]e whatever you want to be," counsels Alston, a young gay man. "If you're young, you have the chance to do what you want, to be what you want, and to feel good about it."[60] Daniel, a white eighteen-year-old from Castro Valley, California, projects the following future for himself:

> I'll have my own business and have made enough money to do what I want . . . I'll have a house in the country . . . I'll have been settled down with somebody for a long time, and have three children. . . . [61]

Kenneth, age seventeen, states it more succinctly, "I'm gay, I'm proud, and I'm gonna get mine!"[62]

What will the future hold for you? I have no idea, but the potential for happiness is wonderful. William, a college student, is celebratory: "[D]espite it all, you have survived. . . . It's about looking at yourself in the mirror and finally being able to say 'I love you.'"[63] You have the ability to love someone else and to experience joy and fulfillment from that love. Whether you do or not is up to you and the work you put into it.

Michael, gay and only twelve years old, offers a final toast: "I know something for sure, . . . It's OK to be gay."[64] "Don't even think about giving up," counsels nineteen-year-old Roy. "The rest of us are rooting for you."[65]

Chapter 12

Conclusion

American culture glorifies sex while repressing all but majority fulfillment of sexual gratification. The assumption is that the only healthy, fulfilling sex is heterosexual. Meanwhile homosexuality and bisexuality are treated as if they are criminal, evil, sinful, and dysfunctional. As proof, a new equation exists: Homosexuality = AIDS = death.

Not all heterosexuals are heterosexist, but where heterosexism exists—and it is widespread—it is usually accompanied by homophobia. Both heterosexism and homophobia are outgrowths of sexism or the notion of male superiority and rigid gender roles. To stray from one's gender role is to risk becoming a vilified "queer." Heterosexism assumes that to be different is to be less, and therefore, queers are less. As less than human, this logic goes, homosexuals and bisexuals do not deserve basic human rights. The use of violence to enforce heterosexism is tacitly approved. Violence by the majority population is to them preferable to the tenderness expressed within the minority population.

Into this mix stride lesbian, gay, and bisexual adolescents, one of the most neglected and disenfranchised of American minorities. After interviewing over a thousand teens, Robert Coles, our foremost child psychologist, and Geoffrey Stokes conclude, "[H]omosexual teens remain likely to face at least strong disapproval and sometimes brutality from their peers."[1] As a group, these teens are recognizing their sexual orientation earlier, acting upon it, and self-identifying earlier. In some cases, their very youth and immaturity are working against them. They are facing challenges of youth and survival unprecedented in recent history.

It is so easy to place the blame on the victim. It is equally easy to propose that queer kids just keep quiet, just remain in the closet. This is misplaced. The problem is not the teens who are coming out earlier, the problem is the unwillingness of families, schools, and society to support that decision. Families seem more willing to accept a daughter with an unwanted pregnancy than a daughter who is lesbian. In the name of family values, we would rather see families torn apart than acknowledge that sexual-minority teens exist.

Sadly, the lesbian, gay, and bisexual community must shoulder some of the blame for the predicament of queer kids. Adults must stop buying into the charge of recruitment and refute the lie that sexual-minority adults cannot be trusted around queer kids. These kids are here and they need role models.

Support groups for queer kids need to move beyond support and to become interest groups run by teens. Certainly, there is a place for problem-solving and learning but there must also be a place for fun and pride-building activity.

Unfortunately, all the support groups and gay role models possible can not erase the hostility of an uncaring society. For the good of all kids, changes are needed. It is time to demand changes in our schools, changes that will benefit all students. It is time to provide options to sexual minority teens, to provide them with role models, education, support, and possibilities. It is time for families to recognize their beautiful, loving sons and daughters who are lesbian, gay, and bisexual. It is time for the bullies who enforce heterosexism to be put in their place.

Educators unwilling to confront the lies perpetuate them. Administrators and teachers overlook harassment and intimidation of sexual-minority teens in a callous disregard for the safety and well-being of these students. Pretending that queer kids do not exist and ignoring ignorance, insensitivity, hostility, and prejudice will not make any of these go away.

An unwillingness by educators to address homosexuality in an open, responsible manner only contributes to homophobia, the same internalized homophobia that leads to self-destructive behaviors. It is difficult to learn to become a healthy sexual-minority adult when there are few supports for being a healthy sexual-minority adolescent. The fact that most queer kids do develop into strong, self-confident adults hardly justifies the process as a character-building exercise.

It is time to correct the drift of American education, to focus on the needs of all young people not on the incessant demands of the American Reich. In their demonizing of lesbians, gays, and bisexuals, the religious and conservative right, who profess a love for the family, have driven a wedge into the very center of that institution, the relationship of parents and children. Parents are being told, "Your child is the enemy. " In the process, something as simple and beautiful as the love between two men or two women has been vilified to a point where it seems corrupt, unclean, and unseemly.

Little doubt exists that, if allowed to prevail, the fanatical, yet all too pervasive, hostilities against sexual minorities would result in genocide. We, as a nation, must stop it before we devour our own young.

There is a corrective alternative. In increasing numbers, queer kids are demonstrating their courage by stepping forward and demanding recognition. Although the issues were very different, the motivation and the drive of queer kids is not unlike that of the freedom riders and voting rights advocates of the 1960s. Progress is occurring slowly. In the process, all teens are benefiting by their increased awareness and acceptance of diversity. For the sake of all children and for the good of tolerance, fairness, understanding, and love, these queer kids deserve our support and encouragement.

Resources

USEFUL BOOKS FOR YOUTH, COUNSELORS, AND FAMILY

Books for Children

Alden, *A boy's best friend*—Bill has asthma and on his birthday his two moms give him a dog. Message: Being different is OK.

Bosche, *Jenny lives with Eric and Martin*—Photo essay of Jenny who lives with her father Eric and his partner Martin.

Brown, *The generous Jefferson Bartleby Jones*—Appreciating diverse (gay) families and your gay parents, Ages 6-10.

Heron, *How would you feel if your dad was gay?*—Examines the concerns of three children with gay parents.

Heron and Maran, *How would you feel if your dad was gay?*—Appreciating diverse (lesbian and gay) families and your lesbian and gay parents, Ages 6-12.

Newman, *Belinda's banquet*—Lesson of acceptance by child of weight taught by lesbian mother of friend, Ages 4-10.

Newman, *Gloria goes to gay pride*—Told from the viewpoint of a young girl, Gloria accompanies her two moms to a gay pride celebration.

Newman, *Heather has two mommies*—Illustrates the loving and supportive family of five-year-old Heather and her two lesbian mothers. So lovingly done, you'll wonder what all the fuss was about in the NYC School Board.

Valentine, *The day they put a tax on rainbows, and other stories*—Fairy tales about kids with lesbian and gay parents, Ages 2-adult.

Valentine, *The duke who outlawed jellybeans, and other stories*—Fairy tales about kids with lesbian and gay parents, Ages 2-adult.

Willhoite, *Daddy's roommate*—Illustrates many family situations with this non-traditional family.

Willhoite, *Families, a coloring book*—Appreciating diverse (racial, generational, cultural, sexual) families, Ages 2-6.

Willhoite, *The entertainer*—Will, a talented juggler, leaves his two moms and seeks fame and fortune until he realizes what's really important.

Books for Adolescents

Self-help

Alyson, *Young, gay, and proud*—Easy reading, gay-positive message for lesbian and gay youth on alienation, self-acceptance, coming out, health concerns, and celebration. Clear, informative, and interesting.

Bass and Kaufman, *Free your mind: The book for gay, lesbian, and bisexual youth—and their allies*—Well-written, straightforward advice for teens, parents, educators, and allies. Lots of firsthand quotes.

Be yourself: Questions and answers for gay, lesbian and bisexual youth—Factual, no-nonsense, homo-positive twenty-two-page pamphlet available from PFLAG.

McNaught, *On being gay: Thoughts on family, faith, and love*—Gay-positive essays on family, faith, and love, and what it means to be gay.

Rench, *Understanding sexual identity: A book for gay teens and their friends*—Discusses coming out, healthy sexuality, homophobia, religious views, and resources.

Stopping antigay abuse of students in public schools: A legal perspective—Step-by-step procedures designed to help students end abuse and antigay violence, pamphlet available from Lambda Legal Defense Fund, New York: 1996.

Novels and Autobiographies

Bauer, *Am I blue? Coming out from the silence*—Sixteen short stories for young adults exploring aspects of growing up lesbian or gay.

Block, *Cherokee Bat and the Goat Guys*—Group of friends forms a rock band.

Block, *Weetzie bat*—The loves and lives of a group of gay and nongay friends.

Brett, *S.P. loves A.D.*—Novel explores the confusion and intense feeling between two girls.

Brimner, *Being different: Lambda youths speak out*—In-depth interviews with adolescents and young adults with some commentary by the author.

Carson, *Brothers in arms*—Young man joins seminary to escape his feelings but finds true peace in acceptance of self. A very funny coming-of-age novel.

Chandler, *Passages of pride*—Autobiographic stories of several lesbian, gay, and bisexual youth.

DiMarco, *Escape to the wind*—A fast-paced science fiction tale of lesbian and gay youths set in the post-Armageddon Pacific Northwest. Written by a nineteen-year-old lesbian novelist.

Due, *Joining the tribe: Growing up gay and lesbian in the 90's*—Interviews with several teens of varied backgrounds.

Durant, *When heroes die*—Novel about young boy who must deal with conflicting feelings concerning his uncle—a gay, former baseball star with AIDS—and his own sexuality.

Fricke, *Reactions of a rock lobster*—Autobiography of growing up gay by the then-sixteen-year-old who "shocked" his school in 1980 when he took another male to his high school prom.

Fricke, *Sudden strangers: The story of a gay son and his father*—Continuation of the Fricke story and reconciliation with his father.

Garden, *Annie on my mind*—Novel about two intelligent high school senior women who fall in love.

Grima, *Not the only one: Lesbian and gay fiction for teens.*

Hanlon, *The wing and the flame*—With the help of a grandfatherly friend, an adolescent accepts and learns to express his love for his best friend. A very sensitive novel.

Heron, *One teenager in ten*—Autiobiographical writings by lesbian and gay youth. Helpful for youth, parents, and counselors.

Heron, *Two teenagers in twenty*—Updated version of *One teenager in ten* with all new autobiographies.

Kerr, *Deliver me from evil*—Family slowly begins to realize that their daughter is a lesbian.

Kerr, *Night kites*—Novel concerning being different and accepting your difference and your brother's gayness.

Klein, *Now that you know*—A fifteen-year-old girl goes through the process of accepting her father's gayness.

Levy, *Come out smiling*—In this novel, a teen struggles with acceptance of her sexual orientation while at summer camp and with two very positive lesbian role models.

Mastoon, *The shared heart: Portraits and stories celebrating lesbian, gay, and bisexual young people.* Originated as a photo exhibit. Beautifully done.

Rees, *In the tent*—Novel in which a gay youth comes to terms with his gayness while confronting a crisis on a camping trip.

Scoppettone, *Happy endings are all alike*—Gripping novel about a crisis faced by two romantically involved high school women and their families.

Singer, *Growing up gay, growing up lesbian*—Biographical writing of teens, poems, and excerpts from novels; designed to help students cope.

Trenchard, *Talking about young lesbians*—Lesbian teens discuss families, school, and relationships.

Walker, *Peter*—An honest novel about a young man who is attracted to his brother's best friend.

Winterson, *Oranges are not the only fruit*—Evangelical family comes to terms with daughter's lesbianism.

Magazines

Inside Out

P.O. Box 460268
San Francisco, CA 94146-0268

Telephone: (415) 487-6870
e-mail: insideout@igc.apc.org
e-mail: insideout2@aol.com

OUT

P.O. Box 1935
Marion, OH 43306-2035

Telephone: (800) 669-1002
e-mail: outmag@aol.com

OutYouth
208 W. 13th St.
New York, NY 10011

Y.O.U.T.H.
P.O. Box 34215
Washington, DC 20043

Telephone: (202)234-3562

General

Allport, *The nature of prejudice.*
Blumenfeld, *Homophobia: How we all pay the price.*
Blumenfeld and Raymond, *Looking at gay and lesbian life*—Textbook-like treatment of socialization, gender roles, sexuality, culture, lifestyles, history, etc.
Clunis and Green, *Lesbian couples*—Excellent resource for counselors and clients.
DeCecco, *Homophobia*—Somewhat dated but most thorough resource.
Henderson, Homosexuality in the college years: Developmental differences between men and women. *Journal of American College Health,* 1984, 32, 216-219.
Herdt, *Gay and lesbian youth*—Multicultural exploration of the experiences of lesbian and gay youth.
Isay, *Being homosexual*—A positive psychodynamic approach to understanding the development of the male homosexual.
Jennings, *Becoming visible: A reader in gay and lesbian history for high school and college students.*
Marcus, *Is it a choice?*—Comprehensive and candid discussion of this question and hundreds of other lesbian and gay issues.
Martin and Hetrick, The stigmatization of the gay and lesbian adolescent. *Journal of Homosexuality,* 1988, 15, 163-183.
Williams, *The spirit and the flesh*—Comprehensive study of sexual diversity in Native American cultures.

Books and Articles for Counselors

American Friends Service Committee, *Bridges of respect: Creating support for lesbian and gay youth*—Analysis of effects of homophobia and approaches to effect constructive change.
Balka and Rose, *Twice blessed: On being lesbian and gay and Jewish*—Proposes integration of gay identity and greater Jewish community. Especially useful for counselors with little experience with the Jewish community.
Bergstrom and Cruz, *Counseling lesbian and gay male youth: Their special lives/ special needs.* Increases counselors' awareness of the issues.

Berzon, *Positively gay: New approaches to gay and lesbian life*—Valuable anthology on living a fulfilling lesbian or gay life.

Brown, Counseling the youthful homosexual. *The School Counselor,* 1975, 22, 325-333—Dated but excellent overview of many of the issues facing lesbian and gay youth.

Clark, *The new loving someone gay*—Mostly addresses gay men's issues but excellent resource for gays and nongays alike, including counselors, teachers, and parents.

Coleman and Remafedi, Gay, lesbian, and bisexual adolescents: A critical challenge to counselors. In *Journal of Counseling and Development,* 1989, 68, 36-40—Best general survey of the school counselor's role.

DeCrescenzo, *Helping gay and lesbian youth: New policies, new programs, new practice*—Insights into helping lesbian and gay youth develop and learn to cope.

Eichberg, *Coming out: An act of love.*

Hanckel and Cunningham, *A way of love, a way of life: A young person's introduction to what it means to be gay.* A little dated (1979) but contains some good information.

Herdt and Boxer, *Children of horizons: How gay and lesbian teens are leading a new way out of the closet*—Data from youth seeking counseling that indicates that lesbian and gay youth are as well adjusted as their heterosexual peers.

Hilgalgo, Peterson, and Woodman (Eds.), *Lesbian and gay issues: A resource manual for social workers* (Published by NASW).

McNaught, *A disturbed peace: Confessions of an Irish Catholic homosexual*—Debunks many myths.

McNeill, *The church and the homosexual*—Argues for a new understanding of the spiritual rewards of loving lesbian and gay relationships.

Paroski, Gay and lesbian teens. In Dus, *Keys to caring: Assisting your gay and lesbian clients.*

Powell, Homosexual behavior and the school counselor. *The school counselor,* 1987, 34, 381-399—Very basic strategies for aiding lesbian and gay youth.

Rofes, Gay issues, schools, and the right-wing backlash. *Rethinking schools,* 1997, 11.

Scroggs, *The New Testament and homosexuality*—Bible does not speak as unequivocally against homosexuality as believed.

Shiman, *The prejudice book: Activities for the classroom*—Although the book does not explicitly mention lesbians and gays, the discussion can certainly address these groups. Excellent vehicle for exploring prejudice, stereotypes, and discrimination.

Slater, Essential issues in working with lesbian and gay male youths. *Professional psychology: Research and practice,* 1988, 19, 226-235—Excellent resource, especially bibliography.

Spong, *Living in sin? A bishop rethinks human sexuality*—Calls for equal, loving, nonexploitive relationships for all, regardless of orientation.

The Campaign to End Homophobia, *I think I might be a lesbian . . . Now what do I do?* (available from The Campaign to End Homophobia, Box 819, Cambridge, MA 02139)—Camera-ready copy may be reproduced and distributed to students. Helps youths explore sexuality.

The Campaign to End Homophobia, *I think I might be a gay . . . Now what do I do?* (available from The Campaign to End Homophobia, Box 819, Cambridge, MA 02139)—Camera-ready copy may be reproduced and distributed to students. Helps youths explore sexuality.

Trenchard and Warren, *Something to tell you*—Extensive interviews with 400 youths explore attitudes and services.

Unks (Ed.), *The gay teen: Educational practice and theory for lesbian, gay, and bisexual adolescents.*

Walling (Ed.), *Open lives, safe schools.* Phi Delta Kappa Educational Foundation.

Weinberg, *Society and the healthy homosexual*—Slightly outdated but gay-positive book that urges lesbians and gay men to be happy, healthy and proud.

Whitlock and Kamel, *Bridges of respect: Creating support for lesbian and gay youth—A resource guide from the American Friends Service Committee*—Handbook for counselors, teachers, parents, religious leaders, and youth workers dealing with issues of homophobia, stereotypes, respecting diversity, and health and sex.

Curricular Materials for Teachers/Counselors

Write to Arthur Lipkin, PhD, Harvard Graduate School of Education, Longfellow Hall 210, Cambridge, MA 02138.

Coming-Out and Parental Acceptance Handbooks

Back, *Are you still my mother? Are you still my family?*—Social worker summaries of stories of parents of gay men and lesbians while addressing the emotional needs of these individuals and their families. Good resource for parents and counselors.

Baetz, *Lesbian crossroads: Personal stories of lesbian struggles and triumphs*—Personal accounts of women from diverse backgrounds with section on family acceptance.

Bernstein, *Straight parents/gay children*—Addresses parental fears and helps parents appreciate their child. Told through the vehicle of author accepting his lesbian daughter.

Borhek, *Coming out to parents: A two-way survival guide for lesbians and gay men and their parents*—Good resource for lesbians and gay men, counselors, and parents. Chapter on religious issues.

Borhek, *My son Erik*—Acceptance after initial difficulty relative to fundamentalist religious beliefs. Good for parents with religious issues.

Cohen and Cohen, *When someone you know is gay.*

Curtis, *Revelations: A collection of gay male coming-out stories*—Popular gay authors and unknowns relate their experiences; some contain sexual content.

Delaney, *The motion of light in water*—Memoirs of a gay, African-American science fiction writer which can serve as an excellent model for coming out.

Dew, *The family heart: A memoir of when our son came out*—Relates a family's experience of coming out.

Fairchild and Hayward, *Now that you know: What every parent should know about homosexuality*—Written by the mother of a gay son and the mother of a lesbian daughter who offer answers to the most commonly asked question in the pre-AIDS era.

Fortunato, *Embracing the exile: Healing journeys of gay Christians*—Kübler-Ross's grieving model of acceptance of one's homosexuality within a Christian context. Chapter 8, "Grieving gay," is very insightful.

Griffin, Wirth, and Wirth, *Beyond acceptance: Parents of lesbians and gays talk about their experiences*—Offers answers and emotional support while debunking myths through the experiences of twenty-three parents.

Harbeck, *Coming out of the classroom closet: Gay and lesbian students, teachers, and curricula.*

Helminiak, *What the Bible really says about homosexuality*—Scholar and theologian uses biblical archaeology and older translations to demonstrate a truer meaning.

Jones, *Understanding gay relatives and friends.*

McDonald and Steinhorn, *Understanding homosexuality: A guide for those who know, love, or counsel gay and lesbian individuals.*

McNeill, *The church and the homosexual*—Upbeat, affirming, liberating resource for lesbians and gays, their lovers, and families.

McNeill, *Taking a chance on God*—Good resource for those struggling to reconcile Christianity and homosexuality.

Muchmore and Hansen, *Coming out right: A handbook for the gay male*—Clear, concise information about choices and life as a gay man.

Muller, *Parents matter: Parents' relationships with lesbian daughters and gay sons*—Insightful study of lesbians and gay men and their parents.

Pennington, *Good news for modern gays*—A more fundamentalist religious acceptance.

Rafkin, *Different daughters: A book by mothers of lesbians*—Designed for parents, this book describes the experiences of twenty-four mothers in their own words.

Silverstein, *A family matter: A parents' guide to homosexuality.*

Sauerman, *Read this before coming out to your parents* (Available from PFLAG, see Resources below). Describes the questions one needs to ask one's self first and the typical reactions of parents on the road to acceptance.

Scanzoni and Mollenkott, *Is the homosexual my neighbor?*—Two fundamentalists reconcile the Bible with homosexuality and love for all God's creations.

Spong, *Rescuing the Bible from judgmentalism*—Episcopalian bishop speaks against parochial homophobic interpretation of the Bible.

Umans, *Like coming home: Coming-out letters*—Letter from lesbians and gay men, age fifteen to sixty-four, coming out to families, friends, and themselves.

Williams, *Just as I am: A practical guide to being out, proud, and Christian*—Sensitive and at times humorous exploration of faith and acceptance of one's homosexuality.

Pamphlets for Parents

About our children (available from PFLAG).
Answers to your questions about sexual orientation and homosexuality (available from the American Psychological Association).
Can we understand? (available from PFLAG).
Teens tell their own stories (available from PFLAG).
Why is my child gay?—Summarizes the conclusions of eleven experts to reassure parents that sexual orientation results from many different factors and that sexual orientation cannot be permanently changed (available from PFLAG).

Peer Acceptance

Barger, *What happened to Mr. Forster?*—Young male is befriended by new teacher who becomes the target of antigay prejudice. Novel explores the basis of prejudice for the secondary school child.
Cohen and Cohen, *When someone you know is gay*—For nongay teens who may have a lesbian or gay friend.
Hall, *Sticks and stones*—Novel describes the process a teen experiences in accepting the homosexuality of a friend.
Meyer, *Elliott and win*—Youth struggles with acceptance of his Big Brother, rumored to be gay, and eventually realizes that sexual orientation is irrelevant to their friendship.
Scoppettone, *Trying hard to hear you*—Novel about a summer theater group for teens, including two gay adolescents. Told from perspective of a young woman who is one of the group members. Explores homophobia and internal strife. Somewhat dated.
Spence, *A candle for Saint Anthony*—In this novel two young men have an intense personal relationship that is neither romantic nor sexual but must still endure the prejudice and discrimination of those who find the relationship unacceptable.
Wersba, *Crazy vanilla*—Novel about a streetwise girl who challenges a young man's attitudes, especially his acceptance of his gay brother.
Wersba, *Just be gorgeous*—In this novel, a young nonlesbian woman matures and becomes self-reliant through her relationship with a gay youth who is determined to be himself.

VIDEOS

Be true to yourself—Gay married couple and human rights activists speak caringly to teens (available through PFLAG).

DeGrassi Junior High: He ain't heavy—Fourteen-year-old boy learns to accept his older brother whom he discovers is gay (available WGBH, Box 222-TV, South Esston, MA 02375).

DeGrassi Junior High: Rumor has it—Young girl struggles with her own sexual orientation while rumors begin that an admired teacher is lesbian. Illustrates the viciousness of rumors and the irrelevance of sexual orientation for being a good teacher (available WGBH, Box 222-TV, South Easton, MA 02375).

Families come out—Includes twenty-four-page educational and resource guide (available through PFLAG).

Gay and lesbian youth making history in Massachusetts—Recounts Governor's Commission and the aftermath (available from Massachusetts Governor's Commission on Gay and Lesbian Youth).

Gay youth—Explores the experiences of two teenagers in detail and six to a lesser extent. Demonstrates how love and acceptance can make a positive difference for a lesbian or gay teen.

Growing up gay and lesbian—Includes strategies for effective living while addressing issues of self-acceptance and coming out (available at 800-561-4300).

Hate, homophobia, and schools—Discussion format of youth and adults (available from Wisconsin Public Television's Cooperative Education Service Agency, 800-633-7445).

Homo teens—Five portraits of very different teens allowed to speak for themselves (available from Joan Jubila, P.O. Box 1966, New York, NY 10013).

It's elementary: Talking about gay issues in school—Explores the teaching of tolerance in six different classrooms. Excellent (available from Women's Educational Media, San Francisco, 415-641-4632).

On being gay—Excerpts from Brian McNaught's acclaimed workshops combating homophobia.

Out: Stories of lesbian and gay youth—Chronicles the struggles and victories of a group of diverse lesbian and gay youth in Canada (available at 800-267-7710).

Pride and prejudice: The life and times of gay and lesbian youth—Focuses on a Toronto weekly youth group showing the significance of this service for teens (available at 416-924-2100).

Safe schools: Making schools safe for gay and lesbian students (available from Donna Brathwaite, Safe Schools Program, Massachusetts Department of Education, 617-388-3300, ext. 409. Plan to send blank tape).

Sexual orientation: Issues facing gay and lesbian youth (available from Wisconsin Public Television's Cooperative Education Service Agency, 800-622-7445).

Straight from the heart—Parents talk about their lesbian and gay offspring.

Teaching respect—Produced by the Gay, Lesbian, and Straight Teachers Network. This video explains why educators should be concerned about homophobia and abuse in school (available at 212-727-0135).

ON-LINE RESOURCES

Elight gay youth 'zine
   http://www.youth.org/elight/
Gay and lesbian teen pen pals
   http://www.chanton.com/gayteens.html
Gay, lesbian, and bisexual youth advisor
   http://www.gcfurball.com/cat/glb/glb.html
National resources for lesbian, gay, and bisexual youth
   http://www.yale.edu/glb/youth.html
Oasis (Teen 'zine)
   http://www.oasismag.com/
Outright
   http://outright.com/
Out Proud, National Coalition for Gay, Lesbian, and Bisexual Youth
   http://www.cyberspaces.com/outproud
PFLAG
   http://abacus.oxy.edu/QRD/orgs/.PFLAG
Pink Triangle Services Youth Group, Ottawa
   http://www.ncf.carleton.ca.12345/freeport/sigs/life/gay/youth/menu
The cool page for queer teens
   http://www.pe.net/~bidstrup/cool.html

TALK LINES/HOTLINES/CRISIS LINES

AIDS Foundation Hotline (English and Spanish)	(800) FOR AIDS
AIDS Project New Haven (CT)	(203) 624-0947
Albuquerque (NM) One in Ten Helpline	(505) 266-8041
Ames (IA) Gay and Lesbian Information Line	(512) 295-2104
Anchorage (AK) Gay Helpline	(907) 258-4777
Ann Arbor (MI) Gay Hotline	(313) 662-1977
Arlington (VA) Whitman-Walker Clinic—Northern Virginia Info/Hotline	(703) 358-9550
Ashville (NC) Gay and Lesbian Information Line	(704) 253-2971
Atlanta (GA) Young Adult Program Helpline	(404) 892-0661
Baltimore (MD) Gay and Lesbian Community Center	(410) 837-8888
Berkeley (CA) Pacific Center Switchboard	(415) 548-8283 841-6224
Birmingham (AL) Gay and Lesbian Information Line	(205) 326-8600
Bloomington (IN) Gay and Lesbian Switchboard	(812) 855-OUT
Boston (MA) Alliance of Gay and Lesbian Youth	(800) 42-BAGLY
Boston (MA) Gay and Lesbian Helpline	(617) 267-9001
Burlington (VT) Outright Vermont Hotline (VT only)	(800) GLB-CHAT
Caribou (ME) Gay/Lesbian Phone Line	(207) 498-2088

Charleston (WV) Young, Gay, and Proud Info/Helpline (304) 340-3690
Charlottesville (VA) Lesbian/Gay Student Union Helpline (804) 971-4942
Chicago Horizons Youth Services Helpline (312) 929-HELP
(TDD) (312) 327-HELP
Chicago In Touch Hotline (University of Illinois) (312) 996-5535
Cleveland (OH) Lesbian and Gay Community
  Services Center (216) 781-6736
Colorado Springs (CO) Helpline (719) 471-4429
Columbia (MO) Gay and Lesbian Helpline (314) 449-4477
Columbus (OH) Stonewall Community Center Hotline (614) 299-7764
Coos Bay (OP) Gay and Lesbian Outreach Hotline (503) 269-4183
Dallas (TX) Gay and Lesbian Young Adults Infoline (214) 621-7440
Danbury (CT) Gay, Lesbian, and Bisexual Youth
  Group, Twenty-four-hour Helpline (203) 426-4922
Denver (CO) Helpline (303) 837-1598
Denver (CO) Youth Crisis Line (303) 461-1650
Denver (CO) Youth Services Program Helpline (303) 324-GAYS
Des Moines (IA) Gay and Lesbian Resource Center
  Information Line (512) 277-1454
El Paso (TX) Lambda Services—Youth Network
  Info/Hotline (915) 562-GAYS
Eugene (OR) Gay and Lesbian Helpline (503) 683-CHAT
Ferndale (MI) Affirmations Lesbian and Gay
  Community Center (313) 398-7105
Fort Myers (FL) Support, Inc. Helpline (813) 275-1400
Fort Wayne (IN) Gay/Lesbian Helpline (219) 744-1199
Gainesville (FL) Gay Switchboard (904) 332-0700
Garden Grove (CA) Gay/Lesbian Community Services
  Hotline (714) 534-3261
Gay, Lesbian, and Bisexual Youth Hotline (800) 347-TEEN
Gay Men's Health Crisis (GMHC)—HIV/AIDS
  information and referral (212) 807-6655
Gay Youth Talk Line (415) 863-3636
(800) 246-PRIDE
outside San Francisco
Glen Ellyn (IL) West Suburban Gay Association Hotline (708) 790-9742
Harrisburg (PA) Gay and Lesbian Switchboard (717) 234-0328
Houston (TX) Gay and Lesbian Switchboard (713) 529-3211
Honolulu (HI) Gay Information Service (808) 926-1000
Indianapolis (IN) Gay/Lesbian Switchboard (317) 253-GAYS
(800) 347-TEEN
Iowa City (IA) Gay Line (University of Iowa) (319) 353-3877
Iowa City (IA) United Action for Youth Helpline (319) 338-0059
(800) 850-3051
Kahului (HI) Gay/Lesbian/Bisexual Information Line (808) 575-2681

Kansas City (MO) Gay Talk Helpline	(816) 931-4470
Knoxville (TN) Gay Helpline	(615) 521-6546
Lancaster (PA) Gay and Lesbian Helpline	(717) 397-0691
Lansing (M1) Lesbian/Gay Hotline	(517) 332-3200
Las Vegas (NV) Gay Switchboard	(702) 733-7990
Lesbian AIDS Project—HIV/AIDS info and referral	(212) 337-3532
Lexington (KN) Gay/Lesbian Services Organization	(606) 231-0335
Lincoln (NE) Gay and Lesbian Youth Talkline	(402) 473-7932
Little Rock (AR) Gay and Lesbian Task Force Switchboard	(501) 666-3340
	(800) 448-8305
Los Angeles (CA) Gay and Lesbian Youth Talkline	(213) 993-7475
	(818) 508-1802
Lowell (MA) Merrimack Valley Lesbian/Gay Support	(508) 452-3679
LYRIC Youth Talkline and Infoline	(800) 246-PRIDE
Madison (WI) Community United	
Gay Line	(608) 255-4297
Lesbian Line	(608) 255-0743
Miami (FL) Lambda Passages Community Hotline	(305) 759-3661
Miami (FL) Switchboard	(305) 358-4357
Milwaukee (WI) Gay Information Line	(414) 444-7331+
Minneapolis (MN) Gay and Lesbian Community	
Action Council Hotline	(612) 822-8661
	(800) 800-0907
Morgantown (WV) Gay and Lesbian Helpline	(304) 292-GAYS
Morristown (NJ) Womyn's Network Helpline	(201) 285-1595
Nashua (NH) Gay Information Line	(603) 595-2650
National Center for Lesbian Rights (Special Project to	
Stop Mental Health Abuse of Lesbian, Gay, Bisexual,	
and Transgender Youth)	(800) 528-6257
National HIV/AIDS Hotline	(800) 342-AIDS
National Lesbian and Gay Crisis Line	(800) 221-7044
National Native American AIDS Prevention Center	(800) 283-AIDS
National Runaway Hotline	(800) 843-5200
National Suicide and Runaway Switchboard	(800) 621-4000
	(24-hour service)
National Suicide Hotline	(800) 882-3386
	(Some area codes)
New Hampshire Gay Information Line	(603) 224-1686
New York (NY) Gay/Lesbian Switchboard	(212) 777-1800
New York (NY) Lesbian Switchboard	(212) 741-2610
Norfolk (VA) Gay Information Line	(804) 622-GAYS
Norwich (CT) Information Line of Southeast Connecticut	(203) 886-0516
Orlando (FL) Gay and Lesbian Community Services Hotline	(407) 649-8615
Out Youth Hotline	(800) 96-YOUTH

Parents and Friends of Lesbians and Gays	(415) 921-8850
	(202) 638-4200
Philadelphia (PA) Gay and Lesbian Switchboard	(215) 546-7000
Philadelphia (PA) Lesbian Hotline	(215) 222-5110
Philadelphia (PA) Penguin Place Youth Group Helpline	(215) 732-2220
Phoenix (AZ) Lesbian/Gay Community Switchboard	(602) 234-2752
Portland (ME) Outright—Maine	(207) 774-HELP
Portland (OR) Youthline (3-5 p.m. M-F)	(503) 233-1113
Project Inform Hotline—HIV/AIDS Information	(800) 822-7422
(In CA)	(800) 334-7422
Providence (RI) Gay and Lesbian Helpline	(401) 751-3322
Raleigh (NC) Gay and Lesbian Helpline of Wade County	(919) 821-0055
Rochester (NY) Gay Alliance of Genesee Valley Infoline	(716) 244-8640
Rutgers University (New Brunswick, NJ) Peer Counseling and Infoline	(908) 932-7886
San Francisco (CA) Gay Area Youth Switchboard	(415) 386-GAYS
San Francisco (CA) Lavender Youth Helpline	(800) 246-PRIDE
San Francisco (CA) Support Services for Gay and Lesbian Youth	(415) 749-3400
Santa Rosa (CA) Helpline	(707) 544-HELP
Seattle (WA) Counseling Service for Sexual Minorities Hotline	(360) 282-9307
Seattle (WA) Gay, Lesbian, and Bisexual Youth Program Infoline	(360) 332-7900
South Hackensack Gay Activists of New Jersey Helpline	(201) 692-1794
Spokane (WA) Odyssey AIDS Hotline (Surrounding WA)	(800) 456-3236
Stamford (CT) Gay and Lesbian Guideline	(203) 327-0767
State College (PA) Gay and Lesbian Switchboard	(814) 237-1950
St. Petersburg (FL) The Line	(813) 586-4297
Tallahassee (FL) Women's Information Line	(904) 656-7884
Tampa (FL) Gay Hotline	(813) 229-8839
Topeka (KS) Gay Rap Telephone Line	(913) 233-6558
Tucson (AZ) Information and Referral Service	(602) 234-2752
Tulsa (OK) TOHR Gay/Lesbian Helpline	(918) 743-GAYS
Urbana (IL) Lesbian, Gay, and Bisexual Switchboard	(217) 384-8040
Washington (DC) Gay and Lesbian Hotline	(202) 833-3234
Washington (DC) Sexual Minority Youth Assistance League	(202) 546-5911
Wichita (KS) Land of Oz Information	(316) 269-0913
Wilmington (DE) Gay and Lesbian Hotline	(800) 292-0429
Winston-Salem (NC) Gay and Lesbian Hotline	(919) 722-4040

NATIONAL ORGANIZATIONS

American Education Gender Information Service
P.O. Box 33724
Decatur, GA 30033-0724

Telephone: (404) 939-2122
Fax: (404) 939-1770
e-mail: aegis@mindspring.com

• Transgender and transexual information center.

American Friends Service Committee, Bridges Project
1501 Cherry St.
Philadelphia, PA 19102-1429

Telephone: (215) 241-7133
e-mail: bridgespro@aol.com

American Indian Gays and Lesbians
P.O. Box 10229
Minneapolis, MN 55458-3229

American Psychological Association,
Committee on Lesbian and Gay Concerns
750 First St., N.E.
Washington, DC 20002

Telephone: (202) 336-6052

Asian/Pacific Lesbians and Gays, Inc.
Box 433, Suite 109
7985 Santa Monica Blvd.
West Hollywood, CA 90046-5111

Black Gay and Lesbian Leadership Forum
1219 S. LaBrea
Los Angeles, CA 90019

Telephone: (213) 964-7820
Fax: (213)964-7830

Coalition for Lesbian and Gay Student Groups
P.O. Box 190712
Dallas, TX 75219

Telephone: (214) 621-6705

• Coordinates campus groups in South and Southwest.

Federation of Parents, Families, and Friends of Lesbians and Gays, Inc. (PFLAG)
P.O. Box 27605
Washington, DC 20038-7605

Telephone: (212) 638-4200
e-mail: PFLAG@aol.com

Friends of Project 10, Inc.
7650 Melrose Ave.
Los Angeles, CA 90006

Telephone: (213) 651-5200

Gay and Lesbian Arabic Society
Box 4971
Washington, DC 20008

• Provides a support network.

International Foundation for Gender Education
P.O. Box 229
Waltham, MA 02254-0229

Telephone: (617) 894-8340
Fax: (617) 899-5703
e-mail: IFGE@world.std.com

• Educational service for transgender community.

Lambda Youth Network
P.O. Box 7911
Culver City, CA 90233

Telephone: (310) 216-1312

• Print material, supply self-addressed envelope and $1 contribution.

National Gay Alliance for Young Adults
P.O. Box 190712
Dallas, TX 75219

Telephone: (214) 701-3455

National Education Association, Gay and Lesbian Caucus
P.O. Box 314
Roosevelt, NJ 08555

Telephone: (609) 448-5215

National Latino/a Lesbian and Gay Organization (LLEGO)
703 G Street SE
Washington, DC 20003

Telephone: (202) 454-0092

National Youth Advocacy Coalition
1711 Connecticut Ave., NW
Suite 206
Washington, DC 20009

North American Multicultural Bisexual Network
584 Castro St., Box 441
San Francisco, CA 94114-2558

Rainbow Alliance of the Deaf
P.O. Box 14182
Washington, DC 20044-4182

• National referral source for gay and lesbian deaf community

Trikone: Gay and Lesbian South Asians
P.O. Box 21354
San Jose, CA 95151

Telephone: (408) 270-8776
Fax: (408) 274-2733
e-mail: trikone@rahul.net

YOUTH GROUPS AND SUPPORT SERVICES

CANADA

BRITISH COLUMBIA

Gay and Lesbian Center
1170 Bute St.
Vancouver, V6E 1Z6

Telephone: (604) 684-6867

ONTARIO

Lesbian, Gay and Bisexual Youth of Toronto
519 Church St.
Toronto, M4Y 2C9

Lesbian, Gay and Bisexual Youth Program
Suite 300, 65 Wellesley St. E.
Toronto M4Y 1G7

UNITED STATES

ALABAMA

Lambda Resource Center
516 S. 27th St.
Birmingham, AL

Telephone: (205) 326-8600

MALAGA
P.O. Box 40326
Mobile, AL 36640

Telephone: (205) 433-3245

Lambda Triangle Center
609 Hull St, P.O. Box 40326
Montgomery, AL 36101

Telephone: (205) 834-0018

ALASKA

SE Alaska Gay/Lesbian Alliance
P. O. Box 211371
Auke Bay, AK 99821

Telephone: (907) 586-4297

ARIZONA

Gay and Lesbian Community Center
P.O. Box 183
Flagstaff, AZ 86002

Telephone: (602) 526-6098

Gay and Lesbian Youth Group
P.O. Box 80174
Pheonix, AZ 85060

Telephone: (602) 280-9927

Wingspan Youth Group
Lesbian, Gay, Bisexual Community Center
422 N. 4th Ave.
Tucson, AR 85705

Telephone: (520) 624-1779

ARKANSAS

Women's Project
2224 S. Main St.
Little Rock, AR 72206

Telephone: (501) 372-5113

CALIFORNIA

Bay Area Sexual Minority Youth Network
P.O. Box 460268
San Francisco, CA 94146-0268

• Newsletter, referrals, and pen pal program for high school youth.

Billy DeFrank Lesbian and Gay Community Center
175 Stockton Ave.
San Jose, CA 95216

Telephone: (408) 293-4525

Chinatown Youth Center
1693 Polk St.
San Francisco, CA 94109

Telephone: (415) 775-2636

• Information and referral

DramaDIVAS

Telephone: (415) 641-7684

• Theatre group for lesbian, gay, and bisexual youth, 21 and younger.

EAGLES Center (High School for Lesbian and gay teens)
7051 Santa Monica Blvd.
Hollywood, CA 90038

Telephone: (213) 957-0348

Eighteenth Street Services
217 Church St.
San Francisco, CA 94114

Telephone: (415) 861-4898 (English)
(415) 861-8803 (Spanish)

• Drug, alcohol and AIDS counseling; youth support services.

Family Workshops
10861 Queensland St.
Los Angeles, CA 90034

Telephone: (310) 274-0219/475-3225

• Support workshops for parents of lesbians, gays, and bisexuals.

Gay and Lesbian Adolescent Social Services (GLASS)
650 Robinson Blvd., Suite A
West Hollywood, CA 90069

Telephone: (310) 358-8727

Gay and Lesbian Center
P.O. Box 6333
San Bernadino, CA 92412

Telephone: (714) 824-7618

Gay and Lesbian Community Services Center
1625 N. Schrader Blvd.
Los Angeles, CA 90028-9998

Telephone: (213) 993-7400
TDD: (213) 464-0029

Gay and Lesbian Resources
P.O. Box 3480
Camarillo, CA 93011

Telephone: (805) 389-1530

Gay Asian/Pacific Islanders (GAPA)

Telephone: (415) 575-3939/863-8927

• Support groups and peer buddies.

Gay United Services, Inc.
P. O. Box 4640
Fresno, CA 93744

Telephone: (204) 268-3541

Gay Youth Alliance San Diego
The Center, P.O. Box 83022
3619 Normal St.
San Diego, CA 92138-3022

Telephone: (619) 233-9309

LagunaOutreach
P.O. Box 1701
Laguna Beach, CA 92652

Telephone: (714) 472-8867

Lambda Youth Family Empowerment (LYFE) Program
1748 Market St. (Suite 201)
San Francisco, CA 94102

Telephone: (415) 565-7681

• A substance abuse prevention program for multi-ethnic, self-identified lesbian, gay, and bisexual youth who need a safe environment.

Lambda Youth Group
Lambda Community Center,
P. O. Box 163654, 1931 L St.
Sacramento, CA 95814

Telephone: (916) 442-0185

Lambda Youth Network
P.O. Box 7911
Culver City, CA 90233

Telephone: (310) 821-1139

• To receive a list of lesbian, gay, and bisexual services in your location, send $2 and a self-addressed envelope.

Larkin Street Center

Telephone: (415) 673-0911/0912

• Education, counseling, confidential HIV testing and treatment, food, clothing, shelter, sexual-minority support groups.

Lavender Youth Recreation and Information Center (LYRIC)
127 Collinswood St.
San Francisco, CA 94114

Telephone: (415) 703-6150
                  (800) 246-PRIDE

• Weekly meetings, discussion groups, social activities, dances for sexual minority youth.

Lesbian and Gay Community Center
1332 Commerce Lane, P.O. Box 8280
Santa Cruz, CA 95061

Telephone: (408) 425-LGCC

Lesbian/Gay Bisexual Community Center
P.O. Box 8265
Stanford, CA 94309

Telephone: (415) 725-4222

Men's Network
903 Pacific Ave. (Suite 207A)
Santa Cruz, CA 95060

Telephone: (408) 427-1441

NEAT Family Project (New Experiences in Affection and Trust)
391 Taylor Blvd. (Suite 120)
Pleasant Hill, CA 94523

Telephone: (510) 687-8980

• Support groups for lesbian and gay youth at risk for substance abuse.

!Out Proud!
P.O. Box 24589
San Jose, CA 95154-4589

e-mail: info@outproud.org

• To receive a resource list for your location, contact via e-mail and list city, state, and zip code.

Positive Images
1023 Fourth St. (Suite C)
Santa Rosa, CA 95404

Telephone: (707) 579-4947/433-5333

Proactive Youth Project

Telephone: (415) 333-HELP

• On-the-job training for sexual-minority youth seventeen and younger.

Project Teens
One East Olive Ave.
Redlands, CA 92373

Telephone: (909) 335-2005

Project 10
Virginia Uribe, Fairfax High School
7850 Melrose Ave.,
Los Angeles, CA 90006

Telephone: (213) 651-5200, ext. 244

Pacific Center for Human Growth
2712 Telegraph Ave.
Berkeley, CA 94705
Telephone: (510) 841-6224/548-2192

• Counseling, discussion groups, social activities, and therapy for sexual minority youth with a special focus on youth of color.

Peninsula Family YMCA—Project FOCYS
1710 S. Amphlett (Suite 216)
San Mateo, CA 94402

Telephone: (415) 349-7969

• Family counseling for lesbian, gay, and bisexual youth.

Rainbow's End
100 Sir Francis Drake Blvd., Room 10
San Anselmo, CA 94960

Telephone: (415) 457-3523

R.A.P. (Real Alternative Program)

Telephone: (415) 282-9984

• Multiservice center for Latino youth, sensitive to sexual minorities.

Stonewall Alliance
P. O. Box 8855
Chico, CA 95927

South Bay Lesbian/Gay Community Center
P.O. Box 2777
Redondo Beach, CA 90278

Telephone: (213) 378-2850

Support Services for Gay, Lesbian, and Bisexual Youth
San Francisco Unified School District
1512 Golden Gate Ave.
San Francisco, CA 94115

Telephone: (415) 749-3400

Voice and Vision: Lutheran Lesbian and Gay Ministry
152 Church St.
San Francisco, CA 94114

Telephone: (415) 553-4026

Young Adult Program
Gay and Lesbian Community Services Center
12832 Garden Grove Blvd. (Suite A)
Garden Grove, CA 92463

Telephone: (714) 741-6501
Hot line: (714) 534-3261

Young Adult Program of Long Beach
The Center—Long Beach
2017 E. 4th St.
Long Beach, CA 90802

Telephone: (310) 434-4455

Youth and Family Assistance
Community Living Room
28 W. 37th Ave.
San Mateo, CA 94403

Telephone: (415) 572-0535

Youth Outreach
1625 N. Hudson Ave.
Los Angeles, CA 90028

Telephone: (213) 993-7451

Youth Outreach Gay and Lesbian Resource Center
126 East Haley (Suite A- 17)
Santa Barbara, CA 93101

Telephone: (805) 963-3636

COLORADO

Gay and Lesbian Association
P.O. Box 244
Delta, CO 81416

Telephone: (303) 874-5510

Gay and Lesbian Community
P. O. Box 3143
Aspen, CO 81612-3143

Telephone: (907) 925-9249

Gay and Lesbian Task Force
P.O. Box 18632
Denver, CO 80218

Telephone: (303) 830-2981

Outright
Community Center of Colorado
1245 E. Colfax Ave., Suite 125
Denver, CO 80218

Telephone: (303) 831-6268

Pikes Peak Gay. Lesbian Community Center
P. O. Box 574
Colorado Springs, CO 80901

Youth Services Program
P.O. Drawer 18E
Denver, CO 80218

Telephone: (303) 831-6268

CONNECTICUT

BGLAD 4 Youth
c/o AIDS Project New Haven
P.O. Box 636,
850 Grand Ave. (Suite 206)
New Haven, CT 06503

Telephone: (203) 624-0114

• Social, educational, and social support group for lesbian, gay, and bisexual youth.

Danbury Gay, Lesbian, and Bisexual Youth Group
105 Garfield Ave.
Danbury, CT 06810

Telephone: (203) 798-0863

Gay, Lesbian, and Bisexual Community Center
1841 Broad St.
Hartford, CT 06114

Telephone: (203) 724-5524

DELAWARE

Gay and Lesbian Alliance
800 West St.
Wilmington, DE 19801

Telephone: (302) 655-5280

DISTRICT OF COLUMBIA

Sexual Minority Youth Assistance League
333 1/2 Pennsylvania Ave SE, 3rd Fl
Washington, DC 20003-1148

Telephone: (202) 546-5940

• Youth services and advocacy; youth group.

FLORIDA

Compass
5405 S. Dixie Hiwy
West Palm Beach, FL 33405

Telephone: (407) 547-2622

Lesbian, Gay, and Bisexual Community Center
1335 Alton Rd.
Miami Beach, FL 33139-3811

Telephone: (305) 531-3666

Teen Closet
Contact through Gainesville Gay Switchboard

Telephone: (904) 332-0700

• High school organization

Your Turf, Delta Youth Alliance
c/o Gay and Lesbian Communiy Services of Central Florida
714 E. Colonial Dr.
Orlando, FL 32803

Telephone: (407) THE-GAYS

• Support and social organization for youth.

GEORGIA

Athens Gay and Lesbian Association
P.O. Box 2133
Athens, GA 30612

Telephone: (404) 548-0580

Atlanta Gay and Lesbian Community Center
63 Twelfth St.
Atlanta, GA 30309

Telephone: (404) 876-5372

Atlanta Lambda Community Center
Box 15180
Atlanta, GA 30333
Telephone: (770) 662-9010

Young Adult Program
Atlanta Gay and Lesbian Community Center
63 12th St.
Atlanta, GA 30309

Telephone: (404) 896-0661

HAWAII

Lesbian, Gay, Bisexual, and Transgender Teen Support Group
Wailuku, HI

Telephone: (808) 575-2681

Youth Outreach Services
Gay Community Center
1820 University Ave., 2nd Fl.,
Honolulu, HI 96822

Telephone: (808) 951-7000

IDAHO

The Community Center
P.O. Box 323
Boise, ID 83701

Telephone: (208) 336-3870

ILLINOIS

Horizons Gay/Lesbian Parents Group/Youth Program
961 W. Montana St.
Chicago, IL 60614

Telephone: (312) 472-6469

Kinheart Women's Center
2214 Ridge Ave.
Evanston, IL 60201

Telephone: (708) 491-1103

Gay and Lesbian Youth Education/Support Group (GALES)
Urbana, IL

Telephone: (217) 328-6068

PLGBC
284 Illini Union
1401 W. Green St.
Urbana, IL 61801

Telephone: (217) 384-8040

PRIDE Youth
North Shore Youth Health Service
1779 Maple St.
Northfield, IL 60093

Telephone: (708) 441-9880

INDIANA

Indianapolis Youth Group
P.O. Box 20716
Indianapolis, IN 46220

Telephone: (317) 541-8726
(800) 347-TEEN

IOWA

Gay and Lesbian Resource Center
Box 1643
Cedar Rapids, IA 52406-1643

Telephone: (319) 366-2055

Gay and Lesbian Resource Center, Youth Program
522 11th St.
Des Moines, IA 50309

Telephone: (515) 281-0634

United Action for Youth
410 Iowa City, IA 52240

Young Women's Resource Center
554 28th St.
Des Moines, IA 50312

Telephone: (515) 244-4901

KANSAS

Gay and Lesbian Services
Box 13, Kansas Union
University of Kansas,
Lawrence, KS 66045

Telephone: (913) 864-3091

KENTUCKY

Louisville Youth Group
Box 4664
Louisville, KY 40204

Telephone: (502) 894-9787

LOUISIANA

St. Louis Community Center
1022 Barrack St.
New Orleans, LA 70116

Telephone: (504) 524-7023

Lesbian and Gay Community Center of New Orleans
816 N. Rampart St.
New Orleans, LA 70116

Telephone: (504) 522-1103

MAINE

Gay/Lesbian Alliance
88 Winslow St.
The Powers House
Portland, ME 04103

Telephone: (207) 874-6596

Gay/Lesbian Community Network
P.O. Box 212
Bangor, ME 04401

Outright
P.O. Box 802
Auburn, ME 04212

Telephone: (207) 783-2557

Outright-Maine
P.O. Box 5077
Portland, ME 04101

Telephone: (207) 774-HELP

MARYLAND

Baltimore Gay Alliance
1504 E. Baltimore St.
Baltimore, MD 21231

Telephone: (410) 276-8468

Black Gay Community Center
c/o 614 W. Lexington St.
Baltimore, MD 21201

Telephone: (410)539-0942

Frostburg Gay, Lesbian, and Bisexual Students
32 Mill St., Suite 3
Frostburg, MD 21532

Telephone: (301) 689-0362

Gay and Lesbian Community Center of Baltimore
241 W. Chase St.
Baltimore, MD 21201

Telephone: (410) 837-5415
TDD: (410) 837-8529

Takoma Park Lesbians and Gays
P.O. Box 5243
Takoma Park, MD 20913

Telephone: (301) 891-DYKE

Upper Count Gay/Lesbian Association
15106-A Frederick Rd. #154
Rockville, MD 20850

Telephone: (301) 340-6241

MASSACHUSETTS

Cape and Islands Gay and Lesbian Youth Group
Box 78
Yarmouth Port, MA 02675

Telephone: (508) 362-2494
(800) 421-7874

Boston Alliance of Gay and Lesbian Youth (BAGLY)
P.O. Box 814
Boston, MA 02103

Telephone: (800) 422-2459

• Has listing for other agencies and organizations in New England.

Boston GLASS (Gay and Lesbian Adolescent Social Services)
93 Massachusetts Ave.
Boston, MA 02115

Telephone: (617) 266-3349
Fax: (617) 457-8133
e-mail: glass@jri.org

Framingham Regional Alliance of Gay and Lesbian Youth
P.O. Box 426
Framingham, MA 01701

Gay and Lesbian Alliance
P.O. Box 329
Dorchester, MA 02112

Telephone: (617) 825-3737

Gay and Lesbian Community Center
338 Newbury St.
Boston, MA 02115

Telephone: (617) 247-2927

Gay, Lesbian, and Straight Society (GLASS), FCAC Youth Project
86 Washington St.
Greenfield, MA 01060

Telephone: (413) 774-1028

North Shore Gay/Lesbian Alliance
P.O. Box 806
Marblehead, MA 01945

Telephone: (617) 745-3848

South Shore Gay/Lesbian Alliance
P.O. Box 712
Bridgewater, MA 02324

Telephone: (508) 293-5183

Supporters of Worcester Area Gay and Lesbian Youth
P.O. Box 592, Westside Station
Worcester, MA 01602

Telephone: (508) 755-0005

MICHIGAN

Affirmations Lesbian and Gay Community Center
195 W. Nine Mile Road, Suite 106-110
Ferndale, MI 48220

Telephone: (313) 398-4297

Michigan Alliance for Lesbian and Gay Youth Services (MALGYS)
617 N. Jenison St.
Lansing, MI 48915

Telephone: (517) 484-0946

Ozone House Gay and Lesbian Youth Group
608 N. Main St.
Ann Arbor, MI 48104

Telephone: (313) 662-2222

PRISM
Gateway Community Services
910 Abbott Rd., Suite 10,
East Lansing, MI 48823

Telephone: (517) 351-4000
(800) 292-4517

Windfire—Grand Rapids
c/o Lesbian and Gay Community Network of Western Michigan
909 Cherry SE
Grand Rapids, MI 49506

Telephone: (616) 241-GAYS

Windfire—Kalamazoo
c/o WMU Alliance for Lesbian and Gay Support
Faunce Student Services
Kalamazoo, MI 49008

Telephone: (616) 387-2134

Windfire—Traverse City
P.O. Box 562
Traverse City, MI 49685

Telephone: (616) 922-4800

MINNESOTA

District 202
2524 Nicollet Avenue South
Minneapolis, MN 55404

Telephone: (612) 871-5559

• Meeting place for youth.

Gay and Lesbian Community Action Council
310 E. 38th St., Suite 204
Minneapolis, MN 55409

Telephone: (612) 822-0127

Gay, Lesbian, and Bisexual Activities
P.O. Box 3511
Mankato, MN 56002

Telephone: (507) 345-7799

Gay, Lesbian, and Bisexual Support Group
Central High School, 275 N. Lexington Pkwy
St. Paul, MN 55104

Telephone: (612) 293-8700

Lesbian and Gay Youth Together
c/o 100 N. Oxford St.
St. Paul, MN 55104

Telephone: (612) 224-3371
           (612) 822-8870

• Meet every Sunday at 4:30 p.m. at 2025 Nicollett Ave. South

Lutheran Social Services Street Program
1299 Arcade St.
St. Paul, MN 55416

Telephone: (612) 774-9507

• Services for homeless youth.

Minnesota Gay, Lesbian, Bisexual, and Transgender Education Fund
Box 7275
Minneapolis, MN 55403

Telephone: (612) 220-4880

Rochester Gay and Lesbian Youth Services
Box 91
Rochester, MN 55903

Telephone: (507) 289-6329

So What If I Am?
2200 Emerson Ave.
Minneapolis, MN 55405

Telephone: (612) 377-8800

South High School's Lesbian, Gay, and Bisexual Student Support Group
South High School
3131 19th Ave. South
Minneapolis, MN 55410

Telephone: (612) 627-2510

University of Minnesota Youth and AIDS Project
428 Oak Grove St.
Minneapolis, MN 55403

MISSOURI

Growing American Youth
11 S. Vanderventer
St Louis, MO 63108

Telephone: (314) 533-5322

In Our Twenties
Metropolitan Community Church
1120 Dolman St.
St. Louis, MO 63104

Telephone: (314) 321-9100

St. Louis Gay and Lesbian Community Center
Box 4589
St. Louis, MO 63108

Telephone: (314) 997-9897

MONTANA

Lambda Alliance/Out in Montana
P.O. Box 8661
Missoula, MT 59807

PRIDE
Box 4815
Butte, MT 59702

Telephone: (406) 723-3339

NEBRASKA

A.N.G.L.E.
Omaha, NE 68131

Telephone: (402) 339-9948

Support Group for Lesbigay Youth
c/o Omaha PFLAG
2912 Lynwood Dr.
Omaha, NE 68123-1957

Telephone: (402) 291-6781

NEVADA

Gay Youth Alliance
117 S. Main St.
Las Vegas, NV

Telephone: (702) 383-8386

Gay Youth Outreach Program
University of Nevada
Mailstop 058
Reno, NV 89557

Telephone: (702) 784-1944

NEW HAMPSHIRE

Seacoast Outright
P.O. Box 842
Portsmouth, NH 03802

Telephone: (603) 431-1013

NEW JERSEY

Gay and Lesbian Youth of New Jersey
P.O. Box 137
Convent Station, NJ 07961-0137

Telephone: (201) 285-1595

Lesbian and Gay Coalition
P.O. Box 1431
New Brunswick, NJ 08903

Telephone: (201) 763-0668

NEW MEXICO

One in Ten
c/o Common Bond YES
4013 Silver SE
Albuquerque, NM 87106

Telephone: (505) 266-8041

Outreach
P.O. Box 682
Albuquerque, NM 87103

Telephone: (505) 256-4316

NEW YORK

Bisexual, Gay, and Lesbian Youth of New York
c/o Gay and Lesbian Community Services Center
208 W. 13th St.
New York, NY 10011-7799

Telephone: (212) 620-7310

Gay and Lesbian Alliance
P. O. Box 3785
Kingston, NY 12401

Telephone: (914) 626-3203

Gay and Lesbian Young Adult Support Group
c/o Capital District Gay and Lesbian Community Council
P.O. Box 131
Albany, NY 12201

Telephone: (518) 462-6138

Gay and Lesbian Youth of Buffalo
190 Franklin St.
Buffalo, NY 14202

Gay/Lesbian Community Network
2316 Delaware #267
Buffalo, NY 14216

Telephone: (716) 883-4750

Harvey Milk High School, Hetrick-Martin Institute
401 West St.
New York, NY 10014

Telephone: (212) 633-8920

Health Outreach to Teens (HOTT)
208 West St.
New York, NY 10011

Telephone: (212) 255-1673

Hetrick-Martin Institute
2 Astor Pl.
New York, NY 10003-6998

Telephone: (212) 674-2400
TDD: (212) 674-8695
Fax: (212) 674-8650

Lesbian and Gay Youth Program of Central New York
Echo Center
826 Euclid Ave.
Syracuse, NY 13210

Telephone: (315) 322-9741

Lesbian and Gay Youth of Rochester
179 Atlantic Ave.
Rochester, NY 14607

Telephone: (716) 244-8640

Lighthouse
Downtown United Presbyterian Church
121 N. Fitzhugh Street, Rm 441
Rochester, NY 14614

Telephone: (716) 251-9604

The Loft
255 Grove St.
White Plains, NY 10601

Telephone: (914) 948-4922

Long Island Gay and Lesbian Youth
P.O. Box 704
Selden, NY 11784

Telephone: (516) 579-0117

The Long Island Center
c/o Unitarian Universalists, 223 Stewart St.,
Garden City, NY 11530

Telephone: (516) 379-9017

The Neutral Zone
162 Christopher St.
New York, NY 10014

Telephone: (212) 924-3294

Ninety-Second Street Y, Teen Division
1395 Lexington Ave.
New York, NY 10128

Telephone: (212) 415-5615

Project First Step
338 W 4th St./24 Horatio St.
New York, NY 10014

Telephone: (212) 633-0887

• Services for homeless youth.

Project Reach Anti-Discrimination Space (ProRADS)
1 Orchard St.
New York, NY 10022

Telephone: (212) 966-4227

Syracuse Lesbian and Gay Youth Program
c/o Lambda Youth Services
P.O. Box 6103
Syracuse, NY 13217

Telephone: (315) 422-9741

The S.P.A.C.E.
213 State St.
Binghamton, NY 13902

Telephone: (607) 724-2582
            (607) 724-3462

Youth Enrichment Services
208 W. 13th St.
New York, NY 10011

Telephone: (212) 620-7310

• Substance abuse prevention for bisexual, gay, and lesbian youth.

Youth Environmental Services
30 Broadway
Massapequa, NY 11758

Telephone: (516) 799-3203

NORTH CAROLINA

Metrolina Community Service Project
P.O. Box 11144
Charlotte, NC 28220

Telephone: (704) 535-6277

Out Greensboro
c/o White Rabbit Books
1833 Spring Garden St.,
Greensboro, NC 27403

Telephone: (919) 272-7604

Outright—Triangle Gay, Lesbian, and Bisexual Youth
P.O. Box 3203
Durham, NC 27715

Telephone: (919) 286-2396
                  (800) 879-2300

Stand Out Youth Alliance
P.O. Box 53751
Fayetteville, NC 28305

Telephone: (910) 487-6535
e-mail: standout@aol.com

NORTH DAKOTA

Prairie Lesbian and Gay Community
P.O. Box 83
Moorhead, ND 56560

Telephone: (701) 237-0556

OHIO

Central United Methodist Church
701 W. Central Ave.
Toledo, OH 43610

Telephone: (419) 241-7729

Greater Cincinnati Gay and Lesbian Center
P.O. Box 19158
Cincinnati, OH 45158

Telephone: (513) 651-0040

Lesbian and Gay Community Services Center
1432 W. 29th St.
Cleveland, OH 44113

Telephone: (216) 781-6736

Serenity Youth Rap Group, Inc.
Dayton, OH

Telephone: (513) 274-1616
                  (513) 522-1999

Stonewall Community Center
47 W. 5th Ave.
Columbus, OH 43201

TGALA
P.O. Box 4642
Old West End St.
Toledo, OH 43610

Telephone: (419) 243-9351

OKLAHOMA

Lesbian, Gay, and Bisexual Youth Support Program
Youth Services of Tulsa
302 S. Cheyenne
Tulsa, OK 74103

Telephone: (918) 582-0061

Oasis Community Center
2135 NW 39th St.
Oklahoma City, OK 73112

Telephone: (405) 525-2437

OREGON

Gay and Lesbian Community Center
3856 Carnes Rd.
Boseburg, OR 97470

Telephone: (503) 672-4126

Gay and Lesbian Outreach
P.O. Box 4212
Coos Bay, OR 97420

Telephone: (503) 269-4183

Metropolitan Community Church of Eugene
The Koinonia Center
1414 Kincaid St.
Eugene, OR 97440

Telephone: (503) 345-5963

Oregon Lesbian, Gay, and Bisexual Campus Union
P.O. Box 4925
Portland, OR 97208

Telephone: (503) 236-2597

Park Avenue Social Club
P.O. Box 2294
Portland, OR 97208

Telephone: (503) 238-0334

Pheonix Rising
620 SW 5th Ave., Suite 710
Portland, OR 97204

Telephone: (503) 233-8299

The Other Side
P.O. Box 5672
Bend, OR 97708

Telephone: (503) 388-2395

Windfire (7-9 p.m. Thursday)
Multonomah County Central Library
801 SW 10th Ave.
Portland, OR

Telephone: (503) 233-8299

PENNSYLVANIA

Bisexual, Gay and Lesbian Youth Association
P.O. Box 872
Harrisburg, PA 17108

Telephone: (717) 397-0691

Gay and Lesbian Community Center
2214 E. Carson St.
Pittsburgh, PA 15206

Telephone: (412) 431-LGCC

Growing Alternative Youth
4120 Brownsville Rd., Suite 16-1416
Pittsburgh, PA 15229

Penguin Place Youth Group
201 S. Camac St.
Philadelphia, PA 19107

Telephone: (215) 732-2220

Susquehanna Lambda
P.O. Box 2510
Williamsport, PA 17703

Telephone: (717) 327-1411

RHODE ISLAND

YouthPride
P.O. Box 603017
Providence, RI 02916

Telephone: (401) 421-5626

SOUTH CAROLINA

Gay/Lesbian/Bisexual Youth Circle
141 S. Shandon St., Suite A
Columbia, SC 29205

Telephone: (803) 771-7713

South Carolina Gay and Lesbian Community Center
P.O. Box 12648
Columbia, SC 29211

Telephone: (803) 771-7713

TENNESSEE

Memphis Gay and Lesbian Community Center
1291 Madison Ave.
Memphis, TN 38104

Telephone: (901) 726-5790

One in Ten Youth Services
703 Berry Rd.
Nashville, TN 37204

Telephone: (615) 297-0008

TGALA
P.O. Box 41305
Nashville, TN 37204

Telephone: (615) 292-4820

TEXAS

Community Outreach Center
102 North Avenue South
Lubbock, TX 79464

Telephone: (806) 762-1019

Gay and Lesbian Young Adults
2701 Reagan St.
Dallas, TX 75219

Telephone: (214) 521-5342, ext 260

Gay Student Network
P. O. Box 2585
Austin, TX 78768

Telephone: (512) 445-7270

Houston Area Teen Coalition for Homosexuals
P.O. Box 667053
Houston, TX 77266-7053

Telephone: (512) 302-FLAG

Lambda Services—Youth Network
P.O. Box 30321
El Paso, TX 79931-0321

Telephone: (915) 562-GAYS

Out Youth Austin
425 Woodward St.
Austin, TX 78704

Telephone: (512) 326-1234

The Resource Center
121 West Woodlawn
San Antonio, TX 78212

Telephone: (512) 732-0751

UTAH

Gay and Lesbian Alliance of Cache Valley
UMC 0100, Box 119
Tagart Student Center
Logan, UT 84322

Telephone: (801) 752-1129

The Youth Group
Utah Stonewall Center
770 South 300 West,
Salt Lake City, UT 84102

Telephone: (801) 539-8800

VERMONT

Coalition of Lesbian and Gay Men
Box 1125
Montpelier, VT 05602

Outright Vermont
P.O. Box 5235
Burlington, VT 05402

Telephone: (802) 865-9677

VIRGINIA

Gay and Lesbian Community Association
P.O. Box 19401
Alexandria, VA 22320

Telephone: (703) 684-0444

Richmond Organization for Sexual Minority Youth (ROSMY)
P.O. Box 5542
Richmond, VA 23220

Telephone: (804) 353-2077

Whitman-Walker Clinic—Northern Virginia
3426 Washington Blvd., Suite 102
Arlington, VA 22201

Telephone: (703) 358-9550

WASHINGTON

Gay and Lesbian Youth Association of Seattle
1818 15th Ave.
Seattle, WA 98128

Telephone: (360) 233-8935

Gay and Lesbian Youth Rap Group
c/o Gay Community Social Services,
Box 22228
Seattle, WA 98122

Telephone: (360) 292-5144

Gay, Lesbian, and Bisexual Youth Program
American Friends Service Committee
814 NE 40th
Seattle, WA 98105

Telephone: (360) 632-0500

Lambert House Gay, Lesbian, and Bisexual Youth Center
1818 15th Ave.
Seattle, WA 98122

Telephone: (360) 322-2735

Lesbian Resource Center
1208 E. Pine St.
Seattle, WA 98122

Telephone: (360) 322-3953

Lesbian and Gay Resource Center
CAB, 305 Evergreen State College
Olympia. WA 98505

Telephone: (360) 866-6000 ext. 6544

Oasis Gay, Lesbian, and Bisexual Youth Association
3629 South D St.
Tacoma, WA 98408

Telephone: (360) 596-2860

Odyssey
Spokane County Health District AIDS Program
1101 W. College Ave., Suite 401
Spokane, WA 99201

Telephone: (509) 324-1547

Seattle Counseling Service for Sexual Minorities
200 W. Mercer, Suite 300
Seattle, WA 98119

Telephone: (360) 282-9314

Stonewall Youth
P.O. Box 7383
Olympia, WA 98507

Telephone: (360) 705-2738

Youth Eastside Services
Bisexual, Gay, and Lesbian Drop-In Group (B-GLAD)
16150 NE 8th
Bellevue, WA 98008

Telephone: (360) 747-4937

WEST VIRGINIA

Young, Gay, and Proud
P.O. Box 3642
Charleston, WV 25336-3642

Telephone: (304) 340-3690

WISCONSIN

Gay and Lesbian Alliance
1411 Ellis Ave., P.O. Box 247A
Ashland, WI 54806

Telephone: (715) 682-1595

Gay Youth Milwaukee
P.O. Box 09441
Milwaukee, WI 53209

Telephone: (414) 265-8500

Madison Community United
310 E. Wilson
Madison, WI 53703

Telephone: (608) 255-8582

Teens Like Us
512 E. Washington
Madison, WI 53703

Telephone: (608) 251-6211

WYOMING

Gay and Lesbian Oriented Youth (GLORY)
P.O. Box 9725
Casper, WY 82609

Telephone: (307) 577-7969

United Gays and Lesbians of Wyoming
P.O. Box 2037
Laramie, WY 82070

Telephone: (307) 635-4301

PEN PAL SERVICES

(Enclose a self-addressed stamped envelope.)

Alyson Publications, Letter Exchange Program
40 Plympton, St.
Boston, MA 02118

Bay Area Sexual Minority Youth Network (ASMYN)
P.O. Box 460268
San Francisco, CA 94146-0268

International Pen-Pal Program, Youth Outreach
Los Angeles Gay and Lesbian Community Services Center
1625 Shrader St.
Los Angeles, CA 90028

Telephone: (213) 993-7471

Lambda Youth Network
P.O. Box 7911
Culver City, CA 90233

Lesbian and Gay Youth Network
P.O. Box 20716
Indianapolis, IN 46220

Telephone: (317) 541-8726
Fax: (317) 545-8594

Out Youth Austin
425 Woodward St.
Austin TX 78704

Telephone: (800) 96-YOUTH
e-mail: youth@out-youth.austin.tx.us

Notes

Preface

1. L. Due, *Joining the tribe.* (New York: Anchor Books, 1995).
2. A. Heron, Ed., *Two teenagers in twenty.* (Boston, MA: Alyson, 1994), p. 9.

Chapter 1

1. R.C. Savin-Williams and R.E. Lenhart, "AIDS prevention among gay and lesbian youth: Psychosocial stress and health care intervention guidelines." In D.G. Ostrow, Ed., *Behavioral Aspects of AIDS.* (New York: Plenum Medical Book Co., 1990), p. 1.

2. R.C. Savin-Williams, *Gay and lesbian youth: Expressions of identity.* (Washington, DC: Hemisphere, 1990).

3. R.A. Isay, "The development of sexual identity in homosexual men." In S.I. Greenspan and G.H. Pollack, Eds., *The course of life: Vol. IV, Adolescence.* (Madison, CT: International Universities Press, 1991).

4. J.C. Gonsiorek, "Psychological adjustment and homosexuality," *JSAS Catalog of Selected Documents in Psychology,* (Volume 7, 1977): 45.

M. Hart, H. Roback, B. Tittler, L. Weitz, B. Walston, and E. McKee, "Psychological adjustment of nonpatient homosexuals: Critical review of the research literature," *Journal of Clinical Psychiatry,* (Volume 39, 1978).

5. R.M. Berger, *Gay and gray.* (Urbana, IL: University of Illinois Press, 1982).

R. Green, *The "sissy boy syndrome" and the development of homosexuality.* (New Haven, CT: Yale University Press, 1987).

P.C. Larson, "Sexual identity and self-concept," *Journal of Homosexuality,* (Volume 7, 1981).

R.A. LaTorre and K. Wendenburg, "Psychological characteristics of bisexual, heterosexual, and homosexual women," *Journal of Homosexuality,* (Volume 9, 1983).

D. Lutz, H. Roback, and M. Hart, "Feminine gender identity and psychological adjustment of male-transexuals and male homosexuals," *Journal of Sex Research,* (Volume 20, 1984).

M. Mervis, "A comparison of lesbians and heterosexual women on the Rorschach," *Dissertation Abstracts International,* (Volume 45, 1985).

M.T. Saghir and E. Robins, *Male and female homosexuality.* (Baltimore, MD: Williams & Wilkins, 1973).

M. Siegelman, "Adjustment of homosexual and heterosexual women," *British Journal of Psychiatry,* (Volume 120, 1972).

P.D. Wayson, "Personality variables in males as they relate to differences in sexual orientation," *Journal of Homosexuality,* (Volume 11, 1985).

6. G.J. Remafedi, "Adolescent homosexuality: Issues for pediatricians," *Clinical Pediatrician*, (Volume 24, 1985).

7. M. Schneider, *Often invisible: Counseling gay and lesbian youth.* (Toronto: Toronto Central Youth Services, 1988).

8. J. Billy, K. Taufer, W. Grady, and D. Klepinger, "The sexual behavior of men in the United States," *Family Planning Perspectives*, (Volume 25, 1993).

A.C. Kinsey, W.B. Pomeroy, and C.E. Martin, *Sexual behavior in the human male.* (Philadelphia, PA: W.B. Saunders, 1948).

R. Sell, J. Wells, and D. Wypig, "The prevalence of homosexual behavior and attraction in the United States, United Kingdom, and France: Results of national population-based samples," *Archives of Sexual Behavior*, (Volume 23, 1994).

9. C. Burr, *A separate creation: The search for the biological origins of sexual orientation.* (New York: Hyperion, 1996).

10. M.E. Hotvedt, and J.B. Mandel, "Children of lesbian mothers." In W. Paul, J.D. Weinrich, J.C. Gonsiorek, and M.E. Hotvedt, Eds., *Homosexuality: Social, psychological, and biological issues.* (Beverly Hills, CA: Sage, 1982).

M. Kirkpatrick, C. Smith, and R. Roy, "Lesbian mothers and their children: A comparative survey," *American Journal of Orthopsychiatry*, (Volume 51, 1981).

J. Marmor, "Overview: The multiple roots of homosexual behavior." In J. Marmor, Ed., *Homosexual behavior.* (New York: Basic Books, 1980a).

C. Warren, "Homosexuality and stigma." In J. Marmor, Ed., *Homosexual behavior.* (New York: Basic Books, 1980).

11. Savin-Williams, 1990.

12. M. Manosevitz, "Early sexual behavior in adult homosexual and heterosexual males," *Journal of Abnormal Psychology*, (Volume 76, 1970).

Savin-Williams, 1990.

13. G. Ross-Reynolds, "Issues in counseling the 'homosexual' adolescent." In J. Grimes, Ed., *Psychological approaches to problems of children and adolescents.* (Des Moines, IA: Iowa Department of Eduation, 1982).

14. Kinsey, Pomeroy, and Martin, 1948.

15. A.K. Malyon, "The homosexual adolescent: Developing issues and social bias," *Child Welfare*, (Volume 60, 1981).

16. C.A. Rigg, "Homosexuality and adolescence," *Pediatric Annual*, (Volume 11, 1982).

R. Sorenson, *Adolescent sexuality in contemporary society.* (New York: World Book, 1973).

17. T.S. Weinberg, *Gay men, gay selves: The social construction of homosexual identities.* (New York: Irvington, 1983).

18. Savin-Williams and Lenhart, 1990.

19. B.M. Dank, "Coming out in the gay world," *Psychiatry*, (Volume 34, 1971).

A.M. Boxer, *Betwixt and between: Developmental discontinuities of gay and lesbian youth.* Paper presented at the Society for Research on Adolescence, Alexandria, VA, (1988, March).

G. J. Remafedi, "Adolescent homosexuality: Psychosocial and medical implications. *Pediatrics*, (Volume 79, 1987a).

20. T. Sullivan and M. Schneider, "Development and identity issues in adolescent homosexuality," *Child and Adolescent Social Work*, (Volume 4, Number 1, 1987).

A.D. Martin, "Learning to hide: The socialization of the gay adolescent," *Adolescent Psychiatry*, (Volume 10, 1982).

21. G.P. Mallon, "Gay and no place to go: Assessing the needs of gay and lesbian adolescents in out-of-home settings," *Child Welfare*, (Volume 71, 1992a).

Schneider, 1988.

22. K. Chandler, *Passages of pride: Gay and lesbian youth come of age.* (New York: Times Books, 1995), p. 148.

23. E. Bass and K. Kaufman, *Free your mind: The book for gay, lesbian, and bisexual youth—and their allies.* (New York: Harper Perennial, 1996), p. 7.

24. Ibid., pp. 7-8.

25. Ross-Reynolds, 1988, p. 229.

26. G.M. Herek, "Beyond 'homophobia': A social psychological perspective on attitudes toward lesbians and gay men," *Journal of Homosexuality*, (Volume 10, Number 1/2, 1984).

Jelen, 1982.

27. V.J. Seidler, "Men, feminism, and power." In J. Hearn and D. Morgan, Eds., *Men, masculinities, and social theory.* (London: Hyman Unwin, 1990).

28. R. Green, "Patterns of sexual identity in childhood: Relationship to subsequent sexual preference." In J. Marmor, Ed., *Homosexual behavior.* (New York: Basic Books, 1980).

J. Marmor, "Epilogue: Homosexuality and the issue of mental illness." In J. Marmor, Ed., *Homosexual behavior.* (New York: Basic Books, 1980b).

B.F. Reiss, "Psychological tests in homosexuality." In J. Marmor, Ed., *Homosexual behavior.* (New York: Basic Books, 1980).

29. G. Herdt, "Introduction: Gay and lesbian youth, emergent identities, and cultural scenes at home and abroad." In G. Herdt, Ed., *Gay and lesbian youth.* (Binghamton, NY: Harrington Park Press, 1989).

30. L. Due, *Joining the Tribe.* (New York: Anchor Books, 1995), p. 69.

31. S.K. Hammersmith, "A sociological approach to counseling homosexual clients and their families," *Journal of Homosexuality*, (Volume 14, 1987).

32. A.D. Martin, "The stigmatization of the gay or lesbian adolescent." In M. Schneider, Ed., *Often invisible: Counseling gay and lesbian youth.* (Toronto: Central Toronto Youth Services, 1988), p. 59.

33. M. Rosario, J. Hunter, and M.J. Rotheram-Borus, *HIV-risk acts of lesbian adolescents.* Unpublished manuscript. Columbia University (1992), p. 17.

34. G. Robinson, "Few solutions for a young dilemma," *Advocate*, (1984), p. 14.

35. Herdt, 1989; Sladkin, 1983.

C. Whitney, "Living amid the ruins of the sexual revolution," *Christopher Street*, (Volume 12, Number 9, 1989).

36. G.J. Remafedi, M. Resnick, R. Blum, and L. Harris, L., "Demography of sexual orientation in adolescents," *Pediatrics*, (Volume 89, 1992).

37. Bass and Kaufman, 1996, p. xvi.

38. R.C. Savin-Williams, "An exploratory study of pubertal maturation timing and self-esteem among gay and bisexual male youths," *Developmental Psychology*, (Volume 31, 1995).

39. R. Tingle, *Gay lessons: How public funds are used to promote homosexuality among children and young people.* (London: Pickwick Books, 1986), p. vii.

40. H. Smith, "Letters to the editor," Lewiston (ME) *Sun-Journal*, (1995, October 5), p. 4A.

41. J.T. Sears, *Growing up gay in the South: Race, gender, and journeys of the spirit.* (Binghamton, NY: Harrington Park Press, 1991a), p. 349.

42. "Under surveillance," *The Advocate*, (1996, April 16).

43. Letters, *Time*, January 11, 1993.

44. G. Rotello, "Trickle-down liberation," *The Advocate*, (1996, February 20).

45. Goodman, Lakey, Lashof, and Thorne, 1983.

46. T.L. Vergura, "Meeting the needs of sexual minority youth: One program's response," *Journal of Social Work and Human Sexuality*, (Volume 2, 1983/84), p. 23.

47. Due, 1995, p. 123.

Chapter 2

1. G.J. McDonald, "Individual differences in the coming-out process for gay men: Implications for theoretical models," *Journal of Homosexuality*, (Volume 8, 1982).

P.K. Rector, "The acceptance of homosexual identity in adolescence: A phenomenological study," Dissertation Abstracts International, (Volume 43, 1982).

2. G.J. Remafedi, M. Resnick, R. Blum, and L. Harris, L., "Demography of sexual orientation in adolescents," *Pediatrics*, (Volume 89, 1992).

3. Dailey, 1979; Peplau, Cochran, Rook, and Pedesky, 1978.

M.T. Saghir and E. Robins, "Clinical aspects of female homosexuality." In J. Marmor, Ed., *Homosexual behavior: A modern reappraisal.* (New York: Basic Books, 1980).

4. M. Kirkpatrick and C. Morgan, "Psychodynamic psychotherapy of female homosexuality." In J. Marmor, Ed., *Homosexual behavior: A modern reappraisal.* (New York: Basic Books, 1981), p. 372-373.

5. R.R. Troiden, "Homosexual identity formation," *Journal of Adolescent Health Care*, (Volume 9, 1988).

6. A.P. Bell, M.S. Weinberg, and S.K. Hammersmith, *Sexual preference: Its development in men and women.* (Bloomington, IN: Indiana University Press, 1981a).

R.C. Savin-Williams, "Memories of childhood and early adolescent sexual feelings among gay and bisexual boys: A narrative approach." In R.C. Savin-Williams and K.M. Cohen, Eds., *The lives of lesbians, gays, and bisexuals.* (Fort Worth, TX: Harcourt & Brace College Publishers, 1996c).

R.R. Troiden, "Becoming homosexual: A model of gay identity acquisition," *Psychiatry*, (Volume 42, 1979).

7. A. Heron, Ed., *One teenager in ten.* (Boston, MA: Alyson, 1983), p. 115.

8. Durby, 1994.

9. L. Heal, "It happened on Main Street." In B.L. Singer, Ed., *Growing up gay/growing up lesbian.* (New York: The New Press, 1994), p. 9.

10. P.J. Gorton, "Different from the others." In R. Luczak, Ed., *Eyes of desire: A deaf gay and lesbian reader.* (Boston, Alyson, 1993), p. 20.

11. Bell, Weinberg, and Hammersmith, 1981a.

12. R. Green, "Gender identity in childhood and later sexual orientation," *American Journal of Psychiatry*, (Volume 142, 1985).

G.B. MacDonald, "Exploring sexual identity: Gay people and their families," *Sex Education Coalition News*, (Volume 5, 1983).

R. Robertson, "Young gays." In J. Hart and J. Richardson, Eds., *The theory and practice of homosexuality.* (New York: Routledge & Kegan Paul, 1981).

B. Zuger, "Early effeminate behavior in boys," *Journal of Nervous and Mental Disorders*, (Volume 172, 1984).

R.C. Savin-Williams, *Gay and lesbian youth: Expressions of identity.* (Washington, DC: Hemisphere, 1990).

R.C. Savin-Williams, "Ethnic- and sexual-minority youth." In R.C. Savin-Williams and K.M. Cohen, Eds., *The lives of lesbians, gays, and bisexuals.* (Fort Worth, TX: Harcourt & Brace College Publishers, 1996b).

13. K. Chandler, *Passages of pride: Gay and lesbian youth come of age.* (New York: Times Books, 1995).

14. Savin-Williams, 1996c, p. 100.

15. Ibid.

16. Bell, Weinberg, and Hammersmith, 1981a.

R.C. Friedman and L.O. Stern, "Juvenile aggressivity and sissiness in homosexual and heterosexual males," *Journal of the Academy of Psychoanalysis*, (Volume 8, 1980).

R. Green, "Childhood cross-gender behavior and subsequent sexual preference," *American Journal of Psychiatry*, (Volume 36, 1979).

17. R.R. Troiden, "Becoming homosexual: A model of gay identity acquisition," *Psychiatry*, (Volume 42, 1979), p. 363.

18. Bell, Weinberg, and Hammersmith, 1981a, p. 74.

19. M.T. Saghir and E. Robins, *Male and female homosexuality.* (Baltimore, MD: Williams & Wilkins, 1973).

20. I. Bieber, *Homosexuality: A psychoanalytic study.* (New York: Basic Books, 1962).

M. Eisner, *An investigation of the coming-out process, lifestyle, and sex-role orientation of lesbians.* Unpublished doctoral dissertation, York University, Toronto (1982).

R.B. Evans, "Childhood parental relationships of homosexual men," *Journal of Counsulting and Clinical Psychology,* (Volume 33, 1969).

E.A. McCauley and A.A. Ehrhardt, "Role expectations and definitions: A comparison of female transsexuals and lesbians," *Journal of Homosexuality,* (Volume 3, 1977).

C. Van Cleave, "Self-identification, self-identification discrepancy, an environmental perspective of women with same-sex preference." *Dissertation Abstracts International,* (Volume 38, 1978).

21. Bell, Weinberg, and Hammersmith, 1981a, p. 148.

22. S.O. Murray, *Social theory, homosexual realities.* (New York: Gai Sabre Books, 1984).

R. Parker, "Youth, identity, and homosexuality: The changing shape of sexual life in contemporary Brazil." In G. Herdt, Ed., *Gay and lesbian youth.* (Binghamton, NY: Harrington Park Press, 1989).

23. R. Green, *The "sissy boy syndrome" and the development of homosexuality.* (New Haven, CT: Yale University Press, 1987).

Whitan, 1983.

24. J.T. Sears, *Growing up gay in the South: Race, gender, and journeys of the spirit.* (Binghamton, NY: Harrington Park Press, 1991a), p. 50.

25. R.C. Savin-Williams and R.E. Lenhart, "AIDS prevention among gay and lesbian youth: Psychosocial stress and health care intervention guidelines." In D.G. Ostrow, Ed., *Behavioral aspects of AIDS.* (New York: Plenum Medical Book Co., 1990).

26. Sears, 1991a, p. 49.

27. Savin-Williams, 1996c.

28. E. Coleman, "Developmental stages of the coming-out process," *Journal of Homosexuality,* (Volume 7, 1982b).

29. Sears, 1991a, p. 49.

30. K. Jennings, "American dreams." In B.L. Singer, Ed., *Growing up gay/growing up lesbian.* (New York: The New Press, 1994).

31. Sanders, 1980.

C.J. Straver, "Research on homosexuality in the Netherlands," *The Netherlands' Journal of Sociology,* (Volume 12, 1976).

32. E. White, *A boy's own story.* (New York: E.P. Dutton, 1982), p. 169.

33. A.M. Boxer, *Betwixt and between: Developmental discontinuities of gay and lesbian youth.* Paper presented at the Society for Research on Adolescence, Alexandria, VA (1988, March).

34. E. Bass and K. Kaufman, *Free your mind: The book for gay, lesbian, and bisexual youth—and their allies.* (New York: Harper Perennial, 1996), p. 24.

35. Coleman, 1982b.

K. Jay and A. Young, *The gay report: Lesbians and gay men speak out about sexual experiences and lifestyles.* (New York: Simon & Schuster, 1979).

A.C. Kinsey, W.B. Pomeroy, and C.E. Martin, *Sexual behavior in the human male.* (Philadelphia, PA: W.B. Saunders, 1948).

H. Kooden, S. Morin, D. Riddle, M. Rogers, B. Sang, and F. Strassburger, *Removing the stigma. Final Report of the Task Force on the Status of Lesbian and Gay Male Psychologists.* (Washington, DC: American Psychological Association, 1979).

MacDonald, 1983; Rector, 1982.

R.A. Rodriguez, *Significant events in gay identity development: Gay men in Utah.* Paper presented at the annual meeting of the American Psychological Association, Atlanta, GA (1988, August).

G. Sanders, "Homosexuals in the Netherlands," *Alternative Lifestyles,* (Volume 3, 1980).

J. Spada, *The Spada Report: The newest survey of gay male sexuality.* (New York: New American Library, 1979).

Troiden, 1979.

36. Heal, 1994.

37. G.J. Remafedi, "Male homosexuality: The adolescent's perspective," *Pediatrics,* (Volume 79, 1987b).

38. S.K. Telljohann and J.H. Price, "A qualitative examination of adolescent homosexuals' life experiences: Ramifications for secondary school personnel," *Journal of Homosexuality,* (Volume 26, 1993).

39. Savin-Williams, 1996c, p. 97.

40. Sears, 1991a, p. 112.

41. Remafedi, 1987b, p. 328.

42. J.T. Sears, "Black-gay or gay-black: Choosing identities and identifying choices." In G. Unks, Ed., *The gay teen.* (New York: Routledge, 1995), p. 142.

43. Chandler, 1995, p. 6.

44. Sears, 1991a, p. 352.

45. P. Singer, "Breaking through," Rochester, NY, *Democrat and Chronicle,* (1993, July 4), p. D-1.

46. Sears, 1991a, p. 84.

47. J. Green, "This school is out," *The New York Times Magazine,* (1991, October 13), p. 18.

48. Savin-Williams, 1996c.

49. Ibid., p. 100.

50. Chandler, 1995, p. 16.

51. Savin-Williams, 1996c, p. 98.

52. D. Kopay and P.D. Young, *The David Kopay Story: An extraordinary self-revelation.* (New York: Donald Fine, 1988).

53. "Starting over: A Chinese teenager comes to a new home and comes out," *Crossroads,* (1996, Winter/Spring), p. 6.

54. Sears, 1991a, p. 205.

55. P. Gibson, "Report of the Secretary's Task Force on Youth Suicide." In M. Feinleib, Ed., *Prevention and intervention in youth suicide.* Washington, DC: U.S. Department of Health and Human Services, Public Health Services; Alcohol, Drug Abuse and Mental Health Administration, (1989), pp. 3-131.

56. Chandler, 1995, p. 82.

57. Sears, 1991a. p. 290.

58. Boxer, 1988.

A.H. Buss, *Self-consciousness and social anxiety.* (San Francisco, CA: W.H. Freeman, 1980).

McDonald, 1982; Remafedi, 1987b.

T. Roesler and R. Deisher, "Youthful male homosexuality," *Journal of the American Medical Association,* (Volume 219, 1972).

Savin-Williams, 1990.

59. Bell, Weinberg, and Hammersmith, 1981a, 1981b.

60. Savin-Williams, 1996c.

61. S. Maguen, "Gay rural youth lack support from the community," *The Advocate,* (1992, November 17), p. 54.

62. Singer, 1993, p. D-1.

63. Heron, 1983, pp. 9-10.

64. Heal, 1994, p. 10.

65. Bass and Kaufman, 1996, p. 17.

66. "Starting over," 1996, p. 6.

67. P.D. Toth, "Realizing it's OK to be gay." Rochester, NY, *Times Union,* (1993, October 12), p. 15.

68. S. Parsavand, "Discussion groups ease acceptance for gay high schoolers," *Schenectady Gazette,* (1993, December 5), p. A-1.

69. D.A. Anderson, "Family and peer relations of gay adolescents." In S.C. Geinstein, Ed., *Adolescent psychiatry: Developmental and clinical studies,* Volume 14. (Chicago: The University of Chicago Press, 1987).

Savin-Williams, 1996c.

70. R.C. Savin-Williams, "Dating and romantic relations among gay, lesbian, and bisexual youths." In R.C. Savin-Williams and K.M. Cohen, Eds., *The lives of lesbians, gays, and bisexuals.* (Fort Worth, TX: Harcourt & Brace College Publishers, 1996a), p. 170.

71. M. Schneider, "Sappho was a right-on adolescent: Growing up lesbian," *Journal of Homosexuality,* (Volume 17, 1989), p. 118.

72. J.L. Norton, "The homosexual and counseling," *Personnel and Guidance Journal,* (Volume 54, 1976).

73. R. Fisher, *The gay mystique: The myth and reality of male homosexuality.* (New York: Stein & Day, 1972), p. 249.

74. B.L. Singer, Ed., *Growing up gay/growing up lesbian.* (New York: The New Press, 1994).

75. Bell, Weinberg, and Hammersmith, 1981a.

V.C. Cass, "Homosexual identity formation: Testing a theoretical model," *Journal of Homosexuality,* (Volume 4, 1979).

J.A. Lee, "Going public: A study of the sociology of homosexual liberation," *Journal of Homosexuality*, (Volume 3, 1977).

A.K. Malyon, "The homosexual adolescent: Developing issues and social bias," *Child Welfare*, (Volume 60, 1981).

A.D. Martin, "Learning to hide: The socialization of the gay adolescent," *Adolescent Psychiatry*, (Volume 10, 1982).

K. Plummer, *The making of the modern homosexual*. (London: Hutchinson, 1981).

Reiche and Dannecker, 1977; Sanders, 1980; Troiden, 1979.

76. Anderson, 1987.

77. G.P. Mallon, "Gay and no place to go: Assessing the needs of gay and lesbian adolescents in out-of-home settings," *Child Welfare*, (Volume 71, 1992a).

78. Cass, 1979; Plummer, 1981.

R.C. Savin-Williams and R.G. Rodriguez, "A developmental, clinical perspective on lesbian, gay male, and bisexual youths." In T.P. Gulotta, G.R. Adams, and R. Montemayor, Eds., *Adolescent sexuality*. (Newbury Park, CA: Sage, 1993).

C.A. Tripp, *The homosexual matrix*. (New York: McGraw-Hill, 1975).

Troiden, 1979.

79. Cass, 1979; Reiche and Dannecker, 1977; Savin-Williams and Rodriguez, 1993; Troiden, 1979.

80. C. DeMontflores and S.J. Schultz, "Coming out: Similarities and differences for lesbians and gay men," *Journal of Social Issues*, (Volume 34, 1978).

Malyon, 1981; Martin, 1982; Tripp, 1975.

81. Malyon, 1981.

82. Troident and Goode, 1980.

83. D.A. Anderson, "Lesbian and gay adolescents: Social and developmental considerations." In G. Unks, Ed., *The gay teen*. (New York: Routledge, 1995).

84. Savin-Williams, 1996c.

85. Ross-Reynolds, 1988.

86. Cass, 1979; Lee, 1977.

G. Sanders, 1980.

87. Sears, 1991a, p. 194.

88. Savin-Williams, 1996c.

89. E.S. Hetrick and A.D. Martin, "Developmental issues and their resolution for gay and lesbian adolescents," *Journal of Homosexuality*, (Volume 14, 1987).

90. Bell, Weinberg, and Hammersmith, 1981; Cass, 1979; Martin, 1982; Lee, 1977.

R. Reich and M. Dannecker, "Male homosexuality in West Germany—A sociological investigation," *Journal of Sex Research*, (Volume 13, 1977).

G. Sanders, 1980.

M.S. Weinberg and C.J. Williams, *Male homosexuals: Their problems and adaptations*. (New York: Penguin, 1974).

91. A.P. Bell and M.S. Weinberg, *Homosexualities: A study of diversity among men and women*. (New York: Simon & Shuster, 1978).

S. Schafer, "Sexual and social problems of lesbians," *Journal of Sex Research*, (Volume 12, 1976).

Spada, 1979.

R.R. Troiden and E. Goode, "Variables related to acquisition of gay identity," *Journal of Homosexuality*, (Volume 5, 1980).

Weinberg and Williams, 1974.

92. B.S. Newman and P.G. Muzzonigro, "The effects of traditional family values on the coming out process of gay male adolescents," *Adolescence*, (Volume 28, 1993).

93. Sears, 1991a, p. 82.

94. L.D. Brimmer, *Being different: Lambda youth speak out.* (New York Franklin Watts, 1995), p. 37.

95. Sears, 1991a, p. 52.

96. L. Due, *Joining the Tribe*, (New York: Anchor Books, 1995), p. 242.

97. C.A. Rigg, "Homosexuality and adolescence," *Pediatric Annual*, (Volume 11, 1982).

98. Sears, 1991a, p. 353.

99. Due, 1995, p. 77.

100. K.M. Cohen and R.C. Savin-Williams, "Developmental perspectives on coming out to self and others. In R.C. Savin-Williams and K.M. Cohen, Eds., *The lives of lesbians, gays, and bisexuals.* (Fort Worth, TX: Harcourt & Brace College Publishers, 1996), p. 126.

101. D. Boyer, "Male prostitution and homosexual identity." In G. Herdt, Ed., *Gay and Lesbian Youth.* (Binghamton, NY: Harrington Park Press, 1989), p. 169.

102. Sears, 1991a, p. 132.

103. Savin-Williams, 1996a, p. 173.

104. Due, 1995, p. 108.

105. G. Herdt and A.M. Boxer, *Children of horizons: How gay and lesbian teens are leading a new way out of the closet.* (Boston: Beacon Press, 1993).

106. Sears, 1991a, p. 327.

107. Herdt and Boxer, 1993.

G.J. Remafedi, "Adolescent homosexuality: Psycho-social and medical implications," *Pediatrics*, (Volume 79, 1987a).

Remafedi, 1987b; Roesler and Deisher, 1972; Savin-Williams, 1990; Sears, 1991a.

108. Savin-Williams, 1996b, p. 172.

109. Sears, 1991a, p. 327.

110. M.S. Schneider and B. Tremble, "Training service providers to work with gay and lesbian adolescents: A workshop," *Journal of Counseling and Development*, (Volume 65, 1986).

111. Heron, 1983, p. 76.

112. Toth, 1993, October 12, p. 15.

113. Bass and Kaufman, 1996, p. 33.

114. J. Gover, "Gay youth in the family," *Journal of Emotional and Behavioral Problems*, (Volume 2, Number 4, 1993), p. 36.

115. Savin-Williams, 1996c, p. 105.

116. Weisberg and Williams, 1974.

117. L.J. Braaten and C.D. Darling, "Overt and covert homosexual problems among male college students," *Genetic Psychology Monographs*, (Volume 71, 1965).

118. F.L. Myrick, "Homosexual types: An empirical investigation," *Journal of Sex Research*, (Volume 10, 1974a), p. 234.

119. Toth, 1993, October 12, p. 15.

120. G. Sanders, 1980.

121. Sears, 1995, p. 140.

122. J. Harry, "Adolescent sexuality: Masculinity-femininity, and educational attainment," ERIC Document No. 237395, (1983a).

123. Sears, 1991a, p. 52.

124. Martin, 1982.

125. Savin-Williams, 1990.

126. Michael, "Different is not bad." In B.L. Singer, Ed., *Growing up gay/ growing up lesbian*. (New York: The New Press, 1994), p. 60.

127. J.A. Cook, A.M. Boxer, and G. Herdt, *First homosexual and heterosexual experiences reported by gay and lesbian youth in an urban community.* Paper presented at the annual meeting of the American Sociological Association. San Francisco, CA, (1989).

128. S.M. Brady, "The relationship between differences in stages of homosexual identity formation and background characteristics, psychological well-being and homosexual adjustment," *Dissertation Abstracts International*, (Volume 45, 1985).

Rodriguez, 1988.

129. Bass and Kaufman, 1996, p. 92.

130. Sears, 1991a.

131. R.A. Isay, "The development of sexual identity in homosexual men." In S.I. Greenspan and G.H. Pollack, Eds., *The course of life: Volume IV, Adolescence*. (Medison, CT: International Universities Press, 1991), p. 477.

132. Heal, 1994, p. 12.

133. Savin-Williams, 1996a, p. 175.

134. Due, 1995, p. 74.

135. Savin-Williams, 1996c.

136. M. Manosevitz, "Early sexual behavior in adult homosexual and heterosexual males," *Journal of Abnormal Psychology*, (Volume 76, 1970).

137. DeMonteflores and Schultz, 1978; Shafer, 1977; Remafedi, 1987a.

138. Saghir and Robins, 1973.

139. J.C. Gonsiorek, "Mental health issues of gay and lesbian adolescents," *Journal of Adolescent Health Care*, (Volume 9, 1988).

140. Cook, Boxer, and Herdt, 1989.

141. G. Ross-Reynolds, "Issues in counseling the 'homosexual' adolescent." In J. Grimes, Ed., *Psychological approaches to problems of children and adolescents*. (Des Moines, IA: Iowa Department of Education, 1982).

142. M. Mac an Ghaill, "Schooling, sexuality and male power: Towards an emancipatory cirriculum," *Gender and Education*, (Volume 3, 1991), p. 298.

143. Gover, 1993.

144. Sears, 1991a, p. 127.

145. Brimmer, 1995, p. 64.

146. Savin-Williams, 1996c, p. 104.

147. Boxer, 1988.

148. C.L. Chng, "Adolescent homosexual behavior and the health educator," *Journal of School Health*, (Volume 61, 1980).

149. Savin-Williams, 1996a, p. 171.

150. M. Glasser, "Homosexuality in adolescence," *British Journal of Medical Psychology*, (Volume 50, 1977).

151. Savin-Williams and Lenhart, 1990.

152. J. Diepold and R.D. Young, "Empirical studies of adolescent sexual behavior: A critical review," *Adolescence*, (Volume 14, 1979).

Kinsey, Pomeroy, and Martin, 1948.

A.C. Kinsey, W.B. Pomeroy, C.E. Martin, and P.H. Gebhard, *Sexual behavior in the human female*. (Philadelphia, PA: W.B. Saunders, 1953).

153. R.E. Fay, C.F. Turner, A.D. Klassen, and J.H. Gagnon, "Prevalence and patterns of same-gender sexual contact among men," *Science*, (Number 243, 1989).

E. Goode and L. Haber, "Sexual correlates of homosexual experience: An exploratory study of college women," *Journal of Sex Research*, (Volume 13, 1977).

R. Sorenson, *Adolescent sexuality in contemporary society*. (New York: World Book, 1973).

154. Mac an Ghaill, 1991, p. 298.

155. Bell, Weinberg, and Hammersmith, 1981a.

A.P. Bell, M.S. Weinberg, and S.K. Hammersmith, *Sexual preference: Its development in men and women*, *(Statistic appendix)*. (Bloomington, IN: Indiana University Press, 1981b).

156. Isay, 1991.

157. R.C. Savin-Williams, "An exploratory study of pubertal maturation timing and self-esteem among gay and bisexual male youths," *Developmental Psychology*, (Volume 31, 1995).

158. D'Augelli, 1991.

J. Harry and W.B. DeVall, *The social organization of gay males*. (New York: Praeger, 1978).

Remafedi, 1987a; G. Sanders, 1980; Savin-Williams, 1990.

159. Sears, 1991a.

160. Stanley and Wolf, 1980, p. 47.

161. W. Curtis, Ed., *Revelations: A collection of gay male coming-out stories*. (Boston, MA: Alyson, 1988), p. 109-110.

162. Due, 1995, p. 74.

163. Ibid., pp. 123-124.

164. Rodriguez, 1988; Savin-Williams and Lenhart, 1990.

165. Remafedi, 1987b; Rodriguez, 1988.

166. D. Offer and A.M. Boxer, "Normal adolescent development: Empirical research findings." In M. Lewis, Ed., *Child and adolescent psychiatry: A comprehensive textbook.* (Baltimore, MD: Williams & Wilkins, 1991).

Rector, 1982.

167. Chandler, 1995, p. 146.

168. Sears, 1991a.

169. Schneider, 1989, pp. 121-122.

170. Isay, 1991.

171. Schneider, 1989, p. 123.

172. Ibid., p. 128.

173. S.M. Jourard, *The transparent self.* (New York: Van Nostrand, 1971).

174. Schneider, 1989, p. 128.

175. Malyon, 1981.

176. M. Sluchan, "Whose world is it anyway?" *The Weekly Pennsylvanian,* (1993, March 30), p. 4.

177. Savin-Williams, 1990.

178. Troiden, 1979.

179. Isay, 1991.

180. Schneider, 1989.

181. Savin-Williams, 1990, p. 182.

182. Remafedi, 1987b.

183. E. Pahe, "Speaking up." In B.L. Singer, Ed., *Growing up gay/growing up lesbian.* (New York: The New Press, 1994), p. 234.

184. A. Heron, Ed., *Two teenagers in twenty.* (Boston, MA: Alyson, 1994), p. 14.

Chapter 3

1. C. DeMontflores and S.J. Schultz, "Coming out: Similarities and differences for lesbians and gay men," *Journal of Social Issues,* (Volume 34, 1978).

2. Amelia, "My coming out story," *ELIGHT Email* (1996, 1997). Out stories collection 1.

3. A.P. Bell and M.S. Weinberg, *Homosexualities: A study of diversity among men and women.* (New York: Simon & Shuster, 1978).

D.W. Cramer and A.J. Roach, "Coming out to Mom and Dad: A study of gay males and their relationships with their parents," *Journal of Homosexuality,* (Volume 15, 1988).

K. Jay and A. Young, *The gay report: Lesbians and gay men speak out about sexual experiences and lifestyles.* (New York: Simon & Schuster, 1979).

H. Kooden, S. Morin, D. Riddle, M. Rogers, B. Sang, and F. Strassburger, *Removing the stigma. Final Report of the Task Force on the Status of Lesbian and Gay Male Psychologists.* (Washington, DC: American Psychological Association, 1979).

K. Plummer, Lesbian and gay youth in England. In G. Herdt, (Ed.), *Gay and lesbian youth.* (Binghamton, NY: Harrington Park Press, 1989).

4. McDonald, 1982.

5. D.W. Cramer, "Coming out the family: An exploration of the role of selected aspects of family functioning in the disclosure decision and outcome," *Dissertation Abstracts International*, (Volume 46, 1986).

G. Fitzpatrick, "Self-disclosure of lesbianism as related to self-actualization and self-stigmatization," *Dissertation Abstracts International*, (Volume 43, 1983).

P.K. Rector, "The acceptance of homosexual identity in adolescence: A phenomenological study," *Dissertation Abstracts International*, (Volume 43, 1982).

6. J.T. Sears, *Growing up gay in the South: Race, gender, and journeys of the spirit*. (Binghamton, NY: Harrington Park Press, 1991a), p. 158.

7. R.C. Savin-Williams, *Gay and lesbian youth: Expressions of identity*. (Washington, DC: Hemisphere, 1990).

8. S.M. Brady, "The relationship between differences in stages of homosexual identity formation and background characteristics, psychological well-being and homosexual adjustment," *Dissertation Abstracts International*, (Volume 45, 1985).

F.L. Myrick, "Homosexual types: An empirical investigation," *Journal of Sex Research*, (Volume 10, 1974a).

G.J. Remafedi, M. Resnick, R. Blum, and L. Harris, L., "Demography of sexual orientation in adolescents," *Pediatrics*, (Volume 89, 1992).

Savin-Williams, 1990.

9. J.T. Sears, "Black-gay or gay-black: Choosing identities and identifying choices." In G. Unks, Ed., *The gay teen*. (New York: Routledge, 1995).

10. Bell and Weinberg, 1978.

A.R. D'Augelli and M.M. Hart, "Gay women, men, and families in rural settings: Toward the development of helping communities," *American Journal of Community Psychology*, (Volume 15, 1987).

A.E. Moses and J.A. Buckner, "The special problems of rural gay clients," *Human Services in the Rural Environment*, (Volume 5, 1980).

11. Sears, 1991a, p. 91.

12. Savin-Williams, 1990.

13. E. Coleman, "Changing approaches to the treatment of homosexuality," *Journal of American Behavioral Sciences*, (Volume 25, 1982a).

M. Schneider, "Sappho was a right-on adolescent: Growing up lesbian," *Journal of Homosexuality*, (Volume 17, 1989).

14. Remafedi, Resnick, Blum, and Harris, 1992.

15. P.E. Elliot, "Lesbian identity and self-disclosure," *Dissertation Abstracts International*, (Volume 42, 1982).

McDonald, 1982.

G.J. McDonald, "Identity congruency and identity management among gay men," *Dissertation Abstracts International*, (Volume 45, 1984).

16. E.M. Ettorre, *Lesbians, women, and society*. (London: Routledge & Kegan Paul, 1980).

B. Ponse, "Lesbians and their worlds." In J. Marmor, Ed., *Homosexual behavior: A modern reappraisal*. (New York: Basic Books, 1980).

D. Richardson, "Lesbian identities." In J. Hart and D. Richardson, Eds., *The theory and practice of homosexuality.* (London: Routledge & Kegan Paul, 1981).

Savin-Williams, 1990.

17. Bell and Weinberg, 1978.

J. Harry and W.B. DeVall, *The social organization of gay males.* (New York: Praeger, 1978).

McDonald, 1982.

F.L. Myrick, "Attitudinal differences between heterosexually and homosexually oriented males and between covert and overt male homosexuals," *Journal of Abnormal Psychology,* (Volume 83, 1974b).

Rector, 1982; Savin-Williams, 1990.

T.S. Weinberg, *Gay men, gay selves: The social construction of homosexual identities.* (New York: Irvington, 1983).

18. Coleman, 1982a.

B.M. Dank, "Coming out in the gay world," *Psychiatry,* (Volume 34, 1971).

R.R. Troiden and E. Goode, "Variables related to acquisition of gay identity," *Journal of Homosexuality,* (Volume 5, 1980).

19. G.J. Remafedi, "Adolescent homosexuality: Psychosocial and medical implications. *Pediatrics,* (Volume 79, 1987a).

20. R. Robertson, "Young gays." In J. Hart and J. Richardson, Eds., *The theory and practice of homosexuality.* (New York: Routledge & Kegan Paul, 1981).

21. L. Nemeyer, "Coming out: Identity congruence and the attainment of adult female sexuality," *Dissertation Abstracts International,* (Volume 41, 1980).

22. Coleman, 1982a.

M. Eisner, *An investigation of the coming out process, lifestyle, and sex-role orientation of lesbians.* Unpublished doctoral dissertation, York University, Toronto, (1982).

H.L. Minton and G.J. McDonald, "Homosexual identity formation as a developmental process," *Journal of Homosexuality,* (Volume 9, 1984).

R.R. Troiden, "Homosexual identity formation," *Journal of Adolescent Health Care,* (Volume 9, 1988).

23. S.K. Hammersmith and M.S. Weinberg, "Homosexual identity: Commitment, adjustment, and significant others," *Sociometry,* (Volume 36, 1973).

J.C. Gonsiorek and J.R. Rudolph, "Homosexual identity: Coming out and other developmental events." In J.C. Gonsiorek and J.D. Weinrich, Eds., *Homosexuality: Research implications for public policy.* (Newbury Park, CA Sage, 1991).

24. P.J. Gorton, "Different from the others." In R. Luczak, Ed., *Eyes of desire: A deaf gay and lesbian reader.* (Boston, Alyson, 1993), p. 22.

25. L. Due, *Joining the tribe.* (New York: Anchor Books, 1995), p. 78.

26. L.D. Brimmer, *Being different: Lambda youth speak out.* (New York: Franklin Watts, 1995), p. 77.

27. S.M. Jourard, *The transparent self.* (New York: Van Nostrand, 1971).

A.D. Martin, "Learning to hide: The socialization of the gay adolescent," *Adolescent Psychiatry*, (Volume 10, 1982).

28. E. Bass and K. Kaufman, *Free your mind: The book for gay, lesbian, and bisexual youth—and their allies*. (New York: Harper Perennial, 1996), p. 63.

29. A. Heron, Ed., *One teenager in ten*. (Boston, MA: Alyson, 1983), p. 51.

30. Due, 1995, p. 225.

31. J. Steffan, *Honor bound*. (New York: Villard Books, 1992), pp. 144-145.

32. Cramer, 1986; Savin-Williams, 1990.

33. Cramer, 1986.

34. A.M. Boxer, J.A. Cook, and G. Herdt, "Double jeopardy: Identity transitions and parent-child relations among gay and lesbian youth." In K. Killemer and K. McCortney, Eds., *Parent child relations through life*. (Hillsdale, NJ: Erlbaum Associates, 1991).

35. Fitzpatrick, 1983.

36. K. Chandler, *Passages of pride: Gay and lesbian youth come of age*. (New York: Times Books, 1995), p. 95.

37. McDonald, 1982.

38. R.R. Troiden, "The formation of homosexual identities," *Journal of Homosexuality*, (Volume 17, 1989).

C. Warren, *Identity and community in the gay world*. (New York: John Wiley, 1974).

39. A. Fricke, *Reflections of a Rock Lobster*. (Boston, MA: Alyson Publications, 1981), p. 70.

40. Ettorre, 1980; Ponse, 1980; Richardson, 1981.

41. D.J. McKirnan and P.L. Peterson, "Chicago survey documents anti-gay bias," *Windy City Times*, (1987a, March 12).

42. M.S. Weinberg and C.J. Williams, *Male homosexuals: Their problems and adaptations*. (New York: Penguin, 1974).

43. J.A. Lee, "Going public: A study of the sociology of homosexual liberation," *Journal of Homosexuality*, (Volume 3, 1977).

44. R. Sohier, "Homosexual mutuality: Variation on a theme by Erik Erikson," *Journal of Homosexuality*, (Volume 12, 1985/1986).

45. J. Harry, "Being out: A general model," *Journal of Homosexuality*, (Volume 26, 1993).

46. P. Davies, "The role of disclosure in coming out among gay men." In K. Plummer, Ed., *Modern homosexualities: Fragments of lesbian and gay experience*. (London: Routledge, 1992).

47. L. Kaahumanu and L. Hutchins, *Bi any other name: Bisexual people speak out*. (Boston: Alyson, 1991).

48. Bass and Kaufman, 1996, p. 67.

49. Cohen and Saven-Williams, 1996.

50. Ibid., p. 122.

51. M. Schneider, "Developing services for lesbian and gay adolescents," *Canadian Journal of Community Mental Health*, (Volume 10, 1991).

52. Ibid., p. 143.

53. J.C. Benitez, "The effect of gay identity acquisition on the psychological adjustment of male homosexuals," *Dissertation Abstracts International*, (Volume 43, 1983).

   Brady, 1985; Elliott, 1982; Nemeyer, 1980.

   R.J. O'Carolan, "An investigation of the relationship between self-disclosure of sexual preference to self-esteem, feminism, and locus of control in lesbians," *Dissertation Abstracts International*, (Volume 43, 1982).

   G. Sanders, "Homosexuals in the Netherlands," *Alternative Lifestyles*, (Volume 3, 1980).

54. Steffen, 1992, p. 145.

55. G. Herdt, "Introduction: Gay and lesbian youth, emergent identities and cultural scenes at home and abroad." In G. Herdt, Ed., *Gay and lesbian youth*. (Binghamton, NY: Harrington Park Press, 1989).

56. M. Kehoe, "Lesbians over 65: A triple invisible minority," *Journal of Homosexuality*, (Volume 12, 1986).

   Ponce, 1978.

57. deMonteflores and Schultz, 1978.

58. A. Heron, Ed., *Two teenagers in twenty*. (Boston, MA: Alyson, 1994), p. 130.

59. D.A. Anderson, "Lesbian and gay adolescents: Social and developmental considerations." In G. Unks, Ed., *The gay teen*. (New York: Routledge, 1995).

60. Brimmer, 1995, p. 59.

61. Savin-Williams, 1990.

62. Boxer, Cook, and Herdt, 1991.

63. J.D. Hencken, "Sexual-orientation self-disclosure," *Dissertation Abstracts International*, (Volume 45, 1985).

   Savin-Williams, 1990.

64. S.K. Telljohann and J.H. Price, "A qualitative examination of adolescent homosexuals' life experiences: Ramifications for secondary school personnel," *Journal of Homosexuality*, (Volume 26, 1993).

65. A.R. D'Augelli, "Gay men in college: Identity processes and adaptations," *Journal of College Student Development*, (Volume 32, 1991).

66. Sears, 1991a, p. 181.

67. V.L. Bender, Y. Davis, O. Glover, and J. Stapp, "Patterns of self-disclosure in homosexual and heterosexual college students," *Sex Roles*, (Volume 2, 1976).

   Cramer, 1986.

   J.C. Grabert, "Homosexual men and their parents: A study of self-disclosure, personality traits and attitudes toward homosexuality," *Dissertation Abstracts International*, (Volume 46, 1985).

   Jay and Young, 1979.

   D.J. McKirnan and P.L. Peterson, "Preliminary social issues survey results," *Windy City Times*, (1986, October 2).

   G.J. Remafedi, "Male homosexuality: The adolescent's perspective," *Pediatrics*, (Volume 79, 1987b).

   Savin-Williams, 1990.

68. P. Singer, "Breaking through," Rochester, NY, *Democrat and Chronicle*, (1993, July 4), p. D-1.

69. Ellenberger, 1966.

70. L.G. Nungesser, *Homosexual acts, actors, and identities.* (New York: Praeger, 1983).

71. Staver, 1976.

72. Savin-Williams, 1990.

73. Ibid.

74. Minton and McDonald, 1984.

75. Nemeyer, 1980.

76. C. Silverstein, *Man to man: Gay couples in America.* (New York: William Morrow, 1981).

77. A.R. D'Augelli and S.L. Hershberger, "Lesbian, gay, and bisexual youth in community settings: Personal challenges and mental health problems," *American Journal of Community Psychology*, (Volume 21, 1993).

78. Boxer, Cook, and Herdt, 1991, p. 61.

79. Singer, 1993, p. D-1.

80. Boxer, Cook, and Herdt, 1991, p. 70.

81. K.M. Cohen and R.C. Savin-Williams, "Developmental perspectives on coming out to self and others. In R.C. Savin-Williams and K.M. Cohen, Eds., *The lives of lesbians, gays, and bisexuals.* (Fort Worth, TX: Harcourt & Brace College Publishers, 1996).

82. Sears, 1995, p. 140.

83. Boxer, Cook, and Herdt, 1991.

84. A.M. Boxer and J.A. Cook, *Developmental discontinuities in the transition to gay and lesbian adult roles: A study of homosexual youth.* Paper presented at the Midcontinental Meeting of the Society for the Scientific Study of Sex, Chicago, IL, 1988.

Boxer, Cook, and Herdt, 1991.

85. M.V. Borhek, "Helping gay and lesbian adolescents and their families," *Journal of Adolescent Health Care*, (Volume 9, 1988).

Savin-Williams, 1990.

86. T. Wise, "Coming out to my mom." In B.L. Singer, Ed., *Growing up gay/growing up lesbian.* (New York: The New Press, 1994), p. 122.

87. Chandler, 1995.

88. Ibid.

89. Sears, 1991a, p. 38.

90. Savin-Williams, 1990.

91. Schneider, 1989.

92. Heron, 1994, p. 174.

93. D'Augelli and Hershberger, 1993.

G.J. Remafedi, "Homosexual youth: A challenge to contermporary society," *Journal of the American Medical Association*, (Volume 258, 1987c).

Telljohann and Price, 1993.

94. Singer, 1993, p. D1.

95. Bass and Kaufman, 1996, p. 195.

96. L. Collins and N. Zimmerman, "Homosexual and bisexual issues." In J.C. Hansen, J.D. Woody, and R.H. Woody, Eds., *Sexual issues in the family*. (Rockville, MD: Aspen Publications, 1983).

J.L. DeVine, "A systematic inspection of affectional preference orientation and the family of origin," *Journal of Social Work and Human Sexuality*, (Volume 2, 1984).

97. B.S. Newman and P.G. Muzzonigro, "The effects of traditional family values on the coming-out process of gay male adolescents," *Adolescence*, (Volume 28, 1993).

Cohen and Savin-Williams, 1996.

98. C. Clarke, "The failure to transform: Homophobia in the Black community." In B. Smith, Ed., *Home girls: A Black feminist anthology*. (New York: Kitchen Table Press, 1983).

O.M. Espin, "Issues of identity in the psychology of Latina lesbians." In Boston Lesbian Psychologies Collective, Eds., *Lesbian psychologies: Explorations and challenges*. (Urbana, IL: University of Illinois Press, 1987).

L. Icard, "Black gay men and conflicting social identities: Sexual orientation versus racial identity," *Journal of Social Work and Human Sexuality*, (Volume 4, 1986).

E.S. Morales, *Third world gays and lesbians: A process of multiple identities*. Paper presented at the 91st Annual Convention of the American Psychological Association, Anaheim, CA, (1983, August).

A.F. Poussaint, "An honest look at black gays and lesbians," *Ebony*, (1990, September).

99. R.C. Savin-Williams, "Ethnic- and sexual-minority youth." In R.C. Savin-Williams and K.M. Cohen, Eds., *The lives of lesbians, gays, and bisexuals*. (Fort Worth, TX: Harcourt & Brace College Publishers, 1996b).

100. C.S. Chan, "Issues of identity development among Asian-American lesbians and gay men," *Journal of Counseling and Development*, (Volume 68, 1989).

H.A. Hidalgo and E. Hidalgo-Christensen, "The Puerto Rican lesbian and the Puerto Rican community," *Journal of Homosexuality*, (Volume 2, 1976/1977).

101. M. Romo-Carmona, "Introduction." In J. Ramos, Ed., *Compameras: Latina lesbians*. (New York: Routledge, 1994), p. xxvi.

102. Savin-Williams, 1996b.

103. E.F. Strommen, "'You're a what?': Family members reactions to the disclosure of homosexuality," *Journal of Homosexuality*, (Volume 18, 1989).

104. Muchmore and Hanson, 1982. In W. Muchmore and W. Hanson, Eds., *Coming out right: A handbook for the gay male*. (Boston, MA: Alyson, 1982).

105. Chandler, 1995, p. 99.

106. Wise, 1994, p. 119.

107. Ibid., p. 121.

108. Cohen and Savin-Williams, 1996, p. 137.

109. Ibid., p. 138.

110. Ibid., p. 137.

111. Ibid., p. 138.

112. R.R. Troiden, "The formation of homosexual identities," *Journal of Homosexuality*, (Volume 17, 1989).

113. Due, 1995, p. 220-221.

114. D.H. Demo, S.A. Small, and R.C. Savin-Williams, "Family relations and self-esteem of adolescents and their parents," *Journal of Marriage and Family*, (Volume 49, 1987).

V. Gecas and M.L. Schwalbe, "Parental behavior and adolescent self-esteem," *Journal of Marriage and the Family*, (Volume 48, 1986).

115. Savin-Williams, 1989a; 1990.

116. B. Grier, "The garden variety lesbian." In J.P. Stanley and S.J. Wolfe, Eds., *The coming out stories*. (Watertown, MA: Persephone Press, 1980), p. 236.

117. Cohen and Savin-Williams, 1996, p. 139.

118. D.J. McKirnan and P.L. Peterson, "Preliminary social issues survey results," *Windy City Times*, (1986, October 2).

D.J. McKirnan and P.L. Peterson, "Chicago survey documents anti-gay bias," *Windy City Times*, (1987a, March 12).

D.J. McKirnan and P.L. Peterson, "Social support and copying resources," *Windy City Times*, (1987b, April 30).

D.J. McKirnan and P.L. Peterson, "A profile of older gay men: A perspective from the social issues survey," *Windy City Times*, (1987c, June 25).

119. Heather, "My coming out story," *ELIGHT Email* (1996, 1997). Out stories collection 1.

120. Salim, "His way," *ELIGHT Email* (1996, 1997). Writings collection 1.

121. V.C. Cass, "Homosexual identity formation: Testing and theoretical model," *Journal of Homosexuality*, (Volume 4, 1979).

Coleman, 1982a.

P. Colgan, "Treatment of identity and intimacy issues in gay males," *Journal of Homosexuality*, (Volume 14, 1987).

B.M. Dank, "The homosexual." In D. Spiegal and P. Keith-Spiegel, Eds., *Outsiders USA*. (San Francisco, CA: Rinehart, 1973).

Hammersmith and Weinberg, 1973; McDonald, 1982; Savin-Williams, 1990.

R.R. Troiden, "Becoming homosexual: A model of gay identity acquisition," *Psychiatry*, (Volume 42, 1979).

Warren, 1974.

122. Anonymous, "Out of the closet," *Heartline*, (1996, October 8), p. 7.

Chapter 4

1. J.T. Sears, *Growing up gay in the South: Race, gender, and journeys of the spirit*. (Binghamton, NY: Harrington Park Press, 1991a), p. 385.

2. C.J. Cohen and T.S. Stein, "Reconceptualizing individual psychotherapy with gay men and lesbians." In C.J. Cohen and T.S. Stein, Eds., *Contemporary*

perspectives on psychotherapy with lesbians and gay men. (New York: Plenum, 1986).

J.C. Gonsiorek, Ed., *Homosexuality: Social, psychological, and biological issues.* (Beverly Hills, CA: Sage Publications, 1982).

3. K. Chandler, *Passages of pride: Gay and lesbian youth come of age.* (New York: Times Books, 1995), p. 38.

4. S. Maguen, "Teen suicide: The government's cover-up and America's lost children," *The Advocate,* (1991, September 24), p. 45.

5. E.S. Hetrick and A.D. Martin, "Ego-dystonic homosexuality: A developmental view." In E. Hetrick and T. Stein, Eds., *Psychotherapy with homosexuals.* (Washington, DC: American Psychiatric Press, 1983).

M. Schneider, *Often invisible: Counseling gay and lesbian youth.* (Toronto: Toronto Central Youth Services, 1988).

6. R.C. Savin-Williams, "Memories of childhood and early adolescent sexual feelings among gay and bisexual boys: A narrative approach." In R.C. Savin-Williams and K.M. Cohen, Eds., *The lives of lesbians, gays, and bisexuals.* (Fort Worth, TX: Harcourt & Brace College Publishers, 1996c), p. 104.

7. E.E. Rofes, "Youth: New identities, new issues," *The Advocate,* (1984, November 27), p. 15.

8. A.M. Boxer, J.A. Cook, and G. Herdt, "Double jeopardy: Identity transitions and parent-child relations among gay and lesbian youth." In K. Pillemer and K. McCortney, Eds., *Parent-child relations through life.* (Hillsdale, NJ: Erlbaum Associates, 1991), p. 62.

9. A. Lipkin, "The case for a gay and lesbian curriculum." In G. Unks, Ed., *The gay teen.* (New York: Routledge, 1995).

10. R. Friend, "Choices, not closets: Heterosexism and homophobia in schools." In L. Weis and M. Fine, Eds., *Beyond silent voices.* (Albany, NY: SUNY Press, 1993), p. 146.

11. G.M. Herek, "The social context of hate crimes: Notes on cultural heterosexism." In G. Herek and K. Berill, Eds., *Hate crimes: Confronting violence against lesbians and gay men.* (Newbury Park, CA: Sage, 1992).

12. A.K. Malyon, "The homosexual adolescent: Developing issues and social bias," *Child Welfare,* (Volume 60, 1981), p. 328.

13. Sears, 1991a, p. 347.

14. G. Herdt, *Sambia: Ritual and gender in New Guinea.* (New York: Holt, Rinehart & Winston, 1987).

15. J.A. Lee, "Going public: A study of the sociology of homosexual liberation," *Journal of Homosexuality,* (Volume 3, 1977).

16. J.N. Baker, "Coming out now," *Newsweek,* (Volume 115:27, Summer 1990), p. 60.

17. Penelope, 1979.

18. Sears, 1991a, p. 112.

19. G.P. Mallon, "Counseling strategies with gay and lesbian youth." In T. DeCrescenzo, Eds., *Helping gay and lesbian youth: New policies, new programs, new practice.* (Binghamton, NY: Harrington Park Press, 1994), pp. 75-76.

20. P.D. Toth, "Realizing it's OK to be gay." Rochester, NY, *Times-Union*, (1993, October 12), p. 15.

21. D. Tievsky, "Homosexual clients and homophobic social workers," *Journal of Independent Social Work*, (Volume 2, Number 3, 1988).

22. K. Butler and T.J. Byrne, "Homophobia among preservice elementary teachers," *Journal of Health Education*, (Volume 23, Number 6, 1992).

23. D. Boyer, "Male prostitution and homosexual identity." In G. Herdt, Ed., *Gay and lesbian youth*. (Binghamton, NY: Harrington Park Press, 1989), p. 161.

24. B.J. Miller, "From silence to suicide: Measuring a mother's loss." In W.J. Blumenfeld, Ed., *Homophobia: How we all pay the price*. (Boston, MA: Beacon Press, 1992), p. 88.

25. J.H. Price, "High school students attitudes toward homosexuality," *Journal of School Health*, (Volume 52, 1982).

H.J. Sobel, "Adolescent attitudes toward homosexuality in relation to self-concept and body satisfaction," *Adolescence*, (Volume 11, 1976).

26. Kunjufu, 1985.

27. A.F. Poussaint, "An honest look at black gays and lesbians," *Ebony*, (1990, September).

28. Sears, 1991a, p. 68.

29. K.P. Monteiro and V. Fuqua, "African-American gay youth: One form of manhood." In G. Unks, Ed., *The gay teen*. (New York: Routledge, 1995).

30. Sears, 1991a, p. 68.

31. Monteiro and Fuqua, 1994.

32. T. Osborn, "The fountain of youth," *The Advocate*, (1994, November 29).

33. M Sluchan, "Whose world is it anyway?" *The Weekly Pennsylvanian*, (1993, March 30), p. 4.

34. Maguen, 1991, p. 42.

35. Sears, 1991a, pp. 110-111.

36. A.P. Kielwasser and M.A. Wolf, "Mainstream television, adolescent homosexuality, and significant silence," *Critical Issues in Mass Communication*, (Volume 9, 1992).

A.P. Kielwasser and M.A. Wolf, "Silence, difference, and annihilation: Understanding the impact of mediated heterosexism on high school students," *The High School Journal*, (Volume 77, Number 1/2, 1994).

37. Ibid., p. 66.

38. Kielwasser and Wolf, 1992.

39. Ibid.

40. Heron, 1983, p. 30.

41. Herek, 1993, p. 90.

42. Sears, 1991a, p. 183.

43. R. Coles, "What makes some kids more vulnerable to the worst of TV?" *TV Guide*, (1986, June 21).

44. G. Gerbner and L. Gross, "Living with television: The violence profile," *Journal of Communication*, (Volume 26, Number 2, 1976).

45. Ibid., p. 21.

46. R. Robertson, "Young gays." In J. Hart and J. Richardson, Eds., *The theory and practice of homosexuality.* (New York: Routledge & Kegan Paul, 1981), p. 174.

47. M. Pawa, "Coming out for Sarah," *The Weekly Pennsylvanian*, (1993, March 23), p. 4.

48. Chandler, 1995, p. 85.

49. A. Heron, Ed., *One teenager in ten.* (Boston, MA: Alyson, 1983), p. 114.

50. Chandler, 1995.

51. Sears, 1991a, p. 176.

52. L. Galst, "Throwaway kids," *The Advocate*, (1992, December 29), p. 56.

53. "Starting over: A Chinese teenager comes to a new home and comes out," *Crossroads*, (1996, Winter/Spring), p. 7.

54. D.A. Anderson, "Family and peer relations of gay adolescents." In S.C. Geinstein, Ed., *Adolescent psychiatry: Developmental and clinical studies,* Volume 14. (Chicago: The University of Chicago Press, 1987).

55. M.F. Myers, "Counseling the parents of young homosexual male parents," *Journal of Homosexuality*, (Volume 7, 1982).

K. Plummer, "Lesbian and gay youth in England." In G. Herdt, Ed., *Gay and lesbian youth.* (Binghamton, NY: Harrington Park Press, 1989).

Robertson, 1981.

R.R. Troiden, "The formation of homosexual identities," *Journal of Homosexuality*, (Volume 17, 1989).

56. G. Powell, J. Yamamoto, A. Romero, and A. Morales, Eds., *The psychosocial development of minority group children.* (New York: Brunner/Mazel, 1983).

57. E.S. Hetrick and A.D. Martin, "Developmental issues and their resolution for gay and lesbian adolescents," *Journal of Homosexuality*, (Volume 14, 1987).

58. J. Gover, "Gay youth in the family," *Journal of Emotional and Behavioral Problems*, (Volume 2, Number 4, 1993).

59. Mercier and Berger, 1989.

60. B. Tremble, M. Schneider, and C. Appathurai, "Growing up gay or lesbian in a multicultural context," *Journal of Homosexuality*, (Volume 17, 1989).

61. Boyer, 1989, p. 162.

62. Sears, 1991a, p. 355.

63. Boyer, 1989, p. 162.

64. J. Harry, *Gay children grown up.* (New York: Praeger, 1982).

65. Maguen, 1991, p. 44.

66. Boxer, Cook, and Herdt, 1991, p. 76.

67. M. Brownley, *Gay youth.* (Minneapolis, MN: Community Intervention, 1988), p. 1.

68. Gover, 1993.

69. E. Kübler-Ross, *On death and dying.* (New York: Macmillan, 1969).

70. Greene and Boxer, 1986.

R.A. Pruchno, F.C. Blow, and M.A. Smyer, "Life-events and interdependent lives," *Human Development*, (Volume 27, 1984).

71. S.J. Weissman, R.S. Cohen, A.M. Boser, and B.J. Cohler, "Parenthood experience and the adolescent's transition to young adulthood: Self-psychological perspectives," *Adolescent Psychiatry*, (Volume 16, 1989).

72. Brownley, 1988.

73. Robinson, Walters, and Skeen, 1989.

74. A. Muller, *Parents matter*. (New York: Naiad Press, 1987).

C.W. Griffin, M.J. Wirth, and A.G. Wirth, *Beyond acceptance: Parents of lesbians and gays talk about their experiences*. (Englewood Cliffs, NJ: Prentice-Hall, 1986).

75. Griffin, Wirth, and Wirth, 1986; Muller, 1987.

76. Boxer, Cook, and Herdt, 1991, p. 79.

77. Mallon, 1994, pp. 83-84.

78. B. Robinson and L. Walters, "The AIDS epidemic hits home," *Psychology Today*, (1987, April).

79. G. Herdt, "Introduction: Gay and lesbian youth, emergent identities and cultural scenes at home and abroad." In G. Herdt, Ed., *Gay and lesbian youth*. (Binghamton, NY: Harrington Park Press, 1989), p. 32.

80. A. O'Conor, "Who gets called queer in school? Lesbian, gay, and bisexual teenagers, homophobia, and high school." In G. Unks, Ed., *The gay teen*. (New York: Routledge, 1995), p. 96.

81. P. Singer, "Breaking through," Rochester, NY, *Democrat and Chronicle*, (1993, July 4), p. D-1.

82. Boxer, Cook, and Herdt, 1991, p. 63.

83. Malyon, 1981.

84. A. Heron, Ed., *Two teenagers in twenty*. (Boston, MA: Alyson, 1993), p. 147.

85. B. Mirken, "A child's worst nightmare," *The Advocate*, (1992, March 10), p. 56.

86. Abinati, 1994.

87. Mirken, 1992, p. 56.

88. L. Due, *Joining the tribe*. (New York: Anchor Books, 1995), p. 14.

89. P. Christopher, "Notes from the inside," *The Advocate*, (1993, December 28).

90. Boxer, Cook, and Herdt, 1991, p. 76.

91. Heron, 1994, p. 173.

92. O'Conor, 1995, p. 97.

93. Sears, 1991a, p. 42.

94. Chandler, 1995.

95. E.F. Strommen, "'You're a what?': Family members reactions to the disclosure of homosexuality," *Journal of Homosexuality*, (Volume 18, 1989).

96. Boxer, Cook, and Herdt, 1991.

97. S. Zitter, "Coming out to Mom: Theoretical aspects of the mother-daughter process." In Boston Lesbian Psychologies Collective, Eds., *Lesbian*

psychologies: Explorations and challenges. (Urbana, IL: University of Illinois, 1987).

98. Brownley, 1988.

99. Gover, 1993.

100. Chandler, 1995, p. 83.

101. N. Adair, and C. Adair, *Word is out.* (Adair Films, 1978).

102. J. Tinney, "Why a gay black church?" In J. Beam, Ed., *In the life: A black gay anthology.* (Boston, MA: Alyson, 1986).

103. M. Schneider, "Developing services for lesbian and gay adolescents," *Canadian-Journal of Community Mental Health,* (Volume 10, 1991).

104. L.D. Brimmer, *Being different: Lambda youth speak out.* (New York: Franklin Watts, 1995), p. 89.

105. Schneider, 1991.

106. E. Bass and K. Kaufman, *Free your mind: The book for gay, lesbian, and bisexual youth—and their allies.* (New York: Harper Perennial, 1996), p. 232.

107. Osborn, 1994, p. 80.

108. Gover, 1993.

109. M. Schneider, "Sappho was a right-on adolescent: Growing up lesbian," *Journal of Homosexuality,* (Volume 17, 1989), p. 126.

110. Chandler, 1995, p. 35.

111. Boyer, 1989.

112. Schneider, 1989, p. 125.

113. E.E. Rofes, "Making our schools safe for sissies." In G. Unks, Ed., *The gay teen.* (New York: Routledge, 1995).

114. J. D'Emilio, *Sexual politics, sexual communities.* (Chicago: University of Chicago Press, 1983).

G. Robinson, "Few solutions for a young dilemma," *The Advocate,* (1984).

115. J. Hunter, "Violence against lesbian and gay male youth," *Journal of Interpersonal Violence,* (Volume 5, 1990).

116. J.C. Gonsiorek, "Mental health issues of gay and lesbian adolescents," *Journal of Adolescent Health Care,* (Volume 9, 1988).

W.R. Greer, "Violence against homosexuals rising, groups seeking wider protection say," *The New York Times,* (1986, November 23).

W. Masters, V. Johnson, and R. Kolodny, *Human sexuality,* Fourth edition. (New York: Harper Collins, 1992).

117. Sears, 1991a, p. 51.

118. Price, 1982.

119. Hunter, 1990.

G.J. Remafedi, "Male homosexuality: The adolescent's perspective," *Pediatrics,* (Volume 79, 1987b).

L. Trenchard and H. Warren, *Something to tell you.* (London: Gay Teenagers' Project, 1984).

120. Sears, 1991a, p. 241.

121. Boyer, 1989, p. 168.

122. O'Conor, 1995, p. 97.

123. Chandler, 1995, p. 196.

124. C. Bull, "Safey net," *The Advocate*, (1993, September 7).

125. "Danger on campus," *The Advocate*, (1994, October 4), p. 21.

126. Chandler, 1995.

127. R.C. Savin-Williams and K.M. Cohen, "Psychosocial outcomes of verbal and physical abuse among lesbian, gay, and bisexual youths." In R.C. Savin-Williams and K.M. Cohen, Eds., *The lives of lesbians, gays, and bisexuals*. (Fort Worth, TX: Harcourt & Brace College Publishers, 1996).

128. O'Conor, 1995, p. 97.

129. Mallon, 1994, p. 85.

130. Due, 1995, p. 224.

131. L. Gross and S.K. Aurand, *Discrimination and violence against lesbian women and gay men in Philadelphia and the Commonwealth of Pennsylvania*, (Philadelphia, PA: Lesbian and Gay Task Force, 1992).

132. Due, 1995, p. 116.

133. *Hostile hallways: The American Association of University Women Survey on Sexual Harassment in American Schools.* (Washington, DC: AAUW Education Foundation, 1993, June).

134. Louis Harris, 1993.

135. K. Gessen, K., "Matt Flynn, high school activist," *The Advocate*, (1993, September 7), p. 69.

136. Anderson, 1987.

137. Baker, 1990.

138. Ibid., p. 60.

139. Governor's Commission on Gay and Lesbian Youth, "Excerpts from public testimony," (Boston, MA, 1992), p. 19.

140. Due, 1995, p. 221.

141. Chandler, 1995, p. 36.

142. J. Green, "This school is out," *The New York Times Magazine*, (1991, October 13).

143. V. Uribe and K.M. Harbeck, *Coming out of the classroom closet: Gay and lesbian students, teachers, and curricula*. (Binghamton, NY: Harrington Park Press, 1992).

144. J. Cart, "Lesbian issue stirs discussion," *Los Angeles Times*, (1992, April 6).

M. Denney, "Homophobia in sports," *Indianapolis News-Sentinel*, (1992, July 15).

R. Lipsyte, "Gay bias moves off the sidelines," *The New York Times*, (1992, May 24).

145. Mac an Ghaill, 1991, p. 301.

146. T. Curry, "Fraternal bonding in the locker room: A profeminist analysis of talk about competition and women," *Sociology of Sport Journal*, (Volume 8, Number 2, 1991).

147. Mac an Ghaill, 1991, p. 302.

148. P. Griffin, "Changing the game: Homophobia, sexism, and lesbians in sports," *Quest*, (Volume 44, 1992).

149. P. Griffin, "Addressing the needs of lesbian and gay high school athletes." In G. Unks, Ed., *The gay teen.* (New York: Routledge, 1995).

150. Kissen, 1991, p. 10.

151. M.C. Cage, "Openly gay students face harassment and physical assaults on some campuses," *The Chronicle of Higher Education*, (1993, March 10).

152. Ibid., p. A23.

153. Ibid.

154. Chandler, 1995.

155. T. Rutten, "Candidate sees gays as enemies," *Los Angeles Times*, (1992, March 5).

156. Hunter, 1990.

157. Mac an Ghaill, 1991, p. 300.

158. Ibid., p. 301.

159. Ibid., p. 302.

160. D. Siminoski, "A killing in a small town," *The Advocate*, (1988).

161. L. Galst, "Throwaway kids," *The Advocate*, (1992, December 29), p. 57.

162. Green, 1991.

163. Chandler, 1995.

164. V.A. Brownworth, "Abused and isolated: Gay and lesbian teens," *The Advocate*, (1992, June 2), p. 63.

165. M. Foucault, *The history of sexuality,* Volume 1. (New York: Random House, 1978).

166. R.C. Savin-Williams, "Dating and romantic relations among gay, lesbian, and bisexual youths." In R.C. Savin-Williams and K.M. Cohen, Eds., *The lives of lesbians, gays, and bisexuals.* (Fort Worth, TX: Harcourt & Brace College Publishers, 1996a).

167. Ibid.

168. Ibid.

169. C.R. Fikar, "Commentary: Thoughts of a gay pediatrician," *Journal of Adolescent Health*, (Volume 13, 1992).

W.C. Matthews, M.W. Booth, J.D. Turner, and L. Kessler, "Physicians' attitudes toward homosexuality—Survey of a California county medical society," *Western Journal of Medicine*, (Volume 144, 1986).

170. Schwanberg, 1990.

171. M. Glasser, "Homosexuality in adolescence," *British Journal of Medical Psychology*, (Volume 50, 1977).

172. Singer, 1993.

173. M. Ross, "Stigma, sex, and society," *Journal of Homosexuality*, (Volume 3, 1978).

C.A. Tripp, *The homosexual matrix.* (New York: McGraw-Hill, 1975).

K. Freund, "Should homosexuality arouse therapeutic concern?" *Journal of Homosexuality*, (Volume 1, 1977).

174. G.P. Jones, "Counseling gay adolescents," *Counselor Education and Supervision*, (Volume 18, 1978).

175. Peroski, 1987.

176. N. Youngstrom, "Minority youth who are gay: A tough road, but there's hope," *APA Monitor*, (1992).

177. Bass and Kaufman, 1996, p. 203.

178. Ross-Reynolds, 1988, p. 219.

179. Singer, 1993, p. D-1.

180. J.T. Sears, "Educators, homosexuality, and homosexual students: Are personal feelings related to professional beliefs?" *Journal of Homosexuality*, (Volume 22, 1992).

Chapter 5

1. B.L. Singer, Ed., *Growing up gay/growing up lesbian.* (New York: The New Press, 1994), p. 222

2. G. Herdt, and A.M. Boxer, *Children of Horizons: How gay and lesbian teens are leading a new way out of the closet.* (Boston: Beacon Press, 1993), p. 222.

3. S. Maguen, "Teen suicide: The government's cover-up and America's lost children," *The Advocate*, (1991, September 24).

4. K. Chandler, *Passages of pride: Gay and lesbian youth come of age.* (New York: Times Books, 1995).

5. J. Gallagher, "The transgender revolution," *The Advocate*, (1996, December 10).

6. C. Bull, "Safety net," *The Advocate*, (1993, September 7), p. 53.

7. Mac an Ghaill, 1991.

J.L. Norton, "Same sex preference." In A.C. Nicholas and J.P. Whittmer, Eds., *Let me be me.* (Muncie, IN: Accelerated Development, 1980).

R.E. Powell, "Homosexual behavior and the school counselor," *School Counselor*, (Volume 34, 1987).

8. D. Reed, *High school gay youth: Invisible diversity.* Paper presented at the annual meeting of the American Educational Research Association, Atlanta, GA, (1993, August).

9. L.D. Brimmer, *Being different: Lambda youth speak out.* (New York: Franklin Watts, 1995), p. 94.

10. Maupin, 1986, p. 295.

11. A. Johnson, "Lesbians and gays in the schools: Teachers, students, and courses of study," *On Our Backs*, (1989).

M. Mac an Ghaill, "Schooling, sexuality and male power: Toward an emancipatory curriculum," *Gender and Education*, (Volume 3, 1991).

H. Warren, *Talking about school.* (London: Gay Teachers Project, 1984).

12. J.T. Sears, "Educators, homosexuality, and homosexual students: Are personal feelings related to professional beliefs," *Journal of Homosexuality*, (Volume 22, 1991b), p. 32.

13. Letters, *Time*, January 11, 1993.

14. V. Uribe, "The silent minority: Rethinking our commitment to gay and lesbian youth," *Theory into Practice*, (Volume 33, 1994).

15. Chandler, 1995, p. 129.
16. Ibid., p. 269.
17. G.M. Leck, "The politics of adolescent sexual identity and queer responses." In G. Unks, Ed., *The gay teen.* (New York: Routledge, 1995).
18. Sears, 1991b.
19. Ibid., p. 31.
20. Ibid.
21. Ibid., p. 32.
22. Mercier and Berger, 1989.
23. Sears, 1991b, p. 36.
24. Ibid., p. 34.
25. Sears, 1991b, p. 35.
26. "Agenda," *The Advocate*, (1997, April 15).
27. "The Nation," *The Advocate*, (1996, July 23).
28. L. Due, *Joining the tribe.* (New York: Anchor Books, 1995), p. 196.
29. Mac an Ghaill, 1991, p. 292.
30. Sears, 1991b.
31. A. O'Conor, "Who gets called queer in school? Lesbian, gay, and bisexual teenagers, homophobia, and high school." In G. Unks, Ed., *The gay teen.* (New York: Routledge, 1995), p. 96.
32. J.T. Sears, *Growing up gay in the South: Race, gender, and journeys of the spirit.* (Binghamton, NY: Harrington Park Press, 1991a), p. 277.
33. Kissen, 1991, p. 9.
34. Ibid.
35. W.P. McFarland, "A developmental approach to gay and lesbian youth," *Journal of Humanistic Education and Development*, (Volume 32, Number 1, 1993).
36. M.S. Schneider and B. Tremble, "Training service providers to work with gay and lesbian adolescents: A workshop," *Journal of Counseling and Development*, (Volume 65, 1986).
37. G.J. Remafedi, J. Farrow, and R. Deisher, "Risk factors for attempted suicide in gay and bisexual youth," *Pediatrics*, (Volume 87, 1991).
38. Sears, 1992.
39. E. Bass and K. Kaufman, *Free your mind: The book for gay, lesbian, and bisexual youth—and their allies.* (New York: Harper Perennial, 1996), p. 203.
40. S.K. Telljohann and J.H. Price, "A qualitative examination of adolescent homosexuals' life experiences: Ramifications for secondary school personnel," *Journal of Homosexuality*, (Volume 26, 1993).
41. Sears, 1991a, p. 104.
42. S. Maguen, "Gay rural youth lack support from the community," *The Advocate*, (1992, November 17), p. 53.
43. Sears, 1991a, p. 395.
44. K. Whitlock, *Bridges of respect.* (Philadelphia, PA: American Friends Service Committee, 1988).
45. Chandler, 1995, p. 322.

46. "Class act," *The Advocate*, (1996, May 28), p. 23.

47. Sears, 1991b.

48. Maguen, 1992, p. 53.

49. The Nation, *The Advocate*, July 23, 1996.

50. "Unsportsmanlike conduct," *The Advocate*, (1996, July 23).

51. G. Unks, "Thinking about the gay teen." In G. Unks, Ed., *The gay teen.* (New York: Routledge, 1995).

52. T. Shepard, "A letter to Aunt Shelley and Uncle Don." In B.L. Singer, Ed., *Growing up gay/growing up lesbian.* (New York: The New Press, 1994), p. 222.

53. Reed, 1993.

54. K.M. Harbeck, *Coming out of the classroom closet: Gay and lesbian students, teachers, and curricula.* (Binghamton, NY: Harrington Park Press, 1992).

T. Phariss, *A bibliography: Gay and lesbian issues in education.* (Lakewood, CO: The Teachers Group of Colorado, 1992).

M. Schoenhals, *Lesbian and gay affirmative education initiatives in seven selected U.S. cities and counties.* (Philadelphia, PA: Philadelphia Lesbian and Gay Task Force, 1992).

55. Telljohann and Price, 1993.

56. J. Gallagher, "Battle of the books," *The Advocate*, (1992, December 29), p. 68.

57. J. Green, "Out and organized," *The New York Times*, (1993, June 13), Sec. 9, p. 7.

58. Green, 1993, p. 9-7.

59. H. Lenskyj, "Beyond plumbing and prevention: Feminist approaches to sex education," *Gender and Education*, (Volume 2, 1990).

60. P. Szirom, *Teaching gender? Sex education and sexual stereotypes.* (Sydney, AU: Allen & Unwin, 1988).

61. Brimner, 1995, p. 93.

62. Woog, 1995, p. 41.

63. W. Gardner and J. Herman, "Adolescents' AIDS risk taking: A rational choice perspective." In W. Gardner, S.G. Millstein, and B.L. Wilcox, Eds., *Adolescents in the AIDS epidemic: New directions in child development.* Monograph No. 50. (San Francisco, CA: Jossey-Bass, 1990), p. 29.

64. P. Aggleton, H. Homans, and I. Warwick, "Health education, sexuality and AIDS." In S. Walker and L. Walker, Eds., *Politics and the process of schooling.* (Milton Keynes, UK: Open University Press, 1989).

65. C.F. Turner, H.G. Miller, and L.E. Moses, *AIDS: Sexual behavior and intravenous drug use.* (Washington, DC: National Academy Press, 1989), p. 373.

66. B. Wilcox, "Federal policy and adolescent AIDS." In W. Gardner, S.G. Millstein, and B.L. Wilcox, Eds., *Adolescents in the AIDS epidemic: New directions in child development.* Monograph No. 50. (San Francisco, CA: Jossey-Bass, 1990).

67. Macan Ghaill, 1991, p. 295.

68. D. Mechanic, "Adolescent health and illness behavior: Review of the literature and a new hypothesis for the study of stress," *Journal of Human Stress*, (Volume 9, 1983).

69. R.C. Savin-Williams and R.E. Lenhart, "AIDS prevention among gay and lesbian youth: Psychosocial stress and health care intervention guidelines." In D.G. Ostrow, Ed., *Behavioral aspects of AIDS*. (New York: Plenum Medical Book Co., 1990).

70. Merki and Merki, 1993.

71. McDermitt, 1993.

72. A. Heron, Ed., *One teenager in ten*. (Boston, MA: Alyson, 1983), p. 147.

73. D.A. Anderson, "Lesbian and gay adolescents: Social and developmental considerations." In G. Unks, Ed., *The gay teen*. (New York: Routledge, 1995), p. 21.

74. Telljohann and Price, 1993, p. 49.

75. K. Snow, "Rebels with a cause," *The Advocate*, (1997, January 21).

76. S. Parsavand, "Discussion groups ease acceptance for gay high schoolers," *Schenectady Gazette*, (1993, December 5), p. A-11.

77. Governor's Commission on Gay and Lesbian Youth, *Making schools safe for gay and lesbian youth: Breaking the silence in schools and families*. (1993), p. 8.

78. J. Barrett, "School's out," *The Advocate*, (1997, September 16).

79. Bass and Kaufman, 1996, p. 45.

80. "Agenda," *The Advocate*, (1997, April 15).

81. Governor's Commission on Gay and Lesbian Youth, 1993, p. 8.

82. F. Kuhr, "Gay, lesbian youth and their allies stage second annual Youth Pride march May 18," Portland, ME. *Bay Windows*, (1996, May 23).

83. Chandler, 1995, pp. 321-322.

84. Ibid., p. 321.

85. Telljohann and Price, 1993, p. 49.

86. Chandler, 1995, p. 341.

87. *Hazelwood School District vs. Kuhlmeier*, 1988.

88. "Writing rights," *The Advocate*, (1996, December 10).

89. C. Jensen and Project Consored, *Censored: The news that didn't make the news and why*. (New York: Seven Stories, 1996).

90. S. Daggett, "Controversial issues possible in student press," *Communication: Journalism Education Today*, (Volume 17, Number 2, 1983, Winter), p. 8.

91. Due, 1995, p. 12.

92. Kissen, 1991, p. 12.

93. Telljohann and Price, 1993.

94. J. Barrett, "School's out," *The Advocate,* (1997, September 16), p. 40.

95. Chandler, 1995, p. 269.

96. Brimner, 1995, p. 85.

Chapter 6

1. Cited in R. Coles, *Erik Erikson: The growth of his work*. (Boston: Little, Brown, 1987), p. 120.

2. R. Bidwell, "The gay and lesbian teen: A case of denied adolescence," *Journal of Pediatric Health Care*, (Volume 2, No. 1, 1988).

A.L. Reynolds and M.J. Koski, "Lesbian, gay, and bisexual teens and the school counselor." In G. Unks, Ed., *The gay teen.* (New York: Routledge, 1995).

3. G.J. Remafedi, "Homosexual youth: A challenge to contemporary society," *Journal of the American Medical Association*, (Volume 258, 1987c).

4. L. Due, *Joining the tribe.* (New York: Anchor Books, 1995), p. 119.

5. D.S. Sanders, "A psychotherapeutic approach to homosexual men." In J. Marmor, Ed., *Homosexual behavior: A modern reappraisal.* (New York: Basic Books, 1980).

6. S.K. Telljohann and J.H. Price, "A qualitative examination of adolescent homosexuals' life experiences: Ramifications for secondary school personnel," *Journal of Homosexuality*, (Volume 26, 1993).

7. N. Adair and C. Adair, *Word is out.* (Adair Films, 1978).

8. K.P. Monteiro and V. Fuqua, "African-American gay youth: One form of manhood." In G. Unks, Ed., *The gay teen.* (New York: Routledge, 1995).

H.A. Ploski and J. Williams, *The Afro-American*, Fourth edition. (New York: Wiley & Sons, 1983).

9. E.S. Hetrick and A.D. Martin, "Developmental issues and their resolution for gay and lesbian adolescents," *Journal of Homosexuality*, (Volume 14, 1987), p. 40.

10. G. Herdt, "Introduction: Gay and lesbian youth, emergent identities and cultural scenes at home and abroad." In G. Herdt, Ed., *Gay and lesbian youth.* (Binghamton, NY: Harrington Park Press, 1989).

11. A.T. Cook, *Who is killing whom?* (Washington, DC: Parents, Families, and Friends of Lesbians and Gays, 1991).

HHS Report, 1989.

12. A.P. Bell and M.S. Weinberg, *Homosexualities: A study of diversity among men and women.* (New York: Simon & Shuster, 1978).

P. Gibson, "Report of the Secretary's Task Force on Youth Suicide." In M. Feinleib, Ed., *Prevention and intervention in youth suicide.* (Washington, DC: U.S. Department of Health and Human Services, Public Health Services; Alcohol, Drug Abuse & Mental Health Administration, 1989).

G.J. Remafedi, "Adolescent homosexuality: Psychosocial and medical implications," *Pediatrics*, (Volume 79, 1987a).

S.G. Schneider, N.L. Farberow, and G.N. Kruks, "Suicidal behavior in adolescent and young adult gay men," *Suicide and Life-Threatening Behavior*, (Volume 19, 1989).

L. Trenchard and H. Warren, *Something to tell you.* (London: Gay Teenagers' Project, 1984).

13. Remafedi, 1987a.

M.J. Rotheram-Borus, M. Rosario, and C. Koopman, "Minority youths at high risk: Gay males and runaways." In M.E. Colten and S. Gore, Eds., *Adolescent stress: Causes and consequences.* (New York: Aldine, 1991).

14. T. Osborn, "The fountain of youth," *The Advocate*, (1994, November 29).

15. Trenchard and Warren, 1984.

16. A.K. Malyon, "The homosexual adolescent: Development issues and social bias," *Child Welfare*, (Volume 60, 1981), p. 328.

17. R.R. Troiden, "Homosexual identity formation," *Journal of Adolescent Health Care*, (Volume 9, 1988).

18. A. Heron, Ed., *One teenager in ten.* (Boston, MA: Alyson, 1983), p. 96.

19. K. Chandler, *Passages of pride: Gay and lesbian youth come of age.* (New York: Times Books, 1995), p. 20.

20. Ibid., p. 29.

21. J.A. Lee, "Going public: A study of the sociology of homosexual liberation," *Journal of Homosexuality*, (Volume 3, 1977).

A.D. Martin, "Leading to hide: The socialization of the gay adolescent," *Adolescent Psychiatry*, (Volume 10, 1982).

22. K. Jennings, "American dreams." In B.L. Singer, Ed., *Growing up gay/growing up lesbian.* (New York: The New Press, 1994), p. 4.

23. L.D. Brimner, *Being different: Lambda youth speak out.* (New York: Franklin Watts, 1995).

24. J.T. Sears, *Growing up gay in the South: Race, gender, and journeys of the spirit.* (Binghamton, NY: Harrington Park Press, 1991a), p. 359.

25. Due, 1995, p. 132.

26. E. Bass and K. Kaufman, *Free your mind: The book for gay, lesbian, and bisexual youth—and their allies.* (New York: Harper Perennial, 1996), p. 18.

27. Ibid., p. 68.

28. D.E. Mitchell and W.G. Spady, "Authority, power, and the legitimation of social control," *Educational Administration Quarterly*, (Volume 19, Number 1, 1983).

29. Governor's Commission on Gay and Lesbian Youth, *Making schools safe for gay and lesbian youth: Breaking the silence in schools and families.* (1993), p. 20.

30. G.P. Mallon, "Gay and no place to go: Assessing the needs of gay and lesbian adolescents in out-of-home settings," *Child Welfare*, (Volume 71, 1992a).

31. Troiden, 1988.

32. Sears, 1991a, p. 362.

33. Remafedi, 1990.

34. Sears, 1991a, p. 127.

35. Ibid., p. 330.

36. P.A. Paroski, "Health care delivery and the concerns of gay and lesbian adolescents," *Journal of Adolescent Health Care*, (Volume 8, 1987).

37. R.C. Savin-Williams, *Gay and lesbian youth: Expressions of identity.* (Washington, DC: Hemisphere, 1990).

38. V. Uribe, "Project 10: A school-based outreach to gay and lesbian youth." In G. Unks, Ed., *The gay teen.* (New York: Routledge, 1995).

39. M. Schneider, "Sappho was a right-on adolescent: Growing up lesbian," *Journal of Homosexuality*, (Volume 17, 1989), p. 123.

40. Due, 1995, p. 55.

41. Brimner, 1995.

42. Heron, 1983, p. 116.

43. S. Maguen, "Teen suicide: The government's cover-up and America's lost children," *The Advocate*, (1991, September 24), p. 44.

44. Governor's Commission on Gay and Lesbian Youth, 1993, p. 8.

45. A. Heron, Ed., *Two teenagers in twenty.* (Boston, MA: Alyson, 1994), p. 146.

46. Mercier and Berger, 1989.

47. N. Youngstrom, "Minority youth who are gay: A tough road, but there's hope," *APA Monitor*, (1992).

48. C.A. Rigg, "Homosexuality and adolescence," *Pediatric Annual*, (Volume 11, 1982).

49. Due, 1995, p. 187.

50. J. Gover, "Gay youth in the family," *Journal of Emotional and Behavioral Problems*, (Volume 2, Number 4, 1993).

51. G.J. Remafedi, "Male homosexuality: The adolescent's perspective," *Pediatrics*, (Volume 79, 1987b).

52. Sears, 1991a, p. 111.

53. Gover, 1993, p. 35.

54. D. Miranda, "School days," *The Advocate*, (1993, September 7), p. 5.

55. Gover, 1993, p. 35.

56. E. Coleman, "Developmental stages of the coming out process," *Journal of Homosexuality*, (Volume 7, 1982b).

57. Chandler, 1995, p. 17.

58. Ross-Reynolds, 1988, p. 219-220.

59. Governor's Commission on Gay and Lesbian Youth, 1993, p. 14.

60. Martin, 1982.

61. Youngstrom, 1992.

62. A. O'Conor, "Who gets called queer in school? Lesbian, gay, and bisexual teenagers, homophobia, and high school." In G. Unks, Ed., *The gay teen.* (New York: Routledge, 1995), p. 98.

63. L. Galst, "Kids in GLASS houses," *Out*, (1993, December/January).

64. J. Hunter and R. Schaecher, "Lesbian and gay youth." In M.J. Rotheram-Borus, J. Bradley, and N. Obolensky, Eds., *Planning to live: Evaluating and treating suicidal teens in community settings.* (Tulsa: University of Oklahoma Press, 1990). Remafedi, 1987a, 1987b; Rotheram-Borus, Rosario, and Koopman, 1991.

65. K. Jay and A. Young, *The gay report: Lesbians and gay men speak out about sexual experiences and lifestyles.* (New York: Simon & Schuster, 1979), p. 701.

66. Governor's Commission on Gay and Lesbian Youth, 1993, p. 19.

67. Remafedi, 1987a.

68. Due, 1995, p. 222.

69. Ibid.

70. P. Nardi, "Alcoholism and homosexuality: A theoretical perspective," *Journal of Homosexuality*, (Volume 4, 1982).

71. Israelstrom and Lambert, 1989.

R.P. Cabaj, "AIDS and chemical dependency: Special issues and treatment barriers for gay and bisexual men," *Journal of Psychoactive Drugs*, (Volume 21, 1989).

R.E. Hellman, M. Stanton, J. Lee, A. Tytun, and R. Vachon, "Treatment of homosexual alcoholics in government-funded agencies: Provider training and attitudes," *Hospital and Community Psychiatry*, (Volume 40, 1989).

Remafedi, 1987b.

72. F. Shifrin and M. Solis, "Chemical dependency in gay and lesbian youth," *Journal of Chemical Dependency Treatment*, (Volume 5, 1992).

73. Schneider, 1989, p. 122.

74. Brimner, 1995, p. 31.

75. Shifrin and Solis, 1992.

76. G.L. Yates, M.D. Mackenzie, J. Pennbridge, and A. Swofford, "A risk profile comparison of homeless youth involved in prostitution and homeless youth not involved," *Journal of Adolescent Health*, (Volume 12, 1991).

77. "HMI launches foster care and youth services training project," *HMI Report Card*, (1995, Winter).

78. Due, 1995.

79. Wellisch, DeAngelis, and Bond, 179.

80. G.P. Mallon, "Serving the needs of gay and lesbian youth in residential treatment centers," *Residential Treatment for Children and Youth*, (Volume 10, Number 2, 1992b).

81. C. McMillen, "Sexual identity issues related to homosexuality in the residential treatment of adolescents," *Residential Treatment for Children and Youth*, (Volume 9, Number 2, 1992).

82. T.A. DeCrescenzo, "Homophobia: A study of the attitudes of mental health professionals toward homosexuality," *Journal of Social Work and Human Sexuality*, (Volume 2, Number 2/3, 1983/1984).

D.L. Graham, E.I. Rawlings, H.S. Halpern, and J. Hermes, "Therapists' needs for training in counseling lesbians and gay men," *Professional Psychology: Research and Practice*, (Volume 15, 1984).

J. Rudolph, "Counselors attitudes toward homosexuality: A selective review of the literature," *Journal of Counseling and Development*, (Number 676, 1988).

J.J. Wisniewski and B.G. Toomey, "Are social workers homophobic?" *Social Work*, (Volume 32, 1987).

83. Sears, 1991a.

84. National Network of Runaway and Youth Services, *To whom do they belong? Runaway, homeless, and other youth in high-risk situations in the 1990s.* (Washington, DC: National Network of Runaway and Youth Services, 1991).

M.J. Rotheram-Borus, H.F. Meyer-Bahlburg, M. Rosario, C. Koopman, C.S. Haignere, T.M. Exner, M. Matthieu, R. Henderson, and R.S. Gruen, "Lifetime sexual behaviors among predominantly minority male runaways and gay/bisexual adolescents in New York City," *AIDS Education and Prevention*, (Supplement, 1992).

85. M.D. Kipke, S. O'Connor, R. Palmer, and R.G. MacKenzie, "Street youth in Los Angeles," *Archives of Pediatric Adolescent Medicine*, (Volume 149, 1995).

86. L. Galst, "Throwaway kids," *The Advocate*, (1992, December 29), p. 55.

87. C. Bull, "Safety net," *The Advocate*, (1993, September 7).

88. Galst, 1992, p. 55.

89. Galst, 1993, p. 55.

90. Galst, 1992, p. 57.

91. Ibid.

92. Schaffer and DeBlaissie, 1984.

93. D.M. Allen, "Young male prostitutes: A psychological study," *Archives of Sexual Behavior*, (Volume 9, 1980).

B. Fisher, D.K. Weisberg, and T. Marotta, *Report on adolescent prostitution*. (San Francisco, CA: Urban and Rural Systems Associates, 1982).

94. Chandler, 1995, p. 229.

95. "Hollywood glamour eludes runaway," Rochester, NY, *Democrat and Chronicle*, (1992, March 29), p. 20-A.

96. Allen, 1980.

D. Boyer, "Male prostitution and homosexual identity." In G. Herdt, Ed., *Gay and lesbian youth*. (Binghamton, NY: Harrington Park Press, 1989).

E. Coleman, "Changing approaches to the treatment of homosexuality," *Journal of American Behavioral Sciences*, (Volume 25, 1982a).

Fisher, Weisberg, and Marotta, 1982.

R. Furnald, "Male juvenile prostitution." Unpublished master's thesis, (University of Southern California, Los Angeles, CA, 1978).

97. Fisher, Weisberg, and Marotta, 1982; Yates, Mackenzie et al., 1991.

98. Yates, Mackenzie, Pennbridge, and Swofford, 1991.

99. Fisher, Weisberg, and Marotta, 1982.

100. P. Freiberg, "Minneapolis: Help for hustlers," *The Advocate*, (1985, November 12).

101. Boyer, 1989, p. 169.

102. Ibid.

103. Bass and Kaufman, 1996, p. 46.

104. Boyer, 1989, p. 172.

105. A.N. Groth and J.H. Birnbaum, *Men who rape: The psychology of the offender*. (New York: Plenum, 1979).

106. C. Bagley, "Child abuse and juvenile prostitution: A commentary on the Bagley report on sexual offenses against children and youth in Canada," *Journal of Public Health*, (Volume 76, 1985).

Furnald, 1978.

M.D. Janus, B. Scanlon, and V. Prince, "Youth prostitution." In A.W. Burgess, Ed., *Sex rings and child pornography*. (Lexington, MA: M.C. Heath, 1984).

107. Boyer, 1989, p. 173.

108. Galst, 1992, p. 56.

109. D. Boyer and J. James, "Prostitutes as victims: Sex and the social order." In D.E. MacNamara and A. Karman, Eds., *Deviants: Victims or victimizers.* (Beverly Hills, CA: Sage Publications, 1983).

110. Fisher, Weisberg, and Marotta, 1982.

111. Ibid.

112. Chandler, 1995, p. 230.

113. Boyer, 1989, p. 177.

114. P. Maloney, "Street hustling: Growing up gay." Unpublished manuscript, (1980).

115. Boyer, 1989, p. 177.

116. Fisher, Weisberg, and Marotta, 1982.

117. E. Coleman, "The development of male prostitution activity among gay and bisexual adolescents." In G. Herdt, Ed., *Gay and lesbian youth.* (Binghamton, NY: Harrington Park Press, 1989).

118. Boyer, 1989, p. 178.

119. Due, 1995, p. 42.

120. D.A. Feldman, "Gay youth and AIDS." In G. Herdt, Ed., *Gay and lesbian youth.* (Binghamton, NY: Harrington Park Press, 1989).

121. R. DiClemente, *Adolescents' avoidance of AIDS information: Counterproductive behavior in the face of a perceived health threat.* Paper presented at the meeting of the American Public Health Association, Las Vegas, NV, (1986, October).

122. J. Green, "Out and organized," *The New York Times*, (1993, June 13), p. 9-7.

123. G.J. Remafedi, "Predictors of unprotected intercourse among gay and bisexual youth: Knowledge, belief, and behavior," (1994).

124. Fisher, Weisberg, and Marotta, 1982.

125. Coleman, 1989.

126. Martin, 1982.

127. Paroski, 1987.

128. M.J. Rotheram-Borus, M. Rosario, H.F. Meyer-Bahlburg, C. Koopman, S. Dopkins, and M. Davies, "Sexual and substance use acts of gay and bisexual male adolescents in New York City," *The Journal of Sex Research*, (Volume 31, 1994).

129. Feldman, 1989.

130. Due, 1995, p. 193.

131. Remafedi, 1987a.

132. H. Amaro, "AIDS/HIV among Hispanics in the Northeast and Puerto Rico," *Migration World*, (Volume 19, No. 4, 1991).

133. Ibid.

134. M.J. Rotheram-Borus, C. Selfridge, S. Koopman, S. Dopkins, and M. Davies, *The relationship of knowledge and attitudes towards AIDS to safe sex among runaway and gay adolescents.* Paper presented at the International Conference on AIDS, Montreal, Canada, (1989).

135. S.G. Millstein, "Risk factors for AIDS among adolescents." In W. Gardner, S.G. Millstein, and B.L. Wilcox, Eds., *Adolescents in the AIDS epidemic: New directions in child development.* Monograph No. 50. (San Francisco, CA: Jossey-Bass, 1990).

136. Bell and Weinberg, 1978; Gibson, 1989; Remafedi, 1987a.

G.J. Remafedi, J. Farrow, and R. Deisher, "Risk factors for attempted suicide in gay and bisexual youth," *Pediatrics*, (Volume 87, 1991).

Rotheram-Borus, Hunter, and Rosario, 1989; Schneider, Farberow, and Kruks, 1989.

137. Bell and Weinberg, 1978.

E. Coleman and G. Remafedi, "Gay, lesbian, and bisexual adolescents: A critical challenge to counselors," *Journal of Counseling and Development*, (Volume 68, 1989).

138. Maguen, 1991, p. 46.

139. Garfinkel, Froese, and Hood, 1982.

A.H. Green, "Self-destructive behavior in battered childred," *American Journal of Psychiatry*, (Volume 135, 1978).

Schneider, Farberow, and Kruks, 1989.

140. Maguen, 1991, 44.

141. M. Brownley, *Gay Youth*, (Minneapolis, MN: Community Intervention, 1988).

J. Hunter and R. Schaecher, R. "Stresses on lesbian and gay adolescents in schools," *Social Work in Education*, (Volume 9, 1987).

142. Brian, "It was a Saturday afternoon," *ELIGHT Email,* (1996, 1997). Writings collection 2.

143. Governor's Commission on Gay and Lesbian Youth, 1993, p. 27.

144. S.L. Hershberger and A.R. D'Augelli, "The impact of victimization on the mental health and suicidality of lesbian, gay, and bisexual youths," *Developmental Psychology*, (Volume 31, 1995).

145. Remafedi, 1987a; Remafedi, Farrow, and Deisher, 1991; Schneider, Farberow, and Kruks, 1989.

146. Pollak, 1985.

147. Remafedi, 1987a.

148. Governor's Commission on Gay and Lesbian Youth, 1993, p. 8.

149. G. Kruks, "Gay and lesbian homeless/street youth: Special issues and concerns," *Journal of Adolescent Health Care*, (Volume 12, 1991).

150. J. Harry, "Parasuicide, gender and gender deviance," *Journal of Health and Social Behavior*, (Volume 24, 1983b).

J. Harry, *Adolescent suicide and sexual identity issues.* Paper presented at the Risk Factors in Adolescent Suicide Conference, National Institute of Mental Health, Washington, DC, (1986 May).

151. Schneider, Farberow, and Kruks, 1989.

152. Sears, 1991a, p. 104.

153. T. Roesler and R. Deisher, "Youthful male homosexuality," *Journal of the American Medical Association*, (Volume 219, 1972).

Schneider, Farberow, and Kruks, 1989.

154. Remafedi, Farrow, and Deisher, 1991.

155. Chandler, 1995, p. 230.

156. E.E. Rofes, *"I thought people like that killed themselves": Lesbians, gay men, and suicide.* (San Francisco, CA: Grey Fox, 1983), p. 148.

157. M. Mac an Ghaill, "Schooling, sexuality, and male power: Toward an emancipatory curriculum," *Gender and Education,* (Volume 3, 1991), p. 304.

158. Boyer, 1989, p. 179.

159. Schneider, 1989, p. 129.

160. P. Walton, "To save our children," *Bay Area Reporter,* (1992, June 25).

Chapter 7

1. S. Maguen, "Teen suicide," *The Advocate,* (1991, September 24), p. 46.

2. Ibid.

3. Taylor, 1994.

4. J. Green, "Out and organized," *The New York Times,* (1993, June 13), Sec. 9, p. 7.

5. G.M. Herek, "Beyond 'homophobia': A social psychological perspective on attitudes toward lesbians and gay men," *Journal of Homosexuality,* (Volume 10, Number 1/2, 1984).

S.F. Morin and E.M. Garfinkle, "Male homophobia," *Journal of Social Issues,* (Volume 34, 1978).

6. P. Singer, "Breaking through," Rochester, NY. *Democrat and Chronicle,* (1993, July 4), p. D-1.

7. Ibid.

8. K. Chandler, *Passages of pride: Gay and lesbian youth come of age.* (New York: Times Books, 1995), p. ix.

9. J. Gover, "Gay youth in the family," *Journal of Emotional and Behavioral Problems,* (Volume 2, Number 4, 1993).

10. E. Bass and K. Kaufman, *Free your mind: The book for gay, lesbian, and bisexual youth—and their allies.* (New York: Harper Perennial, 1996), p. 34.

11. Ibid., p. 33.

12. R. Dyer, Ed., *Gays and film,* Revised edition. (New York: New York Zoëtrope, 1984).

13. Liebertt and Sprafkin, 1988; Nielson Media Research, 1990.

14. C. Bull, "Safety net," *The Advocate,* (1993, September 7), p. 52.

15. Cook and Pawlowski, 1991.

16. *The Advocate,* November 14, 1995, p. 20.

17. Governor's Commission on Gay and Lesbian Youth, "Excerpts from public testimony," (Boston, MA, 1992).

18. W.J. Blumenfeld, Gay/straight alliances: Transforming pain to pride. In G. Unks, Ed., *The gay teen.* (New York: Routledge, 1995), p. 221.

19. "Different strokes," *The Advocate,* (1995, October 31), p. 12.

20. Kissen, 1991, p. 10

21. K. Chandler, "A reluctant hero," *The Advocate*, (1996, May 28).

22. C. Rothman, "A stand for human worth," *Los Angeles Times*, (1997, February 26), p. E-1.

23. K. Snow, "Rebels with a cause," *The Advocate*, (1997, January 21).

24. J. Barrett, "School's out," *The Advocate*, (1997, September 16).

25. LLDEF, "Student sues school for anti-gay violence/harassment," *The Empty Closet*, (1995/96, December/January), p. 5.

26. Chandler, 1996, p. 30.

27. Governor's Commission on Gay and Lesbian Youth, *Making schools safe for gay and lesbian youth: Breaking the silence in schools and families.* (1993), p. 15.

28. K. Gessen, K., "Matt Flynn, high school activist," *The Advocate*, (1993, September 7), p. 69.

29. Kissen, 1991, p. 10.

30. K.M. Harbeck, "Invisibility no more: Addressing the needs of lesbian, gay, and bisexual youth and their advocates." In G. Unks, Ed., *The gay teen.* (New York: Routledge, 1995).

31. Governor's Commission on Gay and Lesbian Youth, 1993, p. 20.

32. Bass and Kaufman, 1996, p. 193.

33. J.T. Sears, *Growing up gay in the South: Race, gender, and journeys of the spirit.* (Binghamton, NY: Harrington Park Press, 1991a), p. 397.

34. Woog, 1995, p. 30-31.

35. Ibid., p. 56.

36. Governor's Commission on Gay and Lesbian Youth, 1993, p. 20.

37. Kissen, 1991, p. 11.

38. "Reading, writing, and suing," *The Advocate*, (1996, April 16), p. 14.

39. F. Kuhr, "Gay, lesbian youth and their allies stage second annual Youth Pride march May 18," Portland, ME, *Bay Windows*, (1996, May 23).

40. Green, 1993, Sec. 9, p. 7.

41. Abinati, 1994.

42. G. Unks, "Thinking about the gay teen." In G. Unks, Ed., *The gay teen.* (New York: Routledge, 1995).

43. V.C. Cass, "Homosexual identity: A concept in need of definition," *Journal of Homosexuality*, (Volume 9, 1983/84).

E. Coleman, "Changing approaches to the treatment of homosexuality," *Journal of American Behavioral Sciences*, (Volume 25, 1982a).

G. Herdt, "Introduction: Gay and lesbian youth, emergent identities and cultural scenes at home and abroad." In G. Herdt, Ed., *Gay and lesbian youth.* (Binghamton, NY: Harrington Park Press, 1989).

R.R. Troiden, "Homosexual identity formation," *Journal of Adolescent Health Care*, (Volume 9, 1988).

44. A. Lipkin, "The case for a gay and lesbian curriculum." In G. Unks, Ed., *The gay teen.* (New York: Routledge, 1995).

45. V. Uribe, "Project 10: A school-based outreach to gay and lesbian youth." In G. Unks, Ed., *The gay teen.* (New York: Routledge, 1995).

46. "Elizabethtown, PA," Associated Press, (1996, October 8), p. 1.

47. D. A. Feldman, "Gay youth and AIDS." In G. Herdt, Ed., *Gay and lesbian youth.* (Binghamton, NY: Harrington Park Press, 1989), p. 191.

48. J. Barrett, "School's out," *The Advocate,* (1997, September 16).

49. G.J. Remafedi, "Preventing the sexual transmission of AIDS during adolescence," *Journal of Adolescent Health Care,* (Volume 9, 1988).

50. M.J. Rotheram-Borus and C. Koopman, "Sexual risk behavior, AIDS knowledge, and beliefs about AIDS among predominantly minority gay and bisexual male adolescents," *AIDS Education and Prevention,* (Volume 3, 1991).

51. A.M. Boxer, J.A. Cook, and G. Herdt, "Double jeopardy: Identity transitions and parent-child relations among gay and lesbian youth." In K. Pillemer and K. McCortney, Eds., *Parent child relations through life.* (Hillsdale, NJ: Erlbaum Associates, 1991).

52. M. Schneider, "Sappho was a right-on adolescent: Growing up lesbian," *Journal of Homosexuality,* (Volume 17, 1989), p. 125.

53. M. Schneider, "Developing services for lesbian and gay adolescents," *Canadian Journal of Community Mental Health,* (Volume 10, 1991).

54. Schneider, 1989, p. 123.

55. Green, 1993, Sec. 9, p. 7.

56. Snow, 1997.

57. Ibid.

58. Maguen, 1991, p. 43.

59. Ibid.

60. K. Jennings, "American dreams." In B.L. Singer, Ed., *Growing up gay/growing up lesbian.* (New York: The New Press, 1994).

61. E.E. Rofes, "Making our schools safe for sissies." In G. Unks, Ed., *The gay teen.* (New York: Routledge, 1995).

62. Singer, 1993, p. D1.

63. Woog, 1995, p. 49.

64. "Hell's Bells," *The Advocate,* (1996, April 2).

65. Chandler, 1996, p. 29.

66. Ibid., p. 31.

67. Abinati, 1994.

68. Uribe, 1995.

69. Z. Gershick, "Virginia is for students," *The Advocate,* (1993, September 7), p. 56.

70. Gershick, 1993, p. 57.

71. J. Green, "This school is out," *The New York Times Magazine,* (1991, October 13), p. 34.

72. D. Miranda, "School days," *The Advocate,* (1993, September 7), p. 5.

73. "High school for gay teens in the works," Austin, TX, *American-Statesman,* (July 16, 1997).

74. L. Due, *Joining the tribe.* (New York: Anchor Books, 1995), p. 196.

75. "Scout's dishonor," 1995, p. 11.

76. "Scout's honor," *The Advocate,* (1997, February 4).

77. J.E. Hardy, "Behind the mask," *The Advocate*, (1994, November 15), p. 6.

78. A. Heron, Ed., *One teenager in ten*. (Boston, MA: Alyson, 1983), p. 175.

79. *Growing up, moving on*, New York: Hetrick-Martin Institute.

80. P. Cicchino, "Legal clinic at HMI," *HMI Report Card*, (1995, Winter).

81. "Project First Step Reaches Out," *HMI Report Card*, (1993, Spring), p. 1.

82. C. Claar, "Put queer youth in their place—United with all gays and lesbians," *The Advocate*, (1992, October 20), p. 96.

83. A.D. Martin, "Learning to hide: The socialization of the gay adolescent," *Adolescent Psychiatry*, (Volume 10, 1982).

M. Hippler, "The problems and promise of gay youth," *The Advocate*, (1986, September 16).

E.S. Hetrick and A.D. Martin, "Developmental issues and their resolution for gay and lesbian adolescents," *Journal of Homosexuality*, (Volume 14, 1987).

84. Claar, 1992, October 20, p. 96.

85. Maguen, 1992, p. 54.

86. M. Rivera-Ortiz, "Young and gay in black and white," Rochester, NY. *Democrat and Chronicle*. (1996, July 29), p. 6C.

87. Maguen, 1992, p. 53.

88. Mercier and Berger, 1989.

89. T. Gabriel, "Some on-line discoveries give gay youths a path to themselves, *The New York Times*, (1995), p. 1.

90. Chandler, 1995, p. 282.

91. Gabriel, 1995, p. 1.

92. "One step closer," *The Advocate*, (1991, September 24), p. 10.

93. D.A. Anderson, "Family and peer relations of gay adolescents." In S.C. Geinstein, Ed., *Adolescent psychiatry: Developmental and clinical studies*, Volume 14. (Chicago: The University of Chicago Press, 1987), p. 172.

94. N. Youngstrom, "Minority youth who are gay: A tough road, but there's hope," *APA Monitor*, (1992), p. 5.

95. Due, 1995, p. 245.

96. Ibid., p. 84.

97. Bass and Kaufman, 1996, p. 30.

98. Anderson, 1987, p. 177.

99. Mercier and Berger, 1989.

100. Due, 1995, p. xxxiv.

101. Mercier and Berger, 1989.

102. L. Galst, "Kids in GLASS houses," *Out*, (1993, December/January), p. 54.

103. Ibid., p. 55.

104. Ibid., p. 57.

105. Ibid., p. 56.

106. L. Galst, "Throwaway kids," *The Advocate*, (1992, December 29).

107. Wellisch, DeAngelis, and Bond, 1979.

108. C. McMillen, "Sexual identity issues related to homosexuality in the residential treatment of adolescents," *Residential Treatment for Children and Youth*, (Volume 9, Number 3, 1992).

109. R.G. Forrester and J. Huggins, "Homosexuality and homosexual behavior," In D.A. Shore and H.L. Gochros, Eds., *Sexual problems of adolescents in institutions*. (Springfield, IL: Thomas, 1981).

110. Galst, 1992, p. 57.

111. Abinati, 1994.

112. Ibid.

113. Ibid.

114. Chandler, 1995.

115. L.D. Brimner, *Being different: Lambda youth speak out*. (New York: Franklin Watts, 1995), p. 120.

116. P.A. Paroski, "Health care delivery and the concerns of gay and lesbian adolescents," *Journal of Adolescent Health Care*, (Volume 8, 1987).

117. W. Dale and D. Soler, "Class acts," *The Advocate*, (1993, September 7).

118. Ibid.

119. M.C. Cage, "Openly gay students face harassment and physical assaults on some campuses," *The Chronicle of Higher Education*, (1993, March 10).

120. J. Rabin, K. Keefe, and M. Burton, "Enhancing services for sexual minority clients: A community mental health approach," *Social Work*, (Volume 31, 1986).

121. M.B. McKee, S.F. Hayes, and I.R. Axiotis, "Challenging heterosexism in college health service delivery," *Journal of American College Health*, (Volume 42, 1994).

122. Chandler, 1995, p. 330.

123. A. Heron, Ed., *Two teenagers in twenty*. (Boston, MA: Alyson, 1994), p. 100.

124. Sears, 1991a, p. 248.

125. R.C. Savin-Williams and R.E. Lenhart, "AIDS prevention among gay and lesbian youth: Psychosocial stress and health care intervention guidelines." In D.G. Ostrow, Ed., *Behavioral aspects of AIDS*. (New York: Plenum Medical Book Co., 1990).

126. Due, 1995, p. 181.

Chapter 8

1. W. Ricketts, "Homosexuality in adolescence: The reification of sexual personalities," *Journal of Social Work and Human Sexuality*, (Volume 5, 1986).

2. G. Robinson, "Few solutions for a young dilemma," *The Advocate*, (1984).

3. Karii, "HMI youth: 'We can be who we are'," *HMI Report Card*, (1995, Winter), p. 6.

4. Hardy, 1990, p. 6.

5. L. Due, *Joining the tribe*. (New York: Anchor Books, 1995), p. 84.

6. A.M. Boxer, J.A. Cook, and G. Herdt, "Double jeopardy: Identity transitions and parent-child relations among gay and lesbian youth." In K. Pillemer and K. McCortney, Eds., *Parent-child relations through life*. (Hillsdale, NJ: Erlbaum Associates, 1991), p. 61.

7. J. Gover, "Gay youth in the family," *Journal of Emotional and Behavioral Problems*, (Volume 2, Number 4, 1993), p. 35.

8. A. Heron, Ed., *One teenager in ten*. (Boston, MA: Alyson, 1983), p. 16.

9. J.T. Sears, *Growing up gay in the South: Race, gender, and journeys of the spirit*. (Binghamton, NY: Harrington Park Press, 1991a), p. 246.

10. L.D. Brimner, *Being different: Lambda youth speak out*. (New York: Franklin Watts, 1995), p. 62.

11. P. Singer, "Breaking through," Rochester, NY. *Democrat and Chronicle*. (1993, July 4), p. D-1.

12. F. Bruni, "A prom night of their own to dance, laugh, reminisce," *Detroit Free Press*, (1992, May 22), p. 10-A.

13. D.A. Anderson, "Family and peer relations of say adolescents." In S.C. Geinstein, Ed., *Adolescent psychiatry: Developmental and clinical studies*, Volume 14. (Chicago: The University of Chicago Press, 1987).

14. E.S. Hetrick and A.D. Martin, "Developmental issues and their resolution for gay and lesbian adolescents," *Journal of Homosexuality*, (Volume 14, 1987).

15. Savin-Williams, 1996a.

16. A. O'Conor, "Who gets called queer in school? Lesbian, gay, and bisexual teenagers, homophobia, and high school." In G. Unks, Ed., *The gay teen*. (New York: Routledge, 1995), p. 97.

17. N.J. Woodman and H.R. Lenna, *Counseling with gay men and women*. (San Francisco, CA: Jossey-Bass, 1980), p. 87.

18. Hardy, 1990, p. 6.

19. M. Sluchan, "Whose world is it anyway?" *The Weekly Pennsylvanian*, (1993, March 30), p. 4.

20. Sears, 1991a, p. 188.

21. O.M. Espin, "Issues of identity in the psychology of Latina lesbians." In Boston Lesbian Psychologies Collective, Eds., *Lesbian psychologies: Explorations and challenges*. (Urbana, IL: University of Illinois Press, 1987).

22. E. Bass and K. Kaufman, *Free your mind: The book for gay, lesbian, and bisexual youth—and their allies*. (New York: Harper Perennial, 1996), p. 111.

23. J. Beam, *In the life*. (Boston: Alyson, 1986), p. 17.

24. J.M. Johnson, "Influences of assimilation on the psychosocial adjustment of Black homosexual men." Unpublished doctoral dissertation, California School of Professional Psychology, Berkeley, *Dissertation Abstracts International*, (Volume 42, 1981).

25. V.M. Mays, S.D. Cochran, and S. Rhue, "The impact of perceived discrimination on the intimate relationships of Black lesbians," *Journal of Homosexuality*, (Volume 25, 1993), p. 9.

26. E.E. Rofes, "Living as all of who I am: Being Jewish in the lesbian/gay community." In C. Balka and A. Rose, Eds., *Twice blessed: Being lesbian, gay, and Jewish.* (Boston: Beacon Press, 1989).

W.S. Wooden, H. Kawasaki, and R. Mayeda, "Lifestyles and identity maintenance among gay Japanese-American males," *Alternative Lifestyles*, (Volume 5, 1983).

27. B. Tremble, M. Schneider, and C. Appathurai, "Growing up gay or lesbian in a multicultural context," *Journal of Homosexuality*, (Volume 17, 1989), p. 263.

28. E. Coleman, "Changing approaches to the treatment of homosexuality," *Journal of American Behavioral Sciences*, (Volume 25, 1982a).

29. R.E. Powell, "Homosexual behavior and the school counselor," *School Counselor*, (Volume 34, 1987).

30. R.M. Berger, "Gaymen." In H.L. Gochros, J.S. Gochros, and J. Fisher, Eds., *Helping the sexually oppressed.* (Englewood Cliffs, NJ: Prentice Hall, 1986).

31. E.E. Levitt and A.D. Klasser, "Public attitudes toward homosexuality," *Journal of Homosexuality*, (Volume 1, 1981).

32. G.J. Krysiak, "A very silent and gay minority," *School Counselor*, (Volume 34, 1987).

Powell, 1987.

R.C. Savin-Williams and R.E. Lenhart, "AIDS prevention among gay and lesbian youth: Psychosocial stress and health care intervention guidelines." In D.G. Ostrow, Ed., *Behavioral aspects of AIDS.* (New York: Plenum Medical Book Co., 1990).

33. Powell, 1987.

34. Ross-Reynolds, 1988.

35. D.L. Graham, E.I. Rawlings, H.S. Halpern, and J. Hermes, "Therapists' needs for training in counseling lesbians and gay men," *Professional Psychology: Research and Practice*, (Volume 15, 1984).

36. J. Hunter and R. Schaecher, R., "Stresses on lesbian and gay adolescents in schools," *Social Work in Education*, (Volume 9, 1987).

A.K. Malyon, "The homosexual adolescent: Developing issues and social bias," *Child Welfare*, (Volume 60, 1981).

G. Robinson, "Few solutions for a young dilemma," *The Advocate*, (1984).

Ross-Reynolds, 1988.

T.G. Russell, "AIDS education, homosexuality, and the counselor's role," *The School Counselor*, (Volume 36, 1989).

J. Wakelee-Lynch, "Gay and lesbian youths face danger and isolation," *AACD Guidepost*, (1989, October 5),

37. M. Marco, "Covering gay youth: From invisibility to trendiness to respect," *Extra*, (1994, March/April), p. 15.

38. J.T. Sears, "Educators, homosexuality, and homosexual students: Are personal feelings related to professional beliefs," *Journal of Homosexuality*, (Volume 22, 1991b).

39. Powell, 1987.

40. S. Christensen and L.M. Sorensen, "Effects of a multi-factor education program on the attitude of child and youth worker students towards gays and lesbians," *Child and Youth Care Forum*, (Volume 23, Number 2, 1994).

41. R. Goldberg, "Attitude change among college students towards homosexuality," *Journal of American College Health*, (Volume 30, 1982).

L.M. Lance, "The effects of interaction with gay persons on attitudes towards homosexuality," *Human Relations*, (Volume 40, 1987).

Pagtolum-An and Clair, 1985.

W.J. Serdahely and G.J. Ziemba, "Changing homophobic attitudes through college sexuality education," *Journal of Homosexuality*, (Volume 10, 1984).

42. Christensen and Sorensen, 1994.

43. T.A. DeCrescenzo, "Homophobia: A study of the attitudes of mental health professionals toward homosexuality," *Journal of Social Work and Human Sexuality*, (Volume 2, Number 2/3, 1983/84).

44. Sears, 1991b, p. 37.

45. M. Lewis and A. Lewis, *Meeting the needs of gay, lesbian, and bisexual youth: Our hidden clients.* Paper presented at the annual convention of the American Counseling Association, Minneapolis, (1993, March).

46. Krysiak, 1987.

M. Mac an Ghaill, "Schooling, sexuality, and male power. Towards an emancipatory curriculum," *Gender and Education*, (Volume 3, 1991).

47. Sears, 1991b, p. 34.

48. S. Parsavand, "Discussion groups ease acceptance for gay high schoolers," *Schenectady Gazette*, (1993, December 5).

49. Krysiak, 1987, p. 307.

50. Malyon, 1982, p. 62.

51. J.C. Gonsiorek, "Mental health issues of gay and lesbian adolescents," *Journal of Adolescent Health Care*, (Volume 9, 1988).

52. E. Rosen and E. Weinstein, "Adolescent sexual counseling." In E. Weinstein and E. Rosen, Eds., *Sexual counseling: Issues and implications.* (Pacific Grove, CA: Brooks/Cole, 1988).

53. Ross-Reynolds, 1988, p. 220.

54. Ibid., p. 219.

55. Krysiak, 1987.

56. Mac an Ghaill, 1991, p. 305.

57. Gonsiorek, 1988.

58. M.S. Schneider and B. Tremble, "Gay or straight? Working with the confused adolescent," *Journal of Social Work & Human Sexuality*, (Volume 4, 1985).

M.S. Schneider and B. Tremble, "Training service providers to work with gay and lesbian adolescents: A workshop," *Journal of Counseling and Development*, (Volume 65, 1986).

59. Gonsiorek, 1988.

60. G.P. Mallon, "Counseling strategies with gay and lesbian youth." In T. DeCrescenzo, Ed., *Helping gay and lesbian youth: New policies, new programs, new practice.* (Binghamton, NY: Harrington Park Press, 1994).

61. Ross-Reynolds, 1988.

62. T. Sullivan and M. Schneider, "Development and identity issues in adolescent homosexuality," *Child and Adolescent Social Work*, (Volume 4, Number 1, 1987), p. 17.

63. Lewis and Lewis, 1993.

64. Sternhorn, 1979.

65. N. Youngstrom, "Minority youth who are gay: A tough road, but there's hope," *APA Monitor*, (1992).

66. G. Robinson and A.D. Martin, *Problems and issues in the delivery of services to gay and lesbian youth: A needs survey.* (New York: IPLGY, Inc., 1983).

67. Powell, 1987.

68. Mallon, 1994.

69. Hunter and Schaecher, 1987.
    J. Washington and N.J. Evans, "Becoming an ally." In N.J. Evans and V.A. Wall, Eds., *Beyond tolerance: Gays, lesbians, and bisexuals on campus.* (Alexandria, VA: American Association of Counseling and Development, 1991).

70. Savin-Williams and Lenhart, 1990.

71. R. Bidwell, "The gay and lesbian teen: A case of denied adolescence," *Journal of Pediatric Health Care*, (Volume 2, Number 1, 1988).

72. M.B. McKee, S.F. Hayes, and I.R. Axiotis, "Challenging heterosexism in college health service delivery," *Journal of American College Health*, (Volume 42, 1994).

73. Savin-Williams and Lenhart, 1990.

74. Mallon, 1994.

75. J. Marmor, "Overview: The multiple roots of homosexual behavior." In J. Marmor, Ed., *Homosexual behavior.* (New York: Basic Books, 1980a).

76. B.O. Silberman and R.O. Hawkins, "Lesbian women and gay men: Issues for counseling." In E. Weinstein and E. Rosen, Eds., *Sexual counseling: Issues and implications.* (Pacific Grove, CA: Brooks/Cole, 1988).
    Woodman and Lenna, 1980.

77. Jackson and Sullivan, 1994.

78. V.C. Cass, "Homosexual identity: A concept in need of defintiion," *Journal of Homosexuality*, (Volume 9, 1983/84).
    Lewis and Lewis, 1993.

79. Ross-Reynolds, 1988.

80. L. Chunovic, "Portrait of Letitia: Officials try to cover a student's lesbian art," *The Advocate*, (1992, June 30), p. 85.

81. Ricketts, 1986.

82. Gonsiorek, 1988.

83. K. Chandler, *Passages of pride: Gay and lesbian youth come of age.* (New York: Times Books, 1995), p. 146.

84. Schneider and Tremble, 1985/1986.

85. Mallon, 1994.

86. Krysiak, 1987.

87. Powell, 1987.

88. M.V. Borhek, "Helping gay and lesbian adolescents and their families," *Journal of Adolescent Health Care*, (Volume 9, 1988).

89. Mallon, 1994.

90. Savin-Williams and Lenhart, 1990.

91. Rosen and Weinstein, 1988.

92. R.C. Savin-Williams, *Gay and Lesbian Youth: Expressions of Identity.* (Washington, DC: Hemisphere, 1990).

93. H.M. Carlson and J. Steuer, "Age, sex-role categorization, and psychological health in American homosexual and heterosexual men and women," *Journal of Social Psychology*, (Volume 125, 1985).

A.R. D'Augelli and M.M. Hart, "Gay women, men, and families in rural settings: Toward the development of helping communities," *American Journal of Community Psychology*, (Volume 15, 1987).

J. Harry and W.B. DeVall, *The social organization of gay males.* (New York: Praeger, 1978).

M.S. Weinberg and C.J. Williams, *Male homosexuals: Their problems and adaptations.* (New York: Penguin, 1974).

94. A.P. Bell and M.S. Weinberg, *Homosexualities: A study of diversity among men and women.* (New York: Simon & Shuster, 1978).

Harry and DeVall, 1978.

D.J. McKirnan and P.L. Peterson, "Social support and coping resources," *Windy City Times*, (1987b, April 30).

T.S. Weinberg, *Gay men, gay selves: The social construction of homosexual identities.* (New York: Irvington, 1983).

Weinberg and Williams, 1974.

95. J. Harry, *Gay couples.* (New York: Praeger, 1984).

Harry and DeVall, 1978.

J.L. Wilkins, "A comparative study of male homosexual personality factors: Brier cruising encounters vs. ongoing relationships," *Dissertation Abstracts International*, (Volume 42, 1981).

M.J. Wong, "Long-term homosexual and heterosexual couple relationship effects on self-concept and relationship adjustment," *Dissertation Abstracts International*, (Volume 41, 1980).

96. Savin-Williams, 1990.

97. Ibid.

98. S.L. Hershberger and A.R. D'Augelli, "The impact of victimization on the mental health and suicidality of lesbian, gay, and bisexual youths," *Developmental Psychology*, (Volume 31, 1995).

99. Savin-Williams, 1990.

100. K.E. Robinson, "Addressing the needs of gay and lesbian students: The school counselor's role," *The School Counselor*, (Volume 41, 1994).

101. Dulaney and Kelly, 1982.

102. Mallon, 1994.

103. Lewis and Lewis, 1993; Powell, 1987; Robinson, 1994; Savin-Williams and Lenhart, 1990.

104. Mallon, 1994.

105. Powell, 1987.

106. Mallon, 1994; Powell, 1987.

107. A.L. Reynolds and M.J. Koski, "Lesbian, gay, and bisexual teens and the school counselor." In G. Unks, Ed., *The gay teen.* (New York: Routledge, 1995).

108. F. Shifrin and M. Solis, "Chemical dependency in gay and lesbian youth," *Journal of Chemical Dependency Treatment*, (Volume 5, 1992).

109. Savin-Williams, 1990.

110. Lewis and Lewis, 1993; Powell, 1987.

J.M. Ussher, "Family and couples therapy with gay and lesbian clients: Acknowledging the forgotten minority," *Journal of Family Therapy*, (Volume 13, 1991).

111. Jackson and Sullivan, 1994.

112. Lewis and Lewis, 1993.

113. Gonsiorek, 1988.

114. T.L. Hammelman, "Gay and lesbian youth: Contributing factors to serious attempts or consideration of suicide," *Journal of Gay and Lesbian Psychotherapy*, (Volume 2, Number 1, 1993).

115. Bidwell, 1988; Coleman, 1982a; Gonsiorek, 1988.

G.J. Remafedi, "Homosexual youth: A challenge to contemporary society," *Journal of the American Medical Association*, (Volume 258, 1987c).

Chapter 9

1. L.D. Brimner, *Being different: Lambda youth speak out.* (New York: Franklin Watts, 1995), p. 40.

2. A.E. Moses and R.O. Hawkins, *Counseling lesbian women and gay men: A life issues approach.* (St. Louis, MO: C.V. Mosby, 1982), p. 82.

3. E. Coleman, "Developmental stages of the coming out process," *Journal of Homosexuality*, (Volume 7, 1982b).

4. B.O. Silberman and R.O. Hawkins, "Lesbian women and gay men: Issues for counseling." In E. Weinstein and E. Rosen, Eds., *Sexual counseling: Issues and implications.* (Pacific Grove, CA: Brooks/Cole, 1988).

5. Ross-Reynods, 1988.

6. Gonsiork, 1988.

7. G.J. Krysiak, "A very silent and gay minority," *School Counselor*, (Volume 34, 1987).

Silberman and Hawkins, 1988.

8. M.V. Borhek, "Helping gay and lesbian adolescents and their families," *Journal of Adolescent Health Care*, (Volume 9, 1988), p. 126.

9. Borhek, 1988; Silberman and Hawkins, 1988.

10. Borhek, 1988.

11. Ibid.

12. L. Due, *Joining the tribe.* (New York: Anchor Books, 1995), pp. 183-184.

13. C. Silverstein, *Family matters: A parents' guide to homosexuality.* (New York: McGraw-Hill, 1977).

14. Silberman and Hawkins, 1988.

15. Borhek, 1988.

16. A. Fricke, *Reflections of a Rock Lobster.* (Boston, MA: Alyson Publications, 1981), pp. 71-72.

17. Borhek, 1988.

18. D.A. Anderson, "Family and peer relations of gay adolescents." In S.C. Geinstein, Ed., *Adolescent psychiatry: Developmental and clinical studies*, Volume 14. (Chicago: The University of Chicago Press, 1987).

19. E. Pahe, "Speaking up." In B.L. Singer, Ed., *Growing up gay/growing up lesbian.* (New York: The New Press, 1994), p. 233.

20. Borhek, 1988.

21. E. Bass and K. Kaufman, *Free your mind: The book for gay, lesbian, and bisexual youth—and their allies.* (New York: Harper Perennial, 1996), p. 125.

22. Shawn, "My best friend is gay." In B.L. Singer, Ed., *Growing up gay/growing up lesbian.* (New York: The New Press, 1994), p. 78.

23. Weinberg, 1972.

24. Anderson, 1987.

25. K. Chandler, *Passages of pride: Gay and lesbian youth come of age.* (New York: Times Books, 1995), p. 94.

Chapter 10

1. G.G. Back, *Are you still my mother? Are you still my family?* (New York: Warner Books, 1985).

2. Back, 1985.

M. Brownley, *Gay Youth.* (Minneapolis, MN: Community Intervention, 1988).

3. Jackson and Sullivan, 1994.

4. K. Chandler, *Passages of pride: Gay and lesbian youth come of age.* (New York: Times Books, 1995), p. 88.

5. A. Heron, Ed., *Two teenagers in twenty.* (Boston, MA: Alyson, 1994), p. 14.

6. Anonymous, "My coming-out herstory." In J.P. Stanley and S.J. Wolfe, Eds., *The coming-out stories.* (Watertown, MA: Persephone Press, 1980), p. 77.

7. Trent, "Coming out story," *ELIGHT Email* (1996, 1997). Out stories collection 2.

8. A.M. Boxer, J.A. Cook, and G. Herdt, "Double jeopardy: Identity transitions and parent-child relations among gay and lesbian youth." In K. Pillemer and K. McCortney, Eds., *Parent-child relations through life.* (Hillsdale, NJ: Erlbaum Associates, 1991), p. 70.

9. Ibid., p. 81.

10. Tristan, "Out story," *ELIGHT Email* (1996, 1997). Out stories collection 1.

11. Durby, 1994, p. 4.

12. L. Due, *Joining the tribe*. (New York: Anchor Books, 1995), p. 98.

13. Boxer, Cook, and Herdt, 1991, p. 83.

14. Governor's Commission on Gay and Lesbian Youth, *Making schools safe for gay and lesbian youth: Breaking the silence in schools and families.* (1993), p. 25.

15. Chandler, 1995, p. 175.

16. Boxer, Cook, and Herdt, 1991.

17. J.C. Gonsiorek, "Mental health issues of gay and lesbian adolescents," *Journal of Adolescent Health Care*, (Volume 9, 1988).

18. L.D. Brimner, *Being different: Lambda youth speak out.* (New York: Franklin Watts, 1995), p. 37.

19. Chandler, 1995, p. 182.

20. Ibid., p. 323.

21. Ibid., p. 175.

22. Boxer, Cook, and Herdt, 1991, p. 84.

23. Ibid., p. 81.

24. K.B. Knapper, "Black, queer, and out." In B.L. Singer, Ed., *Growing up gay/growing up lesbian.* (New York: The New Press, 1994), p. 137.

25. D.A. Anderson, "Family and peer relations of gay adolescents." In S.C. Geinstein, Ed., *Adolescent psychiatry: Developmental and clinical studies*, Volume 14. (Chicago: The University of Chicago Press, 1987).

26. Chandler, 1995, p. 23.

27. Heron, 1994, p. 18.

28. Chandler, 1995, p. 190.

29. P. Singer, "Breaking through," Rochester, NY, *Democrat and Chronicle*, (1993, July 4).

30. J.N. Baker, "Coming out now," *Newsweek*, (Volume 115 Number 27), Summer 1990), p. 61.

31. S. Maguen, "Gay rural youth lack support from the community," *The Advocate*, (1992, November 17), p. 44.

32. Brownley, 1988.

33. J.T. Sears, *Growing up gay in the South: Race, gender, and journeys of the spirit.* (Binghamton, NY: Harrington Park Press, 1991a), p. 308.

34. T. Wise, "Coming out to my mom." In B.L. Singer, Ed., *Growing up gay/growing up lesbian.* (New York: The New Press, 1994), p. 124.

35. R.S. Cohen and S. Weissman, "The parenting alliance." In R.S. Cohen, B.J. Cohen, and S. Weissman, Eds., *Parenthood: A psychodynamic perspective.* (New York: Guilford, 1984).

36. Boxer, Cook, and Herdt, 1991, p. 85.

37. Chandler, 1995, p. 176.

38. Brownley, 1988.

39. Ibid.

40. Chandler, 1995, p. 220.

41. Governor's Commission on Gay and Lesbian Youth, 1993, p. 25.

42. Boxer, Cook, and Herdt, 1991, pp. 73-73.

43. W.J. Blumenfeld, Gay/straight alliances: Transforming pain to pride. In G. Unks, Ed., *The gay teen.* (New York: Routledge, 1995), p. 221.

44. Boxer, Cook, and Herdt, 1991, p. 83.

45. R.A. Bernstein, *Straight parents/gay children.* (Thunder's Mouth Press, 1994), p. 66.

46. Mercier and Berger, 1989.

47. Brownley, 1988.

48. Singer, 1993, p. D1.

49. Brownley, 1988.

50. Ibid.

51. Ibid.

52. E. Marcus, *Making history: The struggle for gay and lesbian equal rights, 1945-1990.* (New York: Harper-Collins, 1992), p. 83.

53. H. Smith, "Letters to the editor," Lewiston, (ME) *Sun-Journal,* (1995, October 5), p. 4-A.

Chapter 11

1. A. Heron, Ed., *One teenager in ten.* (Boston, MA: Alyson, 1983), p. 114.

2. E. Bass and K. Kaufman, *Free your mind.* (New York: Harper Collins, 1996), p. 23.

3. A. Heron, Ed., *Two teenagers in twenty.* (Boston, MA: Alyson, 1994), p. 142.

4. C. Glenn, "In my own space." In B.L. Singer, Ed., *Growing up gay/ growing up lesbian.* (New York: The New Press, 1994), p. 235.

5. K. Chandler, *Passages of pride: Gay and lesbian youth come of age.* (New York: Times Books, 1995), p. 241.

6. P. Singer, "Breaking through," Rochester, NY, *Democrat and Chronicle,* (1993, July 4), p. D-1.

7. L.D. Brimner, *Being different: Lambda youth speak out.* (New York: Franklin Watts, 1995), pp. 48-49.

8. *Growing up, moving on.* New York: Hetrick-Martin Institute.

9. L. Due, *Joining the tribe.* (New York: Anchor Books, 1995), p. 133.

10. E. Bass and K. Kaufman, *Free your mind: The book for gay, lesbian, and bisexual youth—and their allies.* (New York: Harper Perennial, 1996), p. 265.

11. Ibid.

12. Suzanne, "My story," *ELIGHT Email* (1996, 1997). Writings collection 1.

13. J.T. Sears, *Growing up gay in the South: Race, gender, and journeys of the spirit.* (Binghamton, NY: Harrington Park Press, 1991a), p. 229.

14. Bass and Kaufman, 1996, p. 11.

15. Sears, 1991a, p. 166.

16. Bass and Kaufman, 1996, pp. 30, 73.

17. B.L. Singer, Ed., *Growing up gay/growing up lesbian.* (New York: The New Press, 1994), p. xiv.

18. Brimner, 1995, p. 49.

19. G. Stambolian, *A black man.* (New York: Anchor Books, 1984), p. 3.

20. R.C. Savin-Williams, *Gay and lesbian youth: Expressions of identity.* (Washington, DC: Hemisphere, 1990), p. 184.

21. Sears, 1991a, p. 315.

22. Due, 1995, p. 234.

23. Heron, 1994, p. 88.

24. Tristan, "My coming out story," *ELIGHT Email* (1996, 1997). Out stories collection 1.

25. "Life is hard," *ELIGHT Email* (1996, 1997). Speak your mind, rant and rave.

26. Brimner, 1995, p. 113.

27. Woog, 1995, pp. 35-36.

28. Due, 1995, p. 228.

29. K. Plummer, "Lesbian and gay youth in England." In G. Herdt, Ed., *Gay and lesbian youth.* (Binghamton, NY: Harrington Park Press, 1989), p. 211.

30. Sears, 1991a, p. 112.

31. M. Wilson, "Frontlines: Coming out to new perspectives," *Windy City Times,* (1987, April 16), p. 8.

32. I. Ricks, "Ice queen," *The Advocate,* (1995, December 12), p. 34.

33. K. Jennings, "American dreams." In B.L. Singer, Ed., *Growing up gay/growing up lesbian.* (New York: The New Press, 1994), p. 5.

34. Woog, 1995, p. 39.

35. Bass and Kaufman, 1996, p. 48.

36. Heron, 1994, p. 132.

37. Nathan, "My coming out story," *ELIGHT Email* (1996, 1997). Out stories collection 1.

38. Due, 1995, p. 66.

39. Heron, 1994, p. 65.

40. Heather, "My coming out story," *ELIGHT Email* (1996, 1997). Out stories collection 1.

41. *Be yourself: Questions and answers for gay, lesbian, and bisexual youth.* (Washington, DC: Parents, Families, and Friends of Lesbians and Gays, 1994).

42. S. Alyson, Ed., *Young, gay and proud.* (Boston, MA: Alyson Publications, 1985), p.

43. J. Green, "Out and organized," *The New York Times,* (1993, June 13), Sec. 9, p. 7.

44. L. Heal, "It happened on Main Street." In B.L. Singer, Ed., *Growing up gay/growing up lesbian.* (New York: The New Press, 1994), p. 14.

45. S. Bergman, "Letters," *The Advocate,* (1993, October 5), p. 10.

46. Brimner, 1995, pp. 57-58.

47. Ibid., pp. 84-85.

48. Bass and Kaufman, 1996, p. 26.

49. S. Parsavand, "Discussion groups ease acceptance for gay high schoolers," *Schenectady Gazette,* (1993, December 5), p. A-11.

50. Heron, 1994, p. 50.

51. Bass and Kaufman, 1996, p. 96.

52. A. Fricke, 1981, pp. 45-46.

53. Sears, 1991a, p. 305.

54. D. Leavitt, *The lost language of cranes.* (New York: Knopf, 1986), pp. 71-72.

55. Heal, 1994.

56. Michael, "Different is not bad." In B.L. Singer, Ed., *Growing up gay/ growing up lesbian.* (New York: The New Press, 1994), p. 61.

57. Bass and Kaufman, 1996, p. 27.

58. Brimner, 1995, p. 49.

59. Bass and Kaufman, 1996, p. 73.

60. Sears, 1991a, p. 249.

61. J.N. Baker, "Coming out now," *Newsweek,* (Volume 115 Number 27), Summer 1990), p. 60.

62. Heron, 1994, p. 115.

63. William, "Gay and lesbian pride," *ELIGHT Email* (1996, 1997). Speak your mind, rant and rave.

64. Michael, "It's OK to be Gay," *ELIGHT Email* (1996, 1997). Speak your mind, rant and rave.

65. Ibid., p. 67.

Chapter 12

1. R. Coles and G. Stokes. *Sex and the American teenager.* (New York: Harper & Row, 1985), p. 139.

Index

Page numbers followed by the letter "t" indicate tables.

Order Your Own Copy of
This Important Book for Your Personal Library!

QUEER KIDS
The Challenges and Promise for Lesbian, Gay, and Bisexual Youth

_____ in hardbound at $49.95 (ISBN: 0-7890-0439-9)

_____ in softbound at $24.95 (ISBN: 1-56023-929-8)

COST OF BOOKS_____

OUTSIDE USA/CANADA/
MEXICO: ADD 20%_____

POSTAGE & HANDLING_____
*(US: $3.00 for first book & $1.25
for each additional book)
Outside US: $4.75 for first book
& $1.75 for each additional book)*

SUBTOTAL_____

IN CANADA: ADD 7% GST_____

STATE TAX_____
*(NY, OH & MN residents, please
add appropriate local sales tax)*

FINAL TOTAL_____
*(If paying in Canadian funds,
convert using the current
exchange rate. UNESCO
coupons welcome.)*

Prices in US dollars and subject to change without notice.

☐ **BILL ME LATER:** ($5 service charge will be added)
(Bill-me option is good on US/Canada/Mexico orders only;
not good to jobbers, wholesalers, or subscription agencies.)

☐ Check here if billing address is different from
shipping address and attach purchase order and
billing address information.

Signature _____

☐ **PAYMENT ENCLOSED: $**_____

☐ **PLEASE CHARGE TO MY CREDIT CARD.**

☐ Visa   ☐ MasterCard   ☐ AmEx   ☐ Discover
☐ Diner's Club

Account # _____

Exp. Date _____

Signature _____

NAME _____

INSTITUTION _____

ADDRESS _____

CITY _____

STATE/ZIP _____

COUNTRY _____ COUNTY (NY residents only) _____

TEL _____ FAX _____

E-MAIL_____

May we use your e-mail address for confirmations and other types of information? ☐ Yes   ☐ No

Order From Your Local Bookstore or Directly From
The Haworth Press, Inc.
10 Alice Street, Binghamton, New York 13904-1580 • USA
TELEPHONE: 1-800-HAWORTH (1-800-429-6784) / Outside US/Canada: (607) 722-5857
FAX: 1-800-895-0582 / Outside US/Canada: (607) 772-6362
E-mail: getinfo@haworth.com
PLEASE PHOTOCOPY THIS FORM FOR YOUR PERSONAL USE.

BOF96

#3- Gen 911 K